WARSHIP
RECOGNITION GUIDE

Keith Faulkner

Revised and edited by Robert Hutchinson

HarperCollins*Publishers*

In the USA for information address:
HarperCollins*Publishers* Inc
10 East 53rd Street
New York
NY 10022

In the UK for information address:
HarperCollins*Publishers*
77-85 Fulham Palace Road
Hammersmith
London W6 8JB

First Published by HarperCollins*Publishers* 1999

© Jane's Information Group 1999

1 3 5 7 9 10 8 6 4 2

ISBN 0 00 4722116

Design: Rod Teasdale

Printed in Italy

Contents

Ships and submarines are listed by their country of origin

AIRCRAFT CARRIERS

CRUISERS

DESTROYERS

Contents

Contents

Contents

Contents

Foreword

Warship identification has progressed a long way since Admiral Horatio Nelson put his telescope to his blind eye and commented: 'I see no ships'. As well as the traditional visual recognition, we now have thermal imagery, acoustic signatures, electronic emission analysis, magnetic anomalies and even wake detection devices.

In spite of this march of technology, the classification criteria which must be met before a weapon can be released at an intended target remain difficult to achieve. The sequence of detection, classification, localisation and attack (or surveillance) demands an unambiguous recognition of the target at some stage during this process. The trouble with technological solutions is that they are seldom absolutely reliable and are vulnerable to deception and jamming. Often there is no absolute certainty that you have the right target, or even any target at all. Usually only accurate visual recognition can resolve the problem.

Examples of false target analysis are particularly prevalent in anti-submarine warfare, precisely because visual recognition in operational conditions is rarely possible. The result is weapon or decoy expenditure on false alarms, with expensive torpedoes chasing banks of krill or exploding harmlessly against prominent objects on the sea bottom. Surface ship classification by non-visual means ought to be easier, and sometimes is, if the target is in calm, deep, open waters, transmitting on identifiable electronic equipment and well away from other activities. Much more likely is that weather conditions are foul, transmission policies have been planned to generate deception and the whole area is alive with merchant and fishing vessels navigating around complex archipelagos.

Another problem is that many anti-ship weapons have ranges far in excess of the firing platform's ability to make its own classification, so some form of third party targeting may be needed to take advantage of these extended ranges. This brings in all the uncertainties of data transfer which looks easy in the manufacturer's brochures, but requires skilled management and equipment reliability if mistakes are to be avoided. Whether you fire as a result of your own sensor information or on the basis of data provided by others, it is always a great comfort to know the classification has, at some stage, involved visual recognition.

So, in most cases, certain target identification by sighting is just as important as it always has been, not only to avoid needless waste of costly and limited ammunition, but also to prevent the "friendly fire" incidents in which allies hit each other or harmless civilians going about their lawful business on the high seas. Ship recognition may look easy to the desk-bound warrior. In the fog of war, it remains one of the most difficult — and decisive — ingredients of the successful prosecution of a target.

Captain Richard Sharpe OBE RN
Editor, Jane's Fighting Ships

These are challenging, if not frustrating times for the navies of the world. Following the end of the Cold War, new ship construction was cut; strengths of fleets reduced; and equipment upgrades postponed or cancelled in pursuance of the mirage-like 'Peace Dividend.' Reality has come like a cold douche of seawater on many navies, but sadly has not yet dampened the grey suits of their political masters.

The reality is that new missions and roles, particularly for Western navies, place far heavier demands on ships and personnel than ever the Cold War did. First there was the Gulf War, then peace-keeping operations in support of UN missions. Now there is an expeditionary strategy which requires considerable amphibious lift resources, as well as the associated land attack role, for both major surface combatants and submarines. All this with fewer ships and fewer personnel. History has an unfortunate habit of repeating itself and in the planned procurement of 'land attack destroyers' — such as the US Navy's DD 21s — are we so very far away from the concept of the imperial gunboat?

Talking of history, the military at least, has still been keeping a wary eye on Russia, despite the political complacency that followed the collapse of the Soviet Union and the continued support for the Russian leadership by Western politicians, in the hope it will deliver democracy and a healthy market economy. Russian naval equipment is still formidable, but the current state of morale, fleet maintenance and the capability of the shipbuilding industry no longer generates any political stress in Western capitals. Recent events in Russia threaten a return to the centrally controlled economy. There are domestic demands for more efficient armed forces. Perhaps the military's cynicism about the docility of the Russian bear has not been quite so misplaced?

As we approach the Millennium, let's take a brief look at naval developments around the world.

United States of America

The US Navy is devoting substantial effort into developing its planned DD 21 land attack destroyer, which, according to Chief of Naval Operations Admiral Jay Johnson will 'embody the post-Cold War purpose of our Navy — to influence events ashore directly and decisively, anytime and anywhere.' Up to 30 'stealthy' hulls are planned to be acquired, equipped with 'considerable

NIMITZ CLASS CVN: USS DWIGHT D EISENHOWER

offensive punch, ranging from advanced guns to supersonic land attack missiles,' according to Johnson. Meanwhile, the US Navy plans to buy five additional DDG 51 Arleigh Burke class destroyers early next century.

However, budget pressures have forced the US Navy to 're-orientate' plans for a new generation carrier, the 'CVX' to succeed the current Nimitz class. Instead of starting from scratch, the Navy is seeking to introduce new technologies into three new carriers (CVN-77, 78 and 79) which retain the basic Nimitz hull. The choice was stark for the US Navy: the $3.2 billion required for CVX research and development over the next six years could not be afforded if the acquisition of the next Nimitz, CVN-77, was to go ahead at the same time. This way, CVN-77 presses ahead, with an in-service date of 2010, and CVN-78 and CVN-79 in 2013 and 2018 respectively.

The current shipbuilding rate for the US Navy will not sustain the size of the current fleet and even that has dropped by 40% since the end of the Cold War. The decision to pay off most of the surviving ships not equipped with missile Vertical Launch Systems is causing another major reduction in numbers of major operational surface combatants. In addition, SSN numbers are also in steady decline with the slowest rate of submarine building in the 40 years since nuclear propulsion was first introduced. The Pentagon must increase the number of ships it builds per year to maintain a 300-ship navy — the critical level to meet future missions. Without a 300-ship fleet, the navy faces 'serious [operating tempo] problems,' says John Douglas, assistant secretary of the navy for research, development and acquisitions.

TICONDEROGA CLASS (AEGIS) CRUISER: USS MOBILE BAY

At the other end of the Order of Battle, the US Navy is considering permanently stationing four 'Cyclone' class coastal patrol craft in Rota, Spain, to support special operations forces and provide a continuous presence in Europe. US Defense Secretary William Cohen has asked the Navy to speed up its attempts to equip and train its fleet in mine countermeasures (MCM). He believes the proliferation of low-cost/low-risk but highly effective sea mines is one of the 'asymmetric' threats facing US forces in the years ahead. In response, the Navy has been drafting a plan to move away from reliance on a dedicated force of mine countermeasure vessels. The MCM mission will apply to the whole fleet, involving a mix of helicopters and remote-piloted vehicles and sub-surface vehicles.

Russia

In Russia, despite 'extremely limited financing,' a smaller navy will maintain its combat readiness, according to Fleet Admiral Vladimir Kuroyedov, Commander-in-Chief. His force has seen its share of Moscow's defence budget slashed from 23% to 13% in 1996-98, with further reductions expected, and this ignores the problems of Moscow not paying its bills! Although personnel numbers have been cut by 36,000 to 200,000, 85% - 90% of the navy's 1998 budget is expected to be allocated to personnel expenditures. However, he expects to commission two 'multi-purpose submarines' in 1999.

Since 1991, a shortage of funds to pay for dockyard repairs, spare parts and fuel has meant that many major surface warships have rarely been to sea and few have operated away from their local exercise areas. Since 1996, some ships have been 'selected' to go to sea but many remain in commission but permanently in harbour.

The new 'multi-purpose' submarines may be boats from the 'Yasen' class (Type 885) SSN/SSGN of which three are currently building. The 8,600 tons boats will be equipped with the Novator Alfa SS-N-27 submarine-launched cruise missiles fired from vertical launch tubes in the after casing — a first for Russian designs. They will also carry SS-N-15 Starfish (Tsakra) anti-submarine missiles, fired from the canted 533 mm torpedo tubes.

The 17,000 ton strategic missile submarine (SSBN) Yuri Dolgoruky, lead ship of the new 'Borey' (Type 955) class is also under construction at the

Severodvinsk yard, although changes have been made to the design because of the scrapping of the SS-NX-28 Gorm (RSM-52V) ballistic missile, planned for deployment in the boat but which failed on a test launch in 1997. The revised design will be ready early in 1999 and the SSBN is expected to be equipped with a new, lighter missile, with an extended range. The failure of the Gorm missile also impacted on the modernisation of the six remaining 'Typhoon' class SSBNs, which were planned to be equipped with this missile, but will begin decommissioning in 1999 according to some reports.

Russia is also building a new Lada (Amur) class (Type 1650) SSK of 2,600 dived displacement, at the Admiralty Yard, St. Petersburg. One boat is being construction for Russian Navy service, another for export. These new classes of Russian submarines will demonstrate a dramatic reduction in running noise, thus eroding one of the greatest tactical advantages enjoyed by Western submarines.

In terms of surface combatants, the keel of a new Grom (Type 1244.1)

UDALOY (TYPE 1155) DESTROYER: ADMIRAL LEVCHENKO

class frigate was laid with much publicity in 1997 at the Yantar yard, Kaliningrad. As the yard is apparently wrestling with the completion of the second 'Neustrashimy' class frigate, it may be surprising if this hull meets its launch date of 2000. When completed, the 3,000 ton FFG will be armed with 16 SS-N-25 (KH 35 Uran) surface-to-surface missiles and SAM and anti-submarine missiles in a vertical launch system forward of the superstructure. Stealth features are part of the specification. The only other major surface warship nearing completion is the 'Sovremenny' (Sarych) class DDG Ekatarinbury (ex-Sobrazitelny, ex-Buliny) at North Yard, St.Petersburg, due to be commissioned in 2000.

Britain

The Royal Navy has come through the 1998 Strategic Defence Review with plans for two new large aircraft carriers confirmed, creation of a joint RN/RAF fixed-wing force of FA.2s and Harrier GR.7s; acquisition of another four roll-on/roll-off (ro-ro) container ships and the fitting of Tomahawk land attack cruise missiles to all SSNs.

The number of frigates and destroyers will drop from 35 to 32. The Type 42 Batch 1 destroyer Birmingham and five Type 22 Batch 2 frigates (Boxer, Beaver, Brave, London and Coventry) will be retired between 1999 and 2001, at the same time that the last three Type 23 'Duke' class frigates enter service. Given the operational demands on the Royal Navy, it is a pity that these ships were lost in the wrangling over budgetary resources. However, with current personnel levels, it is unlikely the Royal Navy could crew them anyway. Brazil and Chile have emerged as the most likely purchasers of the Type 22s which will have around 50% of their service life left to them after paying off from RN service. Brazil already has four former RN Type 22 Batch 1 frigates in service, purchased in November 1994 as part of a $100 million second-hand package which included three 'River' class minesweepers.

The British Strategic Defence Review also included reductions from 12 to 10 SSNs with the retirement of both Splendid and Spartan although plans to order an additional 'Astute' class boats were confirmed.

The RN's mine countermeasures force will be cut from 25 to 22 through withdrawal of three 'Hunt' class ships early next century. Plans to order a second batch of Merlin HM.1 helicopters, in addition to the 44 on order, were

TYPE 42 DESTROYER: HMS LIVERPOOL

also scrapped, but a further 10 Lynx helicopters will be brought up to the improved HMA.8 standard. As a result, Type 23 frigates will operate the Lynx HMA.8 as standard with Merlins embarked as a substitute when an enhanced ASW capability is required.

The new carriers, 'of the order of 30,000 to 40,000 tonnes and capable of carrying up to 50 fixed wing aircraft and helicopters' will be considerably larger than the three Invincible class they will replace from 2012. The UK Ministry of Defence is now examining the STOVL (short take off/vertical landing) variant of the US Joint Strike Fighter to embark in the carriers, with a total sortie rate of 150 a day — a launch or recovery every 10 minutes. Other candidates to replace the Sea Harriers and GR.7s are a conventional version of the JSF and a navalised Eurofighter/Typhoon. Whether the carriers survive the Treasury's quest for continued stringency in government spending remains to be seen.

The replacement class for the Type 42 air defence destroyers, the 6,500

ton 'Horizon' class, seems as distant as ever. The collaborative project, with France and Italy, was to produce the first three ships by 2002, but work seems to be running at least four years late. The poor old Type 42s, with their Sea Dart SAM system which was obsolescent even in the 1980s, will have to lumber on until at least 2010, when the hulls will be a minimum of 30 years old. With wrangling still going on between the three partners, and the Treasury happily watching as money remains unspent on the construction programme, this is little short of a national scandal.

Meanwhile, a £13 million contract to build a two-thirds size trimaran warship demonstrator for the Royal Navy was awarded to Vosper Thornycroft. The demonstrator, the RV Triton, will be 90 metres long, have a beam of 20 metres and will displace 1,100 tons. After delivery in September 2000, the demonstrator will be used for trials to decide whether a trimaran configuration could be used for the Future Escort to replace the RN's Type 22/Type 23 frigates. A trimaran hull would give the Future Escort larger and higher anti-air warfare radars; increased speed and sea-keeping characteristics and a 'Stealthy' radar signature.

The new primary mission for the Royal Navy is 'maritime enablement for joint force projection,' according to the Strategic Defence Review. Previous commitments to maintain a brigade-sized amphibious lift capability remain unchanged. Previous prevarication on building the resources necessary to achieve that lift, happily has been removed with the amphibious helicopter carrier Ocean joining the fleet, commando carriers Albion and Bulwark now building and two new landing ships logistic planned to replaced RFA Sir Geraint and RFA Sir Percivale. The acquisition of the four ro-ro- ships will bring the strategic sealift force up to six hulls.

France

In France, the latest in a series of expenditure cuts affecting the Marine Nationale's equipment programmes, were announced in April 1998, slicing FFr 20 billion ($3.3 billion) for the period 1999-2002. Achieving these savings would require a decision not to acquire the MILAS stand-off anti-submarine weapon; the postponement by six months of the in-service date for the third Le Triomphant class SSBN and delaying the order for the fourth until 2003. Development of a new generation of heavyweight torpedo would be cancelled, as well as the paying off of the carrier Foch earlier than planned, in late-1999 (when the Charles de Gaulle) is commissioned.

Funding, however, will be available to enable the M51 submarine-launched strategic ballistic missile to enter service two years earlier, in 2008, and to purchase a third E-2C Hawkeye airborne early warning aircraft for the Charles de Gaulle. The decision on building a sister nuclear carrier remains postponed; a second vessel would probably not enter service until 2012-15, even if an order was to be placed at the beginning of the next budget cycle. The problem of carrier capability has been worsened by Foch's early retirement and it will be unavailable to stand in for Charles de Gaulle during its first major refit, scheduled for 2005-07.

The Marine Nationale's procurement plans include a new generation of nuclear attack submarines, the Sous-Marin d'Attaque Futur (SMAF), numbering six to replace the Rubis class on a one-for-one-basis. The diesel-electric Agosta class will be retired in 1999 (leaving another Agosta, the Ouessant, as a trials platform); the survivor of the Daphné class, Psyché paid off in late 1998, although a sister boat, Sirène, completed a long refit in March 1997 and is now up for sale. With these decommissionings, France will follow the UK's example and move to an all-nuclear submarine fleet.

Two more TCDs, the French Landing Ship Docks (LSDs) are planned, but, at present, it is unclear whether they will be based on the Foudre/Sirocco class, or on the through-deck, multi-role designs of the kind produced by French industry. They are due to enter service in 2004 and 2006 so the fate of TCD04 looks less than certain.

China

Having secured its northern borders by diplomatic means, China has moved away from its long-standing defensive ground war doctrine. It is developing a better trained, better armed navy, designed to operate far from the mainland. Despite the beliefs of some politicians, such a process takes time. Chinese naval strategic planners are aiming to achieve a so-called 'green water' capability by around 2002 — i.e. being able to operate out to the 'first island chain' of Japan, the Senkaku islands, Taiwan and the west coast of Borneo. By 2020, the PLA Navy hopes to have extended its operational capability further out to the Kuriles in the north, the Bonin and Marina Islands and Papua

MAESTRALE CLASS FRIGATE: EURO

New Guinea in the south. Already Chinese ships are beginning to operate much further away from home: in March 1997, two destroyers and an oiler from the South Sea Fleet, headquartered at Zhanjiang, visited Hawaii and then Mexico, Peru and Chile. A few days after their departure, a frigate/destroyer task group from the East Sea Fleet, began a similar port visit programme in Malaysia, Thailand and the Philippines.

The current Chinese order of battle comprises more than 50 surface combatants, the majority of which date back to the 1970s with obsolete command and control, anti-submarine warfare systems and sensors. Although most boast surface-to-surface missiles and guns, only around 40% have a surface-to-air missile capability. The pressing priority for the Chinese Navy, therefore, is to redress the lack of air defence, particularly important if China is to fulfil her ambitions to operate at least one carrier.

A first move was the planned acquisition of the last two uncompleted Russian 'Sovremenny' class destroyers, 8,400 tons, with the SA-N-7 Gadfly

Introduction

DE LA PENNE CLASS DDG: LUIGI DURAND DE LA PENNE

(Uragan) or SA-N-17 Grizzly Mach 3 missiles with a range of 13.5 nm. However progress on the ships has been delayed because China wants Kamov Ka-32 Helix ASW helicopters included in the price and the Russians have demanded extra payment for the aircraft.

The new 6,000 ton Luhai class DDG is in series production at Dalian Shipyard, possibly fitted with a VLS launcher for SAM missiles aft of the HQ-7 (Crotale) octuple SAM launcher in the 'B' position on the forecastle.

There continue to be conflicting reports about China's success (or otherwise) in establishing an organic naval air capability — vital to her strategy in establishing a 'blue water' capability. China has announced that its first aircraft carrier will be launched in 2000; whether this will be helicopter-capable rather than a true carrier is debatable. Some unconfirmed reports suggest that prefabrication of a carrier, designed with Russian assistance, began in August

1996 at the Dalian Shipyard, Shanghai. This may, however, resemble the UK Royal Navy's aviation training ship Argus, 26,421 tons, in which the Chinese showed such great interest when she commissioned in 1988. (The Chinese already operate the training ship Shichang, out of the same stable, with two flight-deck spots for Harbin Zhi-9A Haitun (Dauphin 2) helicopters. An alternate containerised hangar arrangement has been seen on board Shichang during air training operations, reminiscent of the US-developed 'Arapaho' scheme in which VSTOL aircraft were stored in containers on deck. This was trialled by the UK aboard RFA Reliant in the mid-1980s). There are other reports that Russian-supplied Sukhoi Su-27 Flankers are being tested in practice take-off and landings on a mock-up concrete deck in preparation for carrier operations sometime in the future.

More has been achieved in the area of amphibious warfare with 6 Type 074'Yuting' 4,800 tank landing ships built between 1992 and 1997, latterly with a large helicopter deck aft of the superstructure to join 8 'Yukan' class 4,170 ton LSTs built from 1980 and the 31 'Yuliang' class 1,100ton LSMs. Construction of three more 799 ton 'Yuhai' class LSMs, to join the nine currently operational, is underway.

Finally, a new SSBN class, the Type 094, is being developed with a longer range strategic missile, to replace the ageing and unreliable single Xia, reported to have been in refit until late 1998. The first of a class of four is expected to begin construction shortly, but may be held up until the JL-2 missile has completed trials from the 30-year-old 'Golf' class boat, based with the Northern Fleet. A new class of nuclear attack submarine (SSN), the Type 093, is also being developed, based on the Russian 'Victor III' class, armed with submarine-launched cruise missiles. Prefabrication began in 1994 and the first launch is expected in 1999-2000 from the Bohai shipyard, with an in-service date of 2002. A second of class will follow two years later.

Italy

The Italian Navy has outlined plans for a new 22,500 ton multi-purpose air-capable ship, planned to begin construction in 2000. Intended to replace the 30-year-old cruiser Vittorio Veneto the new ship will operate alongside the Harrier carrier Giuseppe Garabaldi. Planned roles include light aircraft carrier, amphibious transport dock or civil disaster relief. As such, the concept is similar to that of the three San Giorgio class LPDs, where the first of class, San Giorgio, is specially fitted to cope with civil emergencies and indeed, was paid for by the Ministry of Civil Protection. The design envisages a through-deck ship of 18,500 tons standard displacement with an overall length of 220 metres and a beam of 39 metres. The 5,900 m² flight-deck will be fitted with a ski-jump for short take off/vertical landing aircraft and the hull will contain a well dock at the stern, big enough to accommodate two 60 ton or four 30 ton LCMs. The hangar will be able to house up to 12 EH101-size medium helicopters or eight Harrier II Plus fixed wing aircraft in the primary carrier role. For amphibious warfare lift, the ship could carry about 100 light vehicles or 12 60-ton Ariete main battle tanks.

Italy is also building two Type 212A SSKs of 1,830 tons dived displacement armed with Whitehead A184 and DM2A4 torpedoes, based on a common design produced with Germany of which four will be built for the Deutsche Marine.

Germany

Germany is building four Sachsen class air defence frigates to replace the three venerable Lütjens (Modified 'Charles F Adams') class destroyers currently in service. First of the 5,600 ton new ships, armed with Harpoon SSMs, and vertically-launched Standard SM 2 Block IIIA SAMs, is expected to be commissioned in 2002.

The design emanates from a collaborative effort with the Netherlands, evolved from a common anti-air warfare system. As many examination papers suggest, contrast and compare the success of this project with the ill-starred 'Horizon' destroyer project involving the UK, France and Italy!

Canada

Canada is to lease the four former Royal Navy Upholder class diesel-electric submarines under an eight-year deal, which includes a subsequent option to purchase the boats outright. Ottawa's long-awaited decision follows a three-year quest by the British Government and Vickers Shipbuilding and Engineering to sell the boats, originally designed for a Cold War role in the Greenland-Iceland-UK gap but retired, brand new, under defence cuts announced in 1992. All four submarines, Upholder, Unseen, Ursula and

Unicorn, will now be reactivated and trialled before the first boat is delivered in mid-2000 to Canada for more modification work, including a new communications suite, adaptations to fire the Mk 48 Mod 4 heavyweight torpedo and the retrofit of the Lockheed Martin Librascope fire control system, currently fitted on Canada's three ageing Oberon class.

Australia

Australia's Project Sea 1400 — under which eight new surface combatants will succeed the Adelaide class FFG 7 guided missile frigates — has faced more delays. The plan was excluded from the Australian Department of Defence's capital equipment proposals for 1998-2003, although, according to previous announcements, capability studies for the new ships were to have begun in 1999/2000.

Fourteen ships is the target surface combatant strength of the Royal Australian Navy, achieved by the six upgraded Adelaide class and the eight Anzac class with their planned improvement programme. But it will be many years before all 14 are available for service, and allowing 10 years of further service, the Royal Australian Navy will require its successor, one of the Project

ALBATROS CLASS FAST ATTACK CRAFT: HABICHT

Introduction

HUGIN CLASS FAST ATTACK CRAFT: KAPAREN

Sea 1400 hulls, to join the fleet by 2013. No capability requirement has yet been endorsed and no approval won to build the ships at all.

South Korea

South Korea took delivery of its first KDX 1 'Okpo' destroyer, King Kwanggaeto, 3,900 tons, at the end of July 1998. The first of class is armed with eight Boeing Harpoon Block 1C SSMs in quad launchers; Raytheon RIM-7P Seasparrow SAMs in a Mk 48, 16 cell vertical launch system and ASROC anti-submarine missiles, again in a VLS. Guns include one OTOBreda 5 in (127 mm)/54, and two Signaal Goalkeeper close-in weapon systems. One more unit, Eujimundok is nearing completion and construction work continues on a third. A stretched version of the KDX 1, the KDX 2, 4,800 tons, will include a

full area air defence capability. Up to nine units of this class are planned, the first of which, no 975, is under construction at Hyundai, Ulsan.

Japan

Japan's Maritime Self-Defence Force, now trying to take on a more equal partnership with the US Navy in the region, (including replenishment at sea of US ships and integrated mine warfare operations), is faced with the five year defence budget plan being cut back for the first time since 1955. However, the commissioning of the first through-deck LST/LPD Osumi, 8,900 tons, and the funding of a second of class are pointers in a tentative step towards a more expeditionary capability. STOVL aircraft may not be far behind, although this has great political ramifications and has been officially denied. Given the current budgetary climate, in the short term it looks unlikely.

Japanese naval capability remains the envy of many other navies. The last of the seven 'Harushio' class SSKs commissioned in 1997, and the first two of the new four-strong 'Oyashio' class SSKs have now emerged to join a modern fleet of submarines which will number around 20 by 2002. In terms of destroyers and frigates, where Japan ranks among the top four navies in the number of hulls, the last 'Kongou' class DDG, Choukai, commissioned in March 1998, and two more of the nine-strong 'Marasame' class DDG/DDs are due to commission in March 1999.

India

For many years India has expressed interest to buy from Russia the 44,500 ton modified 'Kiev' (Type 1143.4) air capable cruiser Admiral Gorshkov, at present in Rosta shipyard. Now, the Russian Nevskoye Project Design Bureau and state arms exporter Rosvoorouzhenie have released details of a three-year project to convert the ship into a short take-off but arrested recovery carrier for India at a price of between $700 million and $800 million. Part of the package would be the provision of a new carrier-capable MiG-29K (Type 9-31) Fulcrum fighter, together with Kamov Ka-32 Helix ASW and AEW Kamov Ka-28 and Ka-31 helicopters. The Fulcrums would come armed with the Kh-35 (AS-20 'Kayak') anti-ship missile.

Gorshkov suffered a serious fire in the engine room in 1994 but the damage has been repaired, although the ship's condition, after several years of neglect, is reportedly poor. Conversion plans would remove the SS-N-12 'Sandbox' SSM armament from the forward deck to allow for a 14.3° ski-jump for the fighters, which would number 24, with six helicopters. Inevitably, perhaps, the Indian Air Force is reportedly opposing the carrier plans on the basis that the IAF could more efficiently undertake maritime patrol/naval strike operations.

India is placing high priority on completion of its nuclear-powered submarine programme known as the Advanced Technology Vessel (ATV), under development for more than two decades. Between 1988 and 1991, the Indian Navy leased INS Chakra, a 5,000 ton Charlie I SSN from the Soviet Union. Despite some problems with the submarine, it was decided to seek to acquire between four and six SSNs from Moscow but the collapse of the Soviet Union put paid to that plan and India decided to speed up its own development programme. It is understood that the keel of the first ATV, based on the 'Charlie I' class, will be laid by 2001/2, two years after the end of land tests on its 40-55MW reactor. Fabrication will be at Vishakapatnam, but assembled at the Mazagon Dockyard in Bombay. Launch is planned around 2006/7 and commissioning 12 months later. The new SSN will be armed with the Sagarika (Oceanic) cruise missile, reportedly at an advanced stage of development. Indian sources maintain the missile will have a nuclear warhead and is likely to fulfil a land attack role.

Israel
The Israeli government has approved the continuation of the Nirit upgrade to the 'Hetz' (Saar 4.5) class missile-armed fast attack craft. The upgraded Nirit is said to be a hybrid derivative of the smaller 'Reshef' Saar 4 class with a new hull, low radar signature mast, new fire control directors and four eight-cell vertical launch Barak I point defence SAMs. The Saar 4.5 class Romat and Keshet ships have recently completed the modernisation. One of the Saar 4 class, Yaffo, also competed the upgrade and was handed over to the navy in July 1998.

Chile
Chile signed a contract for two new French designed 'Scorpene' class SSKs, of 1,570 tons dived displacement and probably armed with a SSM, as

KILO CLASS SSK

replacements for the two ageing 'Oberon' class submarines, O'Brien and Hyatt (ex-Condell).

Brazil
As well as building Tikuna, an 'Improved Tupi' (SNAC-1) class SSK, Brazil is also constructing a corvette design, Barroso, 2,350 tons, at the Arsenal de Marinha, in Rio de Janeiro. The corvette will be armed with four Aerospatiale MM 40 Exocet SSMs, a Vickers 4.5 in (115 mm) Mk 8 quick-firing gun, and a Bofors SAK Sea Trinity close-in weapons system for defence against sea-skimming missiles. Commissioning is due in December 2002. A second of class was projected in 1997 but this is likely to be overtaken by a 3,500 ton design frigate being developed.

Robert Hutchinson

About this Book

Jane's Warship Recognition Guide has been published primarily to be a tool to help readers identify any of the ships featured; to provide information on the physical characteristics of the ships and the main weapons and to indicate which helicopters and fixed wing aircraft are embarked.

The most important feature of recognition is the visual impact of, for example, hulls, masts, radar aerials, funnels and major weapons systems. To help the reader to identify a particular ship, three different types of visual aid have been included:-

● Each entry has a photograph on the right-hand page, which has been chosen, where possible, for its clarity and the detail it shows.
● Most entries have a detailed line diagram on the left hand page which will give an impression of the overall outline of the ship, as well as the position of weapons and sensors. They are not to the same scale.
● For all major warships there is a silhouette which can be used in the traditional way to help with horizon or sun-backed views.

Composite diagrams of a theoretical warship and submarine are in the front of the book, designed to help the less experienced reader to identify the relevant parts of a ship and to become familiar with the terminology used in the text.

Despite the sophistication of modern electronic sensors, visual ship recognition remains as important as ever and is still taught to armed forces in most countries. This book is intended to be a lead-in to the subject of recognition for the student and is not a comprehensive volume of ship types with full data on equipment and systems. Jane's Information Group publishes a series of yearbooks and subscription binders covering ships and associated equipment in great detail. Examples are *Jane's Fighting Ships*, *Jane's Naval Weapons Systems*, *Jane's Underwater Warfare Systems*, *Jane's Radar and Electronic Warfare Systems* and *Jane's C4I Systems*. In addition, *Jane's High-Speed Marine Craft* covers civilian applications of high-speed craft. The 10-times a year journal, *Jane's Navy International* covers maritime developments with news and articles on new ships, weapons systems, and tactical and strategic issues.

Ship classes for *Jane's Warship Recognition Guide* have been selected for reasons ranging from those ships which may be the most numerous, the most heavily armed, the most tactically important, to those which are most likely to be seen away from their country's territorial waters. Navies' orders of battle constantly change with deletions from the strength of the fleet, sales to other countries, refits, and the arrival of new designs and constructions. A number of classes have been deleted in this edition of *Jane's Warship Recognition Guide*, because they are about to disappear; others remain, as whilst the country of origin may be paying them off, they stay in the service of other navies.

The book has been structured to make its use as easy as possible. There are nine sections which cover the major types of warships, namely:-

- Aircraft carriers
- Cruisers
- Destroyers
- Frigates
- Corvettes
- Patrol forces
- Mine warfare forces
- Amphibious warfare
- Submarines

There is no significance to a ship's strategic or tactical importance indicated by its position in the book. In a departure from previous editions, each section now includes the country of origin — i.e. the country primarily where the design originated but often of construction as well. In this way, very many more classes of warships and hulls are covered and the reader is able, for the first time, to compare the differences within classes and different navies.

General Notes

In the **Name (Pennant Number)** section of each entry, the names and pennant numbers of the relevant ships will only be included where applicable. Some countries do not use pennant numbers, or change them so frequently that the information would soon be of little value. In the case of submarines, pennant numbers are included where often they are not displayed on the boat's hull.

There are some cases where the ships fall into the **Patrol Forces** category with one country and are designated as **Corvettes** by another, and vice versa. This also can apply in some cases to **Frigates** and **Corvettes** and **Mine Warfare** vessels. To avoid confusion, this has been pointed out in the text.

There are a few instances where a line diagram may not display exactly the same weapons fit as the photograph. This occurs when there are different versions of that class within a navy or a group of navies operating that class of ship.

Composite Warship

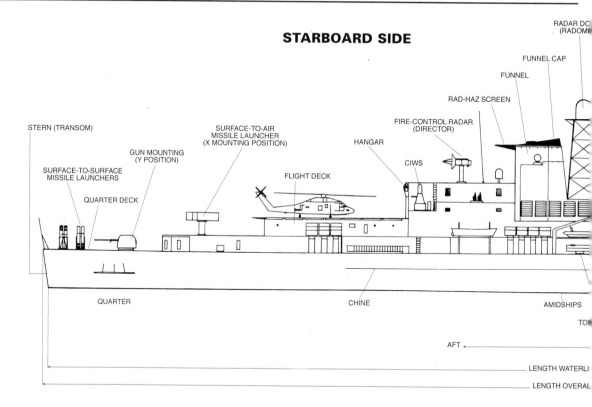

STARBOARD SIDE

RADAR DO
(RADOMI

FUNNEL CAP

FUNNEL

RAD-HAZ SCREEN

STERN (TRANSOM)

SURFACE-TO-AIR
MISSILE LAUNCHER
(X MOUNTING POSITION)

FIRE-CONTROL RADAR
(DIRECTOR)

HANGAR

GUN MOUNTING
(Y POSITION)

CIWS

SURFACE-TO-SURFACE
MISSILE LAUNCHERS

FLIGHT DECK

QUARTER DECK

QUARTER

CHINE

AMIDSHIPS

TO

AFT

LENGTH WATERLI

LENGTH OVERAL

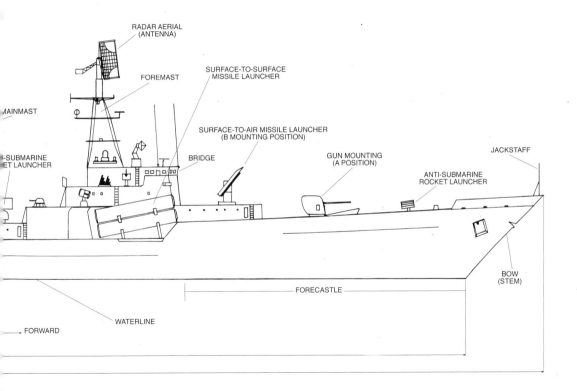

RADAR AERIAL
(ANTENNA)

SURFACE-TO-SURFACE
MISSILE LAUNCHER

FOREMAST

SURFACE-TO-AIR MISSILE LAUNCHER
(B MOUNTING POSITION)

MAINMAST

GUN MOUNTING
(A POSITION)

JACKSTAFF

BRIDGE

ANTI-SUBMARINE
ROCKET LAUNCHER

-SUBMARINE
ET LAUNCHER

BOW
(STEM)

FORECASTLE

WATERLINE

FORWARD

Types of Warship Masts

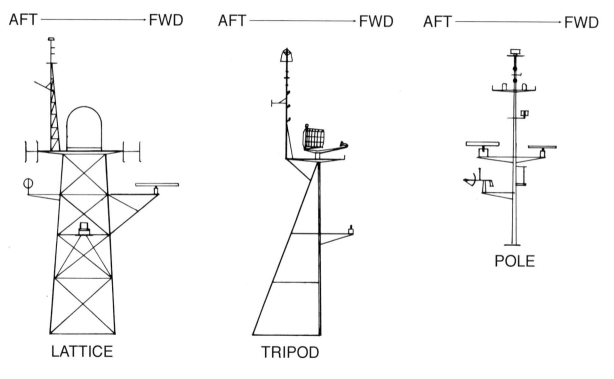

AFT ⟶ FWD   AFT ⟶ FWD   AFT ⟶ FWD

POLE

LATTICE

TRIPOD

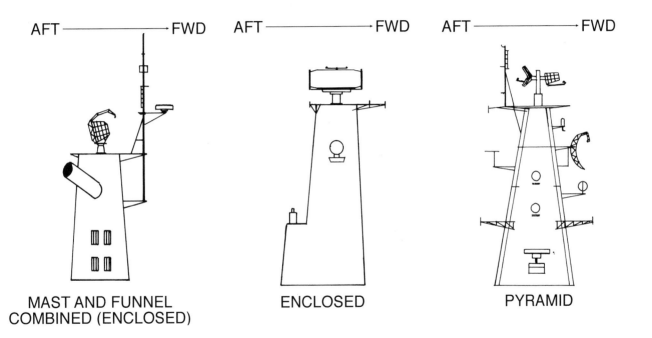

AFT ──────→ FWD

AFT ──────→ FWD

AFT ──────→ FWD

MAST AND FUNNEL
COMBINED (ENCLOSED)

ENCLOSED

PYRAMID

Composite Warship

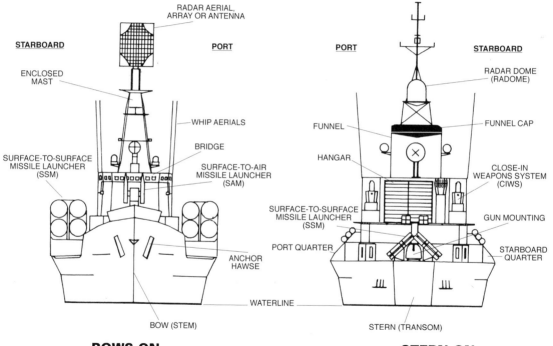

RADAR AERIAL, ARRAY OR ANTENNA

STARBOARD

PORT

ENCLOSED MAST

WHIP AERIALS

BRIDGE

SURFACE-TO-SURFACE MISSILE LAUNCHER (SSM)

SURFACE-TO-AIR MISSILE LAUNCHER (SAM)

ANCHOR HAWSE

BOW (STEM)

BOWS ON

PORT

STARBOARD

RADAR DOME (RADOME)

FUNNEL

FUNNEL CAP

HANGAR

CLOSE-IN WEAPONS SYSTEM (CIWS)

SURFACE-TO-SURFACE MISSILE LAUNCHER (SSM)

GUN MOUNTING

PORT QUARTER

STARBOARD QUARTER

WATERLINE

STERN (TRANSOM)

STERN ON

24

Composite Submarine

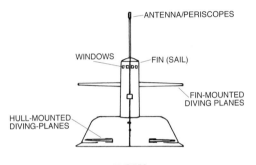

ANTENNA/PERISCOPES

WINDOWS   FIN (SAIL)

FIN-MOUNTED
DIVING PLANES

HULL-MOUNTED
DIVING-PLANES

BOW

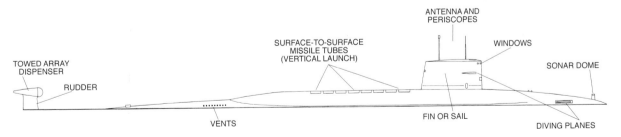

ANTENNA AND
PERISCOPES

WINDOWS

SURFACE-TO-SURFACE
MISSILE TUBES
(VERTICAL LAUNCH)

SONAR DOME

TOWED ARRAY
DISPENSER

RUDDER

VENTS

FIN OR SAIL

DIVING PLANES

Country: FRANCE
Country of origin: FRANCE
Ship type: AIRCRAFT CARRIER
Class: CHARLES DE GAULLE (CVN)
Active: 1 (Sea trials, July 1998; commissioning due December 1999)
Name (Pennant Number): CHARLES DE GAULLE (R 91)

Recognition features:
- Sweeping bow with near vertical stern.
- Very distinctive, clean superstructure, angled surfaces for reduced radar signature.
- Large angular island starboard side, well forward of midships.
- Sturdy enclosed mainmast atop island, supporting tall pole mast.
- Large spherical air-search radar dome atop after end of bridge roof.
- Angled flight deck terminating port side just forward of island.
- Two VLS SAM launchers outboard of flight deck sited amidships, port side and just forward of island, starboard side.

Displacement, tons: 36,600 standard, 40,550 full load.
Length, feet (metres): 857.7 (261.5).
Beam, feet (metres): 211.3 (64.4).

Draught, feet (metres): 27.8 (8.5).
Flight deck length feet (metres): 857.7 (261.5).
Flight deck width feet (metres): 211.3 (64.4).
Speed, knots: 27.

Missiles: SAM - 4 EUROSAM VLS octuple launchers; Aerospatiale ASTER 15 anti-missile system; 2 Matra Sadral PDMS sextuple launchers: Mistral.
Guns: 8 Giat 20F2 20 mm.
Decoys: 4 CSEE Sagaie 10-barrel launchers. Dassault LAD offboard decoys.
Radars:
Air search — Thomson-CSF DRBJ 11B; Thomson DRBV 26D Jupiter
Air/Surface search — Thomson-CSF DRBV 15D Sea Tiger Mk 2.
Navigation — 2 Racal 1229 (DRBN 34A)
Fire control — Thomson-CSF Arabel 3D (SAM).
Sonars: To include SLAT torpedo attack warning.

Fixed wing aircraft: 35/40 including Rafale (M) air defence/strike fighters, Super Étendard strike fighters; E-2C Hawkeye Group 2, AEW.
Helicopters: AS 565MA Panther, (SAR); Super Frelon SA 32 1G (assault/support), NH 90, (from 2005.)

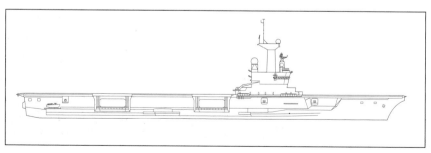

Charles de Gaulle Class

CHARLES DE GAULLE

Clemenceau Class

Country: FRANCE
Country of origin: FRANCE
Ship type: AIRCRAFT CARRIERS
Class: CLEMENCEAU (CV)
Active: 1
Name (Pennant Number): FOCH (R 99)

Recognition features:
- SAM launchers forward of island (starboard) and port side aft.
- Large island just forward of midships, starboard side (three bridges, flag, command and aviation).
- Black-capped, raked funnel atop centre of island.
- Spherical landing approach control (NRBA 51) dome at after end of island.
- Single pole mainmast supporting air/surface search radar aerial forward and air search radar aerial aft.

Displacement, tons: 27,307 standard; 32,780, full load.
Length, feet (metres): 869.4 (265).
Beam, feet (metres): 104.1 (31.7) hull, 168 (51.2) oa.
Draught, feet (metres): 28.2 (8.6).
Flight deck length, feet (metres): 543 (165.5).
Flight deck width, feet (metres): 96.8 (29.5).
Speed, knots: 32.
Range, miles: 7500 at 18 kts., 4,800 at 24 kts.

Missiles: SAM - 2 Thomson-CSF Crotale EDIR octuple launchers; 2 Matra Sadral PDMS sextuple launchers; Mistral.
Guns: 12.7 mm M2 machine-guns
Decoys: 2 CSEE Sagaie 10-barrel trainable launchers.

Radars:
Air search — Thomson-CSF DRBV 23B.
Air/surface search — 2 DRBI 10; Thomson-CSF DRBV 15.
Navigation — Racal Decca 1226.
Fire control — 2 Thomson-CSF DRBC 32B (Sadral); 2 Crotale.
Landing approach control — NRBA 51.
Sonars: Westinghouse SQS-505; hull-mounted, active search.

Fixed wing aircraft: 18 Super Étendard strike fighters; 4 Étendard IV-PM photoreconnaissance (until 1999); 8 LTV F-8P Crusader air defence fighters (until 1999); 7 Br 1050 Alize surveillance aircraft.
Helicopters: 2 SA 365F Dauphin 2.

Note: Sister ship, Clemenceau, deleted in 1997. Foch to be placed in reserve in 2000, returning to full service in 2004 during Charles de Gaulle's refit.

Clemenceau Class

FOCH

French navy

Jeanne D'Arc Class

Country: FRANCE
Country of origin: FRANCE
Ship type: AIRCRAFT CARRIERS (HELICOPTERS)
Class: JEANNE D'ARC (CVH)
Active: 1
Name (Pennant Number): JEANNE D'ARC (ex-La Résolue) (R 97)

Recognition features:
- Long forecastle.
- SSM launcher immediately forward of bridge.
- Main superstructure one third of ship's length from bow.
- Pole mainmast forward of funnel supporting air/surface search and air search radar aerials.
- Tall black-capped funnel at after end of bridge structure.
- Flight deck extending from bridge aft to break at short quarterdeck.
- Four 3.9 in mountings, two on flight deck level in line with forward edge of bridge, port and starboard, two on quarterdeck, port and starboard.

Displacement, tons: 10,000, standard, 13,270, full load.
Length, feet (metres): 597.1 (182.).
Beam, feet (metres): 78.7 (24) (hull).
Draught, feet (metres): 24. (7.3).
Flight deck length, feet (metres): 203.4 (62).
Flight deck width, feet (metres): 68.9 (21).
Speed, knots: 26.5.
Range, miles: 6000 at 15 kts.

Missiles: SSM - 6 Aerospatiale MM 38 Exocet, (2 triple launchers.)
Guns: 4 DCN 3.9 in (100 mm)/55 Mod 1964 CADAM automatic.
Decoys: 2 CSEE/VSEL Syllex 8-barrel trainable chaff launchers. (May not be fitted.)

Radars:
Air search — Thomson-CSF DRBV 22D.
Air/surface search — DRBV 50 (51 version planned.)
Navigation — 2 DRBN 34A (Racal-Decca)
Fire control — 3 Thomson-CSF DRBC 32A.
Sonars: Thomson Sintra DUBV 24C, hull-mounted, active search.

Helicopters: 4 SA 365F Dauphin (SAR); war inventory includes 8 Super Puma and Mk 4 Lynx (ASW).

Note: Used for training officer cadets. After rapid modernisation, could be used as a commando ship, helicopter carrier or troop transport with a 700-strong battalion.

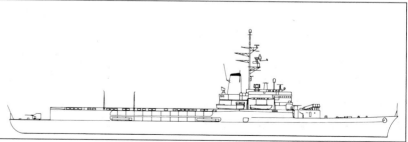

Jeanne D'Arc Class

JEANNE D'ARC

Garibaldi Class

Country: ITALY
Country of origin: ITALY
Ship type: AIRCRAFT CARRIERS
Class: GARIBALDI (CVS)
Active: 1
Name (Pennant Number): GIUSEPPE GARIBALDI (C 551)

Recognition features:
- 6.5° ski jump ramp.
- Large midships island.
- Short mast forward of funnel supporting square profile, long-range air search radar aerial.
- Air search radar aerial atop forward end of bridge.
- Integral, short, black-capped funnel after end of island.
- Two tall pole masts, after one supporting air/surface search radar aerial.
- SSM launchers, two port, two starboard, below after end of flight deck.
- Three 40 mm/70 mountings, one port, one starboard below flight deck just aft of ski jump ramp, one centre-line aft quarterdeck.

Displacement, tons: 10,100 standard, 13,850 full load.
Length, feet (metres): 591 (180).
Beam, feet (metres): 110.2 (33.4).
Draught, feet (metres): 22 (6.7).
Flight deck length, feet (metres): 570.2 (173.8).
Flight deck width, feet (metres): 99.7 (30.4).
Speed, knots: 30.
Range, miles: 7000 at 20 kts.

Missiles: SSM - 4 OTO MELARA Teseo Mk 2 (TG 2). (Mk 3 planned) SAM - 2 Selenia Elsag Albatros octuple launchers: Aspide.

Guns: 6 Breda 40 mm/70 (3 twin) MB.
Torpedoes: 6 - 324 mm B-515 (2 triple) tubes. Honeywell Mk 46 anti-submarine. (Being replaced by A 290.)
Decoys: AN/SLQ-25 Nixie; noisemaker. 2 Breda SCLAR 105 mm 20-barrel trainable chaff launchers.

Radars:
Long range air search — Hughes SPS-52C, 3D.
Air search — Selenia SPS-768 (RAN 3L). SMA SPN-728.
Air/surface search — Selenia SPS-774 (RAN 10S).
Surface search/target indication — SMA SPS-702 UPX; 718 beacon.
Navigation — SMA SPN-749(V)2.
Fire control — 3 Selenia SPG-75 (RTN 30X), (Albatros). 3 Selenia SPG-74 (RTN 20X).
Sonars: Raytheon DE 1160 LF; bow-mounted, active search.

Fixed wing aircraft: 16 AV-8B Harrier II Plus.
Helicopters: 18 Agusta-Sikorsky SH-3D Sea King helicopters (12 in hangar, 6 on deck). Capacity is either 16 Harriers or 18 Sea Kings, but this leaves no space for movement.

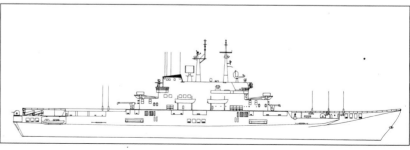

Garibaldi Class

GIUSEPPE GARIBALDI

Country: RUSSIA
Country of origin: RUSSIA
Ship type: AIRCRAFT CARRIERS
Class: KUZNETSOV (OREL) (TYPE 1143.5/6) (CV)
Active: 1
Name (Pennant Numbers): ADMIRAL KUZNETSOV (ex-Tbilisi, ex-Leonid Brezhnev.

Recognition features:
- Typical high, sweeping bow profile.
- 14° ski jump ramp.
- 7° angled flight deck.
- SSM launchers forward end of flight deck in centre, with flush deck covers.
- High freeboard of 16.5 m.
- Large island aft of midships, starboard side.
- Distinctive cylindrical Tacan 'Cake Stand' radar aerial housing forward of funnel atop island/bridge.
- Short, slightly raked funnel at after end of island structure.
- Square stern with clear flight deck overhang.

Displacement, tons: 45,900 standard, 58,500 full load.
Length, feet (metres): 918.6 (280) wl., 999 (304.5) oa.
Beam, feet (metres): 121.4 (37) wl., 229.7 (70) oa.
Draught, feet (metres): 34.4 (10.5).
Flight deck length, feet (metres): 999 (304.5).
Flight deck width, feet (metres): 229.7 (70).
Speed, knots: 30.
Range, miles: 3,850 at 29 kts., 8,500 at 18 kts.

Missiles: SSM - 12 SS-N-19 Shipwreck (Granit 4K-8) launchers (flush mounted).
SAM - 4 Altair SA-N-9 Gauntlet (Klinok) sextuple vertical launchers.
SAM/Guns - 8 Altair CADS-N-1; each with twin 30 mm Gatling combined with 8 SA-N-11 Grisson and Hot Flash/Hot Spot fire control radar/optronic director.
Guns: 6 30 mm/65 AK 630; 6 barrels per mounting.
A/S mortars: 2 RBU 12000.
Decoys: 19 PK 10 and 4 PK 2 chaff launchers.

Radars:
Air search — Sky Watch, 4 planar phased arrays, 3D.
Air/surface search — Top Plate B
Surface search — 2 Strut Pair.
Navigation — 3 Palm Frond.
Fire control — 4 Cross Sword (SAM); 8 Hot Flash.
Aircraft control — Fly Trap B.
Sonars: Bull Horn and Horse Jaw; hull-mounted, active search and attack.

Fixed wing aircraft: 18 Sukhoi Su-27K/Su-33 Flanker D air defence fighters; 4 Sukhoi Su-25UT Frogfoot UTG ground attack fighter used for deck training.
Helicopters: 15 Kamov Ka-27PL Helix, (ASW); 3 Kamov Ka-31 RLD Helix (AEW.)

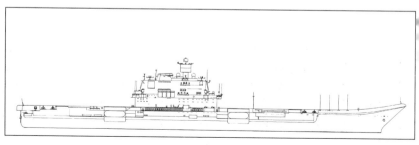

Kuznetsov (Orel) Class

ADMIRAL KUZNETSOV

Country: RUSSIA
Country of origin: RUSSIA
Ship type: AIRCRAFT CARRIERS
Class: MODIFIED KIEV (KRECHYET) (TYPE 1143.4) (CVG)
Active: 0 (In reserve; India reported to be interested in purchase.)
Name (Pennant Number): ADMIRAL GORSHKOV (ex-Baku)

Recognition features:
- Raked bow, square stem.
- Angled flight deck only.
- Two anti-submarine mortars in bows (on forward/aft line).
- Six twin SSM tubular launchers arranged with four forward of two on centreline.
- Two 3.9 in mountings sited on raised sponsons (on forward/aft line) immediately forward of bridge.
- Large island just forward of midships, starboard side.
- Distinctive cylindrical Tacan Cake Stand radar aerial housing centrally sited atop island.
- Squat, low funnel.

Displacement, tons: 32,000, standard; 40,400, full load.
Length, feet (metres): 899 (274) oa.
Beam, feet (metres): 167.3 (51) oa.
Draught, feet (metres): 32.8 (10) (screws).
Flight deck length, feet (metres): 640 (195).
Flight deck width, feet (metres): 68 (20.7).
Speed, knots: 29.
Range, miles: 19,600 at 14 kts.,
    4,000 at 29 kts.

Missiles: SSM - 12 SS-N-12 Sandbox (Basalt P 500) (6 twin) launchers. SAM - 4 SA-N-9 Gauntlet (Klinok) sextuple vertical launchers.
Guns: 2 - 3.9 in (100 mm))/59; 8 30 mm/65 AK 630.
A/S mortars: 2 RBU 12000; 10 tubes per launcher.
Decoys: 2 PK 2 twin chaff launchers. Towed torpedo decoy.
Radars:
Air search — SkyWatch; 4 planar phased array, 3D.
Air/surface search — Plate Steer.
Surface search — 2 Strut Pair.
Navigation — 3 Palm Frond.
Fire control — Front Door, (SS-N-12); Kite Screech, (100 mm guns); 4 Bass Tilt, (Gatlings); 4 Cross Sword., (SA-N-9).
Aircraft control — Fly Trap, Cake Stand.
Sonars: Horse Jaw; hull-mounted, active search and attack; Horse Tail, VDS active search.

Fixed wing aircraft: 12 VSTOL, (Forger aircraft withdrawn from service, 1992.)
Helicopters: 12 Kamov Ka-27 Helix A, (ASW); 2 Kamov Ka-31 Helix RLD, (AEW).

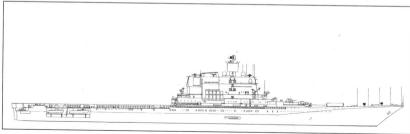

Modified Kiev (Krechyet) Class

ADMIRAL GORSHKOV

Principe de Asturias Class

Country: SPAIN
Country of origin: SPAIN
Ship type: AIRCRAFT CARRIERS
Class: PRINCIPE DE ASTURIAS (CVS)
Active: 1
Name (Pennant Number): PRINCIPE DE ASTURIAS (ex-Almirante Carrero Blanco, (R 11).

Recognition features:
- 12° ski jump ramp fitted.
- Unusual, overhanging aircraft lift at after end of flight deck.
- Two 20 mm/120 mountings at flare of bows, port and starboard.
- Crane gantry forward of island, starboard side.
- Island much further aft of midships than usual, starboard side.
- Large lattice mainmast at forward end of island supporting square profile air search radar aerial.
- Raked funnel mid-island with four protruding individual exhausts at top.
- Aircraft control radar dome at after end of island structure.
- Two 20 mm/120 mountings right aft, port and starboard.

Displacement, tons: 17,188, full load.
Length, feet (metres): 642.7 (195.9) oa.
Beam, feet (metres): 79.7 (24.3).
Draught, feet (metres): 30.8 (9.4).
Flight deck length, feet (metres): 575.1 (175.3).
Flight deck width, feet (metres): 95.1 (29).
Speed, knots: 25.
Range, miles: 6500 at 20 kts.

Guns: 4 Bazán Mod 2A/2B Meroka 12-barrel 20 mm/120; 2 Rheinmetall 37 saluting guns.
Decoys: 4 Loral Hycor SRBOC 6 barrel fixed Mk 36; AN/SLQ-25 Nixie towed torpedo decoy; US Prairie/Masker; hull noise/blade rate suppression.
Radars:
Air search — Hughes SPS-52 C/D, 3D.
Surface search — ISC Cardion SPS-55.
Aircraft control — ITT SPN-35A
Fire control — 1 Selenia RAN 12L (target designation); 4 Sperry/Lockheed VPS 2, (Meroka); 1 RTN 11L/X, (missile warning.)

Fixed wing aircraft: 6-12 BAe/McDonnell Douglas EAV-8B Harrier II/Harrier Plus.
Helicopters: 6-10 Sikorsky SH-3D/G Sea Kings, (ASW/AEW); 2-4 Agusta AB 212EW; 2 Sikorsky SH-60B Seahawks.

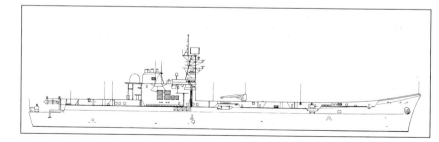

Principe de Asturias Class

PRINCIPE DE ASTURIAS

Jane's/HM Steele

Country: THAILAND
Country of origin: SPAIN
Ship type: AIRCRAFT CARRIER
Class: CHAKRI NARUEBET (CVS)
Active: 1
Name (Pennant Number): CHAKRI NARUEBET (911)

- 12° ski jump ramp.
- Squared, 'chunky' island aft of midships, starboard side.
- Crane gantry forward end of island, starboard side.
- One of two aircraft lifts at after end of flight deck.
- Enclosed mainmast part of funnel structure
- Air search radar, Hughes SPS-52C, atop bridge.

Note: Similarities with Spanish carrier, Principe de Asturias.

Displacement: 11,485 full load.
Length, feet (metres): 599.1 (182.6) oa.
Beam, feet (metres): 73.8 (22.5) wl., 100.1 (30.5) oa.
Draught, (metres): not available.
Flight deck length (metres): 572.8 (174.6).
Flight deck width (metres): 90.2 (27.5).
Speed, knots: 26 (16 on diesels).
Range, miles: 10,000 at 12 kts.

Missiles: SAM — 1 Mk 41 LCHR 8 cell VLS launcher, Sea Sparrow, (to be fitted.) 3 Matra Sadral sextuple launchers, Mistral.
Guns: 4 Vulcan Phalanx CIWS; 2 30 mm (to be fitted.)
Decoys: 4 Tracor Mk 137 chaff launchers. SLQ-32 torpedo decoy, (to be fitted.)

Radars:
    Air search — Hughes SPS-52C.
    Surface search — SPS-64.
    Fire control — Signaal STIR.
    Navigation — Kelvin Hughes.
    Aircraft control — Kelvin Hughes.
Sonars: Type not known; hull-mounted, active search.

Fixed wing aircraft: 6 BAe/McDonnell Douglas AV-8S, (supplied to Spain and transferred in 1996.)
Helicopters: 6 Sikorsky S-70B7 Seahawk, (multi-mission.) Chinook capable.

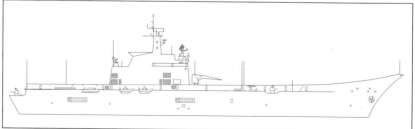

Chakri Naruebet Class

CHAKRI NARUEBET

Aircraft Carrier – Spain   41

Colossus Class

Country: BRAZIL
Country of origin: UK
Ship type: AIRCRAFT CARRIERS
Class: COLOSSUS
Active: 1
Name (Pennant Number): MINAS GERAIS (ex-HMS Vengeance) (A 11)

Recognition features:
- Lattice catapult spur at bows.
- Island forward of midships, starboard side.
- Lattice mainmast immediately forward of funnel supporting large air search radar aerial on platform at half mast.
- Short tapered funnel atop island, sloping aft.
- Angled flight deck.

Displacement, tons: 15,890 standard, 19,890 full load.
Length, feet (metres): 695 (211.8).
Beam, feet (metres): 80 (24.4).
Draught, feet (metres): 24.5 (7.5).
Flight deck length, feet (metres): 690 (210.3).
Flight deck width, feet (metres): 119.6 (36.4).
Speed, knots: 24.
Range, miles: 12,000 at 14 kts; 6,200 at 23 kts.

Missiles: SAM — 2 Matra Sadral twin launchers; Mistral.
Guns: 2 - 47 mm saluting guns.
Decoys: Plessey Shield chaff launcher.

Radars:
Air search — Lockheed SPS-40B.
Air/surface search — Plessey AWS 4.
Navigation — Scanter Mil and Furuno
Fire control — 2 SPG-34.

Fixed wing aircraft: 6 A-4 Skyhawks, (of 23 acquired from Kuwaiti Air Force in 1998,) to be fully operational by end of 1998.
Helicopters: 4-6 Agusta SH-3A/D Sea Kings; 2 Aerospatiale UH-13 Ecureuil II; 3 Aerospatiale UH-14 Super Puma.

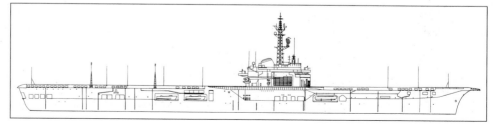

Colossus Class

MINAS GERAIS

Brazilian navy

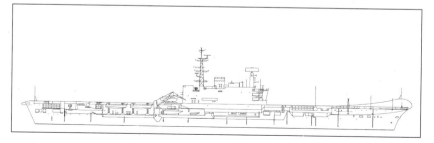

Hermes Class

Country: INDIA
Country of origin: UK.
Ship type: AIRCRAFT CARRIERS
Class: HERMES
Active: 1
Name (Pennant Number): VIRAAT (Ex-HMS Hermes) (R 22)

Recognition features:
- Fitted with 12° ski jump ramp over bows.
- Large midships island, starboard side.
- Medium height, enclosed mast at forward end of island with air search radar aerial atop.
- Short square profile funnel, mid-island.
- Tall lattice mainmast at after end of island supporting radar and communications aerials.
- Crane derrick immediately aft of island starboard side.

Displacement, tons: 23,900, standard; 28,700 full load.
Length, feet (metres): 685 (208.8).
Beam, feet (metres): 90 (27.4).
Draught, feet (metres): 28.5 (8.7).
Speed, knots: 28.

Missiles: None, Seacat SAM removed in 1996.
Guns: 2 Bofors 40 mm/60; 2 USSR 30 mm AK 230 Gatlings on aft sponsons.
Decoys: 2 Knebworth Corvus chaff launchers.

Radars:
Air search — Marconi Type 996.
Air/surface search — Signaal DA05
Navigation — 2 Racal Decca 1006.
Sonars: Graseby Type 184M; hull-mounted, active search and attack.

Fixed wing aircraft: 12 Sea Harriers FRS Mk 51 (capacity for 30).
Helicopters: 7 Sea King Mk 42B/C and Ka-27 Helix.

Note: Life extension refit begun in 1997 to keep ship in service until 2010.

Hermes Class

VIRAAT

Invincible Class

Country: UNITED KINGDOM
Country of origin: UK
Ship type: AIRCRAFT CARRIERS
Class: INVINCIBLE (CVS)
Active: 3
Name (Pennant Number): INVINCIBLE (R 05), ILLUSTRIOUS (R 06), ARK ROYAL (R 07)

Recognition features:

- 12° ski jump ramp fitted on offset, port side deck, (Invincible); 13° on Illustrious, and Ark Royal, post-1998.
- SAM launcher situated outboard, midway along ski jump ramp, starboard side.(Removed from 1998/99.) Starboard side of forecastle roofed in on Illustrious, and Ark Royal post 1998.
- Very long island situated amidships, starboard side.
- Twin funnels, one immediately aft of bridge, one aft of mainmast, forward funnel taller. Both funnels have twin, black painted exhausts atop.
- Two fire control radar domes, one at each extreme of island (fore and aft).
- Central, enclosed mainmast supporting surface search radar aerial, 992R (R 07) or 996(2) (R 05 and R 06). Illustrious has SATCOM terminals midway mast.
- CIWS mountings fitted at bows, port side aft and immediately forward of after funnel. Goalkeeper (R 05 and R 06); Vulcan Phalanx (R 07).

Displacement full load, tons: 20,600.
Length, feet (metres): 685.8 (209.1) oa.
Beam, feet (metres): 118 (36) oa.
Draught, feet (metres): 26 (8).
Flight deck length, feet (metres): 550 (167.8).
Flight deck width, feet (metres): 44.3 (13.5).
Speed, knots: 28.
Range, miles: 7000 at 19 kts.

Missiles: SAM — BAe Sea Dart twin launcher, (removed 1998/99.)
Guns: 3 GE/GD 20 mm Mk 15 Vulcan Phalanx 6-barrels each, (R 07); 3 Signaal/GE 30 mm 7-barrel Gatling Goalkeeper (R 05 and 06); 2 Oerlikon/BMARC 20 mm GAM-B01.
Decoys: Outfit DLJ - 8 Sea Gnat 6-barrel dispensers; Prairie/Masker noise suppression.

Radars:
Air search — Marconi/Signaal Type 1022.
Surface search — Plessey Type 996(2) (R 05 and 06); Marconi Type 992R (R 07).
Navigation — 2 Kelvin Hughes Type 1006 (R 05 and 07); Type 1007 (R 06).
Fire control — 2 Marconi Type 909 or 909(1) (R 06).
Sonars: Plessey Type 2016; hull-mounted, active search and attack.

Fixed wing aircraft: 9 British Aerospace Sea Harrier FA 2 and 6 Harrier GR 7.
Helicopters: Up to 9 Westland Sea King HAS 6 or EH 101 Merlin; 3 Westland Sea King AEW 2.

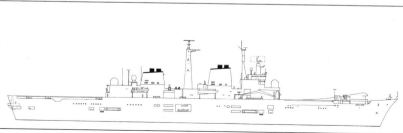

Invincible Class

ILLUSTRIOUS

Jane's/HM Steele

Country: UNITED STATES OF AMERICA
Country of origin: USA
Ship type: AIRCRAFT CARRIERS
Class: ENTERPRISE (CVN)
Active: 1
Name (Pennant Number): ENTERPRISE (CVN 65)

Recognition features:
- Angled flight deck.
- Island aft of midships, starboard side.
- Island comprises unusual box shaped bridge supported on significantly narrower pedestal structure.
- Square profile air search radar aerial mounted atop the bridge, forward.
- SAM launchers mounted port and starboard, at after end of flight deck. Third launcher situated starboard side forward, approximately quarter of ship's length from bows.
- CIWS mountings situated right aft below flight deck overhang.

Displacement, tons: 75,700 standard, 93,970 full load.
Length, feet (metres): 1123 (342.3).
Beam, feet (metres): 133 (40.5).
Draught, feet (metres): 39 (11.9).
Flight deck length, feet (metres): 1088 (331.6).
Flight deck width, feet (metres): 252 (76.8).
Speed, knots: 33.

Missiles: SAM - 3 Raytheon GMLS Mk 29 octuple launchers, NATO Sea Sparrow.
Guns: 3 GE/GD 20 mm Vulcan Phalanx 6-barrel Mk 15.
Decoys: 4 Loral Hycor SRBOC 6-barrel fixed Mk 36; SSTDS; AN/SLQ-36 Nixie.

Radars:
Air search — ITT SPS-48E, 3D; Raytheon SPS-49(V)5; Hughes Mk 23 TAS.
Surface search — Norden SPS-67.
Navigation — Raytheon SPS 64(V)9; Furuno 900.
Fire control — 6 Mk 95, (SAM).

Fixed wing aircraft: 50 TACAIR wing, depending on mission, includes up to 20 Grumman F-14 Tomcat air defence fighters; 36 McDonnell Douglas F/A-18 Hornet (strike/interdiction) ; 4 Grumman EA-6B Prowler (EW) ; 4 Grumman E-2C Hawkeye (AEW); 6 Lockheed S-3B Viking (ASW/ASV) ; 2 Lockheed ES-3A Shadow (ELINT).
Helicopters: 4 Sikorsky SH-60F Seahawk (ASW) and 2 HH-60H Seahawk (strike/special warfare support/SAR).

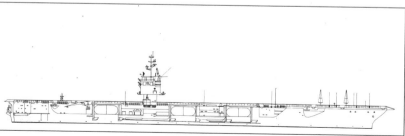

Enterprise Class

ENTERPRISE

Georgio Arra

Kitty Hawk and John F Kennedy Class

Country: UNITED STATES OF AMERICA
Country of origin: USA
Ship type: AIRCRAFT CARRIERS
Class: KITTY HAWK and JOHN F KENNEDY (CV)
Active: 3
Name (Pennant Number): KITTY HAWK (CV 63), CONSTELLATION (CV 64), JOHN F KENNEDY (CV 67) (AMERICA, CV 66, taken out of service 1996).

Recognition features:
- Angled flight deck.
- Complex pole mast central island, housing radar, WT and EW aerials.
- Funnel at rear of island structure, flush with top of bridge.
- Tall lattice mast immediately aft of bridge supporting square profile air search radar aerial.
- Crane derrick starboard, aft of island, outboard of flight deck.
- CIWS mountings, one port side aft below flight deck overhang, one halfway up island structure starboard side and one port side forward sited on platform below round of angled flight deck.
- Two deck-edge lifts fitted forward of island superstructure, a third aft of the island, and a fourth port side quarter.

Displacement full load, tons: 81,123 (CV 63), 81,773 (CV 64), 80,941 (CV 67).
Length, feet (metres): 1062.5 (323.6) (CV 63), 1072.5 (326.9) (CV 64), 1052 (320.6) (CV 67).
Beam, feet (metres): 130 (39.6).
Draught, feet (metres): 37.4 (11.4).
Flight deck length, feet (metres): 1046 (318.8).
Flight deck width, feet (metres): 252 (76.8).
Speed, knots: 32.
Range, miles: 4,000 at 30 kts., 12,000 at 20 kts.

Missiles: SAM - 3 Raytheon GMLS Mk 29 octuple launchers, NATO Sea Sparrow.
Guns: 3 or 4 GE/GD 20 mm Vulcan Phalanx 6-barrel Mk 15.
Decoys: 4 Loral Hycor SRBOC 6-barrelled fixed Mk 36. SSTDS; AN/SLQ-36 Nixie.

Radars:
Air search — ITT SPS-48E, 3D; Raytheon SPS-49(V)5, Hughes Mk 23 TAS.
Surface search — Norden SPS-67.
Navigation — Raytheon SPN-64(V)9; Furuno 900.
Fire control — 6 Mk 95, (SAM).
Sonar: Fitted for SQS-23 (CV-67).

Fixed wing aircraft: 50 TACAIR air wing, depending on mission, including up to 20 Grumman F-14 Tomcat air defence fighters; 36 McDonnell Douglas F/A-18 Hornet (strike/interdiction); 4 Grumman EA-6B Prowler (EW); 4 Grumman E-2C Hawkeye; 6 Lockheed S-3B Viking (ASW/ASV);2 ES-3A Shadow (ELINT).
Helicopters: 4 Sikorsky SH-60F (ASW); 2 HH-60H Seahawk (strike/special forces/SAR).

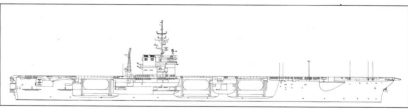

KITTY HAWK

Jane's/HM Steele

Nimitz Class

Country: UNITED STATES OF AMERICA
Country of origin: USA
Ship type: AIRCRAFT CARRIERS
Class: NIMITZ (CVN)
Active: 8
Building: 2 (RONALD REAGAN, CVN 76; —— ,CVN 77).
Name (Pennant Number): NIMITZ (CVN 68), DWIGHT D EISENHOWER (CVN 69), CARL VINSON (CVN 70), THEODORE ROOSEVELT (CVN 71), ABRAHAM LINCOLN (CVN 72), GEORGE WASHINGTON (CVN 73), JOHN C STENNIS (CVN 74), HARRY S TRUMAN, (ex-United States) (CVN 75).

Recognition features:

- Large island well aft of midships. ·
- Square profile air search radar aerial mounted atop forward end of island, above bridge.
- Large complex pole mainmast atop central bridge supporting array of radar, EW and WT aerials.
- Enclosed mast immediately aft of island supporting curved lattice bedstead radar aerial.
- Two CIWS mountings fitted right aft, one port, one starboard below flight deck overhang.
- Second two CIWS mountings, port and starboard, immediately forward of where flight deck narrows.

Displacement, full load, tons: 91,487 (CVN 68-70), 96,386 (CVN 71), 102,000 (CVN 72-76).
Length, feet (metres): 1040 (317).
Beam, feet (metres): 134 (40.8).
Draught, feet (metres): 37 (11.3) CVN 68-70; 38.7 (11.8) CVN 71; 39 (11.9) CVN 72-76.
Flight deck length, feet (metres): 1092 (332.9).
Flight deck angled, feet (metres): 779.8 (237.7).

Flight deck width, feet (metres): 252 (76.8).
Speed, knots: 30.0+
Missiles: SAM - 3 Raytheon GMLS Mk 29 octuple launchers, NATO Sea Sparrow. (RAM to be fitted 1999-2005).
Guns: 4 GE/GD 20 mm Vulcan Phalanx 6-barrel Mk 15 (3 in CVN 68 and 69).
Decoys: 4 Loral Hycor SRBOC 6-barrel fixed Mk 36. SSTDS; SLQ-36 Nixie (Phase I).

Radars:
Air search — ITT SPS-48E, 3D; Raytheon SPS-49(V)5; Hughes Mk 23 TAS.
Surface search — Norden SPS-67V.
Navigation — Raytheon SPS-64(V)9; Furuno 900.
Fire control — 6 Mk 95, (SAM).

Fixed wing aircraft: 50 TACAIR air wing, depending on mission, includes, up to 20 Grumman F-14D Tomcat, air defence fighter; 36 McDonnell Douglas F/A-18E Hornet strike/interdiction; 4 Grumman EA-6B Prowler (EW); 4 Grumman E-2C Hawkeye; 6 Lockheed S-3B Viking (ASW/ASV); 2 ES-3A Shadow, (ELINT).
Helicopters: 4 Sikorsky SH-60F Seahawk (ASW) and 2 HH-60H Seahawk (strike, special warfare support and SAR.)

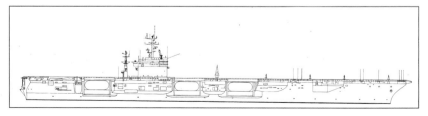

Nimitz Class

ABRAHAM LINCOLN

Vittorio Veneto (CGH)

Country: ITALY
Country of origin: ITALY
Ship type: CRUISERS
Class: VITTORIO VENETO (CGH)
Active: 1
Name (Pennant Number): VITTORIO VENETO (C 550)

Recognition features:
- Two large enclosed masts just forward and aft of midships.
- Twin funnels in 'V' formation at after end of each mast.
- Forward mast supports distinctive, square, SPS-52C long-range air search radar aerial.
- Lattice crane derrick and ship's boat sited between masts.
- Very unusual break in deck level, just aft of bridge, up from main deck to flight deck.
- Breda 40 mm/70 gun mountings situated port and starboard at forward end of long flight deck.
- SAM launcher at after end of forecastle.
- Four SSM launchers amidships, two port two starboard, adjacent to forward funnel.

Displacement, tons: 7,500 standard, 9,500 full load.
Length, feet (metres): 589 (179.6).
Beam, feet (metres): 63.6 (19.4).
Draught, feet (metres): 19.7 (6).
Flight deck length, feet (metres): 131 (40.6).
Flight deck width, feet (metres): 61 (18.6).
Speed, knots: 32.
Range, miles: 5,000 at 17 kts.

Missiles: SSM - 4 OTO MELARA Teseo Mk 2, (TG 2). SAM - GDC Pomona Standard SM-1ER; Aster twin Mk 10 Mod 9 launcher. A/S - Honeywell ASROC launcher.
Guns: 8 OTO MELARA 3 in (76 mm)/62 MMK.

6 Breda 40 mm/70 (3 twin).
Torpedoes: 6 - 324 mm US Mk 32 (2 triple) tubes; Honeywell Mk 46; anti-submarine.
Decoys: 2 Breda SCLAR 20-barrel trainable chaff. SLQ-25 Nixie torpedo decoy.

Radars:
Long range air search — Hughes SPS-52C, 3D.
Air search — Selenia SPS-768 (RAN 3L).
Surface search/target indication — SMA SPS-702.
Navigation — SMA SPS-748.
Fire control — 4 Selenia SPG-70 (RTN 10X). 2 Selenia SPG 74 (RTN 20X). 2 Sperry/RCA SPG 55C (Standard).
Sonars: Sangamo SQS-23G; bow-mounted, active search and attack.

Helicopters: 6 Agusta-Bell AB 212 (ASW).

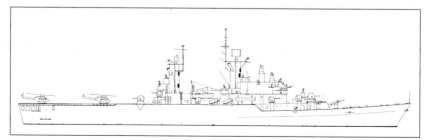

Vittorio Veneto (CGH)

VITTORIO VENETO

De Ruyter Class (CG)

Country: PERU
Country of origin: NETHERLANDS
Ship type: CRUISERS
Class: DE RUYTER (CG)
Active: 1
Name (Pennant Number): ALMIRANTE GRAU (ex-De Ruyter) (CLM 81)

Recognition features:
- Two 6 in gun mountings only forward of bridge.
- Cylindrical after funnel close to midships, sloped slightly aft with lattice mast built around it.
- Forward funnel at after end of forward superstructure with mast above.
- Dome-shaped Signaal WM25 fire control radar on pylon immediately forward of main mast.
- Upper deck superstructure sited astern of after funnel with fire control director atop.
- Two 6 in gun mountings on afterdeck.
- No flight deck.

Displacement, tons: 12,165 full load.
Length, feet (metres): 624.5 (190.3).
Beam, feet (metres): 56.7 (17.3).
Draught, feet (metres): 22 (6.7).
Speed, knots: 32.
Range, miles: 7000 at 12 kts.

Missiles: SSM - 8 OTO MELARA Otomat Mk 2 (TG 1).
Guns: 8 Bofors 6 in (152 mm)/53 (4 twin); 8 Bofors 40 mm/70.
Depth charges: 2 racks.
Decoys: 2 Dagaie and 1 Sagaie chaff launchers.
Radars:
Air search — Signaal LW08.
Surface search/target indication — Signaal DA08.
Navigation — Racal Decca 1226.
Fire control — Signaal WM25, (6 in guns), Signaal STIR.
Sonars: CWE 610; hull-mounted, active search.

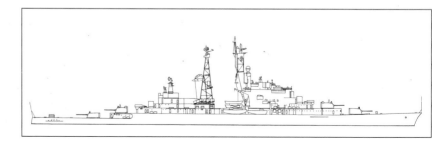

De Ruyter Class (CG)

ALMIRANTE GRAU

Country: PERU
Country of origin: NETHERLANDS
Ship type: CRUISERS
Class: DE RUYTER (CH)
Active: 1
Name (Pennant Number): AGUIRRE (ex-De Zeven Provincien) (CH 84)

Recognition features:
- Two 6 in gun and one 57 mm/60 twin gun mountings forward of bridge. (Grau has just two 6 in twin mountings in same position).
- Forward funnel at after end of forward superstructure with mast above.
- After funnel close to midships, tapered towards top with smoke detector at top after end.
- Signaal LW02 air search radar aerial atop after funnel.
- Lattice mast aft of after funnel.
- Bofors 57 mm/60 twin gun mountings between funnels.
- Helicopter hangar and flight deck aft of lattice mast.

Displacement, tons: 12,250 full load.
Length, feet (metres): 609 (185.6).
Beam, feet (metres): 56.7 (17.3).
Draught, feet (metres): 22 (6.7).
Flight deck length, feet (metres): 115 (35).
Flight deck width, feet (metres): 56 (17).
Speed, knots: 32.
Range, miles: 7,000 at 12 kts.

Guns: 4 Bofors 6in (152 mm)/53 (2 twin); 6 Bofors 57 mm/60 (3 twin); 4 Bofors 40 mm/70.
Depth charges: 2 racks.
Radars:
Air search — Signaal LW02.
Surface search/target indication — Signaal DA02.

Surface search — Signaal ZW03.
Fire control — 3 Signaal M45; 1 Signaal M25.
Navigation — 2 Racal Decca 1226
Sonars: CWE 10N, hull-mounted, active search.

Helicopters: 3 Agusta-Sikorsky ASH-3D Sea King (ASW/ASV).

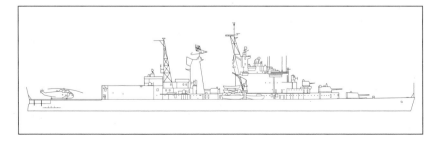

AGUIRRE

Country: RUSSIA
Country of origin: RUSSIA
Ship type: CRUISERS
Class: KARA (BERKOT-B) (TYPE 1134B/BF) (CG)
Active: 2
Name (Pennant Number): KERCH, AZOV.

Recognition features:

- SAM (twin) SA-N-3 Goblet launcher on raised forecastle structure forward of bridge.
- Head Light C fire control director mounted on bridge roof.
- Forward tripod mast aft of bridge supporting air/surface search radar aerial.
- Large pyramid mainmast sited amidships supporting square profile Top Sail air search radar aerial (Azov) or Flat Screen air search radar, (Kerch).
- Two 3-in gun mountings, port and starboard, sited between forward and aftermasts.
- Large, slightly tapered, square section funnel situated immediately aft of mainmast.
- Head Light C fire control director sited aft of funnel, (Kerch). (Top Dome fire control aft in Azov in place of Head Light C)

Displacement, tons: 7,650, standard, 9,900 full load.
Length, feet (metres): 568 (173.2).
Beam, feet (metres): 61 (18.6).
Draught, feet (metres): 22 (6.7).
Speed, knots: 34.
Range, miles: 9,000 at 15 kts, 3,000 at 32 kts.

Missiles: SAM - 2 SA-N-3 Goblet twin launchers (1 in Azov); 6 SA-N-6 Grumble (Rif) vertical launchers (Azov only); 2 SA-N-4 Gecko twin launchers. A/S - 2 SS-N-14 Silex (Rastrub) quad launchers.

Guns: 4 3 in (76 mm)/60 (2 twin). 4 30 mm/65; 6 barrels per mounting.
Torpedoes: 10 or 4 21 in (533 mm) (2 quin) (2 twin in Azov) tubes.
A/S mortars: 2 RBU 6000 12-tubed, trainable. 2 RBU 1000 6-tubed.
Decoys: 2 PK 2 chaff launchers. 1 BAT-1 torpedo decoy.

Radars:
Air search — Top Sail 3D (Azov) or Flat Screen, (Kerch).
Air/surface search — Head Net C, 3D.
Navigation — 2 Don Kay, 2 Palm Frond, Don 2 (not in Azov).
Fire control — 2 Head Light B or C (one in Azov), (for SA-N-3 and SS-N-14); 2 Pop Group, (SA-N-4); Top Dome (SA-N-6) (aft in Azov in place of one Head Light C); 2 Owl Screech, (76 mm guns); 2 Bass Tilt, (30 mm guns).
Sonars: Bull Nose, (Titan 2-MG 332) hull-mounted, active search and attack; Mare Tail; VDS.

Helicopters: 1 Kamov Ka-25 Hormone A, (ASW).

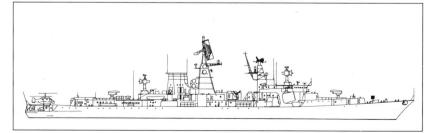

Kara (Berkot-B) Class

AZOV

Kirov (Orlan) Class

Country: RUSSIA
Country of origin: Russia
Ship type: CRUISERS
Class: KIROV (ORLAN) (TYPE 1144.1/1144.2) (CGN)
Active: 2
Name (Pennant Number): ADMIRAL NAKHIMOV (ex-Kalinin), PYOTR
VELIKIY (ex-Yuri Andropov)

Recognition features:

- Very large mast and funnel combined sited amidships supporting Top Pair air search radar aerials.
- Raised bows, sloping forecastle, break in deck aft of superstructure.
- Secondary masts and upper deck structures aft of mainmast supporting (from forward to aft) Top Plate air/surface search and Top Dome fire control radar aerials.
- 130mm/70 gun mounting fitted immediately forward of flight deck.
- CADS-N-1 SAM/gun mounting and Hot Flash/Hot Spot fire control radar/optronic director on raised platforms each side of SS-N-19 launch silos; four more on after superstructure.

Displacement, tons: 19,000 standard, 24,300 full load.
Length, feet (metres): 826.8 (252).
Beam, feet (metres): 93.5 (28.5).
Draught, feet (metres): 29.5 (9.1).
Speed, knots: 30.
Range, miles: 14,000 at 30 kts.

Missiles: SSM - 20 Chelomey SS-N-19
Shipwreck (Granit); SAM - 12 SA-N-6
Grumble (Rif) vertical launchers; 2 SA-N-4
Gecko twin launchers; 2 SA-N-9 Gauntlet
(Klinok) octuple vertical launchers.
SAM/Guns - 6 CADS-N-1 each has a twin
30 mm Gatling, combined with 8 SA-N-11
Grisson missiles. A/S - SS-N-15 (Starfish)

fired from fixed torpedo tubes behind shutters in superstructure.
Guns: 2 130 mm/70 (twin) AK 130.
Torpedoes: 10 - 21 in (533 mm) (2 quin) tubes.
A/S mortars: 1 RBU 12000; 10 tubes per launcher; 2 RBU 1000 6-tubed.
Decoys: 2 twin PK 2 150 mm chaff launchers; towed torpedo decoy.

Radars:

Air search — Top Pair (Top Sail + Big Net) 3D.
Air/surface search — Top Plate 3D.
Navigation — 3 Palm Frond.
Fire control — Cross Sword (SA-N-9); 1 (Velikiy) or 2 Top Dome; 1 Flap Lid or Tomb Stone (Velikiy) (SA-N-6); 2 Pop Group, (SA-N-4); Kite Screech (130 mm guns); 6 Hot Flash (CADS-N-1).
Aircraft control — Flyscreen B.
Sonars: Horse Jaw; hull-mounted, active search and attack; Horse Tail; VDS active search.

Helicopters: 3 Kamov Ka-27PL Helix, (ASW).

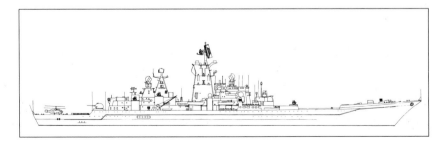

Kirov (Orlan) Class

KIROV

Kynda Class

Country: RUSSIA
Country of origin: RUSSIA
Ship type: CRUISERS
Class: KYNDA (TYPE 58) (CG)
Active: 1
Name (Pennant Number): ADMIRAL GOLOVKO

Recognition features:
- Heavy tubular SS-N-39 Sepal SSM launchers fore and aft of superstructure.
- Twin 3 in mountings, in X and Y positions.
- Twin level deckhouse alongside forward funnel.
- Two pylon masts forward of funnels, both with Head Net A air search radar aerials atop.
- Triple torpedo tubes between funnels.
- Scoop Pair fire control radar aerials midway up both masts.

Displacement, tons: 4,265 standard, 5,412 full load.
Length, feet (metres): 468.2 (142.7).
Beam, feet (metres): 52.5 (16).
Draught, feet (metres): 13.5 (4.1).
Speed, knots: 34.
Range, miles: 3,610 at 18 kts.

Missiles: SSM — 8 SS-N-3B Sepal (2 quad) launchers; SAM — SA-N-1 Goa twin launcher.
Guns: 4 3in (76mm)/60 (2 twin); 4 30mm/65, 6-barrels per mounting.
Torpedoes: 6 21 in (533mm) (2 triple) tubes.
A/S mortars: 2 RBU 6000 12-tube trainable.

Radars:
Air search — 2 Head Net A.
Surface search and navigation — 2 Don 2.
Fire control — 2 Scoop Pair (SS-N-3B); Peel Group (SA-N-1 SAM); Owl Screech (76mm gun); Bass Tilt, (30 mm guns).
Sonars: Herkules-2N (GS 372) hull-mounted, active search and attack.

Helicopters: Platform only.

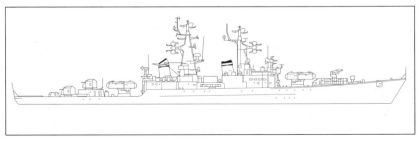

Slava (Atlant) Class

Country: RUSSIA
Country of origin: RUSSIA
Ship type: CRUISERS
Class: SLAVA (ATLANT) (TYPE 1164) (CG)
Active: 4
Name (Pennant Number): MOSKVA (ex-Slava,) MARSHAL USTINOV, VARYAG (ex-Chervona Ukraina), ADMIRAL LOBOV (ex-Ukraina).

Recognition features:
- High bow, sloping forecastle.
- 130 mm/70 gun mounting at after end of forecastle.
- Distinctive angled SSM launchers adjacent to the bridge structure, four pairs port and four pairs starboard.
- Large pyramid mainmast at after end of bridge structure with lattice gantry protruding horizontally astern at the top. Mainmast supports the air/surface search Top Steer or Top Plate radar aerial.
- Smaller aftermast supporting the Top Pair air search radar aerials.
- Short, squat twin funnels, side by side, immediately astern of aftermast.
- Notable gap abaft the twin funnels (SA-N-6 area) is traversed by a large crane which stows between the funnels.
- Prominent Top Dome fire control director aft situated just forward of small flight deck.

Displacement, tons: 9,800 standard, 11,200, full load.
Length, feet (metres): 610.2 (186).
Beam, feet (metres): 70.5 (21.5).
Draught, feet (metres): 24.9 (7.6).
Speed, knots: 32.
Range, miles: 7,500 at 15 kts., 2,500 at 30 kts.

Missiles: SSM — 16 Chelomey SS-N-12 (8 twin) Sandbox (Bazalt) launchers. SAM - 8 SA-N-6 Grumble (Rif) vertical launchers; 2 SA-N-4 Gecko twin launchers.
Guns: 2 - 130 mm/70 (twin) AK 130; 6 - 30 mm/65 AK 650; 6-barrels per mounting.
Torpedoes: 10 - 21 in (533 mm) (2 quin).
A/S mortars: 2 RBU 6000 12-tubed, trainable.
Decoys: 2 PK 2 or 12 PK 10 (Lobov) chaff launchers.

Radars:
Air search — Top Pair (Top Sail + Big Net), 3D.
Air/surface search — Top Steer or Top Plate, (Varyag and Lobov) 3D.
Navigation — 3 Palm Frond.
Fire control — Front Door, (SS-N-12); Top Dome, (SA-N-6 SAM); 2 Pop Group, (SA-N-4 SAM); 3 Bass Tilt, (30 mm guns); Kite Screech, (130 mm gun).
Sonars: Bull Horn and Steer Hide; hull-mounted, active search and attack.

Helicopters: 1 Kamov Ka-27PL Helix, (ASW).

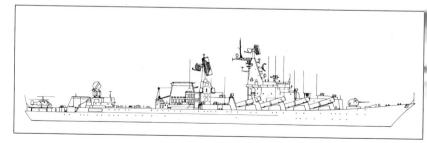

Slava (Atlant) Class

SLAVA

California Class (CGN)

Country: UNITED STATES OF AMERICA
Country of origin: UNITED STATES OF AMERICA
Ship type: CRUISERS
Class: CALIFORNIA (CGN)
Active: 2
Name (Pennant Numbers): CALIFORNIA (CGN 36); SOUTH CAROLINA (CGN 37).

Recognition features:

● Flat deck with slightly raised bows.
● Two pyramid masts with prominent square SPS-48E air search radar aerial atop forward mast; domed SPQ-9A fire control radar facing astern on aft mast.
● SAM launcher aft end of forecastle and on afterdeck.
● Two 5 in gun mountings, far forward of superstructure and immediately aft of superstructure.
● Two ships boats positioned one above each other by aft section of superstructure
● Two distinctive angular SPG-51D fire control directors above bridge and aft superstructure.

Displacement, tons: 9,561 standard, 10,450 full load.
Length, feet (metres): 596 (181.7).
Beam, feet (metres): 61 (18.6).
Draught, feet (metres): 31.5 (sonar) (9.6).
Speed, knots: 30+

Missiles: SSM — 8 McDonnell Douglas Harpoon (2 quad) launchers. SAM — 2 Mk 13 Mod 7 launchers, Standard SM-2MR.
Guns: 2 FMC 5 in (127 mm)/54 Mk 45 Mod 0; 2 GE/GD 20 mm Vulcan Phalanx 6-barrel Mk 15; 4 12.7 mm MGs.
Torpedoes: 4 324 mm Mk 32 (2 twin) fixed tubes. Honeywell Mk 46 Mod 5.

Decoys: 4 Loral Hycor SRBOC 6-barrel fixed Mk 36, IR flares and chaff; SLQ-25 torpedo decoy system.

Radar:
Air search — ITT SPS-48E. 3D, Raytheon SPS-49(V)5.
Surface search — Norden SPS-67(V)1
Navigation — Raytheon SPS-64(V)9
Fire control — 4 Raytheon SPG-51D; Lockheed SPG-60D; Lockheed SPQ-9A.
Sonars: EDO/GE SQS-26CX, bow-mounted, active search and attack.

Helicopters: Platform only.

Note: California planned to pay off to Category B Reserve in late 1998; South Carolina by 1999.

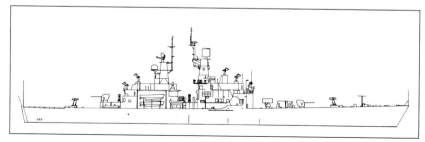

California Class (CGN)

SOUTH CAROLINA

Ticonderoga Class

Country: UNITED STATES OF AMERICA
Country of origin: UNITED STATES OF AMERICA
Ship type: CRUISERS
Class: TICONDEROGA (AEGIS) (CG)
Active: 27

Name (Pennant number): TICONDEROGA (CG 47) (ex-DDG 47),
YORKTOWN (CG 48), VINCENNES (CG 49), VALLEY FORGE (CG 50),
THOMAS S GATES (CG 51), BUNKER HILL (CG 52), MOBILE BAY (CG
53), ANTIETAM (CG 54), LEYTE GULF (CG 55), SAN JACINTO (CG 56),
LAKE CHAMPLAIN (CG 57), PHILIPPINE SEA (CG 58), PRINCETON (CG
59), NORMANDY (CG 60), MONTEREY (CG 61), CHANCELLORSVILLE
(CG 62), COWPENS (CG 63), GETTYSBURG (CG 64), CHOSIN (CG 65),
HUE CITY (CG 66), SHILOH (CG 67), ANZIO (CG 68), VICKSBURG (CG
69), LAKE ERIE (CG 70), CAPE ST GEORGE (CG 71), VELLA GULF (CG
72), PORT ROYAL (CG 73)

Recognition features:
- High raked bow with unusual raised solid sides surrounding forecastle.
- 5 in gun mounting on forecastle at break in maindeck profile.
- Two SAM or A/S Mk 26 Mod 5 launchers (CG 47-51), or two Mk 41 Mod 0 vertical launchers (CG 52 onwards), one between forward turret and bridge structure and one at the after break to quarterdeck. This is the clearest way to differentiate between the two versions of the class.
- Large, boxlike forward superstructure just forward of midships. Bridge at forward end, small lattice mast on bridge roof supporting dome for SPQ-9A fire control radar.
- Twin funnels, both with three exhausts. Forward funnel has two larger diameter exhausts forward of a smaller one, after funnel has smaller diameter exhaust of three at the forward end.
- Tall lattice mainmast supporting radar aerials situated between funnels, exactly amidships.
- Both versions have 5 in mounting on quarterdeck.

Note - Vincennes and later ships have a lighter tripod mainmast instead of the square quadruped of the first two.

Displacement full load, tons: 9,590 (CG 47-48); 9,407 (CG 49-51); 9,516 (remainder).
Length, feet (metres): 567 (172.8).
Beam, feet (metres): 55 (16.8).
Draught, feet (metres): 31 (9.5) (sonar).
Speed, knots: 30+.
Range, miles: 6,000 at 20 kts.

Missiles: SLCM/SSM - GDC Tomahawk (CG 52 onwards). 8 McDonnell
Douglas Harpoon (2 quad).   SAM - GDC Standard SM-2MR.
A/S - Honeywell ASROC, (CG 47-55) and Loral ASROC VLA (CG 56 onwards and CG 52-55 from 1998).
(SAM and A/S missiles are fired from 2 twin Mk 26 Mod 5 launchers (CG 47-51) and 2 Mk 41 Mod 0 vertical launchers (CG 52 onwards). Tomahawk is carried in CG 52 onwards with 8 missiles in each VLS launcher.)
Guns: 2 FMC 5 in (127 mm)/54 Mk 45 Mod 0 (CG 47-50); Mod 1 (CG 51 onwards); 2 GE/GD 20 mm/76 Vulcan Phalanx 6-barrel Mk 15 Mod 2; 2 McDonnell Douglas 25 mm; 4 12.7 mm MGs. (Phalanx to be replaced by RAM Block 1 from 2001.)
Torpedoes: 6 - 324 mm Mk 32 (2 triple) Mk 14 tubes with Honeywell Mk 46 Mod 5.

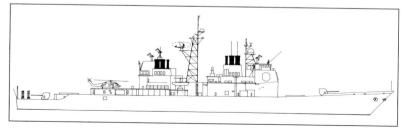

Ticonderoga Class

TICONDEROGA

Decoys: Up to 8 Loral Hycor SRBOC 6-barrel fixed Mk 36, firing IR flares and chaff; SLQ-25 Nixie; towed torpedo decoy.

Radars:
Air search/fire control — RCA SPY-1A phased arrays, 3D. Raytheon SPY-1B phased arrays, 3D (CG 59 on).
Air search — Raytheon SPS-49(V)7 or 8.
Surface search — ISC Cardion SPS-55.
Navigation — Raytheon SPS-64(V)9.
Fire control — Lockheed SPQ-9A. 4 Raytheon/RCA SPG-62.

Sonars: General Electric/Hughes SQS-53A/B (CG 47-55); bow-mounted, active search and attack. Gould SQR-19 (CG 54-55); passive towed array. Gould/Raytheon SQQ-89(V)3 (CG 56 onwards); combines hull-mounted SQS-53B (CG 56-57) or SQS-53C (CG 68-73) and passive towed array SQR-19.

Helicopters: 2 Sikorsky SH-60B Seahawk LAMPS III; 2 Kaman SH-2F LAMPS I (CG 47-48).0

Iroquois Class

Country: CANADA
Ship type: DESTROYERS
Class: IROQUOIS (DDG)
Active: 4
Name (Pennant Number): IROQUOIS (280), HURON (281), ATHABASKAN (282), ALGONQUIN (283)

Recognition features:
- SAM VLS at after end of forecastle.
- 3 in gun mounting (B position).
- Distinctive, curved, Signaal SPQ-502 air search radar aerial atop after end of bridge structure.
- Tall lattice mainmast immediately forward of funnel.
- Unusual, large, square funnel amidships.
- CIWS mounting immediately aft of funnel atop after superstructure.
- Helicopter flight deck raised above quarterdeck level with torpedo tubes visible below.

Displacement full load, tons: 5,100.
Length, feet (metres): 426 (129.8) oa.
Beam, feet (metres): 50 (15.2).
Draught, feet (metres): 15.5 (4.7).
Speed, knots: 27.
Range, miles: 4,500 at 15 kts.

Missiles: SAM - 1 Martin Marietta Mk 41 VLS, Standard SM-2MR Block III.
Guns: 1 OTO Melara 3 in (76 mm)/62 Super Rapid. 1 GE/GD 20 mm/76 6-barrel Vulcan Phalanx Mk 15.
Torpedoes: 6   324 mm Mk 32 (2 triple) tubes. Honeywell Mk 46, Mod 5 Neartip.
Decoys: 2 Plessey Shield Mk 2 6-tubed trainable launchers.; chaff or IR flares. SLQ-25 Nixie; torpedo decoy.

Radars:
Air search — Signaal SPQ-502 (LW08).
Surface search — Signaal SPQ-501 (DA08).
Navigation — 2 Raytheon Pathfinder. Koden MD 373 (Iroquois only, on hangar roof).
Fire control — 2 Signaal SPG-501 (STIR 1.8).
Sonars: Westinghouse SQS-510; combined VDS and hull-mounted, active search and attack.

Helicopters: 2 Sikorsky CH-124A Sea King (ASW).

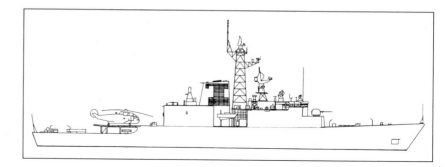

Iroqouis Class

IROQUOIS

Luda I/II Class

Country: CHINA
Country of origin: CHINA
Ship type: DESTROYERS
Class: LUDA I/II (TYPE 051) (DDG)
Active: 15
Name (Pennant Number): JINAN (105) (Type II), XIAN (106), YINCHUAN (107), XINING (108), KAIFENG (109), DALIAN (110) (Type II), NANJING (131), HEFEI (132), CHONGQING (133), ZUNYI (134), CHANGSHA (161), NANNING (162), NANCHANG (163), GUILIN (164), ZHANJIANG (165).

Recognition features:
- High bow with sweeping forecastle aft to bridge. One maindeck level through to stern.
- Large distinctive 5.1 in gun mounting (A position) with 37mm/63 mounting (B position).
- Lattice mainmast with sloping forward edge just forward of forward funnel. Smaller lattice tapered aftermast about midships.
- Twin, black-capped funnels angled astern.
- Two large HY-2 SSM missile launchers. One set immediately aft of forward funnel, the second immediately aft of after funnel.
- Isolated after superstructure supports Rice Lamp fire control director at forward end and 37mm/63 mounting.
- 5.1 in gun mounting (Y position).

Note - Type I/II varies mainly from the Type III in that the HY-2 SSM launchers are substituted by the smaller YJ-1 SSM launchers.

Displacement, tons: 3,250, standard, 3670, full load.
Length, feet (metres): 433.1 (132).
Beam, feet (metres): 42 (12.8).
Draught, feet (metres): 15.1 (4.6).
Speed, knots: 32.
Range, miles: 2,970 at 18 kts.
Missiles: SSM - 6 HY-2 (C-201) (CSS-C-3A Seersucker) (2 triple) launchers. SAM - HQ-7 Crotale octuple launcher (Kaifeng and Xian).
Guns: 4 (Type I) or 2 (Type II) USSR 5.1 in (130 mm)/58; (2 twin) (Type

1). 8 China 57 mm/70 (4 twin). Fitted in some of the class, the others have 37 mm. 8 China 37 mm/63 (4 twin) (some Type I and Type III). 8 USSR 25 mm/60 (4 twin).
Torpedoes: 6 - 324 mm Whitehead B5 15 (2 triple tubes) (fitted in some Type I). Yu-2 (Mk 46 Mod 1).
A/S mortars: 2 FQF 2500 12-tubed launchers. Similar in design to the RBU 1200.
Depth charges: 2 or 4 BMB projectors; 2 or 4 racks. (Type I).
Decoys: Chaff launchers (fitted to some).

Radars:

Air search — Knife Rest or Cross Slot, or Bean Sticks or Pea Sticks. Rice Screen, 3D (on mainmast in some).
Surface search — Eye Shield or Thomson-CSF Sea Tiger. Square Tie (not in all).
Navigation — Fin Curve or Racal Decca 1290.
Fire control — Wasp Head (Wok Won) or Type 343 Sun Visor B (Series 2). 2 Rice Lamp (series 2) or 2 Type 347G. Thomson-CSF Castor II (Crotale)
Sonars: Pegas 2M and Tamir 2; hull-mounted, active search and attack.

Helicopters: 2 Harbin Zhi-9A Haitun (Dauphin 2) (Type II). (ASW/ASV).

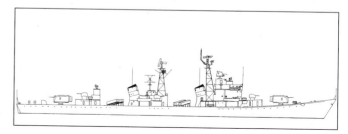

Luda I/II Class

NANJING

Country: CHINA
Country of origin: CHINA
Ship type: DESTROYERS
Class: LUDA III (DDG)
Active: 1
Name (Pennant Number): ZHUHAI (166 — 168 when out of area)

Recognition features:

- High bow with sweeping forecastle aft to bridge. One maindeck level through to stern.
- Large distinctive 5.1 in gun mounting (A position) with turreted 37mm/63 mounting (B position).
- Lattice mainmast with sloping forward edge just forward of forward funnel. Smaller lattice tapered aftermast about midships.
- Twin, black-capped funnels angled astern.
- Two large YJ-1 Eagle Strike missile launchers. One set immediately aft of forward funnel, the second immediately aft of after funnel.
- Isolated after superstructure supports Type 347G fire control director at forward end and turreted 37mm/63 mounting.
- 5.1 in gun mounting (Y position).

Note - Type I/II varies mainly from the Type III in that the YJ-1 SSM launchers are substituted by the larger HY-2 SSM launchers.

Displacement, tons: 3,250, standard, 3,730, full load.
Length, feet (metres): 433.1 (132).
Beam, feet (metres): 42 (12.8).
Draught, feet (metres): 15.3 (4.7).
Speed, knots: 32.
Range, miles: 2,970 at 18 kts.

Missiles: SSM — 8 YJ-1 Eagle Strike (C-801) (CSS-N-4 Sardine) (4 twin launchers). SAM - LY 60N planned. A/S - The after launchers may also be used for CY-1 anti-submarine missile in the future.
Guns: 4 USSR 5.1 in (130 mm)/58; (2 twin). 8 China 37 mm/63 Type 76A (4 twin).
Torpedoes: 6 - 324 mm Whitehead B5 15 (2 triple tubes) Yu-2 (Mk 46 Mod 1).
A/S mortars: 2 FQF 2500 12-tubed fixed launchers. Similar in design to the RBU 1200.
Decoys: 2 15-tubed fixed chaff /IR flare launchers

Radars:

Air search — Rice Screen, 3D. (Similar to Hughes SPS-39A).
Surface search — China ESR 1.
Navigation — Racal Decca 1290.
Fire control — Type 343 Sun Visor B; 2 Type 347G.
Sonars: DUBV 23; hull-mounted, active search and attack VDS.

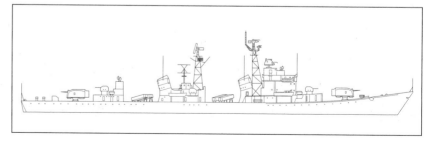

Luda III Class

ZHUHAI

Country: CHINA
Country of origin: CHINA
Ship type: DESTROYERS
Class: LUHAI (DDG)
Active: 0 (Sea trials were expected for 1 unit, mid-1998;)
Building: 1
Name (Pennant Number): – (167).

Recognition features:

- Raised bow with one maindeck level through to stern
- Tall superstructure, forward and helicopter hangar aft of midships with two funnels separated by aft pylon mast and two C-802 SSM missile launchers
- Short forward mast atop bridge superstructure with vertical lattice pylon behind Type 363 air/surface search radar aerial.
- 4 Twin 37 mm/63 Type 64A gun turret mountings atop hangar superstructure.
- Triple torpedo tubes just aft of forward funnel.

Displacement, full load, tons: 6,000.
Length, feet (metres): 502 (153).
Beam, feet (metres): 54.1 (16.5).
Draught, feet (metres): 19.7 (6).
Speed, knots: 29.
Range, miles: 14,000 at 15 kts.

Missiles: SSM — C-802 (CSS-N-8 Saccade), 2 octuple box launchers. SAM — 1 HQ-7 (Crotale) octuple launcher.
Guns: 2 3.9 in (100 mm)/56 (twin); 8 37 mm/63 Type 76A (4 twin).
Torpedoes: 6 324 mm B5 15 (2 triple) tubes with Yu-2.
Decoys: Chaff launchers.

Radars:
Air search — Rice Shield 3D.
Air/surface search — China Type 363.
Fire control — Type 347G (SSM/100 mm guns); 2 EFR-1 Rice Lamp. Thomson-CSF Castor II (Crotale).
Sonars: DUBV-23; hull-mounted, active search and attack.

Helicopters: 2 Harbin Zhi-9A Haitun (Dauphin 2) (ASW/ASV)

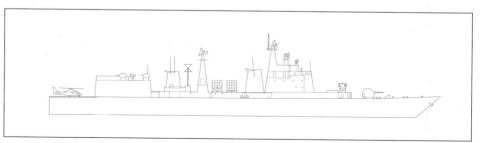

Luhai Class

LUHAI

Luhu Class

Country: CHINA
Country of origin: CHINA
Ship type: DESTROYERS
Class: LUHU (TYPE 052) (DDG)
Active: 2
Name (Pennant Number): HARIBING (112), QUINGDAO (113)

Recognition features:
- Acute angled high bow. Single maindeck level from stem to stern.
- Sloping forecastle with 3.9 in gun mounting (A position).
- Crotale SAM octuple launcher (B mounting position).
- 2 37 mm/63 gun mountings immediately forward of bridge.
- Short, tapered, lattice mainmast at after end of main superstructure.
- Single funnel amidships with black, wedge-shaped, Rad-Haz screen at after end.
- Two SSM missile launchers. One set between enclosed aftermast and funnel, second aft of aftermast.
- Square after superstructure supports large curved Hai Ying air search radar aerial at forward end and 37 mm/63 gun mounting at after end.
- Helicopter flight deck aft with open quarterdeck below.

Displacement full load, tons: 4,200.
Length, feet (metres): 468.2 (142.7).
Beam, feet (metres): 49.5 (15.1).
Draught, feet (metres): 16.7 (5.1).
Speed, knots: 31.
Range, miles: 5,000 at 15 kts.

Missiles: SSM - 8 YJ-1 (Eagle Strike) (C-801) (CSS-N-4 Sardine). SAM - 1 HQ-7 (Crotale) octuple launcher.
Guns: 2 — 3.9 in (100 mm)/56 (twin). 8 37 mm/63 Type 64A (4 twin).
Torpedoes: 6 - 324 mm Whitehead B5 15 (2 triple) tubes. YU-2 (Mk 46 Mod 1).
A/S mortars: 2 FQF 2500 12-tubed fixed launchers.
Decoys: 2 SRBOC Mk 36 6-barrel chaff launchers. 2 China 26-barrel chaff launchers

Radars:
Air search — Hai Ying or God Eye.
Air/surface search — Thomson-CSF TSR 3004 Sea Tiger.
Surface search — China ESR 1.
Navigation — Racal Decca 1290.
Fire control — Type 347G, (for SSM and 100 mm gun); 2 EFR 1 Rice Lamp (37 mm gun); Thomson-CSF Castor II (Crotale).
Sonars: DUBV-23. Hull-mounted, active search and attack. DUBV-43 VDS, active attack.

Helicopters: 2 Harbin Zhi-9A Haitun (Dauphin 2) (ASW/ASV).

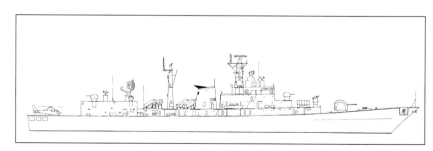

Luhu Class

QUINGDAO

Cassard Class

Country: FRANCE
Country of origin: FRANCE
Ship type: DESTROYERS
Class: CASSARD (TYPE F 70(A/A)) (DDG)
Active: 2
Name (Pennant Number): CASSARD (D 614), JEAN BART (D 615)

Recognition features:
- Continuous maindeck from stem to stern.
- Long forecastle with 3.9 in gun mounting (A position), close to bridge superstructure.
- High forward superstructure with tall lattice mainmast towards after end.
- Large curved DRBV 26C air/surface search radar aerial immediately forward of mainmast.
- High superstructure amidships with very distinctive, domed DRBJ 11B air search radar dome atop.
- Two SPG-51C fire control directors on after end of central superstructure.
- Mk 13 Mod 5 SAM launcher aft of central superstructure.
- Matra Sadral PDMS SAM sextuple launchers outboard at after end of hangar.
- Hangar and small flight deck right aft.

Displacement, tons: 4,230, standard, 4,730, full load.
Length, feet (metres): 455.9 (139).
Beam, feet (metres): 45.9 (14).
Draught, feet (metres): 21.3 (6.5) (sonar).
Speed, knots: 29.5
Range, miles: 8,200 at 17 kts.

Missiles: SSM - 8 Aerospatiale MM 40 Exocet. SAM - GDC Pomona Standard SM-1MR; Mk 13 Mod 5 launcher. 2 Matra Sadral PDMS sextuple launchers; Mistral.
Guns: 1 DCN 3.9 in (100 mm)/55 Mod 68 CADAM automatic. 2 Oerlikon 20 mm. 4 12.7 mm MGs.
Torpedoes: 2 fixed launchers model KD 59E. ECAN L5 Mod 4.
Decoys: 2 CSEE Dagaie and 2 Sagaie 10-barrel Chaff/IR launchers. AN//SLQ-25 Nixie; towed torpedo decoy.

Radars:
Air search — Thomson-CSF DRBJ 11B, 3D.
Air/surface search — DRBV 26C.
Navigation — 2 Racal DRBN 34A.
Fire control — Thomson-CSF DRBC 33A, (guns). 2 Raytheon SPG-51C (missiles).
Sonars: Thomson-Sintra DUBA 25A (D 614) or DUBV 24C (D 615); hull-mounted, active search and attack.

Helicopters: 1 Aerospatiale AS 565MA Panther (SSM targeting).

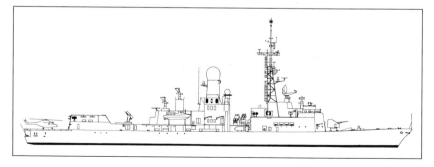

Country: FRANCE
Country of origin: FRANCE
Ship type: DESTROYERS
Class: GEORGES LEYGUES (TYPE 70 (ASW)) (DDG)
Active: 7
Name (Pennant Number): GEORGES LEYGUES (D 640), DUPLEIX (D 641), MONTCALM (D 642), JEAN DE VIENNE (D 643), PRIMAUGUET (D 644), LA MOTTE-PICQUET (D 645), LATOUCHE-TRÉVILLE (D 646).

Recognition features:

- Long forecastle with 3.9 in gun mounting (A position) close to superstructure.
- Tall lattice mainmast at after end of bridge with vertical after edge and sloping forward edge.
- Funnel amidships with vertical forward edge and sloping after edge, funnel cap angled down at after end.
- Two Exocet SSM launchers atop forward end of after superstructure immediately aft of funnel.
- Crotale SAM launcher atop after superstructure.
- Flight deck aft of hangar.
- VDS towing equipment on quarterdeck.

Note - Bridge raised one deck in the last three of the class. INMARSAT aerial can be fitted forward of the funnel or between the Syracuse domes.

Displacement full load, tons: 4,300 (D 640-643), 4,580 (D 644-646).
Length, feet (metres): 455.9 (139).
Beam, feet (metres): 45.9 (14).
Draught, feet (metres): 18.7 (5.7).
Speed, knots: 30; 21on diesels.
Range, miles: 8,500 at 18 kts. on diesels.

Missiles: SSM - 4 Aerospatiale MM 38 Exocet (MM 40 in D 642-646). SAM - Thomson-CSF Crotale Naval EDIR octuple launcher. 2 Matra Sadral/Mistral sextuple launchers being fitted to D 644-646. (2 Matra Simbad twin launchers may be mounted in place of 20 mm guns.)
Guns: 1 - 3.9 in (100 mm)/55 Mod 68 CADAM automatic. 2 Breda/Mauser 30 mm guns being fitted to D 640-643. 2 Oerlikon 20 mm, (see note under 'Missiles.') 4 M2HB 12.7 mm MGs.
Torpedoes: 2 fixed launchers, ECAN L5; Honeywell Mk 46 or Eurotorp Mu 90 for helicopters in due course.
Decoys: 2 CSEE Dagaie 10-barrel double trainable chaff/IR flare launcher.

Radars:

Air search — Thomson-CSF DRBV 26 (not in D 644-646).
Air/surface search — Thomson-CSF DRBV 51C (DRBV 15A in D 644-646).
Navigation — 2 Decca 1226.
Fire control — Thomson-CSF Vega with DRBC 32E (D 640-643), DRBC 33A (D 644-646),(Crotale.)
Sonars: Thomson-Sintra DUBV 23D (DUBV 24C in D 644-646); bow-mounted active search and attack. DUBV 43B (43C in D 643-646) VDS; paired with DUBV 23D/24.

Helicopters: 2 Westland Lynx Mk 4 (FN). (ASW).

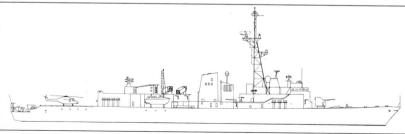

Georges Leygues Class

LA MOTTE-PIQUET

Suffren Class

Country: FRANCE
Country of origin: FRANCE
Ship type: DESTROYERS
Class: SUFFREN (DDG)
Active: 1 (+ 1 in refit in 1999)
Name (Pennant Number): SUFFREN (D 602), DUQUESNE (D 603)

Recognition features:
- Two 3.9 in gun mountings (A and B positions).
- Very large and distinctive air search radome at after end of bridge structure.
- Solid, rounded mast and funnel combined amidships with main engine exhausts at top.
- Malafon A/S missile launcher immediately aft of mainmast.
- Exocet SSM launcher on slightly raised after superstructure immediately forward of short lattice aftermast.
- Masurca SAM twin launcher at forward end of quarter deck.
- VDS towing equipment at after end of quarter deck.

Note: Malafon A/S missile non-operational.

Displacement, tons: 5,090 standard, 6,910 full load.
Length, feet (metres): 517.1 (157.6).
Beam, feet (metres): 50.9 (15.5).
Draught, feet (metres): 20 (6.1).
Speed, knots: 34.
Range, miles: 5,100 at 18 kts., 2,400 at 29 kts.

Missiles: SSM - 4 Aerospatiale MM 38 Exocet. SAM - ECAN Ruelle Masurca twin launcher.   A/S - Latecoere Malafon; payload L4 torpedo, (non-operational).
Guns: 2 DCN 3.9 in (100 mm)/55 Mod 1964 CADAM automatic. 4 or 6 Oerlikon 20 mm.
Torpedoes: 4 launchers (2 each side). 10 ECAN L5.
Decoys: 2 CSEE Sagaie 10-barrel trainable chaff/IR flare launchers. 2 Dagaie launchers.

Radars:
Air search (radome) — DRBI 23.
Air/surface search — DRBV 15A.
Navigation — Racal Decca 1226.
Fire control — 2 Thomson-CSF DRBR 51.(Masurca). Thomson-CSF DRBC 33A, (guns.)
Sonars: Thomson-Sintra DUBV 23; hull-mounted, active search/attack. DUBV 43; VDS.

Note: Duquesne in 'reduced' service until refit in 1999.

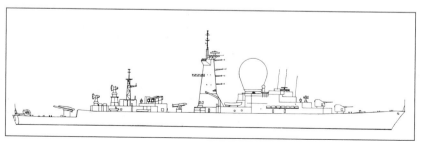

Suffren Class

DUQUESNE

Tourville Class

Country: FRANCE
Country of origin: FRANCE
Ship type: DESTROYERS
Class: TOURVILLE (TYPE F 67) (DDG)
Active: 3
Name (Pennant Number): TOURVILLE (D 610); DUGUAY-TROUIN (D 611), DE GRASSE (D 612)

Recognition features:
- Two 3.9 in gun mountings (A and B positions).
- Short lattice mast atop after end of forward superstructure.
- Exocet SSM launchers immediately aft of forward superstructure.
- Large solid combined mainmast and funnel amidships.
- Distinctive DRBV 26 air search radar aerial supported on projecting gantry forward end of mainmast.
- Two domed SATCOM aerials, port and starboard, immediately aft of mainmast.
- Crotale SAM launcher atop raised after superstructure.
- VDS towing gear on quarterdeck down from after end of flight deck.

Displacement, tons: 4,580 standard, 5,950 full load.
Length, feet (metres): 501.6 (152.8).
Beam, feet (metres): 52.4 (16).
Draught, feet (metres): 18.7 (5.7).
Speed, knots: 32.
Range, miles: 5,000 at 18 kts.

Missiles: SSM - 6 Aerospatiale MM 38 Exocet. SAM - Thomson-CSF Crotale Naval EDIR octuple launcher.
Guns: 2 DCN 3.9 in (100 mm)/55 Mod 68 CADAM automatic. 2 Giat 20 mm.
Torpedoes: 2 launchers, 10 ECAN L5.
Decoys: 2 CSEE/VSEL Syllex 8-barrel trainable chaff launchers.
Radars:
Air search — DRBV 26.
Air/surface search — Thomson-CSF DRBV 51B.
Navigation — 2 Racal Decca Type 1226.
Fire control — Thomson-CSF DRBC 32D, (Crotale.)
Sonars: Thomson-Sintra DUBV 23; bow-mounted, active search/attack. DUBV 43 VDS; DSBV 62C, passive linear towed array.

Helicopters: 2 Westland Lynx Mk 4 (FN). (ASW).

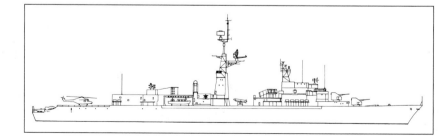

Tourville Class

TOURVILLE

Almirante Brown Class

Country: ARGENTINA
Country of origin: GERMANY
Ship type: DESTROYERS
Class: ALMIRANTE BROWN (MEKO 360) (DDG)
Active: 4
Name (Pennant Number): ALMIRANTE BROWN (D 10), LA ARGENTINA (D 11), HEROINA (D 12), SARANDI (D 13).

Recognition features:

- Short forecastle, 5 in gun mounting (A position).
- 40 mm/70 gun mountings immediately forward of bridge (B position).
- Short, stubby pyramid mast at after end of bridge structure housing WM25 fire control radome.
- Exocet SSM launchers, port and starboard, immediately forward of funnels.
- Two side-by-side funnels angled outboard in 'V' formation with pole mast at forward edge.
- DAO8A Air/surface search and fire control radars sited on raised superstructure aft of funnels.
- Short flight deck right aft with open quarterdeck below.

Note Also operated by Nigeria (1 unit, rated FFG). Most obvious difference is solid deckhouse supporting lattice pylon aft of funnels on Argentine ships, missing on Nigerian hull.

Displacement, tons: 2,900 standard, 3,360 full load.
Length, feet (metres): 413.1 (125.9).
Beam, feet (metres): 46 (14).
Draught, feet (metres): 19 (5.8) (screws)
Speed, knots: 30.5.
Range, miles: 4,500 at 18 kts.

Missiles: SSM - 8 Aerospatiale MM 40 Exocet (2 quad) launchers. SAM - Selenia/Elsag Albatros launcher; Aspide.

Guns: 1 OTO Melara 5 in (127 mm)/54 automatic. 8 Breda/Bofors 40 mm/70 (4 twin).
Torpedoes: 6 324 mm ILAS 3 (2 triple) tubes; Whitehead A 244.
Decoys: CSEE Dagaie double mounting. Graseby G1738 towed torpedo decoy system. 2 Breda 105 mm SCLAR chaff launchers.

Radars:
Air/surface search — Signaal DA08A.
Surface search — Signaal ZW06.
Navigation — Decca 1226.
Fire control — Signaal STIR.
Sonars: Atlas Elektronik 80 DSQS-21BZ; hull-mounted, active search and attack.

Helicopters: 2 Aerospatiale SA 319B Alouette III or Aerospatiale AS 555 Fennec, (ASW/ASV).

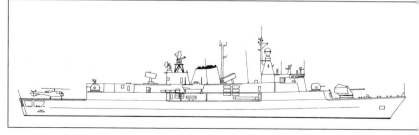

ALMIRANTE BROWN and LA ARGENTINA (background)

Delhi class

Country: INDIA
Country of origin: INDIA
Ship type: DESTROYERS
Class: DELHI (DDG)
Active: 2
Building: 1
Name (Pennant Number): DELHI (D 61), MYSORE (D 62), BOMBAY (D 63).

Recognition features:
- High bow with sweeping forecastle aft to bridge. One maindeck level through to stern.
- Squat 3.9 in gun mounting in 'A' position on forecastle.
- SA-N-7 SAM launcher in B position with 2 RBU 6000 A/S launchers aft.
- Four angled, tubular quad launcher tubes for SS-N-25 SSM, (two port, two starboard) alongside and forward of bridge superstructure.
- Prominent square Half Plate air/surface search radar aerial at top of short mainmast atop bridge superstructure.
- Second low pyramid mast between two squared funnels, with Bharat/Signaal RALW (LW08) air search aerial atop.
- Long, low helicopter hangar aft of second funnel.

Displacement, full load, tons: 6,700.
Length, feet (metres): 534.8 (163).
Beam, feet (metres): 55.8 (17).
Draught, feet (metres): 21.3 (6.5).
Speed, knots: 28.

Missiles: SSM — 16 Zvezda SS-N-25 (4 quad) (KH 35 Uran). SAM — 2 SA-N-7 Gadfly (Uragan).
Guns: 1 USSR 3.9 in (100 mm)/59 AK 100. 4 USSR 30 mm/65 AK 630, 6-barrels per mounting.
Torpedoes: 5 533 mm (quin) tubes.
A/S mortars: 2 RBU 6000, 12 tubed trainable.
Depth charges: 2 rails.
Decoys: 2 PK 2 chaff launchers.

Radars:
Air search — Bharat/Signaal RALW (LW08).
Air/surface search — Half Plate.
Navigation — Bharat Rashmi.
Fire control — 6 Front Dome (SAM), Kite Screech (100 mm gun), 2 Bass Tilt (30 mm guns), Plank Shave, (Garpun B) (SSM).
Sonars: Bharat APSOH, hull mounted, active search.

Helicopters: 2 Westland Sea King Mk 42B (ASV) or 2 Hindustan Aeronautics ALH, (ASW/ASV).

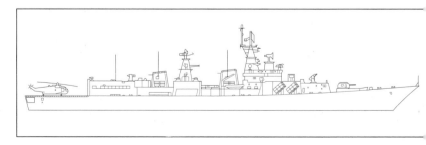

Delhi class

DELHI

Audace Class

Country: ITALY
Country of origin: ITALY.
Ship type: DESTROYERS
Class: AUDACE (DDG)
Active: 2
Name (Pennant Number): ARDITO (D 550), AUDACE (D 551).

Recognition features:
- Continuous maindeck from stem to stern.
- 5 in gun mounting (A position) with Aspide SAM launcher (B position).
- Unusually high forward superstructure.
- Forward mast and funnel, combined at after end of forward superstructure, supports air search radar aerial. Twin exhausts in 'V' protruding aft.
- Aftermast and funnel combined has sloping forward edge supporting large, angled square-shaped long-range air search radar aerial.
- Teseo SSM launchers sited between funnels, above 76 mm gun mountings.
- Standard SAM launcher atop forward end of hangar.
- Flight deck right aft with open quarterdeck below.

Displacement, tons: 3,600 standard, 4,400 full load.
Length, feet (metres): 448 (136.6).
Beam, feet (metres): 46.6 (14.2).
Draught, feet (metres): 15.1 (4.6).
Speed, knots: 34.
Range, miles: 3,000 at 20 kts.

Missiles: SSM - 8 OTO Melara/Matra Teseo Mk 2 (TG 2) (4 twin). SAM - GDC Pomona Standard SM-1MR; Mk 13 Mod 4 launcher. Selenia Albatros octuple launcher for Aspide.
Guns: 1 OTO Melara 5 in (127 mm)/54. 3 OTO Melara 3 in (76 mm)/62 Compact (Ardito) and 1 (Ardito) or 4 (Audace) Super Rapid.
Torpedoes: 6 324 mm US Mk 32 (2 triple) tubes. Honeywell Mk 46.
Decoys: 2 Breda 105 mm SCLAR 20-barrel chaff launchers. SLQ-25 Nixie; towed torpedo decoy.

Radars:
Long range air search — Hughes SPS-52C, 3D.
Air search — Selenia SPS-768 (RAN 3L).
Air/surface search — Selenia SPS-774 (RAN 10S).
Surface search — SMA SPQ-2D.
Navigation — SMA SPN-748.
Fire control — 3 Selenia SPG-76 (RTN 30X), 2 Raytheon SPG-51, (Standard SAM).
Sonars: CWE 610; hull-mounted, active search and attack.

Helicopters: 2 Agusta-Bell AB 212 (ASW).

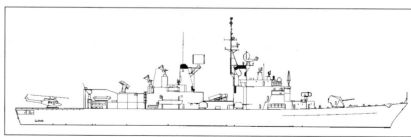

ARDITO

De La Penne Class

Country: ITALY
Country of origin: ITALY
Ship type: DESTROYERS
Class: DE LA PENNE (ex-ANIMOSO) (DDG)
Active: 2
Name (Pennant Number): LUIGI DURAND DE LA PENNE (ex-Animoso) (D 560), FRANCESCO MIMBELLI (ex-Ardimentoso) (D 561).

Recognition features:

● High bow, continuous maindeck from stem to stern.
● 5 in gun mounting (A position) with Aspide SAM octuple launcher (B mounting position).
● Slim pyramid foremast atop forward superstructure.
● Slightly shorter, enclosed aftermast supporting square long range air search 3D radar aerial on platform protruding aft. Pole mast atop aftermast with air/surface search radar atop.
● Three square section funnels, one at after end of forward superstructure and twin 'V' funnels just abaft aftermast. Both sets slightly tapered towards top.
● Teseo SSM launchers amidships between forward funnel and aftermast.
● Standard SAM launcher and 3 in gun mounting atop after superstructure.
● Flight deck right aft with open quarterdeck below.

Displacement, tons: 4,330 standard, 5,400 full load.
Length, feet (metres): 487.4 (147.7).
Beam, feet (metres): 52.8 (16.1).
Draught, feet (metres): 28.2 (8.6) (sonar).
Speed, knots: 31.
Range, miles: 7,000 at 18 kts.

Missiles: SSM - 4 or 8 OTO Melara/Matra Teseo Mk 2 (TG 2) (2 or 4 twin). SAM - GDC Pomona Standard SM-1MR; Mk 13 Mod 4 launcher. Selenia Albatros Mk 2 octuple launcher for Aspide. A/S - OTO MELARA/Matra Milas launcher with Mk 46 Mod 5 or Mu 90 torpedoes planned to be fitted by 2002.
Guns: 1 OTO Melara 5 in (127 mm)/54. 3 OTO Melara 3 in (76 mm)/62 Super Rapid.
Torpedoes: 6 324 mm B5 15 (2 triple) tubes. Honeywell Mk 46.
Decoys: 2 CSEE Sagaie chaff launchers. SLQ-25 Nixie anti-torpedo system.

Radars:

Long range air search — Hughes SPS-52C, 3D.
Air search — Selenia SPS-768 (RAN 3L).
Air/surface search — Selenia SPS-774 (RAN 10S).
Surface search — SMA SPS-702.
Navigation — SMA SPN-748.
Fire control — 4 Selenia SPG-76 (RTN 30X). 2 Raytheon SPG-51D. (SAM).
Sonars: Raytheon DE 1164 LF-VDS; integrated hull and VDS, active search/attack.

Helicopters: 2 Agusta-Bell AB 212 (ASW); SH-3D Sea King and EH 101 capable.

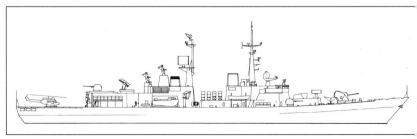

Asagiri Class

Country: JAPAN
Country of origin: JAPAN
Ship type: DESTROYERS
Class: ASAGIRI (DDG/DD)
Active: 8
Name (Pennant Number): ASAGIRI (DD 151), YAMAGIRI (DD 152), YUUGIRI (DD 153), AMAGIRI (DD 154), HAMAGIRI (DD 155), SETOGIRI (DD 156), SAWAGIRI (DD 157), UMIGIRI (DD 158).

Recognition features:

- Continuous maindeck line from stem to stern with rising bows.
- 3 in gun mounting (A position).
- ASROC A/S missile octuple box launcher immediately forward of bridge.
- Two black-capped funnels, after one partially obscured by superstructure.
- Lattice mainmast at aft of bridge supporting several radar aerials. Lattice aftermast just abaft after funnel.
- Fire control radome sited aft of aftermast on tall superstructure.
- Helicopter deck aft, raised above maindeck with Sea Sparrow SAM box launcher right aft at maindeck level.

Note - The mainmast now offset to port, as is the forward funnel but the after funnel has been offset to starboard, all to reduce IR signature and damage to electronic systems on the mainmast.

Displacement full load, tons: 4,200.
Length, feet (metres): 449.4 (137).
Beam, feet (metres): 48 (14.6).
Draught, feet (metres): 14.6 (4.5).
Speed, knots: 30.

Missiles: SSM - 8 McDonnell Douglas Harpoon (2 quad) launchers. SAM - Raytheon Sea Sparrow Mk 29 (Type 3/3A) octuple launcher. A/S - Honeywell ASROC Mk 112 octuple launcher; payload, Mk 46 Mod 5 Neartip torpedoes.

Guns: 1 OTO Melara 3 in (76 mm)/62 compact. 2 GE/GD 20 mm Phalanx Mk 15 CIWS.
Torpedoes: 6 324 mm Type 68 (2 triple) HOS 301 tubes. Honeywell Mk 46 Mod 5 Neartip.
Decoys: 2 Loral Hycor SRBOC 6-barrel Mk 36 chaff launchers. 1 SLQ-51 Nixi or Type 4; towed anti-torpedo decoy.

Radars:

Air search — Melco OPS-14C (DD 151-154). Melco OPS-24 (DD 155-158), 3D.
Surface search — JRC OPS-28C. (DD 151, 152, 155-158). JRC OPS-28C-Y (DD 153-154.)
Fire control — Type 2-22, (guns). Type 2-12E (DD 151-154). Type 2-12G (for SAM), (DD 155-158).
Sonars: Mitsubishi OQS-4A (II); hull-mounted, active search/attack. OQR-1 towed array.

Helicopters: 1 Sikorsky/Mitsubishi SH-60J Sea Hawk (ASW).

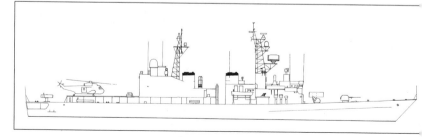

AMAGIRI

Haruna Class

Country: JAPAN
Country of origin: JAPAN.
Ship type: DESTROYERS
Class: HARUNA (DD/DDH)
Active: 2
Name (Pennant Number): HARUNA (DD 141), HIEI (DD 142).

Recognition features:
● Continuous maindeck line from bows to stern.
● Forecastle identical to Shirane class.
● Similar large central superstructure to Shirane class. Main difference is single mast funnel combined offset slightly to port.
● Lattice mast and curved Melco OPS-11C air search radar aerial atop funnel.
● Prominent fire control radome aft of mainmast and funnel.
● Aft of funnel almost identical to Shirane class.
Note 1- A heavy crane is fitted atop the hangar, starboard side.
Note 2 - Appearance of weapons fit on forecastle is very similar in appearance to Shirane class.

Displacement standard, tons: 4,950 (5,050, DD 142).
Length, feet (metres): 502 (153).
Beam, feet (metres): 57.4 (17.5).
Draught, feet (metres): 17.1 (5.2).
Speed, knots: 31.

Missiles: SAM - Raytheon Sea Sparrow Mk 29 (Type 3A) octuple launcher. A/S - Honeywell ASROC Mk 112 octuple launcher; payload, Mk 46 Mod Neartip torpedoes.
Guns: 2 FMC 5 in (127 mm)/54 Mk 42 automatic. 2 GE/GD 20 mm Phalanx Mk 15 CIWS.
Torpedoes: 6 324 mm Type 68 (2 triple) tubes. Honeywell Mk 46 Mod 5 Neartip.
Decoys: 4 Loral Hycor SRBOC 6-barrel Mk 36 chaff launchers.

Radars:
Air search — Melco OPS-11C.
Surface search — JRC OPS-28C/28C-Y.
Fire control — 1 Type 1A, (guns); 1 Type 2-12, (SAM).
Sonars: Sangamo/Mitsubishi OQS-3; bow-mounted, active search/attack.

Helicopters: 3 Sikorsky/Mitsubishi SH-60J Seahawk, (ASW).

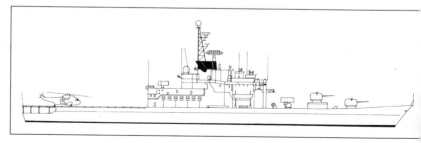

HIEI

Hatakaze Class

Country: JAPAN
Country of origin: JAPAN
Ship type: DESTROYERS
Class: HATAKAZE (DDG)
Active: 2
Name (Pennant Number): HATAKAZE (DD 171), SHIMAKAZE (DD 172).

Recognition features:

- Break in upper deck profile just aft from bow, continuous maindeck from stem to stern.
- Three weapons fitted on long forecastle, from forward to aft, Standard SAM launcher, raised 5 in gun mounting, ASROC A/S missile launcher.
- Central superstructure with lattice mainmast atop after end supporting square profile SPS-52C air search radar aerial.
- Black-capped, slightly tapered funnel just aft of midships.
- Short lattice aftermast supporting curved, OPS-11C air search radar.
- 5 in gun mounting forward end flight deck (Y position).
- Long flight deck with open quarterdeck below.

Displacement full load, tons: 5,500.
Length, feet (metres): 492 (150).
Beam, feet (metres): 53.8 (16.4).
Draught, feet (metres): 15.7 (4.8).
Speed, knots: 30.

Missiles: SSM - 8 McDonnell Douglas Harpoon. SAM - GDC Pomona Standard SM-1MR; Mk 13 Mod 4 launcher. A/S - Honeywell ASROC Mk 112 octuple launcher; payload Mk 46 Mod 5 Neartip torpedoes.
Guns: 2 FMC 5 in (127 mm)/54 Mk 42 automatic. 2 GE/GD 20 mm Phalanx Mk 15 CIWS.
Torpedoes: 6   324 mm Type 68 (2 triple) tubes. Honeywell Mk 46 Mod 5 Neartip.
Decoys: 2 Loral Hycor SRBOC 6-barrel Mk 36 chaff launchers.

Radars:

Air search — Hughes SPS-52C, 3D. Melco OPS-11C.
Surface search — JRC-OPS 28B.
Fire control — 2 Raytheon SPG-51C. Melco 2-21. Type 2-12.
Sonars: Nec OQS 4 Mod 1; bow-mounted, active search/attack.

Helicopters: Platform for 1 Sikorsky/Mitsubishi SH-60J Seahawk, (ASW).

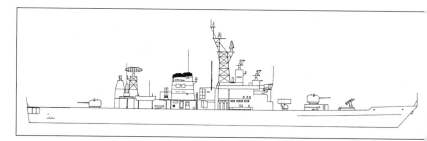

Hatakaze Class

HATAKAZE

Country: JAPAN
Country of origin: JAPAN
Ship type: DESTROYERS
Class: HATSUYUKI (DDG/DD)
Active: 12
Name (Pennant Number): HATSUYUKI (DD 122), SHIRAYUKI (DD 123), MINEYUKI (DD 124), SAWAYUKI (DD 125), HAMAYUKI (DD 126), ISOYUKI (DD 127), HARUYUKI (DD 128), YAMAYUKI (DD 129), MATSUYUKI (DD 130), SETOYUKI (DD 131), ASAYUKI (DD 132), SHIMAYUKI (DD 133).

Recognition features:
- Continuous maindeck with break down to quarterdeck.
- 3 in gun mounting (A position).
- ASROC A/S missile box launcher immediately forward of bridge.
- Large black-capped funnel, slightly tapered, amidships.
- Lattice mainmast at after end of bridge structure supporting several radar aerials.
- Fire control radome mounted atop hangar, offset to starboard.
- Flight deck aft raised above maindeck level.
- Sea Sparrow SAM launcher just forward of quarterdeck.

Displacement full load, tons: 3,700 (3,800 DD 129 onwards).
Length, feet (metres): 426.4 (130).
Beam, feet (metres): 44.6 (13.6).
Draught, feet (metres): 13.8 (4.2), (14.4 (4.4) DD 129 onwards).
Speed, knots: 30.

Missiles: SSM - McDonnell Douglas Harpoon (2 quad) launchers. SAM - Raytheon Sea Sparrow Type 3A launcher. A/S - Honeywell ASROC Mk 112 octuple launcher; payload Mk 46 Mod 5 Neartip torpedoes.
Guns: 1 OTO Melara 3 in (76 mm)/62 compact. 2 GE/GD 20 mm Phalanx Mk 15 CIWS.
Torpedoes: 6 324 mm Type 68 (2 triple) tubes. Honeywell Mk 46 Mod 5 Neartip.
Decoys: 2 Loral Hycor SRBOC 6-barrel Mk 36 chaff launchers.

Radars:
Air search — Melco OPS-14B.
Surface search — JRC OPS-18.
Fire control — Type 2-12 A, (SAM). 2 Type 2-21/21A (guns).
Sonars: Nec OQS 4A (II) (SQS-23 type); bow-mounted active search/attack. OQR 1 TACTASS (in some) passive.

Helicopters: 1 Sikorsky/Mitsubishi SH-60J Seahawk, (ASW).

Hatsuyuki Class

HATSUYUKI

Kongou Class

Country: JAPAN
Country of origin: JAPAN
Ship type: DESTROYERS
Class: KONGOU (DDG)
Active: 4
Name (Pennant Number): KONGOU (DD 173), KIRISHIMA (DD 174), MYOUKOU (DD 175), CHOUKAI (DD 176).

Recognition features:

- Continuous maindeck line from stem to stern.
- Sole visible armament on long foredeck 5 in gun mounting (A position).
- CIWS mounting immediately forward of bridge and at after end of after superstructure.
- High forward superstructure topped by lattice mast sloping aft.
- Two unusually large angular funnels, close together amidships. Funnels tapered and with several black exhausts protruding at top.
- Harpoon SSM launchers between funnels.
- Standard SAM VLS cells at after end foredeck and forward end flight deck; not obvious from side aspect of ship.
- Long flight deck aft.

Note - This is an enlarged and improved version of the US Arleigh Burke class with lightweight version of the Aegis system.

Displacement, tons: 7,250 standard, 9,485 full load.
Length, feet (metres): 528.2 (161)
Beam, feet (metres): 68.9 (21).
Draught, feet (metres): 20.3 (6.2), 32.7 (10) sonar.
Speed, knots: 30.
Range, miles: 4,500 at 20 kts.

Missiles: SSM - 8 McDonnell Douglas Harpoon (2 quad) launchers. SAM - GDC Pomona Standard SM-2MR, FMC Mk 41 (29 cells) forward, Martin Marietta Mk 41 VLS (61 cells) aft. A/S - Vertical launch ASROC; payload Mk 46 torpedoes.
Guns: 1 OTO Melara 5 in (127 mm)/54 Compatto. 2 GE/GD 20 mm/76 Mk 15 Vulcan Phalanx.
Torpedoes: 6 324 mm (2 triple) tubes. Honeywell Mk 46 Mod 5 Neartip.
Decoys: 4 Loral Hycor SRBOC 6-barrel Mk 36 chaff launchers. SLQ-25 towed torpedo decoy.

Radars:
Air search — RCA SPY-1D, 3D.
Surface search — JRC OPS-28D.
Navigation — JRC OPS-20.
Fire control — 3 SPG-62; 1 Mk 2/21.
Sonars: Nec OQS 102 (SQS-53B/C) bow-mounted, active search/attack; Oki OQR 2 (SQR- 19A(V)) TACTASS; towed array, passive.

Helicopters: Platform and refuelling facilities for Sikorsky/Mitsubishi SH-60J Seahawk.

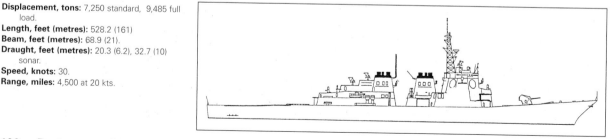

Kongou Class

MYOUKOU

Country: JAPAN
Country of origin: JAPAN
Ship type: EX-DESTROYERS, NOW TRAINING SHIPS
Class: MINEGUMO (AX/TV)
Active: 3

Name (Pennant Number): MINEGUMO (TV 3509 ex-DD 116), NATSUGUMO (TV 3510 ex-DD 117), MURAKUMO (TV 3511 ex-DD 118).

Recognition features:
- High bow, sweeping continuous maindeck to stern.
- 3 in gun mounting (A position).
- Bofors 4-barrel A/S mortar launcher (B mounting position).
- Single tapered funnel amidships.
- Gun mounting atop aft superstructure.
- ASROC A/S missile octuple box launcher on afterdeck.

Note - Almost identical to and easily confused with Yamagumo class from bow to mainmast.

Displacement standard, tons: 2,050.
Length, feet (metres): 373.9 (114).
Beam, feet (metres): 38.7 (11.8).
Draught, feet (metres): 13.1 (4).
Speed, knots: 27.
Range, miles: 7,000 at 20 kts.
Missiles: A/S - Honeywell ASROC Mk 112 octuple launcher; payload Mk 46 Mod 5 Neartip torpedoes.
Guns: 4 USN 3 in (76 mm)/50 Mk 33 (2 twin).
Torpedoes: 6 324 mm Type 68 (2 triple) tubes. Honeywell Mk 46 Mod 5 Neartip.
A/S mortars: 1 Bofors 375 mm Type 71 4-barrel launcher.

Radars:
Air search — Melco OPS-11-Y.
Surface search — JRC OPS-17.
Fire control — 2 Type 1A.
Sonars: Sangamo SQS-23 hull-mounted active search/attack; EDO SQS-35(J); VDS.

Note: Converted, 1995-98 from DD to training ships.

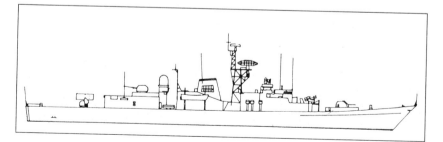

MURAKUMO

Murasame Class

Country: JAPAN
Country of origin: JAPAN
Ship type: DESTROYERS
Class: MURASAME (DDG/DD)
Active: 2
Building: 2 (commissioning due 1999).
Proposed: 5
Name (Pennant Number): MURASAME (DD 101), HARUSAME (DD 102), YUUDACHI (DD 103), KIRISAME (DD 104), (DD 105 — DD 109).

Recognition features:

- Curved, sweeping bow, square, near vertical stern.
- 3 in gun mounting sited at mid-forecastle.
- ASROC abaft forward gun mounting.
- CIWS mounting on raised platform immediately forward of bridge.
- Slab-like forward superstructure has winged bridge; large lattice mainmast at after end.
- Two large, twin, square profile funnels, one at after end of forward superstructure and one at forward end of after superstructure.
- Large flight deck at after end of superstructure.
- CIWS mounting on helicopter hangar.

Displacement, tons: 4,550 standard, 5,100 full load.
Length, feet (metres): 495.4 (151).
Beam, feet (metres): 57.1 (17.4).
Draught, feet (metres): 17.1 (5.2).
Speed, knots: 30.

Missiles: SSM - 8 SSM-1B Harpoon. SAM - Raytheon Mk 48 VLS Sea Sparrow. A/S — Mk 41 VL ASROC.

Guns: 1 OTO MELARA 3 in (76 mm)/62 compact. (May be replaced by 5 in (127 mm) in later ships. 2 GE/GD 20 mm Vulcan Phalanx.
Torpedoes: 6 324 mm Type 68 (2 triple) tubes Mk 46 Mod 5 Neartip.
Decoys: 4 Mk 36 SRBOC chaff launchers, AN/SLQ-25 Nixie towed torpedo decoy.

Radars:
Air search — Melco OPS-24, 3D.
Surface search — JRC OPS-28D.
Navigation — OPS-20.
Fire control — Two Type 2-31.
Sonars: Mitsubishi OQS-5; hull-mounted, active search/attack. OQR-1 towed array, passive search.

Helicopters: 1 Sikorsky/Mitsubishi SH-60J Seahawk (ASW).

Murasame Class

HARUSAME

Shirane Class

Country: JAPAN
Country of origin: JAPAN
Ship type: DESTROYERS
Class: SHIRANE (DD/DDH)
Active: 2
Name (Pennant Number): SHIRANE (DD 143), KURAMA (DD 144).

Recognition features:

- High bow, sweeping continuous maindeck line from stem to stern.
- Two 5 in gun mountings (A and B positions) with ASROC A/S missile octuple box launcher between after mounting and bridge.
- High centrally sited superstructure.
- Two funnels and masts combined with distinctive black, wedge-shaped exhaust diffusers/RAD-HAZ screens atop. The after funnel is set to starboard and the forward one to port.
- Lattice mast mounted atop forward funnel and WM25 fire control radar dome atop after one.
- Long flight deck with open quarterdeck below.
- Sea Sparrow SAM octuple box launcher atop hangar.

Note - Almost identical to and easily confused with Haruna class from bow to bridge.

Displacement standard, tons: 5,200.
Length, feet (metres): 521.5 (159).
Beam, feet (metres): 57.5 (17.5).
Draught, feet (metres): 17.5 (5.3).
Speed, knots: 31.

Missiles: SAM - Raytheon Sea Sparrow Mk 25 octuple launcher. A/S - Honeywell ASROC Mk 112 octuple launcher; payload Mk 46 Mod 5 Neartip torpedoes.
Guns: 2 FMC 5 in (127 mm)/54 Mk 42 automatic. 2 GE/GD 20 mm Phalanx Mk 15 CIWS.

Torpedoes: 6 324 mm Type 68 (2 triple) tubes. Honeywell Mk 46 Mod 5 Neartip.
Decoys: 4 Mk 36 SBROC chaff launchers. Prairie Masker; blade rate suppression system.

Radars:
Air search — Nec OPS-12, 3D.
Surface search — JRC OPS-28.
Navigation — Koden OFS-2D.
Fire control — Signaal WM 25. Two Type 72-1A FCS.
Sonars: EDO/Nec SQS-35(J); VDS active/passive search. Nec OQS-101; bow-mounted. EDO/Nec SQR-18A; towed array, passive.

Helicopters: 3 Sikorsky/Mitsubishi SH-60J Sea Hawk, (ASW).

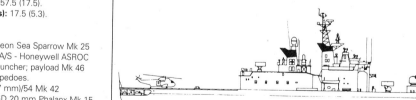

Shirane Class

SHIRANE

Country: JAPAN
Country of origin: JAPAN
Ship type: DESTROYERS
Class: TACHIKAZE (DDG)
Active: 3
Name (Pennant Number): TACHIKAZE (DD 168), ASAKAZE (DD 169), SAWAKAZE (DD 170)

Recognition features:

- High bow, continuous sweeping maindeck line from stem to stern.
- 5 in gun mounting (A position).
- ASROC A/S missile octuple box launcher immediately forward of bridge.
- Forward mast and funnel combined at after end of main superstructure topped by lattice mast.
- Aftermast and funnel combined has SPS-52B/C square profile radar aerial mounted atop.
- Two sets of triple torpedo tubes mounted between funnels.
- After 5 in gun mounting (X position).
- Standard SAM launcher on long afterdeck.

Displacement standard, tons: 3,850 (3,950, DD 170).
Length, feet (metres): 469 (143).
Beam, feet (metres): 47 (14.3).
Draught, feet (metres): 15.4 (4.7).
Speed, knots: 32.

Missiles: SSM - 8 McDonnell Douglas Harpoon. SAM - GDC Pomona Standard SM-1MR; Mk 13 Mod 1 or 4 launcher. A/S - Honeywell ASROC Mk 112 octuple launcher; payload Mk 46 Mod 5 Neartip torpedoes.
Guns: 2 FMC 5 in (127 mm)/54 Mk 42 automatic. 2 GE/GD 20 mm Phalanx CIWS Mk 15.

Torpedoes: 6   324 mm Type 68 (2 triple) tubes. Honeywell Mk 46 Mod 5 Neartip.
Decoys: 4 Loral Hycor SRBOC 6-barrel Mk 36 chaff launchers. SLQ-25 Nixie towed torpedo decoy.

Radars:

Air search — Melco OPS-11C. Hughes SPS-52B or C (DDG 170), 3D.
Surface search — JRC OPS-16D. JRC OPS-28 (DD 170). JRC OPS-18-3, (DDG 169).
Fire control — 2 Raytheon SPG 51. Type 2 FCS.
Sonars: Nec OQS-3A (Type 66); bow-mounted, active search/attack.

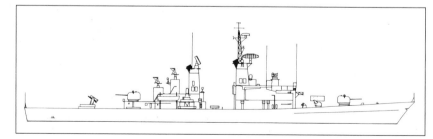

Tachikaze Class

ASAKAZE

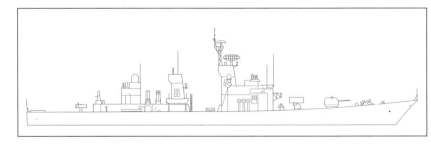

Takatsuki Class

Country: JAPAN
Country of origin: JAPAN
Ship type: DESTROYERS
Class: TAKATSUKI (DDG/DDA)
Active: 2
Name (Pennant Number): TAKATSUKI (DDA 164), KIKUZUKI (DDA 165).

Recognition features:
- High bow, continuous sweeping maindeck line from stem to stern.
- 5 in gun mounting (A position), with Bofors 375 mm Type 71 A/S mortar forward on forecastle.
- ASROC A/S missile octuple box launcher immediately forward of bridge
- Tall forward bridge superstructure with forward mast and short funnel combined at after end, topped by lattice mast
- Two black-topped funnels, with Harpoon SSM quad launchers aft of second funnel.
- Gap between forward and aft superstructures, with triple torpedo tubes between.
- Type 2-12B fire control radome atop tall raised platform on after superstructure.
- Sea Sparrow SAM octuple box launcher in Y position.

Displacement, tons: 3,250 standard.
Length, feet (metres): 446.1 (136).
Beam, feet (metres): 44 (13.4).
Draught, feet (metres): 14.8 (4.5).
Speed, knots: 31.
Range, miles: 7,000 at 20 kts.

Missiles: SSM — McDonnell Douglas Harpoon (2 quad) launchers. SAM — Raytheon Sea Sparrow Type 3 or 3A octuple launchers. A/S — Honeywell ASROC Mk 112 octuple launcher with payload Mk 46 Mod 5 Neartip torpedo.

Guns: 1 FMC 5 in (127 mm)/54 Mk 42 automatic. 1 GE/GD 20 mm Phalanx CIWS.
Torpedoes: 6 324 mm Type 68 (2 triple) tubes. Honeywell Mk 46 Mod 5 Neartip.
A/S mortars: 1 375 mm Bofors Type 71 4-barrel trainable rocket launcher.
Decoys: 2 Loral Hycor SBROC 6-barrel Mk 36 chaff launchers.

Radar:
Air search — Melco OPS-11B-Y.
Surface search — JRC OPS-17.
Fire control — Type 2-12B. 2 GE Mk 35.
Sonars: Nec SQS-35J, hull-mounted active search/attack. EDO SQR-18 TACTASS, passive.

Note: Mochizuki (ex-DD 166) of this class, converted to an auxiliary patrol ship in 1995. Not fitted with Harpoon, Sea Sparrow, or CIWS. Now bears pennant number ASU 7019.

Takatsuki Class

KIKUZUKI

Yamagumo Class

Country: JAPAN
Country of origin: JAPAN
Ship type: DESTROYERS
Class: YAMAGUMO (DD/DDK)
Active: 3
Name (Pennant Number): AOKUMO (DDK 119), AKIGUMO (DDK 120), YUUGUMO (DDK 121).

Recognition features:

- High bow, continuous sweeping maindeck line from stem to stern.
- 3 in gun mountings in A and Y positions.
- Bofors 375 mm Type 71m 4-barrel A/S mortar on raised platform immediately forward of bridge superstructure.
- Lattice mainmast supporting Melco OPS-11B/11C air search radar and surface search radar on gantries.
- Two rounded, tapering funnels with second, short lattice mast forward of squat, aft funnel.
- ASROC A/S missile octuple box launcher between funnels.

Displacement, tons: 2,150 standard.
Length, feet (metres): 377.2 (114.9).
Beam, feet (metres): 38.7 (11.8).
Draught, feet (metres): 13.1 (4).
Speed, knots: 27.
Range, miles: 7,000 at 20 kts.

Missiles: A/S Honeywell ASROC Mk 112 octuple launcher with payload, Mk 46 Mod 5 Neartip.
Guns: 4 USN 3 in (76mm)/50 (2 twin).
Torpedoes: 6 324 mm Type 68 (2 triple) tubes with Honeywell Mk 46 Mod 5 Neartip.
A/S mortars: 1 Bofors 375 mm Type 71 4-barrel trainable rocket launcher.

Radars:

Air search — Melco OPS-11B/11C.
Surface search — JRC OPS-17 (DDK 119); JRC OPS-16D (DDK 120); JRC OPS-18-3 (DDK 121).
Fire control — 2 GE Mk 35.
Sonars: Nec OQS-3A, hull-mounted, active search/attack. EDO SQS-35(J) (DDK 120,121). VDS, active/passive search.

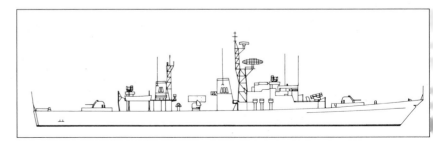

Yamagumo Class

YUUGUMO

Hachiro Nakai

Marasesti Class

Country: ROMANIA
Country of origin: ROMANIA
Ship type: DESTROYERS
Class: MARASESTI (DDG)
Active: 1
Name (Pennant Number): MARASESTI (ex-Muntenia) (111)

Recognition features:

- Continuous sweeping maindeck line from stem to stern with open quarterdeck below. Small break at forward SSM position.
- 3 in gun mountings in A and B positions with Styx SS-N-2C SSM in box-like angled launchers alongside B position and facing astern at aft end of superstructure.
- Tall, box-like bridge superstructure topped by short lattice mast and, immediately above bridge, Hawk Screech fire control radar on raised platform.
- Second lattice mast, aft, on raised platform, forward of square, tapering funnel.

Displacement, tons: 5,790 full load.
Length, feet (metres): 474.4 (144.6).
Beam, feet (metres): 48.6 (14.8).
Draught, feet (metres): 23 (7).
Speed, knots: 27.

Missiles: SSM — 8 SS-N-2C Styx.
Guns: 4 USSR 3 in (76 mm)/60, (2 twin). 4 30mm/65 6-barrelled.
Torpedoes: 6 21 in (533 mm) (2 triple) tubes. Russian 53-65.
A/S mortars: 2 RBU 6000 12-tubed trainable launchers.
Decoys: 2 PK 16 chaff launchers.

Radars:
Air/surface search — Strut Curve.
Surface search — Plank Shave.
Navigation — Nayada.
Fire control — 2 Drum Tilt. Hawk Screech.
Sonars: Hull-mounted, active search/attack.

Helicopters: 2 IAR-316B Alouette III (ASW)

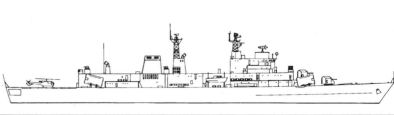

Marasesti Class

MARASESTI

Kashin, Kashin II and Modified Kashin Classes

Country: RUSSIA, INDIA, POLAND
Country of origin: RUSSIA
Ship type: DESTROYERS (DDG)
Class: KASHIN (TYPE 61) KASHIN II (RAJPUT, TYPE 61ME), MODIFIED KASHIN (TYPE 61M/61MP), (DDG).
Active: 2 (Russia) (Kashin Type 61/Modified Kashin Type 61M). 5 (India) (Kashin II/Rajput class). 1 (Poland) (Modified Kashin Type 61MP).

RUSSIA
Name (pennant Number): SMETLIVY (—) , SDERZHANNY (—) .
INDIA
Name (Pennant Number): RAJPUT (ex-Nadiozny) (D 51), RANA (ex-Gubitielny), (D 52) RANJIT (ex-Lovky), (D 53) RANVIR (ex-Twiordy), (D 54), RANVIJAY (ex-Tolkovy), (D 55).
POLAND
Name (Pennant Number): WARSZAWA (ex-Smely), (271).

Recognition features:
Russian and Polish units -
- High bow sloping down to stern.
- 3 in gun in A position and SA-N-1 Goa SAM in B position.
- Owl Screech fire control dish immediately forward of bridge.
- Two isolated, massive lattice masts, with Head Net C air/surface radar aerial atop forward mast.
- Two slab-sided squat funnels, aft well back from midships.
- Gun mounting in Y position, SA-N-1 SAM in X position.
- Angled, tubular Styx tubular launchers, facing astern, port and starboard, alongside aft funnel.

Indian units, as Russian except for —
- Helicopter hangar replaces Y position gun mounting.
- SS-N-2D Mod 2 Styx tubular launchers forward of bridge.
- Aft Owl Screech fire control director omitted.

Displacement, tons: 4,010 standard, 4,750 full load (Kashin); 4,974 (mod. Kashin/Kashin II).
Length, feet (metres): 479.7 (146.2), 480.5 (146.5) Indian.
Beam, feet (metres): 51.8 (15.8).
Draught, feet (metres): 15.4 (4.7).
Speed, knots: 35 (Russian and Indian), 32 (Polish).
Range, miles: 4,000 at 18 kts.

Missiles: SSM - 4 SS-N-2C Styx (Russian and Polish); 4 SS-N-2D Mod 2 Styx (Indian). SAM — 2 SA-N-1 Goa twin launchers.
Guns: 4 3 in (76 mm)/60 (2 twin) AK 762 (2 only in Indian ships); 4 30 mm/65 AK 630 6-barrel, (8 with 4 twin AK 230, in Indian ships, Rajput, Rana and Ranjit, and 4 30mm/65 ADG 630 in Ranvir and Ranvijay).
Torpedoes: 5 21 in (533 mm) (quin tubes).
A/S mortars: 2 RBU 6000 12-tubed trainable, (RBU 1000 6-tubed in Smetlivy).
Decoys: 4 16-tubed chaff launchers; 2 towed torpedo decoys. (4 PK 16 chaff launchers in Indian and Polish ships).

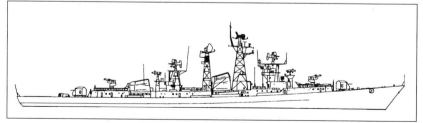

Kashin, Kashin II and Modified Kashin Classes

KASHIN

Radars:
Air / surface search — Head Net C, Big Net. (Big Net A in Indian ships for air search).
Navigation — 2 Don 2/Don Kay/Palm Frond, (Russian); 2 SRN 7453 and 1 SRN 207 (Polish); 2 Don Kay (Indian).
Fire control — 2 Peel Group (SA-N-1); Owl Screech (guns); 2 Bass Tilt (Sderzhany) (30 mm guns). (Drum Tilt in Indian D 51-53).

Sonar: Bull Nose or Wolf Paw, hull-mounted, active search/attack. Mare Tail VDS. Vcheda MG 311 (Indian ships)

Helicopters: Platform only (Sderzhany and Polish) 1 Kamov Ka-27/28 Helix (ASW), (Indian).

Sovremenny (Sarych) Class

Country: RUSSIA, CHINA
Country of origin: RUSSIA
Ship type: DESTROYERS
Class: SOVREMENNY (Sarych) (TYPE 956/956A) (DDG)
Active: 11 (Russia)
Building: 1 (Russia) + 2 (China)

RUSSIA
Name (Pennant Number): BEZUPRECHNY, BOYEVOY, BURNY, GREMYASHCHY, (ex-Vieduzczy), BYSTRY, RASTOROPNY, BEZBOYAZNENNY, BEZUDERZHNY, BESPOKOINY, NASTOYCHIVY, (ex-Moskowski Komsomolets) BESSTRASHNY, EKATARINBURY, (ex-Sobrazitelny, ex-Buliny) (building).

CHINA
Name (Pennant Number): ——(ex-Vazhny), —— (ex-Alexander Nevsky), (building).

Recognition features:
● High bow. Sweeping maindeck aft to break at bridge where tubular quad SSM launchers are fitted, port and starboard.
● 130 mm/70 gun mounting (A position).
● SA-N-7 Gadfly SAM launcher (B mounting position).
● Prominent Band Stand weapons control dome atop bridge.
● High forward superstructure with large enclosed mainmast at its after end. Large distinctive Top Plate air search radar aerial atop.
● Single, large, square funnel just aft of midships.

Displacement, tons: 6,600 standard, 7,940 full load.
Length, feet (metres): 511.8 (156).
Beam, feet (metres): 56.8 (17.3).

Draught, feet (metres): 21.3 (6.5).
Speed, knots: 32.
Range, miles: 14,000 at 14 kts
Missiles: SSM - Raduga SS-N-22 Sunburn (3M-80 Zubr) (2 quad) launchers. SAM - 2 SA-N-7 Gadfly 3K 90 (Uragan). (From Bespokoiny onwards, same launcher is used for SA-N-17 Grizzly/SA-N-12 Yezh.)
Guns: 4 130 mm/70 AK 130 (2 twin). 4 30 mm/65 6-barrel AK 630.
Torpedoes: 4 21 in (533 mm) (2 twin) tubes.
A/S mortars: 2 RBU 1000 6-barrelled.
Mines: Rails for up to 40.
Decoys: 8 PK 10 and 2 PK 2 chaff launchers.

Radars: Air search — Top Plate 3D.
Surface search — 3 Palm Frond.
Fire control — 6 Front Dome. (SA-N-7/17); Kite Screech, (130 mm guns); 2 Bass Tilt, (30 mm guns)
Sonars: Bull Horn (MGK-335 Platina) and Whale Tongue ; hull-mounted active search/attack.

Helicopters: 1 Kamov Ka-27PL Helix. (ASW). 2 Harbin Zhi-9A Haitun (Dauphin 2) (ASW/ASV)(Chinese units)

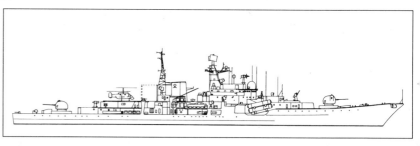

Sovremenny (Sarych) Class

SOVREMENNY

Udaloy (Fregat) Class

Country: RUSSIA
Country of origin: RUSSIA
Ship type: DESTROYERS
Class: UDALOY (FREGAT) (TYPE 1155) (DDG)
Active: 7
Name (Pennant Number): MARSHAL VASILEVSKY, MARSHAL SHAPOSHNIKOV, SEVEROMORSK (ex-Simferopol, ex-Marshal Budienny), ADMIRAL LEVCHENKO, (ex-Kharbarovsk), ADMIRAL VINOGRADOV, ADMIRAL KHARLAMOV, ADMIRAL PANTELEYEV.

Recognition features:
- High bow with sweeping maindeck aft to break at after funnel.
- 3.9 in gun mountings (A and B positions).
- SA-N-9 Gauntlet SAM VLS launcher set into the ship's structure on the forecastle.
- 2 SS-N-14 Silex A/S missile square, tubular quad launchers on maindeck level, beneath bridge, port and starboard.
- Two square section, twin funnels with tapered RAD-HAZ screens at after end.
- Two lattice masts forward of funnels. After mainmast is larger with Top Plate air search radar aerial atop.
- Smaller pyramid mast on bridge roof supports Kite Screech fire control radar.
- Large crane derrick aft of after funnels.
- Two hangars set side by side with inclined elevating ramps to the flight deck.

Note: UDALOY II class (1 unit).

Displacement, tons: 6,700 standard, 8,500 full load.
Length, feet (metres): 536.4 (163.5).
Beam, feet (metres): 63.3 (19.3).
Draught, feet (metres): 24.6 (7.5).
Speed, knots: 29.
Range, miles: 7,700 at 18 kts.

Missiles: SAM - 8 SA-N-9 Gauntlet (Klinok) vertical launchers. A/S — 2 Raduga SS-N-14 Silex (Rastrub) quad launchers; payload nuclear or Type E53-72 torpedo.
Guns: 2   3.9 in (100 mm)/59. 4 30 mm/65 6-barrelled.
Torpedoes: 8   21 in (533 mm) (2 quad) tubes.
A/S mortars: 2 RBU 6000 12-tubed, trainable.
Mines: Rails for 26 mines.
Decoys: 2 PK 2 and 8 PK 10 chaff launchers. US Masker type noise reduction.

Radars:
Air search — Strut Pair, Top Plate 3D.
Surface search — 3 Palm Frond.
Fire Control — 2 Eye Bowl, (SS-N-14); 2 Cross Sword, (SA-N-9); Kite Screech, (100 mm guns); 2 Bass Tilt, (30 mm guns).
Sonars: Horse Jaw (Polinom) hull-mounted, active search/attack. Mouse Tail; VDS, active search.

Helicopters: 2 Kamov Ka-27 Helix A (ASW).

Udaloy (Fregat) Class

UDALOY

Udaloy II (Fregat) Class

Country: Russia
Country of origin: Russia
Ship type: DESTROYERS
Class: UDALOY II (FREGAT) (TYPE 1155.1) (DDG)
Active: 1
Name (Pennant Number): ADMIRAL CHABANENKO.

Recognition features:

- As UDALOY I class, except —
- 130 mm gun only in A position.
- PK 2 chaff launchers in place of gun mounting in B position.
- Full length of SS-N-22 Sunburn SSM tubular quad launchers exposed, port and starboard, below bridge.
- Torpedo tubes protected by hinged flap in hull above chine aft of second funnel.
- Crane deck forward of deck break, which is further after than Udaloy I.

Displacement, tons: 7,700 standard, 8,900 full load.
Length, feet (metres): 536.4 (163.5).
Beam, feet (metres): 63.3 (19.3).
Draught, feet (metres): 24.6 (7.5).
Speed, knots: 28.
Range, miles: 4,000 at 18 kts.

Missiles: SSM — Raduga SS-N-22 Sunburn (3M-82 Moskit) (2 quad launchers); SAM — SA-N-9 Gauntlet (Klinok) VLS. SAM/guns — 2 CADS-N-1 (Kashtan) each with 30 mm 6-barrel gun, combined with SA-N-11 (Grisson) SAMs and Hot Flash/Hot Spot fire control radar/optronic director. A/S — Novator SS-N-15 Starfish, Type 40 torpedo.
Guns: 130 mm/70 (twin) AK 130.
Torpedoes: 8 21 in (533 mm) (2 quad tubes).
A/S mortars: 2 RBU 6000, 12-tubed trainable.
Decoys: 8 PK 10 and 2 PK 2 chaff launchers.

Radar:
Air search — Strut Pair II; Top Plate 3D.
Surface search — 3 Palm Frond.
Fire control — 2 Cross Swords (SA-N-9); Kite Screech (100 mm gun).
Sonars: Horse Jaw (Polinom) hull-mounted, active search/attack; Horse Tail VDS, active search.

Helicopters: 2 Kamov KA-27 Helix A (ASW).

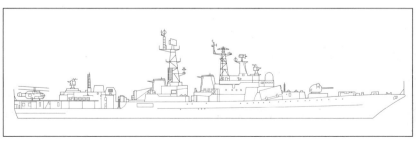

Engel

Daring Class

Country: PERU
Country of origin: UNITED KINGDOM
Ship type: DESTROYERS
Class: DARING (DDG)
Active: 1
Name (Pennant Number): FERRÉ (ex-Decoy), (DM 74).

Recognition features:

- Main deck break aft of bridge superstructure.
- 4.5 in guns at A, B and Y positions.
- Slim pyramid mast behind bridge with pole mast atop.
- Single funnel aft of midships.
- Exocet SSM launchers aft of funnel.
- Raised helicopter landing platform at stern.

Displacement, tons: 2,800 standard, 3,600 full load.
Length, feet (metres): 390 (118.9).
Beam, feet (metres): 43 (13.1).
Draught, feet (metres): 18 (5.5).
Speed, knots: 32.
Range, miles: 3,000 at 20 kts.

Missiles: SSM — 8 Aerospatiale MM 38 Exocet.
Guns: 6 (3 twin) Vickers 4.5 in (114 mm)/45 Mk 5; 4 Breda 40mm/70 (2 twin

Radars:
Air/surface search — Plessey AWS 1.
Surface search — Racal Decca TM 1226.
Fire control — Selenia RTN 10X.

Helicopters: Platform only.

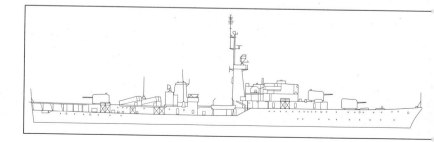

ERRÉ

Peruvian navy

Prat Class

Country: CHILE
Country of origin: UNITED KINGDOM
Ship type: DESTROYERS
Class: PRAT (Ex-COUNTY)
Active: 4
Name (Pennant Number): PRAT (ex-Norfolk) (11), COCHRANE (ex-Antrim) (12), LATORRE (ex-Glamorgan) (14), BLANCO ENCALADA (ex-Fife) (15)

Recognition features:
- High freeboard.
- 4.5 in gun mounting (A position) immediately forward of SSM launchers (B mounting position).
- Slim pyramid mast aft of bridge.
- Squat funnels with pyramid mainmast centrally situated between them. Double bedstead air search radar aerial atop.
- Seaslug SAM director on raised structure forward of flight deck with lattice Seaslug launcher on quarterdeck (Prat and Latorre only).
- Blanco Encalada and Cochrane are different in appearance with greatly enlarged hangar and flight deck continued right aft making them effectively flush-decked. Obsolete Seaslug system has been removed.

Displacement full load, tons: 6,200.
Length, feet (metres): 520.5 (158.7).
Beam, feet (metres): 54 (16.5).
Draught, feet (metres): 20.5 (6.3).
Speed, knots: 30.
Range, miles: 3,500 at 28 kts.

Missiles: SSM - 4 Aerospatiale MM 38 Exocet. SAM - Short Bros Seaslug M 2 (11 and 14 only). 2 octuple IAI/Rafael Barak 1
Guns: 2 Vickers 4.5 in (115 mm) Mk 6 semi-automatic twin mounting. 2 or 4 Oerlikon 20 mm Mk 9.
Torpedoes: 6 324 mm Mk 32 (2 triple) tubes. Honeywell Mk 46 Mod 2.
Decoys: 2 Corvus 8-barrel trainable launchers; 2 Wallop Barricade double layer chaff launchers.

Radars:
Air search — Marconi Type 965 M or 966 (14 and 15); Admiralty Type 277 M; Elta LM 2228S (11 and 12)
Surface search — Marconi Type 992 Q or R.
Navigation — Decca Type 978/1006.
Fire control — Plessey Type 903 (guns); Marconi Type 901 (11 and 14) (Seaslug); 2 Elta EL/M-2221GM.
Sonars: Kelvin Hughes Type 162 M; hull-mounted. Graseby Type 184 M or Type 184 S (in 16); hull-mounted; active search and attack.

Helicopters: 1 Bell 206B JetRanger (11 and 14), 2 Nurtanio NAS 332C Cougar (ASW/ASV) (12 and 15).

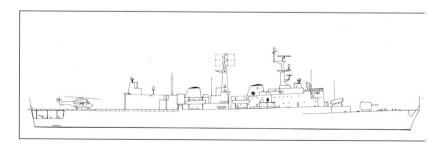

COCHRANE

Type 42 Class (Batch 1 and 2)

Country: UNITED KINGDOM, ARGENTINA.
Country of origin: UNITED KINGDOM
Ship type: DESTROYERS
Class: UK - TYPE 42 (BATCH 1 and 2) ARGENTINA - HERCULES (DDG)
Active: 8 UK; 1 + 1 reserve, Argentina

UNITED KINGDOM BATCH I
Name (Pennant Number): BIRMINGHAM (D 86), NEWCASTLE (D 87), GLASGOW (D 88), CARDIFF (D 108)
BATCH II
Name (Pennant Number): EXETER (D 89), SOUTHAMPTON (D 90), NOTTINGHAM (D 91), LIVERPOOL (D 92)
ARGENTINA
Name (Pennant Number): HERCULES (D 1, ex-28), SANTISIMA TRINIDAD (D 2).

Recognition features:
- Continuous maindeck line from stem to stern, high freeboard.
- 4.5 in gun mounting half way between bows and bridge.
- Sea Dart SAM twin launcher immediately forward of bridge.
- High forward superstructure with large Type 909/9091 fire control radar dome atop.
- Large single, black-capped funnel with sloping after end, just aft of midships.
- Large lattice Type 1022 air search radar aerial at after end of forward superstructure.
- Tall, black-topped pole foremast forward of funnel.
- Tall, enclosed, black-topped mainmast aft of funnel, supporting Type 996 surface search radar aerial.
- Hangar superstructure at forward end of flight deck with large fire Type 909 control radar dome at forward end.
- Open quarterdeck below after end of flight deck.

Argentine ships —
- Most obvious differences are Type 965P air search bedstead radar aerial atop forward superstructure, large black exhausts on side of funnel.
- Exocet SSM launchers outboard of funnels.

Note See Type 42 Batch 3.

Displacement full load, tons: 4,100.
Length, feet (metres): 412 (125) oa.
Beam, feet (metres): 47 (14.3).
Draught, feet (metres): 19 (5.8) (screws).
Speed, knots: 29.
Range, miles: 4,000 at 18 kts.

Missiles: SSM — 4 Aerospatiale MM 38 Exocet (Argentine ships only). SAM - British Aerospace Sea Dart twin launcher. (Mk 30, Argentine ships).
Guns: Vickers 4.5 in (114 mm)/55 Mk 8. 2 or 4 Oerlikon/BMARC 20 mm GAM-BO1. (2 Oerlikon 20 mm only in Argentine ships). 2 Oerlikon 20 mm Mk 7A (in those British ships with only 2 GAM-BOI). 2 GE/GD 20 mm Vulcan Phalanx Mk 15 (British ships only).
Torpedoes: 6 324 mm Plessey STWS Mk 3 (2 triple) tubes. 6 324 mm ILAS 3 (2 triple tubes) in Argentine ships.
Decoys: 4 Marconi Sea Gnat 130/102 mm 6-barrel launchers or SRBOC and Corvus (D 86 and Argentine ships.) Graseby Type 182 towed torpedo decoy. Graseby GI 738 towed torpedo decoy in Argentine ships.

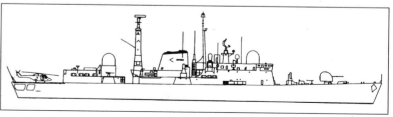

CARDIFF

Jane's/HD Steele

Radars:
Air search — Marconi/Signaal Type 1022. (Marconi Type 965P, Argentine ships)
Air/surface search — Plessey Type 996 or 992 (D 86).
Surface search — Marconi Type 992Q (Argentine ships).
Navigation — Kelvin Hughes Type 1006 or Racal Decca Type 1008.
Fire control — 2 Marconi Type 909 or 9091.

Sonars: Ferranti Type 2050 or Plessey Type 2016; hull-mounted. Graseby Type 184M hull-mounted, active search/attack (Argentine). Kelvin Hughes Type 162M.

Helicopters: 1 Westland Lynx HMA 3/8. (ASV/ASW). 1 Aerospatiale SA 319B Alouette III (ASW/ASV) Argentine ships.

Type 42 Class (Batch 3)

Country: UNITED KINGDOM
Country of origin: UNITED KINGDOM
Ship type: DESTROYERS
Class: TYPE 42 (BATCH 3) (DDG)
Active: 4
Batch 3
Name (Pennant Number): MANCHESTER (D 95), GLOUCESTER (D 96),
EDINBURGH (D 97), YORK (D 98)

Recognition features:
Note - See also Type 42 Batch 1 and 2.
● Extremely long forecastle, some 50 ft more than UK Type 42 Batches 1
and 2. Otherwise very similar to Batch 1 and 2 of the class.
● Stretched Batch 3s are fitted with a strengthening beam on each side
which increases width by 2 feet.

Displacement full load, tons: 4,675.
Length, feet (metres): 462.8 (141.1).
Beam, feet (metres): 49 (14.9).
Draught, feet (metres): 19 (5.8) (screws).
Speed, knots: 30+.
Range, miles: 4,000 at 18 kts.

Missiles: SAM - British Aerospace Sea Dart twin launcher.
Guns: Vickers 4.5 in (114 mm)/55 Mk 8. 2 or 4 Oerlikon/BMARC 20 mm
GAM-BO1. 2 Oerlikon 20 mm Mk 7A (in those with only 2 GAM-BO1) 2
GE/GD 20 mm Vulcan Phalanx Mk 15.
Torpedoes: 6 324 mm STWS Mk 2 (2 triple) tubes. Marconi Stingray.
Decoys: 4 Sea Gnat 130/102 mm 6-barrel launchers. Graseby Type 182;
towed torpedo decoy.

Radars:
Air search — Marconi/Signaal Type 1022.
Air/surface search — Plessey Type 996.
Navigation — Kelvin Hughes Type 1007 or Racal Decca Type 1008..
Fire control — 2 Marconi Type 909 or 909 Mod 1.
Sonars: Ferranti/Thomson Type 2050 or Plessey Type 2016; hull-mounted.
Kelvin Hughes Type 162M; hull-mounted.

Helicopters: 1 Westland Lynx HMA 3/8. (ASV/ASW).

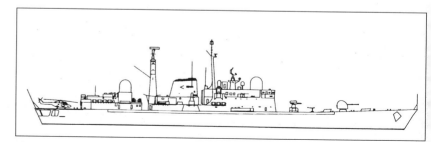

DINBURGH

Jane's/HD Steele

Country: AUSTRALIA, GERMANY, GREECE.
Country of origin: UNITED STATES OF AMERICA
Ship type: DESTROYERS
Class: PERTH (MODIFIED CHARLES F ADAMS) LÜTJENS (MODIFIED CHARLES F ADAMS - TYPE 103B), KIMON (CHARLES F ADAMS) (DDG).
Active: 3 (Perth), 3 (Lütjens), 4 (Kimon).
AUSTRALIA
Name (Pennant Number): PERTH (38), HOBART (39), BRISBANE (41)
GERMANY
Name (Pennant Number): LÜTJENS (D 185, ex-DDG 28), MÖLDERS (D 186, ex-DDG 29), ROMMEL (D 187, ex-DDG 30).
GREECE – Name (Pennant Number): KIMON (ex-Semmes) (D 218 ex-DDG 18), NEARCHOS (ex-Waddell) (D 219, ex-DDG 24), FORMION (ex-Miltiadis, ex-Strauss) (DDG 220 ex-DDG 16), THEMISTOCLES (ex-Konon, ex-Berkeley) (DDG 221, ex-DDG 15).

Recognition features:

- High bow, sweeping forecastle to 5 in mounting (A position).
- High bridge structure with SATCOM dome atop (SATCOM Australian ships only in this position, SATCOM atop short lattice pylon in German ships).
- Twin funnels sloped aft. Tripod mainmast astride forward funnel.
- Distinctive SPS-52C air search radar aerial (SPS-39 in Greek ships) mounted on aftermast and funnel combined.
- Two Raytheon SPG-51C/D fire control radar aerials immediately aft of after funnel.
- Standard SAM launcher immediately forward of quarterdeck, aft of 5 in gun mounting in X position. In German ships, RAM launchers on quarterdeck.
- Unusual tapered black tops to funnels.
- Australian ships have a broad deckhouse

between the funnels, not present in the German or Greek units which have an ASROC box launcher in this position.

Displacement full load, tons: 4,500, German, 4, 618, Australian, 4,825 Greek.
Length, feet (metres): 440.8 (134.3), Australian; 437 (133.2), German, Greek.
Beam, feet (metres): 47.1 (14.3)
Draught, feet (metres): 20.1 (6.1) 21, Greek (sonar).
Speed, knots: 30+ (Australian), 30, (Greek), 32, (German).
Range, miles: 6,000 at 15 kts, 4,500 miles at 20 kts., (German).

Missiles: SAM - GDC Pomona Standard SM-1MR; Mk 13 Mod 6 launcher. (Dual capability launcher for SSM.) (Mod 0 launcher in German ships). RAM 21 cell Mk 49 launchers (German ships only). SSM — McDonnell Douglas Harpoon (German and Greek ships; Australian, fitted for but not carried). Honeywell ASROC Mk 16 octuple launcher (Greek ships only). Mk 112 in German ships.
Guns: 2 FMC 5 in (127 mm) 54 Mk 42 Mod 10. 2 GE/GD 20 mm Mk 15 Vulcan Phalanx, (latter, Australian ships only.) Up to 6 - 12.7 mm MGs. (4 in Greek ships, none in German ships). 2 Rheinmetall 20 mm Rh 202 (German ships only).
Depth charges: 1 projector. (German ships only).

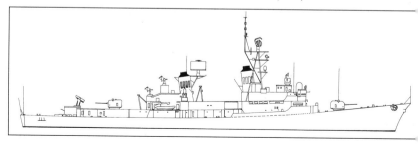

HOBART

Torpedoes: 6 324 mm Mk 32 Mod 5 (2 triple) tubes; Honeywell Mk 46 Mod 5.

Decoys: 2 Loral Hycor SRBOC 6-barrel fixed Mk 36. (4 in Greek ships.) Mk T-6 Fanfare torpedo decoy, (Greek ships only). Nulka quad decoy launcher and SLQ-25; towed torpedo decoy. (Australian ships only).

Radars:

Air search — Hughes SP5-52C. Lockheed SPS-40C. (SPS-39, SPS-40B/D in Greek ships, SPS-39, SPS-40 in German).

Surface search — Norden SPS-67V. (Raytheon SPS-10D/F or SPS-64 in German and Greek ships).

Navigation — Marconi LN66 (Greek ships).

Fire control — 2 Raytheon SPG-51C, (Standard), Western Electric SPG-53F, (guns). (SPG-51, Lockheed SPQ-9 and SPG-60 in German ships.) (SPG-51D, SPG-53A, Greek ships).

Sonars: Sangamo SQS-23KL hull-mounted (Australia) Sangamo or Raytheon DE 1191 (Greek). Atlas Elektronik DSQS-21B hull-mounted, (German ships).

Arleigh Burke Class (Flights I, II and IIA)

Country: UNITED STATES OF AMERICA
Country of origin: UNITED STATES OF AMERICA
Ship type: DESTROYERS
Class: ARLEIGH BURKE (FLIGHTS I,II, IIA) - (AEGIS) (DDG).
Active: 25 (Flights I and II).
Building: 3 (Flights I and II), 5 (Flight IIA).
Proposed: 5 (Flight IIA).

FLIGHTS I AND II

Name (Pennant Number): ARLEIGH BURKE (DDG 51), BARRY (ex-John Barry)(DDG 52), JOHN PAUL JONES (DDG 53), CURTIS WILBUR (DDG 54), STOUT (DDG 55), JOHN S McCAIN (DDG 56), MITSCHER (DDG 57), LABOON (DDG 58), RUSSELL (DDG 59), PAUL HAMILTON (DDG 60), RAMAGE (DDG 61), FITZGERALD (DDG 62), STETHEM (DDG 63), CARNEY (DDG 64), BENFOLD (DDG 65), GONZALEZ (DDG 66), COLE (DDG 67), THE SULLIVANS (DDG 68), MILIUS (DDG 69), HOPPER (DDG 70), ROSS (DDG 71), MAHAN (DDG 72), DECATUR (DDG 73) McFAUL (DDG 74), DONALD COOK (DDG 75), HIGGINS (DDG 76), O'KANE (DDG 77), PORTER (DDG 78).

FLIGHT IIA

Name (Pennant Number): OSCAR AUSTIN (DDG 79), ROOSEVELT (DDG 80), WINSTON CHURCHILL (DDG 81), LASSEN (DDG 82), HOWARD (DDG 83).

Only ships building named.

Recognition features:

- High bow with sweeping maindeck aft to break down to flight deck.
- Only obvious armament on forecastle is 5 in gun mounting mid-way between bow and bridge.
- Missile VLS tubes situated between forward gun mounting and bridge and just forward of flight deck.
- High main superstructure with aft-sloping pole mainmast atop.

- Large twin funnels of unusual square section with black exhausts protruding at top. Funnels sited either side of midships.
- CIWS mountings on raised platform immediately forward of bridge and forward of Harpoon SSM launcher.
- Flight deck right aft.

Note 1 - Helicopter hangars to be incorporated in Flight IIA version with extended transom to increase size of flight deck.

Note 2 - Japan operates an improved Arleigh Burke class named 'Kongou' class, see Japanese entry.

Displacement full load, tons: 8, 422, (9,003 from DDG 72 and 9,217, Flight IIA).
Length, feet (metres): 504.5 (153.8) oa. (509.5, (155.3) oa, Flight IIA).
Beam, feet (metres): 66.9 (20.4).
Draught, feet (metres): 20.7 (6.3), 32.7 (9.9) sonar.
Speed, knots: 32.
Range, miles: 4,400 at 20 kts.

Missiles: SLCM - 56 GDC/Hughes Tomahawk. SSM - 8 McDonnell Douglas Harpoon (2 quad). SAM - GDC Standard SM-2MR Block 4. (Evolved Sea Sparrow in Flight IIA). A/S — Loral ASROC VLA; payload Mk 46 Mod 5

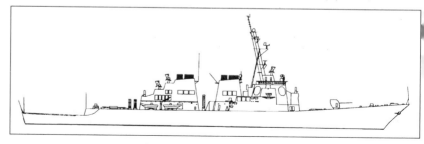

Arleigh Burke Class (Flights I, II and IIA)

CURTIS WILBUR

Neartip torpedoes. 2 Martin Marietta Mk 41 Vertical Launch Systems (VLS) for Tomahawk, Standard and ASROC (and Evolved Sea Sparrow in Flight IIA).

Guns: FMC/UDLP 5 in (127 mm)/54 Mk 45 Mod 1 (or Mod 2 in DDG 79-80, Mod 4 in DDG 81 onwards) 2 GE/GD 20 mm Vulcan Phalanx 6-barrel Mk 15.

Torpedoes: 6   324 mm Mk 32 Mod 14 (2 triple) tubes. Alliant Mod 46 Mod 5.

Decoys: 2 Loral Hycor SRBOC 6-barrel fixed Mk 36, Mod 12. AN/SLQ 25 Nixie; torpedo decoy.
NATO Sea Gnat SLQ-95 AEB, SLQ-39 chaff buoy.

Radars:
Air search/fire control — RCA SPY-1D, 3D. (SPY-1D(V) phased arrays in Flight IIA).
Surface search — Norden SPS-67(V)3.
Navigation — Raytheon SPS-64(V)9.
Fire control — 3 Raytheon/RCA SPG-62.
Sonars: Gould/Raytheon/GE SQQ-89(V)6; combines SQS-53C, bow-mounted active search/attack with SQR-19B passive towed array. (SQQ-89(V)10 in DDG 79 onwards).
Helicopters: Platform facilities to refuel/re-arm Sikorsky SH-60F (LAMPS III) (ASW). Hangar facilities for 2 LAMPS II in DDG 79 onwards.

Destroyers – USA   141

Fletcher/Allen M Sumner Class

Country: MEXICO, TAIWAN
Country of origin: UNITED STATES OF AMERICA
Ship type: DESTROYERS (DD/DDG)
Class: FLETCHER/ALLEN M SUMNER
Active: 1 Mexico, 7 Taiwan
MEXICO
Name (Pennant Number): CUITLAHUAC (ex-John Rodgers) (E 01, ex-E 02, ex-F 2, ex-DD 574).
TAIWAN
Name (Pennant Number): HUEI YANG (ex-English) (906 ex-DD 696), KUEI YANG (ex-Twining) (908 ex-DD 540), CHIN YANG (ex-Mullany) (909 ex-DD 528), LOA YANG (ex-Taussig) (914 ex-DD 746), NAN YANG (ex-Thomason) (917 ex-DD 760), AN YANG (ex-Kimberley) (918 ex-DD 521), KUN YANG (ex-Yarnell) (919 ex-DD 541).

Recognition features:
- High bow, sweeping maindeck from stem to stern .
- 5 in single gun mountings in A, B, X and Y positions with additional mounting, abaft aft funnel. (Mexico). 5 in gun in A and Y position with 3 in gun in B mounting and Hsiung Feng I SSM in X positions. (Taiwan).
- Squat, square bridge superstructure with fire control aerial atop.
- Thin pole mast just aft of superstructure. (Mexico). Two lattice masts forward of forward funnel and abaft aft funnel (Taiwan).
- Two black-topped funnels, forward and aft of midships.

Displacement, tons: 2,100 standard, 3,050 full load.
Length, feet (metres): 376.5 (114.8).
Beam, feet (metres): 39.5 (12).
Draught, feet (metres): 18 (5.5).
Speed, knots: 35 (Taiwan), 12 (Mexico).
Missiles: None.(Mexico). SSM — Hsiung Feng I. SAM — Sea Chaparral quad launcher/Sidewinder missile. (Taiwan).
Guns: 5 USN 5 in (127 mm)/38 Mk 30. (2 5 in, Taiwan). 1 OTO MELARA 3 in (76 mm)/62 (Taiwan). 10 Bofors 40 mm/60 (5 twin) Mk 2. (Mexico).
Torpedoes: 5 21 in (5 33 mm) (quin) tubes. (Mexico). 6 324 mm US Mk 32 (2 triple tubes) (Taiwan).

Radars:
Air Search — Lockheed SPS-40 (Taiwan only)
Air/surface search — Westinghouse SPS-58 (Taiwan only)
Surface search — Kelvin Hughes 17/9 (Mexico only)
Navigation — Kelvin Hughes 14/9 (Mexico only)
Fire control — Western Electric Mk 25. (Mexico). 2 RCA HR 76 (Taiwan).
Sonar: Atlas Elektronik DSQS-21CZ, hull-mounted, active search/attack.

Fletcher/Allen M Sumner Class

CUITLAHUAC

Gearing Class (FRAM I and II)

Country: SOUTH KOREA, MEXICO, PAKISTAN, TAIWAN, TURKEY
Country of origin: UNITED STATES OF AMERICA.
Ship type: DESTROYERS
Class: GEARING (FRAM I/II) (WU CHIN I/II/III CONVERSION) (DD/DDG)
Active: 3 (South Korea); 2 (Mexico); 3 (Pakistan), 4 (Taiwan, Wu Chin I and II)
7 (Taiwan Wu Chin III); 2 (Turkey).

SOUTH KOREA
Name (Pennant Number): KWANG JU (ex-Richard E Kraus) (DD 921 ex DD
849); KANG WON (ex-William R Rush) (DD 922 ex-DD 714); JEON JU
(ex-Rogers) (DD 925 ex-DD 876).

MEXICO
Name (Pennant Number): ILHUICAMINA (ex-Quetzalcoatl, ex-Vogelgesang)
(E 10, ex-E 03); NETZAHUALCOYOTL (ex-Steinaker) (E 11, ex-E 04).

PAKISTAN
Name (Pennant Number): ALAMGIR (ex-Cone) (D 160, ex-DD 866), TAIMUR
(ex-Epperson) (DD 166, ex-DD 719), TUGHRIL (ex-Henderson), (D 167,
ex-DD 785).

TAIWAN
Name (Pennant Number): (Wu Chin I/II) — FU YANG (ex-Ernest G Small)
(907, ex-DD 838), HAN YANG (ex-Herbert J Thomas) (915, ex-DD 833),
KAI YANG (ex-Richard B Anderson) (924, ex-DD 786), SHUEI YANG (ex-
Hawkins) (926, ex-DD 873). Wu Chin III - CHIEN YANG (ex-James E
Kyes) (912 ex-DD 787), LIAO YANG (ex-Hanson) (921, ex-DD 832), SHAO
YANG (ex-Hollister) (929 ex-DD 788), TE
YANG (ex-Sarsfield) (925, ex-DD 837)),
CHEN YANG (ex-Johnston) (928 ex-DD 821),
SHEN YANG (ex-Power) (923 ex-DD 839),
YUN YANG (ex-Hamner) (927 ex-DD 718).

TURKEY
Name (Pennant Number): KILIÇ ALI PASA (ex-
Robert H McCard) (DD 349, ex-DD 822),
PIYALE PASA (ex-Fiske) (DD 350, ex-DD
842).

Recognition features:
- Blunt bow, low freeboard.
- Continuous maindeck from stem to stern.
- 5 in twin gun mounting (A position). (OTO MELARA 3in (76 mm) in Wu
  Chin III conversions).
- Twin funnels sloping aft with distinctive black tapered tops.
- Large lattice mainmast astride forward funnel, smaller lattice mast aft of
  after funnel.

Note 1 - The general recognition features above apply to all of the class.
There are too many variants to be covered in this publication. Further
details can be obtained from Jane's Fighting Ships yearbook.

Displacement full load, tons: approx. 3500, 3,690 (Mexican).
Length, feet (metres): 390.5 (119).
Beam, feet (metres): 41.2 (12.6), 41.9 (12.7) (Mexican).
Draught, feet (metres): 19 (5.8), 15 (4.6) (Mexican).
Speed, knots: 30 (South Korea), 15 (Mexico), 32 (Pakistan), 32.5 (Taiwan and
Turkey).
Range, miles: 5,800 at 15 kts. 6,080 at 15 kts (Taiwan, Wu Chin III).

Missiles: SSM McDonnell Douglas Harpoon (South Korean, 2 quad, and
Pakistani ships 2 twin, Turkey, 2 single); Hsiung Feng I or II or Gabriel II
(1 triple) (Taiwan, Wu Chin I/II) Hsiung Feng II (Taiwan, Wu Chin III). SAM

Gearing Class (FRAM I and II)

- 1 Sea Chaparral quad launcher (Taiwan Wu Chin I/II). General Dynamics Standard SM1-MR (2 triple; 2 twin), (Taiwan Wu Chin III). A/S - Honeywell ASROC Mk 112 octuple launcher; payload Mk 46 torpedoes., (South Korea, Pakistan, Taiwan and Turkish ships).
Note: No missiles fitted to Mexican ships.
Guns: 4 USN 5 in (127 mm)/38 (2 twin) Mk 38. (South Korea, Mexico, Turkey). 2 or 4 USN 5 in (127 mm/38 Mk 38 (Taiwan Wu Chin I/II). 2 USN 5 in (127 mm)/38 Mk 38 (Pakistan). 1 OTO Melara 3 in (76 mm)/62. (Taiwan Wu Chin I/II/III) 1 GE/GD 20 mm Vulcan Phalanx Block 1, 6-barrel Mk 15, (South Korea, Pakistan, Taiwan Wu Chin III) 2 or 4 Bofors 40 mm/70. (Taiwan). USN/Bofors 40mm/56 (twin) (South Korea.) 1 57 mm/70 Mk 2 (Mexico). 2 Oerlikon 35 mm/90 (twin), (Turkey). 8 23mm./87 (2 quad) (Pakistan). 4 or 6 12.7 mm MGs. (Taiwan, Wu Chin III).
Torpedoes: 6 324 mm US Mk 32 (2 triple) tubes. Honeywell Mk 46. (Not Mexican ships).
Depth charges: 1 Mk IX rack. (South Korean, Turkish only)
Decoys: 2 Plessey Shield 6-barrel fixed chaff launchers (Pakistan). 2 or 4 20-barrel Breda 105 mm SCLAR Mk 2 or SRBOC chaff launchers. (Turkish ships.) 4 Kung Fen 6 16-tubed chaff launchers. Mk T-6 Fanfare torpedo decoy. (Taiwan ships).
Radars:
Air search — SPS-40 (South Korean, Mexican, Pakistani, Taiwanese Wu Chin I/II, Turkish ships). Signaal DA-08, (Taiwan Wu Chin III). Westinghouse SPS-29 (Mexico and Taiwanese Wu Chin I/II).
Surface search — Raytheon SPS 10/SPS 58. Kelvin Hughes 17/9 (Mexican).
Navigation — Marconi LN66 (Mexican). Racal Decca TM 1226 (Pakistani, Turkish).
Fire control — Western Electric Mk 12/12 (Mexican ships), Western Electric Mk 25 (South Korean, Pakistani, Taiwan Wu Chin I, Turkish ships)

NETZAHUALCOYOTL

Van Gunderen collection

Selenia RTN-10X (Taiwanese Wu Chin II), 2 RCA HR 76 (Taiwanese Wu Chin I/II), Signaal STIR (Standard and 76mm) (Taiwanese Wu Chin III). Westinghouse W-160, (Bofors guns) (Taiwanese Wu Chin III).

Sonars: Sangamo SQS-23, hull-mounted, (South Korea, Pakistan, Turkey); Atlas Elektronik DSQS-21CZ (Taiwan, 907); Raytheon SQS-23 H; hull-mounted. (Remainder of Taiwanese Wu Chin I/II/III). No sonar in Mexican ships.

Helicopters: Aerospatiale SA 316B Alouette III (marine support) or Westland Super Lynx Mk 99/100, (ASW/ASV), (South Korea, except for DD 925). MBB BO 105CB (Mexico). Aerospatiale SA 319B Alouette III facilities (Pakistan). McDonnell Douglas MD 500 (ASW) (Taiwan).

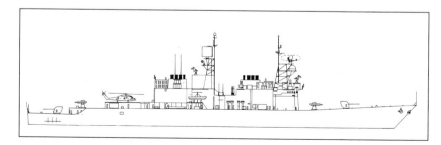

Kidd Class

Country: UNITED STATES OF AMERICA
Country of origin: UNITED STATES OF AMERICA
Ship type: DESTROYERS
Class: KIDD (DDG)
Active: 2
Name (Pennant Number): SCOTT (ex-Iranian Nader) (DDG 995), CHANDLER (ex-Iranian Anoushirvan) (DDG 996).

Recognition features:

- High bow, high freeboard, sweeping maindeck aft to break at flight deck.
- 5 in gun mounting forward of SAM/A/S missile launcher on forecastle.
- Unusually high and long main superstructure giving a slab-sided profile.
- Two funnels, just proud of superstructure, each with several black exhausts protruding at the top.
- Complex lattice foremast supporting various aerials atop bridge roof.
- Large, central mainmast between funnels supporting the square, SPS-48E air search radar aerial.
- Raised flight deck immediately aft of superstructure.
- SAM/A/S missile launcher aft of flight deck with 5 in mounting (Y position).

Displacement full load, tons: 9574.
Length, feet (metres): 563.3 (171.7).
Beam, feet (metres): 55 (16.8).
Draught, feet (metres): 20 (6.2), 33 (10) sonar.
Speed, knots: 33.
Range, miles: 8,000 at 17 kts.

Missiles: SSM - McDonnell Douglas Harpoon (2 quad) launchers. SAM - 52 GDC Standard SM-2MR Block II. 2 twin Mk 26 (Mod 3 and Mod 4) launchers. A/S - 16 Honeywell ASROC; payload Mk 46 Mod 5 Neartip torpedoes. Fired from SAM launchers.
Guns: 2 FMC 5 in (127 mm)/54 Mk 45 Mod 0. 2 GE/GD 20 mm Vulcan Phalanx 6-barrel Mk 15. 4 - 12.7 mm MGs.
Torpedoes: 6 324 mm Mk 32 (2 triple) tubes. Honeywell Mk 46.
Decoys: 4 Loral Hycor SRBOC 6-barrel fixed Mk 36. AN/SLQ-25 Nixie; torpedo decoy.

Radars:

Air search — ITT SPS-48E, 3D. Raytheon SPS-49(V)5.
Surface search — ISC Cardion SPS-55.
Navigation — Raytheon SPS-64.
Fire control — Two SPG-51D, 1 SPG-60, 1 SPQ-9A.
Sonars: General Electric/Hughes SQS-53A; bow-mounted. Gould SQR-19 (TACTAS); passive towed array (may be fitted).

Helicopters: 1 Sikorsky SH-60B LAMPS III. I(ASW).

Kidd Class

KIDD

Spruance Class

Country: UNITED STATES OF AMERICA
Country of origin: UNITED STATES OF AMERICA
Ship type: DESTROYERS
Class: SPRUANCE (DD/DDG)
Active: 24
Name (Pennant Number): SPRUANCE (DD 963), PAUL F FOSTER (DD 964),
KINKAID (DD 865), HEWITT (DD 966), ELLIOTT (DD 967), ARTHUR W
RADFORD (DD 968), PETERSON (DD 969), CARON (DD 970), DAVID R
RAY (DD 971), OLDENDORF (DD 972), JOHN YOUNG (DD 973),
O'BRIEN (DD 975), BRISCOE (DD 977), STUMP (DD 978),
MOOSBRUGGER (DD 980), JOHN HANCOCK (DD 981), NICHOLSON
(DD 982), CUSHING (DD 985), O'BANNON (DD 987), THORN (DD 988),
DEYO (DD 989), FIFE (DD 991), FLETCHER (DD 992), HAYLER (DD 997)

Recognition features:

- High bow, high freeboard, sweeping maindeck aft to break at flight deck.
- 5 in gun mounting on forecastle forward of A/S missile launcher and SSM or VLS tubes (on some).
- Large, square section twin funnels just proud of superstructure, each with several exhausts protruding at the top. After funnel offset to starboard.
- Complex lattice foremast immediately atop bridge roof.
- Large central, lattice mainmast between funnels supporting air search radar aerial.
- Raised flight deck immediately aft of superstructure.

Displacement full load, tons: 8,040.
Length, feet (metres): 563.2 (171.7).
Beam, feet (metres): 55.1 (16.8).
Draught, feet (metres): 19 (5.8).
Speed, knots: 33.
Range, miles: 6,000 at 20 kts.

Missiles: SLCM/SSM - GDC Tomahawk. 8
McDonnell Douglas Harpoon (2 quad).

SAM - Raytheon GMLS Mk 29 octuple launcher. GDC RAM quadruple
launcher (being fitted). A/S - Honeywell ASROC Mk 16 octuple launcher;
payload Mk 46/Mk 50 torpedoes.
Guns: 2 FMC 5 in (127 mm)/54 Mk 45 Mod 0. 2 GE/GD 20 mm/76 6-barrel
Mk 15 Vulcan Phalanx. 4 12.7 mm MGs.
Torpedoes: 6 324 mm Mk 32 (2 triple) tubes. Honeywell Mk 46. AN/SLQ-25
Nixie; torpedo decoy.

Radars:

Air search — Lockheed SPS-40B/C/D (not in DD 997). Raytheon SPS-49V (DD
997). Hughes Mk 23 TAS.
Surface search — ISC Cardion SPS-55.
Navigation — Raytheon SPS-64(V)9.
Fire control — Lockheed SPG-60. Lockheed SPQ-9A. Raytheon Mk 95.
Sonars: SQQ-89(V)6 including GE/Hughes SQS-53B/C; bow-mounted; Gould
SQR-19 (TACTAS); passive towed array.

Helicopters: 2 Sikorsky SH-60B LAMPS III or 1 Kaman SH-2G Seasprite.

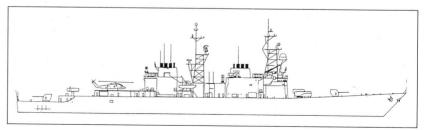

Spruance Class

DEYO

Wielingen Class

Country: BELGIUM
Country of origin: BELGIUM
Ship type: FRIGATES
Class: WIELINGEN (E-71)
Active: 3
Name (Pennant Number): WIELINGEN (F 910), WESTDIEP (F 911),
WANDELAAR (F 912)

Recognition features:
- High freeboard with continuous maindeck from bow aft to break for very short quarterdeck.
- 3.9 in gun mounting ('A' position).
- Creusot-Loire 375 mm A/S mortar launcher ('B' mounting position).
- Enclosed mainmast atop superstructure supporting Signaal WM25 search/fire control radar dome.
- Large distinctive funnel amidships with large central exhaust and smaller exhausts protruding at top.
- Short enclosed aftermast supporting DA05 air/surface search radar aerial.
- Two Exocet SSM launchers ('X' mounting position).
- Sea Sparrow SAM box launcher forward of quarterdeck.

Displacement full load, tons: 2,430.
Length, feet (metres): 349 (106.4).
Beam, feet (metres): 40.3 (12.3).
Draught, feet (metres): 18.4 (5.6).
Speed, knots: 26.
Range, miles: 6,000 at 15 kts.

Missiles: SSM - 4 Aerospatiale MM 38 Exocet (2 twin) launchers. SAM - Raytheon Sea Sparrow Mk 29 octuple launcher.
Guns: 1 Creusot-Loire 3.9 in (100 mm)/55 Mod 68.
Torpedoes: 2   21 in (533 mm) launchers. ECAN L5 Mod 4.
A/S Mortars: Creusot-Loire 375 mm 6-barrel, trainable.
Decoys: 2 Tracor MBA SRBOC 6-barrel Mk 36. Nixie SLQ-25; towed anti-torpedo decoy.

Radars:
Air/surface search — Signaal DA05.
Surface search/fire control — Signaal WM25.
Navigation — Raytheon TM 1645/9X or Signaal Scout.
Sonars: Westinghouse SQS-505A; hull-mounted or Computing Devices Canada SQS-510, hull-mounted active search/attack.

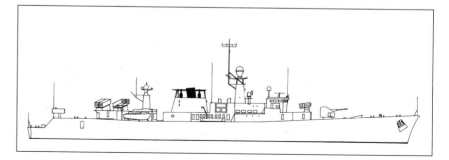

WESTDIEP

Annapolis Class

Country: CANADA
Country of origin: CANADA
Ship type: FRIGATES
Class: ANNAPOLIS (DDH)
Active: 1 + 1 Reserve
Name (Pennant Number): ANNAPOLIS (265), NIPIGON (266)

Recognition features:
- Rounded, contoured forecastle from bow to breakwater.
- 3 in gun mounting aft of breakwater ('A' position).
- Low forward superstructure with very tall lattice mainmast at after end.
- Small, twin, side-by-side funnels aft of mainmast at forward end of hangar.
- Flight deck raised above maindeck level.
- Torpedo tubes, port and starboard, midway along flight deck length at maindeck level.
- Unusual shaped stern, sloping away (aft) from quarterdeck.

Displacement full load, tons: 2,930.
Length, feet (metres): 371.0 (113.1).
Beam, feet (metres): 42 (12.8).
Draught, feet (metres): 14.4 (4.4).
Speed, knots: 28.
Range, miles: 4,570 at 14 kts.

Guns: 2 FMC 3 in (76 mm)/50 Mk 33 (twin).
Torpedoes: 6   324 mm Mk 32 (2 triple) tubes. Honeywell Mk 46 Mod 5 Neartip.
Decoys: 4 Loral Hycor SRBOC 6-barrel Mk 36 chaff launchers.

Radars:
Air/surface search — Marconi SPS-503 (CMR 1820).
Surface search — Norden SPS-502.
Navigation — Sperry 127E.
Fire control — Bell SPG-515.
Sonars: Westinghouse SQS-505 (Annapolis), SQS-510 (Nipigon); hull-mounted. SQS 501; hull-mounted.

Helicopters: 1 Sikorsky CH-124A Sea King (ASW).

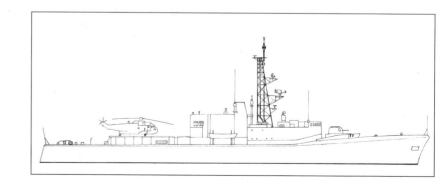

Annapolis Class

ANNAPOLIS

Halifax Class

Country: CANADA
Country of origin: CANADA
Ship type: FRIGATES
Class: HALIFAX (FFH/FFG)
Active: 12
Name (Pennant Number): HALIFAX (330), VANCOUVER (331), VILLE DE QUÉBEC (332), TORONTO (333), REGINA (334), CALGARY (335), MONTREAL (336), FREDERICTON (337), WINNIPEG (338), CHARLOTTETOWN (339), ST JOHN'S (340), OTTAWA (341)

Recognition features:
- Squat 57 mm/70 gun mounting mid-forecastle.
- Short lattice mast supporting large SPS-49(V)5 air search radar aerial mid-forward superstructure.
- Tall lattice mainmast after end of forward superstructure.
- Unusually large, square section funnel amidships, offset to port with grilled intakes top, forward.
- High after superstructure with CIWS mounting at after end.
- Flight deck aft of hangar with small break down to short, shallow quarterdeck.

Displacement full load, tons: 4,770.
Length, feet (metres): 441.9 (134.7) oa.
Beam, feet (metres): 53.8 (16.4).
Draught, feet (metres): 16.4 (5).
Speed, knots: 29.
Range, miles: 9,500 at 13 kts.

Missiles: SSM - 8 McDonnell Douglas Harpoon Block 1C (2 quad) launchers. SAM - 2 Raytheon Sea Sparrow Mk 48 octuple vertical launchers.
Guns: 1 Bofors 57 mm/70 Mk 2. 1 GE/GD 20 mm Vulcan Phalanx Mk 15 Mod 1. 8 12.7 mm MGs.
Torpedoes: 4 324 mm Mk 32 Mod 9 (2 twin) tubes. Honeywell Mk 46 Mod 5.
Decoys: 4 Plessey Shield Mk 2 decoy launchers. Nixie SLQ-25; towed acoustic decoy.

Radars:
Air search — Raytheon SPS-49(V)5.
Air/surface search — Ericsson Sea Giraffe 150HC.
Navigation — Sperry Mk 340.
Fire control — 2 Signaal SPG-503 STIR 1.8.
Sonars: Westinghouse SQS-505(V)6; hull-mounted. CDC SQR-501 CANTASS towed array.

Helicopters: 1 Sikorsky CH-124A ASW or 1 CH-124B Heltas Sea King.

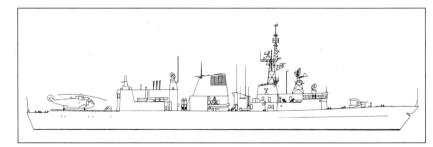

Halifax Class

CALGARY

Country: THAILAND
Country of origin: CHINA
Ship type: FRIGATES
Class: CHAO PHRAYA (TYPES 053 HT and 053 HT(H)) (Modified Jianghu III) (FFG)
Active: 4
Name (Pennant Number): CHAO PHRAYA (455), BANGPAKONG (456), KRABURI (457), SAIBURI (458)

Recognition features:
- RBU 1200 A/S mortar mounting forward of 100 mm/56 gun twin mounting in 'A' position.
- 37 mm/76 gun mounting in 'B' position.
- High forward superstructure with distinctive Sun Visor fire control director atop.
- Pyramid mainmast at after end of forward superstructure with slim lattice mast atop its after end.
- YJ-1 SSM angled, ribbed launchers forward and aft of funnel.
- Single, angular low profile funnel well aft of midships.
- Short lattice mast aft of after SSM launchers with 37 mm/76 gun mounting immediately astern.
- 100 mm/76 gun mounting ('Y' position) in two of class. The other two have a raised flight deck over open quarterdeck.

Note: See Modified Jianghu III class, China

Displacement full load, tons: 1, 924.
Length, feet (metres): 338.5 (103.2).
Beam, feet (metres): 37.1 (11.3).
Draught, feet (metres): 10.2 (3.1).
Speed, knots: 30.

Range, miles: 3,500 at 18 kts.

Missiles: SSM - 8 YJ-1(C-801). SAM — HQ-61 launcher for PL-9 or Matra Sadral/Mistral to be fitted.
Guns: 2 (457 and 458) or 4 China 100 mm/56 (1 or 2 twin). 8 China 37 mm/76 (4 twin) H/PJ 76A.
A/S mortars: 2 RBU 1200 (China Type 86) 5-tubed launchers.
Depth charges: 2 BMB racks.
Decoys: 2 China Type 945 GPJ 26-barrel chaff launchers.

Radars:
Air/surface search — China Type 354 Eye Shield.
Surface search/fire control — China Type 352C Square Tie.
Navigation — Racal Decca 1290 A/D ARPA.
Fire control — China Type 343 Sun Visor.   China Type 341 Rice Lamp.
Sonars: China Type SJD-5A; hull-mounted, active search/attack.

Helicopters: Bell 212 (Commando assault/support). (457 and 458).

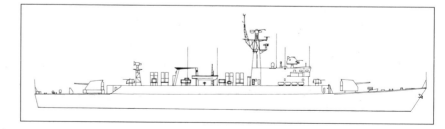

KRABURI

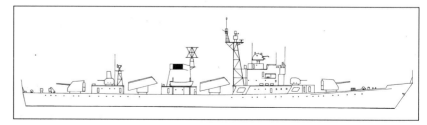

Jianghu I/II Class

Country: BANGLADESH, CHINA, EGYPT.
Country of origin: CHINA
Ship type: FRIGATES
Class: JIANGHU I/II (TYPE 053) (FFG)
Active: 1 Bangladesh (Osman Jianghu I/Type 053 H1), 27 China (Jianghu I), 1 China (Jianghu II), 2 Egypt (Jianghu I)

BANGLADESH
Name (Pennant Number): OSMAN (ex-Xiangtan) (F 18 ex-556).

CHINA
Name (Pennant Number): .(Jianghu I): CHANG DE (509), SHAOXING (510), NANTONG (511), WUXI (512), HUAYIN (513), ZHENJIANG (514), XIAMEN (515), JIUJIANG (516), NANPING (517), JIAN (518), CHANGZHI (519), NINGPO (533), JINHUA (534), DANDONG (543), LINFEN (545), MAOMING (551), YIBIN (552), SHAOGUAN (553), ANSHUN (554), ZHAOTONG (555), JISHOU (557), ZIGONG (558), KANGDING (559), DONGGUAN (560), SHANTOU (561) —— (562) —— (563). (Jianghu II): SIPING (544).

EGYPT
(Name (Pennant Number): NAJIM AL ZAFFER (951), EL NASSER (956).

Recognition features:
- Long slim hull with a high bow, low in water.
- 3.9 in gun single or twin mounting in 'A' position. (Creusot-Loire 3.9 in gun in Jianghu II; Egyptian ships have 57mm/70 twin mounting).
- Squat funnel aft of midships.
- Box-like HY-2 SSM launchers forward and aft of funnel. (Only one in Jianghu II, forward of funnel)
- Tall lattice mainmast aft of forward superstructure.
- 2 37 mm/63 gun mountings forward of bridge, two outboard of mainmast (in some) and two atop after superstructure in 'X'

position (in some).) (Dongguan has 37mm/63 turrets in 'B' and 'X' positions. In Jianghu II, 'X' position mounting omitted in lieu of helicopter hangar; 37mm/63 gun mountings just aft of funnel).
- 3.9 in twin gun mounting in 'Y' position. (Omitted in Jianghu II, in lieu of flight deck. (Egyptian ships have 57mm/70 twin gun mountings in 'Y' position).

Note 1 - There are several variants of the Jianghu I class, but the basic outline is similar.

Note 2 - Jianghu II are similar to Jianghu I except that aft of the funnel, is a through deck with hangar forward of flight deck.

Displacement full load, tons: 1702, 1820 (Jianghu II).
Length, feet (metres): 338.5 (103.2).
Beam, feet (metres): 35.4 (10.8).
Draught, feet (metres): 10.2 (3.1).
Speed, knots: 26.
Range, miles: 4,000 at 15 kts.

Missiles: SSM - 4 HY-2 (C-201) (2 twin) launchers (CSSC-3 Seersucker). (2 twin in Jianghu II).
Guns: 2 or 4 China 3.9 in (100 mm)/56 (2 twin). 1 Creusot-Loire 3.9 in (100 mm)/55 (Jianghu II). 4 China 57mm/70 (2 twin) in Egyptian ships. 12 China 37 mm/63 (6 twin) (8 (4 twin) in some).

Jianghu I/II Class

SHAOGUAN

Torpedoes: 6 - 324 mm ILAS (2 triple) tubes (Jianghu II).Yu-2 (Mk 46 Mod 1).
  (None in Jianghu I or Bangladesh or Egyptian ships).
A/S mortars: 2 RBU 1200 5-tubed fixed launchers (4 in some).
Depth charges: 2 BMB-2 projectors; 2 racks.
Decoys: 2 SRBOC 6-barrel Mk 33 chaff launchers or 2 China 26-barrel
  launchers. 2 Loral Hycor SRBOC Mk 36 6-barrel chaff launchers
  (Bangladesh ship)

Radars:
Air/surface search — MX 902 Eye Shield (Type 354). Type 765 (Egyptian
  ships). Rice Screen/Shield.
Surface search/fire control — Square Tie.
Navigation — Don 2 or Fin Curve or Racal Decca. (Decca RM 1290A in
  Egyptian ships).
Fire control — Wok Won or Rice Lamp. Sun Visor, with Wasp Head (some
  Jianghu I). Fog Lamp. (Egyptian ships).
Sonars: Echo Type 5; hull-mounted, active search/attack.

Helicopters: Harbin Zhi-9A Haitun (Dauphin 2) (ASV, in Jianghu II).

Jianghu III/IV Class

Country: CHINA
Country of origin: CHINA
Ship type: FRIGATES
Class: JIANGHU III/IV (TYPE 053 HT) (FFG)
Active: 4
Name (Pennant Number): (Jianghu III): HUANGSHI (535), WUHU (536).
(Jianghu IV): ZHOUSHAN (537), — (538).

Recognition features:
- High bow, with 3.9 in gun twin mounting in 'A' position.
- Maindeck higher in the midships section.
- Forward superstructure with enclosed mainmast at after end, enclosed lower section lattice top.
- Large, low funnel aft of midships with ship's boats in davits outboard.
- Two 37 mm/63 gun mountings forward of bridge and two at after end of maindeck level, port and starboard, outboard of short mast with Rice Lamp fire control radar atop.
- YJ-1 SSM launchers in pairs, trained outboard, port and starboard, forward and aft of funnel.
- 3.9 in gun twin mounting in 'Y' position.

Note: See modified Jianghu III, Chao Phraya class of Thailand.

Displacement full load, tons: 1,924.
Length, feet (metres): 338.5 (103.2).
Beam, feet (metres): 35.4 (10.8).
Draught, feet (metres): 10.2 (3.1).
Speed, knots: 28.
Range, miles: 4,000 at 15 kts.

Missiles: SSM - 8 YJ-1 (Eagle Strike) (C-801) (CSS-N-4 Sardine). Jianghu IV fitted for improved C-802 (CSS-N-8 Saccade).
Guns: 4 China 3.9 in (100 mm)/56 (2 twin). 8 China 37 mm/63 (4 twin).
A/S mortars: 2 RBU 1200 5-tubed launchers.
Depth charges: 2 BMB-2 projectors; 2 racks.
Mines: Can carry up to 60.
Decoys: 2 China 26-barrel chaff launchers.

Radars:
Air/surface search — MX 902 Eye Shield.
Surface search/fire control — Square Tie.
Navigation — Fin Curve.
Fire Control — Rice Lamp, Sun Visor B (with Wasp Head).
Sonars: Echo Type 5; hull-mounted active search/attack.

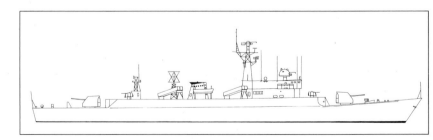

Jianghu III/IV Class

ZHOUSHAN

Ships of the World

Jiangwei I/II Class

Country: CHINA
Country of origin: CHINA
Ship type: FRIGATES
Class: JIANGWEI I (Type 053 H2G) JIANGWEI II (FFG)
Active: 4 (Jiangwei I), 1 (Jiangwei II)
Building: 2 (Jiangwei II)
Name (Pennant Number): (Jiangwei I): ANQING (539), HUAINAN (540) (548 out of area), HUAIBEI (541), TONGLING (542). (Jiangwei II): —— (597) , —— (522), —— (—).

Recognition features:

- Long forecastle, one third length of ship. (Shorter forecastle in Jiangwei II).
- Weapons on forecastle from forward to aft, RBU 1000 A/S mortar launcher, 3.9 in gun twin mounting and HQ-61 SAM tubular launchers, in two banks. (Jiangwei II has rounded turret for 3.9 gun twin mounting; LY 60 SAM box launcher in raised 'B' position).
- Stepped superstructure with 37 mm/63 gun mountings, port and starboard, outboard at forward end of bridge.
- Large Sun Visor fire control radome atop bridge. (Type 347G director in Jiangwei II).
- Mainmast, enclosed bottom lattice topped, at after end of forward superstructure. (More hidden in Jiangwei II).
- Single, squat funnel just aft of midships.
- Ship's boats in davits, port and starboard, adjacent to funnel.
- YJ-1 SSM angled triple launchers forward (trained to starboard) and aft (trained to port) of funnel.
- Large hangar with flight deck right aft and open quarterdeck below. (37mm/63 Type 76A mounting atop hangar in Jiangwei II, outboard of hangar on sponsons, Jiangwei I).

Displacement, (full load, tons): 2,250.
Length, feet (metres): 366.5 (111.7).
Beam, feet (metres): 39.7 (12.1).
Draught, feet (metres): 15.7 (4.8).
Speed, knots: 25.
Range, miles: 4,000 at 18 kts.

Missiles: SSM - 6 YJ-1 (Eagle Strike) (C-801) (CSSN-4 Sardine) or C-802 (2 triple) launchers. SAM - 1 HQ-61 sextuple launcher, (Jiangwei I), LY 60 (Jiangwei II).
Guns: 2 China 3.9 in (100 mm)/56 (twin). 8 China 37 mm/63 Type 76A (4 twin).
A/S mortars: 2 RBU 1200; 5-tubed fixed launchers.
Decoys: 2 SRBOC Mk 33 6-barrel chaff launchers. 2 China 26-barrel launchers.

Radars:
Air/surface search —Knife Rest.
Navigation — Racal Decca 1290 and Chine Type 360.
Fire Control — Sun Visor (with Wasp Head), (Jiangwei I). Type 347G, (Jiangwei II) Rice Lamp. Fog Lamp.
Sonars: Echo Type 5; hull-mounted, active search/attack.

Helicopters: 1 Harbin Zhi-9A Haitun (Dauphin 2). (ASV).

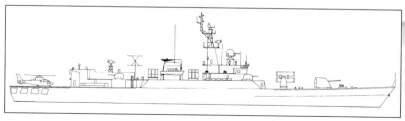

Jiangwei I/II Class

HUAINAN

Naresuan Class

Country: THAILAND
Country of origin: CHINA
Ship type: FRIGATES
Class: NARESUAN (TYPE 25T) (FFG)
Active: 2
Name (Pennant Number): NARESUAN (421, ex-621), TAKSIN (422, ex-622)

Recognition features:

- High bow, 5 in gun mounting in 'A' position.
- Sea Sparrow SAM VLS launchers below maindeck level between forward mounting and bridge.
- High, slab-sided forward superstructure with lattice mainmast atop at after end of bridge.
- Harpoon SSM launchers aft of forward superstructure.
- Large platform amidships supporting Signaal LW08 air search radar aerial.
- Square section funnel with wedge shaped smoke deflector atop.
- After superstructure has Signaal STIR fire control radar at forward end, China 374 G fire control director on low enclosed pylon, and JM-83H optical fire control director aft.
- 37 mm/76 gun mountings, port and starboard, outboard of STIR fire control radar and one deck level down.
- Flight deck aft with open quarterdeck below.

Displacement full load, tons: 2,980.
Length, feet (metres): 393.7 (120).
Beam, feet (metres): 42.7 (13).
Draught, feet (metres): 12.5 (3.8).
Speed, knots: 32.
Range, miles: 4000 at 18 kts.

Missiles: SSM - 8 McDonnell Douglas Harpoon (2 quad) launchers. SAM - Mk 41 LCHR 8 cell VLS launcher, Sea Sparrow.
Guns: 1 FMC 5 in (127 mm)/54 Mk 45 Mod 2. 4 China 37 mm/76 (2 twin) H/PJ 76A.
Torpedoes: 6 324 mm Mk 32 Mod 5 (2 triple) tubes. Honeywell Mk 46.
Decoys: China Type 945 GP J 26-barrel chaff launchers.

Radars:
Air search — Signaal LW08.
Surface search — China Type 360.
Navigation — 2 Raytheon SPS-64(V)5.
Fire control — 2 Signaal STIR, (SSM and 5 in gun). China 374 G, (37 mm gun.
Sonars: China SJD-7; hull-mounted, active search/attack.

Helicopters: 1 Kaman SH-2G Seasprite (in due course).

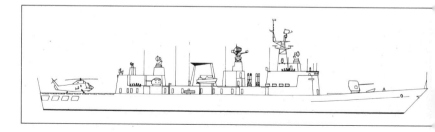

Naresuan Class

NARESUAN

Luis Adell

Niels Juel Class

Country: DENMARK
Country of origin: DENMARK
Ship type: FRIGATES
Class: NIELS JUEL (FFG)
Active: 3
Name (Pennant Number): NIELS JUEL (F 354), OLFERT FISCHER (F 355), PETER TORDENSKIOLD (F 356)

Recognition features:

- Unusual profile and easily identified frigate.
- Low forecastle with 3 in gun mounting ('A' position).
- High midships maindeck section, slab-sided.
- Unusually robust enclosed mainmast amidships, supporting 9GR 600 surface search radar aerial, on forward gantry, and AWS 5 or DASA TRS-3D air search radar atop.
- Large, black-capped funnel with sloping top sited well aft of midships.
- Harpoon SSM angled launchers, port and starboard, aft of funnel.
- 2 fire control directors mounted on sturdy pedestals aft of bridge and forward of quarterdeck.
- Sea Sparrow SAM octuple or VLS modular launcher on quarterdeck.

Displacement full load, tons: 1,320.
Length, feet (metres): 275.5 (84).
Beam, feet (metres): 33.8 (10.3).
Draught, feet (metres): 10.2 (3.1).
Speed, knots: 28.
Range, miles: 2,500 at 18 kts.

Missiles: SSM - 8 McDonnell Douglas Harpoon (2 quad) launchers. SAM - Raytheon NATO Sea Sparrow Mk 29 octuple launcher or MK 48 VLS modular launchers.
Guns: 1 OTO Melara 3 in (76 mm)/62 compact. 4 Oerlikon 20 mm (1 each side of the funnel and 2 abaft the mast), can be fitted.
Depth charges: 1 rack.
Decoys: 2 DL-12T Sea Gnat 12-barrel chaff launchers.

Radars:

Air search — Plessey AWS 5, 3D.
Surface search — Philips 9GR 600.
Navigation — Burmeister & Wain Elektronik Scanter Mil 009.
Fire control — 2 Mk 95,(SAM). Philips 9LV 200. (guns, SSM).
Sonars: Plessey PMS 26; hull-mounted, active search/attack.

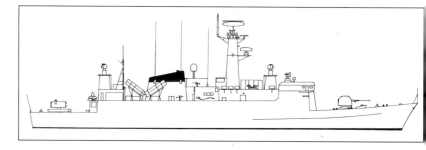

Niels Juel Class

OLFERT FISCHER

Country: DENMARK
Country of origin: DENMARK
Ship type: FRIGATES
Class: THETIS (FF)
Active: 4
Name (Pennant Number): THETIS (F 357), TRITON (F 358), VAEDDEREN (F 359), HVIDBJØRNEN (F 360)

Recognition features:

- Short forecastle with 3 in gun mounting ('A' position).
- High, slab-sided midships section.
- Large enclosed mainmast at after end of forward superstructure with distinctive AWS 6 air/surface search radome atop.
- Large, squat, black-capped funnel amidships.
- Ship's boats in davits outboard of funnel, port and starboard.
- Long flight deck with domed SATCOM aerial on pedestal atop hangar roof.

Note - Thetis has a modified stern for seismological equipment.

Displacement full load, tons: 3,500.
Length, feet (metres): 369.1 (112.5) oa.
Beam, feet (metres): 47.2 (14.4).
Draught, feet (metres): 19.7 (6).
Speed, knots: 20.
Range, miles: 8,500 at 15.5 kts.

Guns: 1 OTO Melara 3 in (76 mm)/62 Super Rapid. 1 or 2 Oerlikon 20 mm.
Depth charges: 2 Rails (door in stern).
Decoys: 2 DL-12T Sea Gnat 12-barrel chaff/IR flares.

Radars:
Air/surface search — Plessey AWS 6.
Surface search — Terma Scanter Mil.
Navigation — Furuno FR 1505DA.
Fire control — Bofors Electronic 9LV Mk 3.
Sonars: Thomson-Sintra TSM 2640 Salmon; hull-mounted and VDS.

Helicopters: 1 Westland Lynx Mk 91.

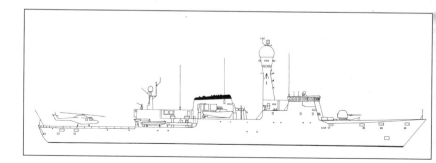

HVIDBJØRNEN

Comandante João Belo/Commandant Rivière Class

Country: PORTUGAL, URUGUAY
Country of origin: FRANCE
Ship type: FRIGATES
Class: COMANDANTE JOÃO BELO (FF), COMMANDANT RIVIÈRE (ffg)
Active: 4 Portugal (João Belo), 3 Uruguay (Commandant Rivière)

PORTUGAL
Name (Pennant Number): COMANDANTE JOÃO BELO (F 480), COMANDANTE HERMENEGILDO CAPELO (F 481), COMANDANTE ROBERTO IVENS (F 482), COMANDANTE SACADURA CABRAL (F 483)

URUGUAY
Name (Pennant Number): URUGUAY (ex-Commandant Bourdais) (1), GENERAL ARTIGAS (ex-Victor Schoelcher) (2), MONTEVIDEO (ex-Admiral Charner) (3, ex-4).

Recognition features:

- Long forecastle with high forward superstructure and high freeboard.
- 3.9 in gun turret ('A' position).
- Mortier 305 mm 4 barrel A/S launcher on Uruguay ships ('B' position).
- Large lattice mainmast at after end of forward superstructure.
- Single large, black-capped funnel well aft of midships.
- DRBC 31D fire control director atop after superstructure.
- 3.9 in gun mountings aft ('X' positions). (Also in 'Y' position in some Portuguese ships).
- Exocet SSM launchers aft of funnel in Uruguay ships.

Displacement full load, tons: 2,250.
Length, feet (metres): 336.9 (102.7).
Beam, feet (metres): 38.4 (11.7).
Draught, feet (metres): 14.4 (4.4), (Portugal). 14.1 (4.3), (Uruguay).
Speed, knots: 25.
Range, miles: 7,500 at 15 kts.

Missiles: 4 Exocet MM 38 Exocet. (Uruguay ships only).
Guns: 2 or 3 Creusot-Loire or DCN 3.9 in (100 mm)/55 Mod 1953. 2 Bofors 40 mm/60, (Portugal). 2 Hispano Suiza 30 mm/70 (Uruguay).
Torpedoes: 6 324 mm Mk 32 Mod 5 (2 triple tubes). Honeywell Mk 46 Mod 5 Neartip, (Portugal). 6 21.7 mm (550 mm) (2 triple) tubes; ECAN L3. (Uruguay).
A/S mortars: 1 Mortier 305 mm 4-barrel launcher. (Uruguay ships only).
Decoys: 2 Loral Hycor SRBOC 6-barrel Mk 36 SBROC chaff launchers. SLQ-25 Nixie; towed torpedo decoy. (Portuguese ships only).

Radars:
Air search — Thomson-CSF DRBV 22A.
Surface search — Thomson-CSF DRBV 50. (Portugal only)
Navigation — Kelvin Hughes KH 1007.(Portugal) Racal Decca 1226 (Uruguay).
Fire control — Thomson-CSF DRBC 31D. (Portugal). DRBC 32C (Uruguay).
Sonars: CDC SQS-510 (after modernisation); hull-mounted. (Portugal). EDO SQS-17, hull-mounted, (Uruguay). Thomson-Sintra DUBA 3A; hull-mounted. (Both classes).

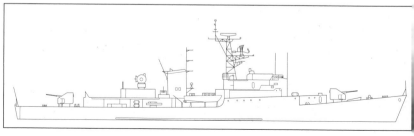

Comandante João Belo/Commandant Rivière Class

COMANDANTE HERMENEGILDO CAPELO

D'Estienne D'Orves (Type A 69) Class

Country: ARGENTINA, FRANCE
Country of origin: FRANCE
Ship type: FRIGATES
Class: D'ESTIENNE D'ORVES (TYPE A69)/DRUMMOND (FFG)
Active: 3 Argentina (Drummond), 16 France

ARGENTINA
Name (Pennant Number): DRUMMOND (ex-Good Hope, ex-Lieutenant de Vaisseau le Hénaff) (31, ex-F 789), GUERRICO (ex-Transvaal, ex-Commandant l'Herminier) (31, ex-F 791), GRANVILLE (33).

FRANCE
Name (Pennant Number): D'ESTIENNE D'ORVES (F 781), AMYOT D'INVILLE (F 782), DROGOU (F 783), JEAN MOULIN (F 785), QUARTIER MAÎTRE ANQUETIL (F 786), COMMANDANT DE PIMODAN (F 787), SECOND MAÎTRE LE BIHAN (F 788), LIEUTENANT DE VAISSEAU LE HÉNAFF (F 789), LIEUTENANT DE VAISSEAU LAVALLÉE (F 790), COMMANDANT L'HERMINIER (F 791), PREMIER MAÎTRE L'HER (F 792), COMMANDANT BLAISON (F 793), ENSEIGNE DE VAISSEAU JACOUBET (F 794), COMMANDANT DUCUING (F 795), COMMANDANT BIROT (F 796), COMMANDANT BOUAN (F 797)

Recognition features:
- Low profile forecastle with 3.9 in gun mounting ('A' position).
- Substantial forward superstructure.
- Single funnel just aft of midships with vertical forward and sloping after end.
- Mast and funnel combined with lattice mainmast atop.
- Break in deck level aft of funnel, with low deckhouse continuing in some ships.
- Exocet SSM launchers, port and starboard, just aft of funnel.
- Ship's boat stowed in davits aft of SSM launchers.
- 375mm A/S mortar launcher atop after superstructure. 40 mm/70 turret vice A/S

mortar launcher on after superstructure in Argentine ships and Syracuse SATCOM dome in some French ships.
- Torpedo tubes in 'Y' position in Drummond class.

Displacement full load, tons: 1,170 (Argentine ships) 1,250 (1,330 on later ships).
Length, feet (metres): 262.5 (80) (Argentine ships) 264.1 (80.5) (French ships).
Beam, feet (metres): 33.8 (10.3).
Draught, feet (metres): 18 (5.5) (sonar).
Speed, knots: 23.
Range, miles: 4,500 at 15 kts.

Missiles: SSM - 4 Aerospatiale MM 40 (or 2 MM 38) Exocet. (4 MM 38, twin launchers, in Argentine ships). SAM — Matra Simbad twin launcher for Mistral can be fitted aft of A/S mortar or Syracuse SATCOM, (French ships).
Guns: 1 DCN 3.9 in (100 mm)/55 Mod 68 CADAM automatic. (Creusot-Loire 3.9 in (100mm)/55 Mod 1953 Drummond class.)2 Giat 20 mm. (2 Oerlikon 20 mm, 2 Breda 40 mm/70 (twin) Argentine ships and 2 12.7 MGs.).(4 12.7 mm MGs, French ships).

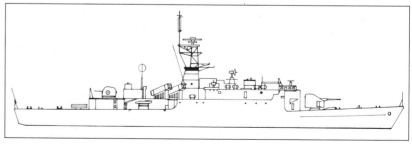

D'Estienne D'Orves (Type A 69) Class

JEAN MOULIN

Torpedoes: 4 fixed tubes. ECAN L5. (French ships). 6 324 mm Mk 32 (2 triple tubes), Whitehead A 244, Argentine ships.

A/S mortars: 1 Creusot-Loire 375 mm Mk 54 6-tubed launcher. (French ships only, removed from F 792-794, 796.)

Decoys: 2 CSEE Dagaie 10-barrel trainable chaff/IR launchers. Nixie SLQ-25 torpedo decoy. (French ships). CSEE Dagaie double mounting, chaff, decoys. Corvus sextuple chaff launchers, (Argentine ships).

Radars:
Air/surface search — Thomson-CSF DRBV 51A.
Navigation — Racal Decca 1226.
Fire control — Thomson-CSF DRBC 32E.
Sonars: Thomson-Sintra DUBA Diodon/25; hull-mounted, active search/attack.

Frigates – France   173

Type F 2000S/Madina Class

Country: SAUDI ARABIA
Country of origin: FRANCE
Ship type: FRIGATES
Class: MADINA (TYPE F 2000S) (FFG)
Active: 4
Name (Pennant Number): MADINA (702), HOFOUF (704), ABHA (706), TAIF (708)

Recognition features:
- Long forecastle. Continuous maindeck profile with break down to quarterdeck.
- 3.9 in gun mounting ('A' position).
- Forward superstructure has slim tripod mainmast at after end.
- Unusually large funnel with large black, wedge shaped smoke deflector at after end, sited just aft of midships.
- Otomat SSM launchers between funnel and forward superstructure.
- Crotale SAM launcher atop after superstructure.
- Small flight deck.
- Short quarterdeck with VDS operating gear.

Displacement full load, tons: 2,870.
Length, feet (metres): 377.3 (115).
Beam, feet (metres): 41 (12.5).
Draught, feet (metres): 16 (4.9) (sonar).
Speed, knots: 30.
Range, miles: 8,000 at 15 kts; 6,500 at 18 kts.

Missiles: SSM - 8 OTO MELARA/Matra Otomat Mk 2 (2 quad). SAM - Thomson-CSF Crotale Naval octuple launcher.
Guns: 1 Creusot-Loire 3.9 in (100 mm)/55 compact. 4 Breda 40 mm/70 (2 twin).
Torpedoes: 4   21 in (533 mm) tubes. ECAN F17P.
Decoys: CSEE Dagaie double mounting.

Radars:
Air/surface search/IFF — Thomson-CSF Sea Tiger (DRBV 15).
Navigation — Racal Decca TM 1226.
Fire control — Thomson-CSF Castor IIB. Thomson-CSF DRBC 32.
Sonars: Thomson-Sintra Diodon TSM 2630; hull-mounted, integrated Sorel VDS.

Helicopters: 1 Aerospatiale SA 365F Dauphin 2. (SSM targeting).

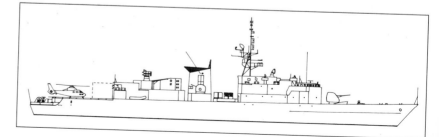

Type F 2000S/Madina Class

MADINA

DCN Toulon

Floréal Class

Country: FRANCE
Country of origin: FRANCE
Ship type: FRIGATES
Class: FLORÉAL
Active: 6
Name (Pennant Number): FLORÉAL (F 730), PRAIRIAL (F 731), NIVÔSE (F 732), VENTÔSE (F 733), VENDÉMAIRE (F 734), GERMINAL (F 735)

Recognition features:
- Low forecastle with 3.9 in gun mounting raised above ('B' position).
- High central superstructure with complex enclosed mainmast at after end of bridge.
- Unusual, twin, rectangular side-by-side funnels with exhausts protruding at top.
- Exocet SSM angled launchers sited between funnel and mainmast.
- Syracuse II SATCOM atop slab-sided platform adjacent funnels.
- 20 mm gun mounting on hangar roof.
- Long flight deck with break down to small quarterdeck.
- Ship's boat in starboard side davits adjacent to SSM launcher.

Displacement full load, tons: 2,950.
Length, feet (metres): 306.8 (93.5).
Beam, feet (metres): 45.9 (14.4).
Draught, feet (metres): 14.1 (4.3).
Speed, knots: 20.
Range, miles: 10,000 at 15 kts.

Missiles: SSM - 2 Aerospatiale MM 38 Exocet. SAM — 2 Matra Simbad twin launchers can replace 20 mm guns or Dagaie launcher.
Guns: 1 DCN 3.9 in (100 mm)/55 Mod 68 CADAM. 2 Giat 20 F2 20 mm.
Decoys: 2 CSEE Dagaie Mk II; 10-barrel trainable chaff/IR launchers.

Radars:
Air/surface search — Thomson-CSF Mars DRBV 21A.
Navigation — 2 Racal Decca 1229 (DRBN 34A)

Helicopters: 1 Aerospatiale AS 565MA Panther or platform for 1 AS 332F Super Puma.

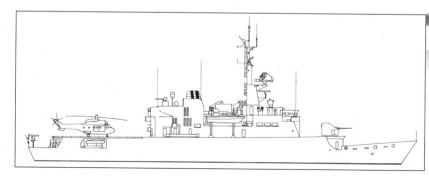

NIVÔSE

Country: FRANCE, SAUDI ARABIA, TAIWAN
Country of origin: FRANCE
Ship type: FRIGATES
Class: LA FAYETTE/KANG DING (KWANG HUA PROJECT II) (FFG)
Active: 3 France, 6 Taiwan (Kang Ding).
Building: 2 France, 2 Saudi Arabia (+ 1 ordered). (Type 3000S)
FRANCE
Name (Pennant Number): LA FAYETTE (F 710), SURCOUF (F 711),
COURBET (F 712), ACONITE (ex-Jauréguiberry) (F 713), GUÉPRATTE (F
714).

TAIWAN
Name (Pennant Number): KANG DING (1202), SI NING (1203), KUN MING
(1205), DI HUA (1206), WU CHANG (1207), CHEN TE (1208).

SAUDI ARABIA
Name (Pennant Number): none allocated.

Recognition features:

- 3.9 in gun mounting ('A' position). (OTO MELARA 76mm/62 in Taiwanese ships). (Giat 3.9 in/55 in Saudi ships).
- High, flush central superstructure with pyramid mainmast amidships. (Short mainmast in Taiwanese ships).
- Unusual forward-sloping mast and funnel combined, supporting air/surface search radar aerial.
- Saudi ships have additional pylon mast, aft of midships, with Thomson-CSF Arabel 3D surveillance/fire control radome atop.
- Crotale Naval CN 2 SAM launcher at after end of main superstructure in French ships. CIWS in Taiwanese.
- Long flight deck right aft.

Note 1 - All superstructure inclines at 10o to the vertical to reduce radar echo area.
Note 2 - External equipment such as capstans and bollards are either hidden or installed as low as possible.

Note 3 - Unusual smooth uncluttered profile for a warship.

Displacement full load, tons: 3,600, (French), 3,800 (Taiwanese), 4,500 (Saudi).
Length, feet (metres): 407.5 (124.2) oa, (French and Taiwanese) 442.9 (135), (Saudi).
Beam, feet (metres): 50.5 (15.4), (French and Taiwanese.) 56.4 (17.2), (Saudi).
Draught, feet (metres): 19.4 (5.9) (French), 18 (5.5) (Taiwanese), 13.5 (4.1), (Saudi).
Speed, knots: 25.
Range, miles: 9,000 at 12 kts.

Missiles: SSM - 8 Aerospatiale MM 40 Block II Exocet. (French and Saudi). Hsiung Feng II (2 quad) (Taiwanese). SAM - Thomson-CSF Crotale Naval CN 2 octuple launcher, (French). Eurosam SAAM octuple VLS for Aster 15. (Saudi). Sea Chaparral quad launcher, (Taiwanese).
Guns: 1 DCN 3.9 in (100 mm)/55 Mod 68 CADAM. (French) 1 Giat 3.9 in (100 mm)/55 Compact Mk 2 (Saudi). 1 OTO MELARA 76 mm/62 Mk 75 (Taiwanese). 2 Giat 20F2 20 mm, 2 12.7 mm MGs, (French and Saudi ships). 1 Hughes 20 mm/76 Vulcan Phalanx Mk 15 Mod 2, 2 Bofors 40mm/70; 2 CS 20 mm Type 75, (Taiwanese ships).

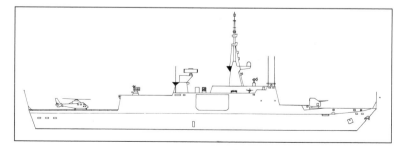

La Fayette Class

SURCOUF

Torpedoes: 4 21 in (533 mm) tubes, ECAN F17P. (Saudi ships). 6 324 mm
    Mk 32 (2 triple) tubes, Alliant Mk 36 Mod 5. (Taiwanese)
Decoys: 2 CSEE Dagaie Mk 2 10-barrel launchers, (all ships). SLAT anti-wake
    homing torpedoes system. (French and Saudi ships).

Radars:
Air/surface search — Thomson-CSF Sea Tiger (DRBV 15C).(French ships).
    DRBV 26D Jupiter II (Saudi and Taiwanese ships).
Surface search — Thomson-CSF Triton G (Taiwanese ships)
Surveillance/Fire control — Arabel 3D (Saudi ships)

Navigation — 2 Racal Decca 1226, (DRBN 34A). 2 Racal Decca 20V90
    (Taiwanese).
Fire control — Thomson-CSF Castor 2J. Arabel (for SAAM after
    modernisation).
Sonars: Thomson Marconi CAPTAS 20. (Saudi ships). BAe/Thomson-Sintra
    ATAS(V)2 active towed array; Thomson-Sintra Spherion B, bow-mounted
    active search. (Taiwanese)

Helicopters: 1 Aerospatiale AS565 MA Panther. 1 Aerospatiale SA 365
    Dauphin 2 (Saudi) 1 Sikorsky S-70C(M)1 (ASW) (Taiwanese).

Brandenburg Class

Country: GERMANY
Country of origin: GERMANY
Ship type: FRIGATES
Class: BRANDENBURG (TYPE 123) (FFG)
Active: 4
Name (Pennant Number): BRANDENBURG (F 215), SCHLESWIG-HOLSTEIN (F 216), BAYERN (F 217), MECKLENBURG-VORPOMMERN (F 218).

Recognition features:
- High freeboard, continuous maindeck from bow to break down to flight deck.
- 76 mm/62 gun mounting ('A' position).
- RAM SAM box launcher ('B' position).
- High central superstructure with bridge well aft from bows.
- NATO Sea Sparrow SAM (VLS) tubes immediately forward of bridge.
- Large, sturdy, enclosed mainmast forward of midships.
- Large twin angled funnels between forward and after superstructures.
- After superstructure with aftermast atop, supporting large Signaal LW08 air search radar aerial.
- Exocet SSM twin launchers between funnel and mainmast.
- RAM SAM box launcher atop hangar.
- Flight deck right aft with open quarterdeck below.

Displacement full load, tons: 4,700.
Length, feet (metres): 455.7 (138.9) oa.
Beam, feet (metres): 54.8 (16.7).
Draught, feet (metres): 22.3 (6.8).
Speed, knots: 29.
Range, miles: 4,000 at 18 kts.

Missiles: SSM - 4 Aerospatiale MM 38 Exocet, (2 twin). SAM - Martin Marietta VLS Mk 41, for NATO Sea Sparrow. 2 RAM 21 cell Mk 49 launchers.
Guns: 1 OTO Melara 76 mm/62. 2 Rheinmetall 20 mm Rh 202.
Torpedoes: 4 324 mm Mk 32 Mod 9 (2 twin) tubes. Honeywell 46 Mod 2.
Decoys: 2 Breda SCLAR.

Radars:
Air search — Signaal LW08.
Air/surface search — Signaal SMART, 3D.
Navigation — 2 Raypath.
Fire control — 2 Signaal STIR 180 trackers.
Sonars: Atlas Elektronik DSQS-23BZ; hull-mounted, active search/attack.

Helicopters: 2 Westland Sea Lynx Mk 88. (ASW/ASV).

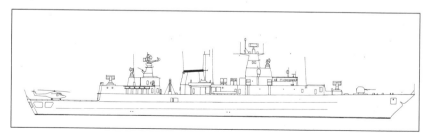

Brandenburg Class

MECKLENBURG-VORPOMMERN

Type FS 1500 Almirante Padilla /Kasturi Class

Country: COLOMBIA, MALAYSIA
Country of origin: GERMANY
Ship type: FRIGATES
Class: ALMIRANTE PADILLA (TYPE FS 1500) KASTURI (FSG)
Active: 4 Columbia, 2 Malaysia*
*Rated as corvettes.
COLUMBIA
Name (Pennant Number): ALMIRANTE PADILLA (CM 51), CALDAS (CM 52), ANTIOQUIA (CM 53), INDEPENDIENTE (CM 54).
MALAYSIA
Name (Pennant Number): KASTURI (25), LEKIR (26).

Recognition features:

- Low forecastle with break up to high midships maindeck and down to short quarterdeck.
- 3 in gun mounting ('A' position, Colombian ships). 3.9 in gun mounting, (Malaysian ships).
- Bofors twin 375 mm A/S/ mortar in 'B' position in Malaysian ships.
- Tall flat fronted bridge structure with large enclosed mainmast at after end. Pole mast atop after end of mainmast. WM22 radome atop mainmast in Malaysian ships.
- Large, tapered funnel with wedge shaped smoke deflector atop.
- Exocet SSM launchers between funnel and forward superstructure.
- Flight deck aft of after superstructure at maindeck level.
- 40 mm/70 gun mounting ('Y' position) (Colombian ships). 57 mm/70 mounting in Malaysian ships.
- DA08 air/surface search radar aerial on raised platform atop after superstructure in Malaysian ships.

Displacement full load, tons: 2,100, (Colombian). 1,850 (Malaysian).
Length, feet (metres): 325.1 (99.1). 319.1 (97.3), (Malaysian).
Beam, feet (metres): 37.1 (11.3).
Draught, feet (metres): 12.1 (3.7). 11.5 (3.5, (Malaysian)
Speed, knots: 27. 28 (Malaysian).
Range, miles: 7000 at 14 kts. 5,000 at 14 kts., (Malaysian).

Missiles: SSM - 8 Aerospatiale MM 40 Exocet. (Colombian). 4 MM 38 Exocet, (Malaysian).
Guns: 1 OTO Melara 3 in (76 mm)/62 Compact, (Colombian). 1 Creusot-Loire 3.9 in (100 mm)/55 Mk 2 Compact, (Malaysian). 2 Breda 40 mm/70 (twin); 4 Oerlikon 30 mm/75 Mk 74 (2 twin), (Colombian). 1 Bofors 57 mm/70 and 4 Emerson Electric 30 mm (2 twin), (Malaysian).
Torpedoes: 6 - 324 mm Mk 32 (2 triple) tubes. (None in Malaysian ships).
A/S mortars: 1 Bofors 375 mm twin trainable launcher. (Malaysian ships only).
Decoys: 1 CSEE Dagaie double mounting. (2 in Malaysian ships).

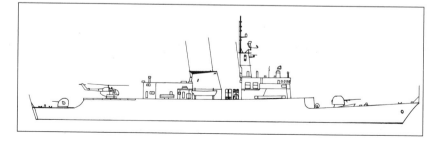

Type FS 1500 Almirante Padilla /Kasturi Class

ALMIRANTE PADILLA

Radars:
Combined search — Thomson-CSF Sea Tiger. (Colombian ships).
Air/Surface search — Signaal DA08. (Malaysian ships).
Navigation — Decca TM 1226C (Malaysian).
Fire control — Castor II B, (Colombian). Signaal WM22, (Malaysian).

Sonars: Atlas Elektronik ASO-4-2; hull-mounted, (Colombian). Atlas Elektronik DSQS-21C, hull-mounted, (Malaysian).

Helicopters: 1 MBB BO 105 CB, (ASW). (Colombian). Platform for Westland Wasp HAS 1 (Malaysian)

Espora (MEKO 140) Class

Country: ARGENTINA
Country of origin: GERMANY
Ship type: FRIGATES
Class: ESPORA (MEKO 140) (FFG)
Active: 4
Planned : 2
Name (Pennant Number): ESPORA (41), ROSALES (42), SPIRO (43), PARKER (44), ROBINSON (45), GOMEZ ROCA (46)

Recognition features:

- Blunt bow. Maindeck level raised for the length of the superstructure.
- 3 in gun mounting ('A' position).
- 40 mm/70 gun twin mountings ('B' and 'Y' positions).
- Exocet SSM ribbed launchers forward of 40 mm/70 gun mounting on quarterdeck.
- Low integral funnel at after end of upper superstructure. Black exhaust protrudes from centre of main funnel.
- Tripod style mainmast atop after end of bridge structure supporting fire control radome.
- Raised flight deck.
- Parker and later ships fitted with a telescopic hangar.

Displacement full load, tons: 1,790.
Length, feet (metres): 299.1 (91.2).
Beam, feet (metres): 36.4 (11.1).
Draught, feet (metres): 11.2 (3.4).
Speed, knots: 27.
Range, miles: 4,000 at 18 kts.

Missiles: SSM - 4 Aerospatiale MM 38 Exocet.
Guns: 1 OTO Melara 3 in (76 mm)/62 Compact. 4 Breda 40 mm/70 (2 twin). 2 - 12.7 mm MGs.
Torpedoes: 6 - 324 mm ILAS 3 (2 triple) tubes. Whitehead A 244/S.
Decoys: CSEE Dagaie double mounting.

Radars:
Air/surface search — Signaal DA045.
Navigation — Decca TM 1226.
Fire Control — Signaal WM28.
Sonars: Atlas Elektronik ASO-4; hull-mounted, active search/attack.

Helicopters: 1 Aerospatiale SA 319B Alouette III or Aerospatiale AS 555 Fennec. (ASW).

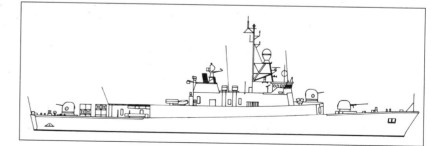

Espora (MEKO 140) Class

ESPORA

MEKO 200 ANZAC/Hydra/Vasco da Gama/ Yavuz/Barbaros Class

Country: AUSTRALIA, GREECE, NEW ZEALAND, PORTUGAL, TURKEY
Country of origin: GERMANY
Ship type: FRIGATES
Class: ANZAC, HYDRA (MEKO 200HN) VASCO DA GAMA, YAVUZ, BARBAROS (MODIFED MEKO 200) (FF/FFG)
Active: 2 Australia (ANZAC), 3 Greece (Hydra), 1 New Zealand (ANZAC), 3 Portugal (Vasco da Gama), 3 Turkey (Barbaros class), 4 Turkey (Yavuz class)
Building: 2 (Australia), 1 (Greece), 1 (New Zealand), 1 (Turkey)
Proposed: 4 (Australia)

AUSTRALIA
Name (Pennant Number): ANZAC (150), ARUNTA (ex-Arrernte) (151) WARRAMUNGA (ex-Warumungu) (152), STUART (153), PARRAMATTA (154), BALLARAT (155), TOOWOOMBA (155), PERTH (157).

GREECE
Name (Pennant Number): HYDRA (F 452), SPETSAI (F 453), PSARA (F 454), SALAMIS (F 455).

NEW ZEALAND
Name (Pennant Number): TE KAHA (F 77), TE MANA (F 111).

PORTUGAL
Name (Pennant Number): VASCO DA GAMA (F 330), ALVARES CABRAL (F 331), CORTE REAL (F 332).

TURKEY (BARBAROS CLASS)
Name (Pennant Number): BARBAROS (F 244), ORUCREIS (F 245), SALIHREIS (F 246), KEMALREIS (F 247).

TURKEY (YAVUZ CLASS)
Name (Pennant Number): YAVUZ (F 240), TURGUTREIS (ex-Turgut) (F 241), FATIH (F 242), YILDIRIM (F 243).

Recognition features:
- High bow with break down to after end of forecastle.
- 5 in gun mounting ('A' position). (3.9 in gun mounting, Portuguese ships).
- CIWS mounting ('B' mounting position) Greek ships.

25 mm Sea Zenith CIWS in Turkish ships in same position. SRBOC chaff launchers in Australian/NZ ships. Space left for VLS SAM, Portuguese ships.
- High, flat sided superstructure extending from bridge aft to flight deck.
- Lattice mainmast at after end of bridge structure.
- Harpoon SSM launchers immediately aft of mainmast. (Greek, Turkish and Portuguese ships. Absent in Australian and NZ units.
- Twin, outward sloping, side-by-side funnels aft of midships.
- Ship's boats hoisted unusually high on midship davits.
- CIWS mounting at after end of hangar roof. (Greek and Portuguese ships). Sea Zenith/Sea Guard CIWS (Turkish ships). Absent in Australian/NZ units.
- Flight deck right aft with open quarterdeck below.

Displacement full load, tons: 3,600 (Australia/NZ), 3,200 (Greece), 3,300 (Portugal). 3,350 (Turkey). 2,919 (Turkish Yavuz class)
Length, feet (metres): 380.3 (115.9), (Portugal). 382.9 (116.7), (Turkey). 383.9 (117), (Greece). 387.1 (118), (Australia/NZ). 378.9 (115.5), (Turkish Yavuz class).
Beam, feet (metres): 48.6 (14.8) (Greece, Turkey, Australia/NZ). 48.7 (14.8), (Portugal). 46.6 (14.2), (Turkish Yavuz class).
Draught, feet (metres): 13.5 (4.1), (Greece, Turkish Yavuz class). 14.1 (14.8), (Turkey). 14.3 (4.4), (Australia/NZ). 20 (6.1), (Portugal)

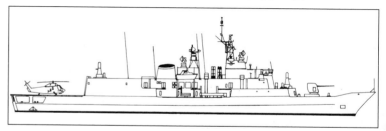

MEKO 200 ANZAC/Hydra/Vasco da Gama/ Yavuz/Barbaros Class

Speed, knots: 27 (Australia/NZ, Turkish Yavuz class) 31 (Greece). 32 (Portugal/Turkey).

Range, miles: 4,100 at 16 kts (Greece). 4,100 at 18 kts. (Turkey).

Missiles: SSM - 8 McDonnell Douglas Harpoon (2 quad launchers) (Greece, Portugal, Turkey). (None in Australian/NZ units.) SAM - Raytheon NATO Sea Sparrow Mk 48 vertical launcher. (Greece). Mk 29 Mod 1 octuple launcher (Portugal). (Aspide, Turkey F 244 and F 245, and Yavuz class). Sea Sparrow RIM-7NP Mk 41 Mod 5 octuple VLS. (Australia/NZ), (Turkey F 246 and F 247, with Aspide missiles).

Guns: 1 FMC Mk 45 Mods 2/2A/4 5 in (127 mm)/54. (Australia/NZ, Greece, Turkey. Mod 1 in Turkish Yavuz class). Creusot-Loire 3.9 in (100 mm)/55 Mod 68 CADAM (Portugal). 2 GD/GE Vulcan Phalanx 20 mm Mk 15 Mod 12. (Greece, 1 only in Portuguese ships). 3 Oerlikon-Contraves 25 mm Sea Zenith, 4-barrels. (Turkish ships).

Torpedoes: 6 324 mm Mk 32 Mod 5 (2 triple) tubes. Honeywell Mk 46 Mod 5 Neartip.

Decoys: SRBOC 6-barrelled Mk 36. (Also, Nulka quad expendable decoy launchers, Australian/NZ ships only). SLQ-25 Nixie; torpedo decoy. 2 Loral Hycor 6-tubed fixed Mk 36, (Portugal, Turkish Yavuz class).

ANZAC

Radars:

Air search — Raytheon SPS-49(V)8 (Australia/NZ). Signaal MW08, 3D. (Greek, Portuguese ships). Siemens/Plessey AWS 9 (Turkish ships). Signaal DA08 (Turkish Yavuz class)

Air/surface search — CelsiusTech 9LV 453 TIR (Australia/NZ). Signaal/Magnavox; DA08. (Greek, Portuguese ships). Siemens/Plessey AWS 6 Dolphin (Turkish ships).

Navigation — Atlas Electronik 9600 ARPA (Australia/NZ).Racal Decca 2690 BT, (Greek, Turkish Barbaros class). Kelvin Hughes Type 1007 (Portuguese ships). Racal Decca TM 1226, (Turkish Yavuz class).

Fire control — CelsiusTech 9LV 453 (Australia/NZ). 2 Signaal STIR. (Greek, Portuguese and Turkish ships). Seaguard (for 25 mm), (Turkish ships). Signaal WM25 (Turkish Yavuz class).

Sonars: Thomson-Sintra Spherion B Mod 5 (Australia/NZ).Raytheon SQS-56/DE 1160; hull-mounted and VDS. (Greek, Turkish ships). CDC SQS-510(V), (Portuguese ships).

Helicopters: 1 Sikorsky S-70B6 Seahawk (Greek). 2 Westland Super Sea Lynx Mk 95 (Portugal). Agusta AB 212 (ASW), (Turkey). 1 Kaman SH-2G Seasprite (Australia/NZ).

Godavari/Modified Godavari Class

Country: INDIA
Country of origin: INDIA
Ship type: FRIGATES
Class: GODAVARI/MODIFIED GODAVARI (PROJECT 16A) (FFG)
Active: 4
Building: 2
Name (Pennant Number): GODAVARI (F 20), GOMATI (F 21), GANGA (F 22), BRAHMAPUTRA (F 23), BEAS (F 24), BETWA (F 25)

Recognition features:

- Unusually long forecastle,.
- Three major weapons systems forward of the bridge; from the bow aft, 57 mm/70 gun mounting, Styx SSM launchers (F 20-22). (SS-N-25, F 23 onwards), SA-N-4 SAM launchers.
- Bows are flared to accommodate the large SSM launchers sited either side of the Muff Cob fire control director.
- Midships superstructure with pyramid mainmast at after end.
- Small, tapered funnel just aft of midships, (resembles 'Leander' class.)
- Slab-sided after superstructure (hangars) with small enclosed aftermast at forward end and LW08 air search radar aerial atop.
- Flight deck with break down to short quarterdeck.

Note - First three further modification of original 'Leander' class design. The second three Modified Godavari class will be larger and with different profile.

Displacement full load, tons: 3,850. 5,100, (Modified Godavari)
Length, feet (metres): 414.9 (126.5). 426.9 (130.5), (Modified Godavari).
Beam, feet (metres): 47.6 (14.5). 50 (16), (Modified Godavari).
Draught, feet (metres): 14.8 (4.5).
Speed, knots: 27.
Range, miles: 4,500 at 12 kts.

Missiles: SSM - 4 SS-N-2D Styx. (F 20 —22) SS-N-25 (4 quad) Sapless (Kh 35 Uran) (F 23-25). SAM - SA-N-4 Gecko twin launcher.
Guns: 2   57 mm/70 (twin). (Replaced by 76 mm gun in Mod. Godavari). 8 30 mm/65 (4 twin) AK 230. (Replaced by AK 630 in Mod. Godavari).
Torpedoes: 6 324 mm ILAS 3 (2 triple) tubes. Whitehead A244S.
Decoys: 2 chaff launchers. Graseby G738 towed torpedo decoy.

Radars:
Air search — Signaal LW 08.
Air/surface search — Head Net C, 3D.
Navigation/helo control — 2 Signaal ZW 06; or Don Kay.
Fire control — 2 Drum Tilt. (30 mm), (F 20-22). Contraves Seaguard (30 mm), (F 23-25). Pop Group. (SA-N-4). Muff Cob (57 mm). Garfun (SS-N-25), (F23-25).
Sonars: Bharat APSOH. Thomson-Sintra DSBV 62 (Ganga) passive towed array. Fathoms Oceanic VDS. Type 162M.

Helicopters: 2 Westland Sea King Mk 42A or 1 Sea King and 1 HAL SA 319B Chetak, (Alouette III).

GOMATI

Lupo/Artigliere/Carvajal/Modified Lupo Class

Country: ITALY, PERU, VENEZUELA
Country of origin: ITALY
Ship type: FRIGATES
Class: LUPO, ARTIGLIERE, carvajal, MODIFIED LUPO (FFG)
Active: 4 Italy (Lupo), 4 Italy (Artigliere), 4 Peru (Carvajal), 6 Venezuela (Modified Lupo)

ITALY (LUPO)
Name (Pennant Number): LUPO (F 564), SAGITTARIO (F 565), PERSEO (F 566), ORSA (F 567)

ITALY (ARTIGLIERE)
Name (Pennant Number): ARTIGLIERE (ex-Hittin) (F 582, ex-F 14), AVIERE (ex-Thi Qar) (F 583 ex-F 15), BERSAGLIERE (ex-Al Yarmouk), (F 584 ex-F 17), GRANATIERE (ex-Al Qadisiya) (F 585 ex-F 16)

PERU
Name (Pennant Number): CARVAJAL (FM 51), VILLAVICENCIO (FM 52), MONTERO (FM 53), MARIATEGUI (FM 54).

VENEZUELA
Name (Pennant Number): MARISCAL SUCRE (F 21), ALMIRANTE BRIÓN (F 22), GENERAL URDANETA (F 23), GENERAL SOUBLETTE (F 24), GENERAL SALOM (F 25), ALMIRANTE GARCIA (ex-José Felix Ribas) (F 26).

Recognition features:
- High bow, sweeping forecastle with 5 in gun mounting ('A' position).
- High forward superstructure. Distinctive surface search/target indication radome atop bridge roof in Italian Lupo class only.
- Enclosed mast, with pole mast at after end, atop bridge superstructure.
- Shorter pyramid aftermast immediately forward of funnel with RAN 10S air search radar atop (all ships). (Lattice mast in Peruvian ships.)
- After superstructure (hangar) with SAM box launcher on roof. (Sea Sparrow, Italian ships. Aspide, Peruvian and Venezuelan ships.)
- Forward-trained, angled SSM launchers on maindeck level, port and starboard, immediately aft and forward of funnel. (Teseo, Italian and Venezuelan ships. Otomat, Peruvian ships.)
- Two 40mm/70 gun mountings on maindeck level, port and starboard, abaft aft SSM launchers. (Peruvian and Venezuelan ships have raised mountings).
- Flight deck right aft with open quarterdeck below. Peruvian and Venezuelan ships have extended flight deck with break down to short quarterdeck.

Note - Italian Artigliere class almost identical. Originally built for Iraq and then transferred in 1992.

Displacement full load, tons: 2,525, (Italian Lupo/Artigliere). 2,500, (Peru), 2,520, (Venezuela).
Length, feet (metres): 371.3 (113.2).
Beam, feet (metres): 37.1 (11.3).
Draught, feet (metres): 12.1 (3.7).
Speed, knots: 35.

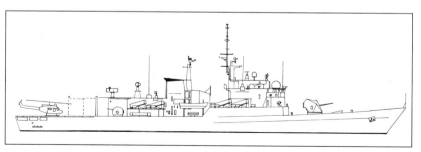

Missiles: SSM - 8 OTO Melara
Teseo Mk 2 (TG 2). (Italian and
Venezuelan ships; 16 in Lupo
class). 8 OTO MELARA/Matra
Otomat Mk 2 (TG 1), (Peruvian
ships). SAM - Raytheon NATO
Sea Sparrow Mk 29 octuple
launcher, (Italian Lupo class).
Albatros/Aspide octuple
launcher (Artigliere class,
Peruvian and Venezuelan ships).

Guns: 1 OTO Melara 5 in (127
mm)/54. 4 Breda 40 mm/70 (2
twin) Compact. 2 Oerlikon 20
mm can be fitted in Italian ships
of both classes.

Torpedoes: 6 324 mm US Mk 32
tubes. Honeywell Mk 46. (Italian
Lupo class; no torpedoes fitted
in Artigliere class.) 6 324 mm
ILAS (2 triple) tubes; Whitehead
A244, (Peruvian and Venezuelan
units).

Decoys: 2 Breda 105 mm SCLAR
20-tubed. (All ships). SLQ-25
Nixie; towed torpedo decoy,
(Italian Lupo class only).

LUPO

Radars:
Air search — Selenia SPS-774 (RAN 10S).
Surface search/target indication — SMA SPS-702, (Italian Lupo class).
Surface search — SMA SPQ-2 F, (Italian Lupo class). SPQ-712 (RAN 12L/X),
(Artigliere), Selenia RAN 11LX, (Peru). SMA SPQ-2F (Venezuela).
Navigation — SMA SPN-748. (Italian Lupo class). SMA SPN-703 (Artigliere).
SMA 3RM 20R. (Peruvian and Venezuelan).

Fire control — Selenia SPG-70 (RTN 10X). 2 Selenia SPG-74 (RTN 20X). (All
ships but also 2 Orion RTN 10XP in Venezuelan ships). US Mk 95 Mod
1, (Italian Lupo class only, for SAM).
Sonars: Raytheon DE 1160B; hull-mounted, (Italian Lupo class.) EDO SQS-29
Mod 610E in Peruvian and Venezuelan ships. None fitted in Artigliere class.

Helicopters: 1 Agusta AB 212 (ASW.)

Country: ITALY
Country of origin: ITALY
Ship type: FRIGATES
Class: MAESTRALE (FFG)
Active: 8
Name (Pennant Number): MAESTRALE (F 570), GRECALE (F 571), LIBECCIO (F 572), SCIROCCO (F 573), ALISEO (F 574), EURO (F 575), ESPERO (F 576), ZEFFIRO (F 577)

Recognition features:
- Bridge well aft from bows.
- 5 in gun mounting ('A' position).
- Albatros/Aspide SAM launcher ('B' mounting position).
- High forward superstructure with pointed pyramid mainmast atop.
- Single, rectangular funnel with wedge shaped, black smoke diffuser at top.
- Teseo SSM launchers, two port, two starboard, angled outboard sited immediately aft of funnel.
- Small, white, domed SATCOM aerial atop hangar roof.
- Flight deck right aft with open quarterdeck below.

Displacement full load, tons: 3,200.
Length, feet (metres): 405 (122.7).
Beam, feet (metres): 42.5 (12.9).
Draught, feet (metres): 15.1 (4.6).
Speed, knots: 32.
Range, miles: 6,000 at 16 kts.

Missiles: SSM - 4 OTO Melara Teseo Mk 2 (TG 2). SAM - Selenia Albatros octuple launcher; Aspide.
Guns: 1 OTO Melara 5 in (127 mm)/54 automatic. 4 Breda 40 mm/70 (2 twin) Compact. 2 Oerlikon 20 mm.
Torpedoes: 6 324 mm US Mk 32 (2 triple) tubes. Honeywell Mk 46. 2 21 in (533 mm) B516 tubes in transom. Whitehead A184.
Decoys: 2 Breda 105 mm SCLAR 20-tubed rocket launchers. SLQ-25; towed torpedo decoy. Prairie Masker; noise suppression system.

Radars:
Air/surface search — Selenia SPS-74 (RAN 10S).
Surface search — SMA SPS-702.
Navigation — SMA SPN-703.
Fire control — Selenia SPG-75 (RTN 30X).   2 Selenia SPG-74 (RTN 20X).
Sonars: Raytheon DE 1164; hull-mounted; VDS.

Helicopters: 2 Agusta AB 212 (ASW).

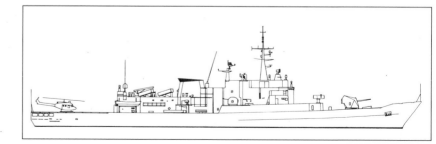

BECCIO

Country: JAPAN
Country of origin: JAPAN
Ship type: FRIGATES
Class: ABUKUMA (FFG/DE)
Active: 6
Name (Pennant Number): ABUKUMA (DE 229), JINTSU (DE 230), OHYODO (DE 231), SENDAI (DE 232), CHIKUMA (DE 233), TONE (DE 234)

Recognition features:

- Long, sweeping, uncluttered forecastle with 3 in gun mounting midway between bow and vertical bridge front.
- High forward superstructure with large lattice mainmast at after end, top half offset.
- Distinctive curved, OPS-14C lattice air search radar aerial on platform at forward end of mast.
- Two rectangular shaped black-capped funnels, forward one slightly taller.
- ASROC A/S missile box launcher sited between funnels.
- Gas turbine air intakes aft of after funnel, port and starboard.
- Short lattice aftermast atop after superstructure.
- Harpoon SSM angled launchers on raised structure immediately aft of aftermast.
- CIWS mounting on afterdeck.

Note - Non-vertical and rounded surfaces are employed for stealth reasons.

Displacement full load, tons: 2,550.
Length, feet (metres): 357.6 (109).
Beam, feet (metres): 44 (13.4).
Draught, feet (metres): 12.5 (3.8).
Speed, knots: 27.

Missiles: SSM - 8 McDonnell Douglas Harpoon (2 quad) launchers. A/S - Honeywell ASROC Mk 112 octuple launcher; payload Mk 46 Mod 5 Neartip torpedoes.
Guns: 1 OTO Melara 3 in (76 mm)/62 Compact. 1 GE/GD 20 mm Phalanx CIWS Mk 15.
Torpedoes: 6 324 mm Type 68 (2 triple) tubes. Honeywell Mk 46 Mod 5 Neartip.
Decoys: 2 Loral Hycor SRBOC 6-barrel Mk 36.

Radars:

Air search — Melco OPS-14C.
Surface search — JRC OPS-28C/D.
Fire control — Type 2-21.
Sonars: Hitachi OQS-8; hull-mounted.

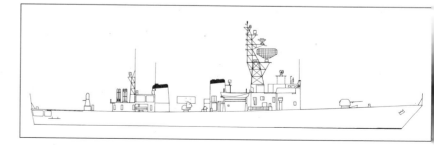

Abukuma Class

CHIKUMA

Country: JAPAN
Country of origin: JAPAN
Ship type: FRIGATES
Class: CHIKUGO (FF/DE)
Active: 8
Name (Pennant Number): TOKACHI (DE 218), IWASE (DE 219), CHITOSE (DE 220), NIYODO (DE 221), TESHIO (DE 222), YOSHINO (DE 223), KUMANO (DE 224), NOSHIRO (DE 225)

Recognition features:

- High bow with continuous sweeping maindeck through to stern.
- 3 in gun mounting within high breakwater ('A' position).
- High forward superstructure with large lattice mainmast at after end.
- Mainmast supports air search and air/surface search radar aerials.
- Single, sloping, black-capped funnel amidships.
- Small lattice aftermast.
- ASROC A/S missile box launcher sited between funnel and aftermast.
- 40 mm/60 gun mounting on sponson on afterdeck.

Displacement standard, tons: 1,470 (DE 218-219 and 221); 1,480 (DE 220); 1,500 (DE 222 onwards).
Length, feet (metres): 305 (93).
Beam, feet (metres): 35.5 (10.8).
Draught, feet (metres): 11.5 (3.5).
Speed, knots: 24.
Range, miles: 10,900 at 12 kts.

Missiles: A/S - Honeywell ASROC Mk 112 octuple launcher; payload Mk 46 Mod 5 Neartip torpedoes.
Guns: 2 USN 3in (76 mm)/50 Mk 33 (twin). 2 Bofors 40 mm/60 Mk 1 (twin).
Torpedoes: 6   324 mm Type 68 (2 triple) tubes. Honeywell Mk 46 Mod 5 Neartip.

Radars:

Air search — Melco OPS-14/14B
Surface search — JRC OPS-16C/D/18-3.
Fire control — Type 1B.
Sonars: Hitachi OQS-3A; hull-mounted, active search and attack. EDO SPS (35(J) (in last five ships only); VDS.

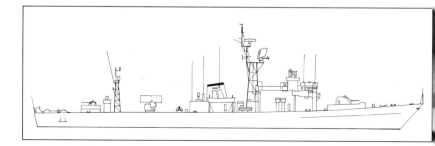

IWASE

Ulsan Class

Country: KOREA, SOUTH
Country of origin: KOREA, SOUTH
Ship type: FRIGATES
Class: ULSAN (FFG)
Active: 9
Name (Pennant Number): ULSAN (FF 951), SEOUL (FF 952), CHUNG NAM (FF 953), MASAN (FF 955), KYONG BUK (FF 956), CHON NAM (FF 957), CHE JU (FF 958), BUSAN (FF 959), CHUNG JU (FF 961)

Recognition features:
- High bows with continuous maindeck from stem to stern.
- 3 in gun mounting ('B' position).
- High superstructure at forward end with lower continuous superstructure to afterdeck.
- Single sloping funnel aft of midships.
- Large pyramid mainmast, supporting radome, at after end of bridge structure.
- Slim, enclosed aftermast supporting DA05 air/surface search radar aerial.
- Harpoon SSM angled twin launchers aft of funnel.
- 3 in gun mounting ('Y' position).

Note - The first five ships are the same but Kyong Buk has four Emerson Electric 30 mm guns replaced by three Breda 40 mm, and the last four of the class have a built-up gun platform aft.

Displacement, full load, tons: 2,180 (2,300 for FF 957 onwards).
Length, feet (metres): 334.6 (102).
Beam, feet (metres): 37.7 (11.5).
Draught, feet (metres): 11.5 (3.5).
Speed, knots: 34.
Range, miles: 4,000 at 15 kts.

Missiles: SSM - 8 McDonnell Douglas Harpoon (4 twin) launchers.
Guns: 2 3 in OTO Melara (76 mm)/62 Compact. 8 Emerson Electric 30 mm (4 twin) (FF 951-955). 6 Breda 40 mm/70 (3 twin) (FF 956-961).
Torpedoes: 6 324 mm Mk 32 (2 triple) tubes. Honeywell Mk 46 Mod 1.
Depth charges: 12.
Decoys: 4 Loral Hycor SRBOC 6-barrel Mk 36. SLQ-25 Nixie; towed torpedo decoy.

Radars:
Air/surface search — Signaal DA05.
Surface search — Signaal ZW06 (FF 951-956). Marconi S 1810 (FF 957-961).
Fire control — Signaal WM28 (FF 951-956). Marconi ST 1802 (FF 957-961).
Navigation — Raytheon SPS-10C (FF 957-961).
Sonars: Signaal PHS-32; hull-mounted active search and attack.

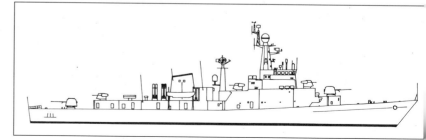

Ulsan Class

CHUNG NAM

Fatahillah Class

Country: INDONESIA
Country of origin: NETHERLANDS
Ship type: FRIGATES
Class: FATAHILLAH (FFG)
Active: 3
Name (Pennant Number): FATAHILLAH (361), MALAHAYATI (362), NALA (363)

Recognition features:

- 4.7 in gun mounting ('A' position) with Bofors 375 mm A/S mortar launcher ('B' mounting position).
- Low, slab-sided superstructure centred forward of midships.
- Very substantial pyramid mainmast with pole mast atop its after end.
- WM28 fire control radome atop short pyramid mainmast above bridge.
- Large, square-shaped, low profile funnel well aft of midships.
- Exocet SSM launchers between funnel and after superstructure.
- Large DA05 air/surface search radar aerial on pedestal atop small after superstructure.
- 40 mm/70 gun mounting aft of maindeck at break down to small quarterdeck.

Note - Nala has no after mounting and the maindeck is extended to provide a hangar and flight deck.

Displacement full load, tons: 1,450.
Length, feet (metres): 276 (84).
Beam, feet (metres): 36.4 (11.1).
Draught, feet (metres): 10.7 (3.3).
Speed, knots: 30.
Range, miles: 4,250 at 16 kts.

Missiles: SSM - 4 Aerospatiale MM 38 Exocet.
Guns: 1 Bofors 4.7 in (120 mm)/46. 1 or 2 Bofors 40 mm/70 (2 in Nala). 2 Rheinmetall 20 mm.
Torpedoes: 6   324 Mk 32 or ILAS 3 (2 triple) tubes (none in Nala). 12 Mk 46 (or A244S).
A/S mortars: 1 Bofors 375 mm twin-barrelled.
Decoys: 2 Knebworth Corvus 8-tubed trainable launchers.1 T-Mk 6 torpedo decoy.

Radars:
Air/surface search — Signaal DA05.
Surface search — Racal Decca AC 1229.
Fire control — Signaal WM28.
Sonars: Signaal PHS-32; hull-mounted active search/attack.

Helicopters: 1 Westland Wasp HAS (Mk 1). (ASW). (Nala only).

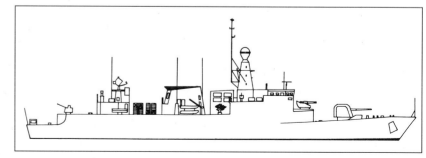

FATAHILLAH

Jacob van Heemskerck Class

Country: NETHERLANDS
Country of origin: NETHERLANDS
Ship type: FRIGATES
Class: JACOB VAN HEEMSKERCK (FFG)
Active: 2
Name (Pennant Number): JACOB VAN HEEMSKERCK (F 812), WITTE DE WITH (F 813)

Recognition features:
- Continuous maindeck from stem to stern.
- No weapons on forecastle.
- Sea Sparrow SAM octuple launcher ('B' mounting position).
- Forward superstructure has large pyramid mast at after end supporting Signaal Smart 3D air/surface search radar aerial.
- Pole mast aft of mainmast.
- Harpoon angled quad SSM launchers immediately aft of mainmast.
- Large funnel with sloping top just aft of midships.
- After superstructure with raised forward section supporting large LW08 air search radar aerial at forward end and STIR 240 fire control radar aft.
- Standard SM-1MR SAM launcher aft of raised superstructure.
- Goalkeeper CIWS mounting on quarterdeck.

Displacement full load, tons: 3,750.
Length, feet (metres): 428 (130.5).
Beam, feet (metres): 47.9 (14.6).
Draught, feet (metres): 14.1 (4.3).
Speed, knots: 30.
Range, miles: 4,700 at 16 kts.

Missiles: SSM - 8 McDonnell Douglas Harpoon (2 quad) launchers. SAM - 40 GDC Pomona Standard SM-1MR; Mk 13 Mod 1 launcher. Raytheon Sea Sparrow Mk 29 octuple launcher.
Guns: 1 Signaal SGE-30 Goalkeeper CIWS with General Electric 30 mm. 2 Oerlikon 20 mm.
Torpedoes: 4 324 mm US Mk 32 (2 twin) tubes. Honeywell Mk 46 Mod 5 Neartip.
Decoys: 2 Loral Hycor SRBOC 6-barrel Mk 36 (quad) launchers.

Radars:
Air search — Signaal LW08.
Air/surface search —Signaal Smart.
Surface search — Signaal Scout.
Fire control — 2 Signaal STIR 240. Signaal STIR 180.
Sonars: Westinghouse SQS-509; hull-mounted, active search/attack.

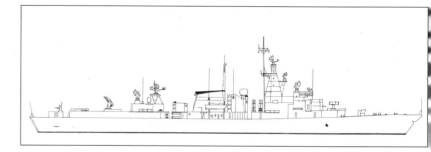

Jacob van Heemskerck Class

WITTE DE WITH

Karel Doorman Class

Country: NETHERLANDS
Country of origin: NETHERLANDS
Ship type: FRIGATES
Class: KAREL DOORMAN (FFG)
Active: 8
Name (Pennant Number): KAREL DOORMAN (F 827), WILLEM VAN DER ZAAN (F 829), TJERK HIDDES (F 830), VAN AMSTEL (F 831), ABRAHAM VAN DER HULST (F 832), VAN NES (F 833), VAN GALEN (F 834), VAN SPEIJK (F 828)

Recognition features:

- Continuous maindeck from stem to stern.
- 3 in gun mounting ('A' position).
- High forward superstructure topped by tall enclosed mainmast at after end supporting SMART air/surface search radar aerial.
- Squat, square shaped funnel with sloping after end, just aft of midships.
- After superstructure has distinctive pedestal mounted LW08 air search radar aerial at forward end. Small, white SATCOM dome immediately forward.
- Large hangar with Goalkeeper CIWS mounting atop at after end.
- Long flight deck with open quarterdeck below.

Displacement full load, tons: 3,320.
Length, feet (metres): 401.2 (122.3) oa.
Beam, feet (metres): 47.2 (14.4).
Draught, feet (metres): 14.1 (4.3).
Speed, knots: 30.
Range, miles: 5,000 at 18 kts.

Missiles: SSM - McDonnell Douglas Harpoon Block 1C (2 quad) launchers. SAM - Raytheon Sea Sparrow Mk 48 vertical launchers.

Guns: 1 OTO Melara 3 in (76 mm)/62 Compact Mk 100. 1 Signaal SGE-30 Goalkeeper with General Electric 30 mm. 2 Oerlikon 20 mm.
Torpedoes: 4 324 mm US Mk 32 (2 twin) tubes (mounted inside the after superstructure). Honeywell Mk 46 Mod 5 Neartip.
Decoys: 2 Loral Hycor SRBOC 6-barrel Mk 36 (quad) fixed launchers. SLQ-25 Nixie towed torpedo decoy.

Radars:
Air/surface search — Signaal SMART, 3D.
Air search — Signaal LW08.
Surface search — Signaal Scout.
Navigation — Racal Decca 1226.
Fire control — 2 Signaal STIR.
Sonars: Signaal PHS-36; hull-mounted active search/attack. Thomson-Sintra Anaconda DSBV 61; towed array.

Helicopters: 1 Westland SH-14D Lynx.

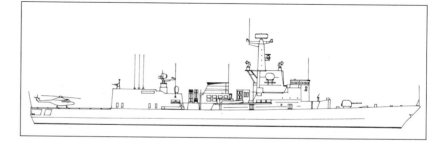

Karel Doorman Class

ABRAHAM VAN DER HULST

Country: GERMANY, GREECE, NETHERLANDS, UNITED ARAB EMIRATES (UAE).

Ship type: FRIGATES

Country of origin: NETHERLANDS

Class: KORTENAER/BREMEN (MODIFIED KORTENAER TYPE 122)/ELLI (FFG)

Active: 8 Germany (Bremen/Modified Kortenaer/Type 122), Greece (Elli), Netherlands (Kortenaer), 2 UAE (Kortenaer)

GERMANY

Name (Pennant Number): BREMEN (F 207), NIEDERSACHSEN (F 208), RHEINLAND-PFALZ (F 209), EMDEN (F 210), KÖLN (F 211), KARLSRUHE (F 212), AUGSBURG (F 213), LÜBECK (F 214)

GREECE

Name (Pennant Number): ELLI (ex-Pieter Florisz) (F 450, ex-F 812), LIMNOS (ex-Witte de With) (F 451, ex-F 813), AEGEON (ex-Banckert) (F 460, ex-F 810), ADRIAS (ex-Callenburgh), (F 459, ex-F 808), NAVARINON (ex-Van Kinsbergen) (F 461, ex-F 809), KOUNTOURIOTIS (ex-Kortenaer), (F 462, ex-F 807).

NETHERLANDS

Name (Pennant Number): PHILIPS VAN ALMONDE (F 823), BLOYS VAN TRESLONG (F 824), JAN VAN BRAKEL (F 825), PIETER FLORISZ (ex-Willem van der Zaan) (F 826)

UNITED ARAB EMIRATES

Name (Pennant Number): ABU DHABI (ex-Abraham Crijnssen) (F 01, ex-F 816), AL EMIRAT (ex-Piet Heyn) (F 02, ex- F 811).

Recognition features:

- Similar hull and basic profile to the Jacob Van Heemskerck class.
- Easily identifiable differences are: 3 in gun mounting ('A' position), WM25 fire control radar dome atop mainmast, Pomona Standard SAM launcher not fitted, low hanger, flight deck with open quarterdeck below.

- Sea Sparrow SAM box launcher in 'B' position.
- LW08 air search radar atop short open pylon, forward edge of hangar, aft of funnel.
- Greek ships have 3 in gun mounting atop hangar.
- Bremen class has tall lattice mast immediately forward of funnel and main deck not continuous. Taller hangar aft.

Displacement full load, tons: 3,630 (3,680, German ships).
Length, feet (metres): 428 (130.5) (426.4 (130), German ships).
Beam, feet (metres): 47.9 (14.6). (47.6 (14.5) German ships).
Draught, feet (metres): 20.3 (6.2), (screws). (21.3 (6.5) German ships).
Speed, knots: 30.
Range, miles: 4,700 at 16 kts.

Missiles: SSM - McDonnell Douglas Harpoon (2 quad) launchers. SAM - Raytheon Sea Sparrow Mk 29 octuple launcher. 2 GDC RAM (German ships only).
Guns: 1 OTO Melara 3 in (76 mm)/62 Compact. (2 in some Greek ships) Signaal SGE-30 Goalkeeper with General Electric 30 mm. (Dutch and UAE ships). GE/GD Vulcan Phalanx 20 mm Mk 15. (Greek ships). 2 Oerlikon 20 mm, (Dutch and UAE ships only). 2 Rheinmetall 20 mm Rh 202, (German ships only).

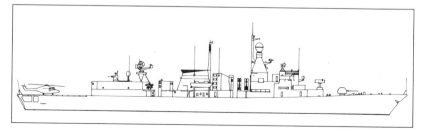

BREMEN

Torpedoes: 4 324 mm US Mk 32 (2 twin) tubes. Honeywell Mk 46 Mod 5 Neartip. (Mod 2 in German ships, to be replaced by Mu 90; Mod1/2 in Greek ships).

Decoys: 2 Loral Hycor SRBOC 6-barrel Mk 36 chaff launchers. (4 in German ships). SLQ-25 Nixie towed torpedo decoy; Prairie Bubble noise reduction, (German ships).

Radars:
Air search — Signaal LW08. (Dutch, Greek and UAE units).
Air/surface search — Signaal DA08, being replaced by DASA TRS-3D/32. (German ships only).

Surface search — Signaal ZW06, (Dutch, Greek units). Signaal Scout (UAE ships).
Navigation — SMA 3 RM 20, (German ships only).
Fire control — Signaal STIR. Signaal WM25.

Sonars: Westinghouse SQS-509, bow-mounted active search/attack, (Dutch ships). SQS-505, hull-mounted, (Greek and UAE ships). Atlas Elektronik DSQS-21BZ (BO), (German ships).

Helicopters: 2 Westland Sea Lynx Mk 88 (ASW/ASV), (German ships). 2 Agusta AB 212 (ASW), (Greek). 2 Westland SH-14D Lynx (ASW), (Dutch). 2 Eurocopter AS 545 Panther, (ASW), (UAE).

Tromp Class

Country: NETHERLANDS
Country of origin: NETHERLANDS
Ship type: FRIGATES
Class: TROMP (FFG)
Active: 2
Name (Pennant Number): TROMP (F 801), DE RUYTER (F 806)

Recognition features:

- 4.7 in gun twin mounting ('A' position). Sea Sparrow SAM launcher ('B' mounting position).
- WM25 fire control radome forward of bridge.
- High forward superstructure dominated by very large MTTR/SPS-01 air/surface search radome.
- Low profile twin, side-by-side, 'V' formation funnels amidships.
- Harpoon SSM angled launchers sited between funnels and forward superstructure.
- Large enclosed mainmast atop main superstructure aft of funnels and immediately forward of SPG-51C fire control director on pedestal.
- After superstructure with Standard SM-1MR SAM launcher at forward end and Goalkeeper CIWS mounting starboard side aft on hangar roof.
- Short flight deck with open quarterdeck below.

Displacement full load, tons: 4,308.
Length, feet (metres): 454 (138.4).
Beam, feet (metres): 48.6 (14.8).
Draught, feet (metres): 15.1 (4.6).
Speed, knots: 30.
Range, miles: 5,000 at 18 kts.

Missiles: SSM - McDonnell Douglas Harpoon (2 quad) launchers. SAM - 40 GDC Pomona Standard SM-1MR; Mk 13 Mod 4 launcher. Raytheon Sea Sparrow Mk 29 octuple launcher.
Guns: 2 Bofors 4.7 in (120 mm)/50 (twin). Signaal SGE-30 Goalkeeper with GE 30 mm. 2 Oerlikon 20 mm.
Torpedoes: 6 324 mm US Mk 32 (2 triple) tubes. Honeywell Mk 46 Mod 5 Neartip.
Decoys: 2 Loral Hycor SRBOC 6-barrel Mk 36.

Radars:
Air/surface search — Signaal MTTR/SPS-01, 3D.
Navigation — 2 Decca 1226.
Fire control — 2 Raytheon SPG-51C. Signaal WM25.
Sonars: CWE 610; hull-mounted, active search and attack.

Helicopters: 1 Westland SH-14D Lynx (ASW).

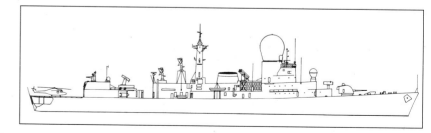

Tromp Class

TROMP

Van Speijk/Ahmad Yani Class

Country: INDONESIA
Country of origin: NETHERLANDS
Ship type: FRIGATES
Class: VAN SPEIJK/AHMAD YANI (FFG)
Active: 6
Name (Pennant Number): AHMAD YANI (ex-Tjerk Hiddes) (351), SLAMET RIYADI (ex-Van Speijk) (352), YOS SUDARSO (ex-Van Galen) (353), OSWALD SIAHAAN (ex-Van Nes) (354), ABDUL HALIM PERDANAKUSUMA (ex-Evertsen) (355), KAREL SATSUITUBUN (ex-Isaac Sweers) (356)

Recognition features:
- Similar to British Leander class.
- Long, raised forecastle with OTO MELARA 3 in (76 mm)/62 Compact gun mounting ('A' position).
- Midships superstructure with pyramid mainmast atop, just aft of bridge.
- Single, 'capped' funnel just aft of midships.
- Short aftermast supporting large LW03 air search radar aerial.
- Mistral SAM Simbad launchers on hangar roof, (replacing Seacat quad launchers).
- Torpedo tubes, port and starboard, on maindeck at forward end of long flight deck.

Displacement full load, tons: 2,835.
Length, feet (metres): 372 (113.4).
Beam, feet (metres): 41 (12.5).
Draught, feet (metres): 13.8 (4.2).
Speed, knots: 28.5.
Range, miles: 4,500 at 12 kts.

Missiles: SSM - 8 McDonnell Douglas Harpoon. SAM - 2 Short Bros Seacat quad launchers. (Being replaced by 2 Matra Simbad twin launchers for Mistral).
Guns: 1 OTO Melara 3 in (76 mm)/62 Compact. 2 12.7 mm MGs.
Torpedoes: 6 324 mm Mk 32 (2 triple) tubes. Honeywell Mk 46.
Decoys: 2 Knebworth Corvus 8-tubed trainable launchers.

Radars:
Air search — Signaal LW03.
Air/surface search — Signaal DA05.
Navigation — Racal Decca 1229.
Fire control — Signaal M 45.   2 Signaal M 44.
Sonars: Signaal CWE 610; hull-mounted; VDS.

Helicopters: 1 Westland Wasp HAS Mk 1 (ASW).

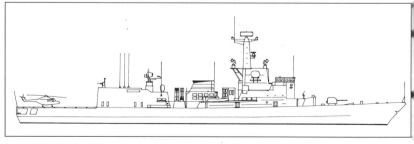

ABDUL HALIM PERDANAKUSUMA

Oslo Class

Country: NORWAY
Country of origin: NORWAY
Ship type: FRIGATES
Class: OSLO (FFG)
Active: 4
Name (Pennant Number): BERGEN (F 301), TRONDHEIM (F 302), STAVANGER (F 303), NARVIK (F 304)

Recognition features:

- High bow with continuous sweeping maindeck from stem to stern.
- Long forecastle with 3 in gun twin mounting forward of Kongsburg Terne III 6-tube A/S mortar launchers.
- High superstructure with large pedestal-mounted AWS-9 air search radar aerial atop.
- Unusual tripod/pole mainmast configuration at after end of forward superstructure sloping at an angle aft.
- Low, slim, black-capped angled funnel below angled mainmast.
- After superstructure has tall slim pedestal-mounted Mk 95 fire control radar aerial atop.
- Sea Sparrow SAM box launcher at after end of after superstructure.
- 40 mm/70 gun mounting ('Y' position).
- Penguin SSM launcher right aft on quarterdeck.

Displacement full load, tons: 1,950.
Length, feet (metres): 317 (96.6).
Beam, feet (metres): 36.8 (11.2).
Draught, feet (metres): 18 (5.5) (screws).
Speed, knots: 25+.
Range, miles: 4,500 at 15 kts.

Missiles: SSM - 4 Kongsberg Penguin Mk 1. SAM - Raytheon RIM-7M Sea Sparrow Mk 29 octuple launcher.
Guns: 2 US 3 in (76 mm)/50 Mk 33 (twin). 1 Bofors 40 mm/70. 2 Rheinmetall 20 mm/20 (not in all).
Torpedoes: 6 324 mm US Mk 32 (2 triple) tubes. Marconi Stingray.
A/S mortars: Kongsberg Terne III 6-tubed.
Decoys: 2 chaff launchers.

Radars:

Air search — Siemens/Plessey AWS-9.
Surface search — Racal Decca TM 1226.
Navigation — Decca.
Fire control — NobelTech 9LV 218 Mk 2. Raytheon Mk 95, (Sea Sparrow).
Sonars: Thomson-Sintra/Simrad TSM 2633; combined hull and VDS, Simrad Terne III.

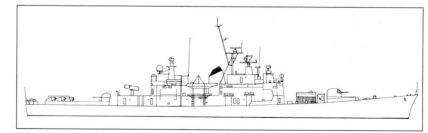

TRONDHEIM

Tetal/Improved Tetal Class

Country: ROMANIA
Country of origin: ROMANIA
Ship type: FRIGATES (FF)
Class: TETAL/IMPROVED TETAL
Active: 4 (Tetal), 2 (Improved Tetal)
Name (Pennant Number): ADMIRAL PETRE BARBUNEANU (260), VICE ADMIRAL VASILE SCODREA (261), VICE ADMIRAL VASILE URSEANU (262), VICE ADMIRAL EUGENIU ROSCA (263). Improved Tetal - CONTRE ADMIRAL EUSTATIU SEBASTIAN (264), ADMIRAL HORIA MACELARIU (265)

Recognition features:
- Regular profile hull with continuous maindeck from stem to stern.
- Very long forecastle with 3 in gun mounting ('A' position).
- A/S mortar mounting ('B' mounting position).
- Long superstructure centred well aft of midships.
- Large mainmast amidships, with enclosed bottom half and lattice top. (Lattice throughout in Improved Tetal).
- Hawk Screech fire control radar aerial atop after end of bridge structure in Tetal class. Drum Tilt in Improved Tetal.
- Drum Tilt fire control radar aerial mounted atop tall pedestal towards after end of superstructure, (Tetal class only).
- Short, squat black-capped funnel aft of mainmast and aft of superstructure in Improved Tetal.
- 30 mm/65 gun mountings at after end of after superstructure, one port one starboard.
- 3 in gun mounting ('Y' position) in Tetal class. Missing from Improved Tetal — long helicopter deck substituted.

Note - Heavily modified Soviet 'Koni' design.

Displacement full load, tons: 1,440. 1,500 (Improved Tetal).
Length, feet (metres): 303.1 (95.4).
Beam, feet (metres): 38.4 (11.7).
Draught, feet (metres): 9.8 (3). 10 (3.1) (Improved Tetal).
Speed, knots: 24.
Guns: 4 USSR 3 in (76 mm)/60 (2 twin), (Tetal). 1 USSR 3 in (76 mm)/60, (Improved Tetal). 4 USSR 30 mm/65 (2 twin), (Tetal). 4 30 mm/65 AK 630, (Improved Tetal). 2 - 14.5 mm MGs, (Tetal).
Torpedoes: 4 21 in (533 mm) (twin) tubes. Russian Type 53-65.
A/S mortars: 2 RBU 2500 16-tubed, (Tetal). 2 RBU 6000 (Improved Tetal).
Decoys: 2 PK 16 chaff launchers

Radars:
Air/surface search — Strut Curve.
Navigation — Nayada.
Fire control — Drum Tilt. Hawk Screech. (Drum Tilt only in Improved Tetal).
Sonars: Hercules (MG 322) hull-mounted, active search/attack.

Helicopters: 1 IAR 316B Alouette III (ASW). (Improved Tetal only).

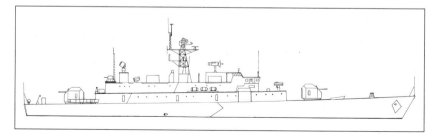

Tetal/Improved Tetal Class

Grisha I-V/KASZUB (Type 620) Class

Country: LITHUANIA, POLAND, RUSSIA, UKRAINE
Country of origin: RUSSIA
Ship type: FRIGATES
Class: GRISHA I (TYPE 1124) (ALBATROS) (FFL)
   Active: 6 (Russia), 2 (Ukraine)
Class: GRISHA II (TYPE 1124P) (ALBATROS) (FFL)
   Active: 8 (Russia), 2 (Ukraine)
Class: GRISHA III (TYPE 1124M) (ALBATROS) (FFL)
   Active: 2 (Lithuania), 21 (Russia)
Class: GRISHA V (TYPE 1124EM) (ALBATROS) (FFL)
   Active: 30 (Russia), 1 (Ukraine)
Class: KASZUB (TYPE 620) (FF)
   Active: 1 (Poland).

LITHUANIA
Name (Pennant Number): ZEMAITIS (F 11 ex-MPK 108), AUKSTAITIS (F 12 ex-MPK 44).

RUSSIA
Name (Pennant Number): AMETYST, BRILLIANT, IZUMRUD, PREDANNY, RUBIN, ZHEMCHUG, PROVORNY, NADEZHNY. (All Grisha II class, Border Guard)
DOZORNY, SMELY, BDITELNY, RESITELNY. (All Grisha III, Border Guard).

UKRAINE
Name (Pennant Number): Grisha I — SUMY (U 209), KHERSON (U 210). Grisha II — CHERNIGIV (U 205), VINNITSA (U 206). Grisha V — Lutsk (U 200, ex-400).

POLAND
Name (Pennant Number): KASZUB (240).

Recognition features:
- High bow with sweeping lines to stern.
- SA-N-4 Gecko SAM launcher ('A' mounting position). (57mm/80 gun twin mounting in this position in Grisha II).
- Two A/S mortar launchers, port and starboard ('B' mounting position).
- Pyramid mainmast at after end of forward superstructure.
- Small 'Y' shaped (in profile) lattice mast at top after end of mainmast. (Enclosed in Grisha II).
- Pop Group fire control radar aerial atop forward superstructure, forward of mainmast. (except Grisha II).
- Single, low profile, square shaped funnel just aft of midships.
- Small after superstructure with slender lattice mast at forward end, and Muff Cob fire control radar aerial atop after end. (Bass Tilt in Grisha III/V with 30mm/65 mountings).
- 57 mm/80 gun mounting ('Y' position).

Note 1 - Most obvious identification of Grisha II is 57 mm/80 gun mounting ('A' position). Grisha III same as Grisha I except for raised after superstructure with Bass Tilt fire control radar aerial atop. Grisha V is the only type with 3 in gun mounting ('Y' position).

Note 2 - Kaszub, based on Grisha design, has 3 in gun mounting in 'A' position, long low superstructure aft of mainmast and no obvious funnel. ZU-23-2M Wrobel 23 mm/87 twin gun mountings fitted on aft superstructure in 'X' position and aft of mainmast.

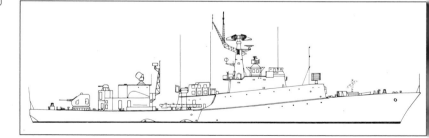

Grisha I — V/KASZUB (Type 620) Class

GRISHA I

Displacement full load, tons: 1,200. (1,150, Ukraine). (1,183, Kaszub).
Length, feet (metres): 233.6 (71.2). (270 (82.3) Kaszub).
Beam, feet (metres): 32.2 (9.8). (32.8 (10) Kaszub).
Draught, feet (metres): 12.1 (3.7). (10.2 (3.1) Kaszub).
Speed, knots: 30. (27, Kaszub).
Range, miles: 2,500 at 14 kts. (3,500 at 14 kts., Kaszub).

Missiles: SAM - SA-N-4 Gecko twin launcher (Grisha I, III and V classes). 2 SA-N-5 quad launchers, (Kaszub).
Guns: 2 57 mm/80 (twin) (2 twin in Grisha II class). 1 3 in (76 mm)/60 (Grisha V). 1 30 mm/65 (Grisha III and V classes). 1 USSR 3 in (76 mm)/66 AK 176 and 6 ZU-23-2M Wrobel 23 mm/87 (3 twin), (Kaszub).
Torpedoes: 4 21 in (533 mm) (2 twin) tubes. (Tubes removed from Lithuanian ships F 12 and F 11).

A/S mortars: 2 RBU 6000 12-tubed. (Only 1 in Grisha Vs.)
Depth charges: 2 racks/rails.
Decoys: 2 PK 16 chaff launchers or 4 PK 10.

Radars:
Air/surface search — Strut Curve (Strut Pair in early Grisha Vs). Half Plate Bravo (in the later Grisha Vs).
Surface search — Nogat SRN 7453 (Kaszub only). (Racal Decca RM 1290, Lithuania).
Navigation — Don 2. (SRN 441XT, Kaszub only). Terma Scanter (Lithuania).
Fire control — Pop Group (Grisha I, III and V). Muff Cob (except in Grisha III and V). Bass Tilt (Grisha III and V).
Sonars: Bull Nose (MGK 335MS) hull-mounted. Elk Tail, VDS. (Grisha). (MG 322T bow-mounted, MG 329M stern-mounted dipping type, Kaszub).

Koni/Mourad Rais class

Country: ALGERIA, BULGARIA, CUBA, LIBYA, YUGOSLAVIA
Country of origin: RUSSIA
Ship type: FRIGATES
Class: KONI I/III (TYPE 1159) (FF)
Active: 1 (Bulgaria), 2 (Cuba), 1 + 1 reserve (Libya) (FFG)
BULGARIA
Name (Pennant Number): SMELI (ex-Delfin) (11).
CUBA
Name (Pennant Number): (350), (383, ex-353).
LIBYA
Name (Pennant Number): AL HANI (F 212), AL QIRDABIYAH (F 213).

Class: MOURAD RAIS (KONI II) (TYPE 1159.2) (FF)
Active: 3 (Algeria)
ALGERIA
Name (Pennant Number): MOURAD RAIS (901), RAIS KELLICH (902), RAIS KORFOU (903)

Class: KONI (SPLIT AND KOTOR) CLASSES (FFG)
Active: 2 (Split/Koni) 2 (Kotor) (Yugoslavia)
YUGOSLAVIA
Name (Pennant Number): BEOGRAD (ex-Split) (31), PODGORICA (ex-Kopar) (32), ZAGREB (ex-Kotor) (33), NOVI SAD (ex-Pula) (34).

Recognition features:

- High bow, sweeping maindeck line through to stern.
- 3 in gun twin mounting ('A' position).
- RBU 6000 A/S mortar in 'B' mounting position.
- Stepped main superstructure with enclosed mast at after end supporting Strut Curve air/surface or air search radar aerials.
- Single, squat funnel just aft of midships.
- Short enclosed pyramid mast just forward of

funnel supporting Drum Tilt fire control radar aerial.
- SA-N-4 Gecko SAM launcher in 'X' position.
- 3 in gun twin mounting ('Y' position).
- Pop Group fire control director just forward of SAM launcher at aft end of superstructure.

Note 1 - The above features apply to Algerian, Bulgarian and Cuban ships which could easily be confused. Obvious differences in Libyan ships are, forward end of superstructure removed to fit SS-N-2C SSM launcher and lattice mast fitted forward of Pop Group fire control director. Camouflage paint applied to Libyan ships in 1991. Algerian, Cuban and Libyan ships have extended deck housing aft of funnel.

Note 2 - First two Yugoslav units have SS-N-2C Styx in four launchers, two port and two starboard, facing forward alongside bridge superstructure and 'B' position. First two have them aft of the funnel, facing astern. In the last pair, the funnel is considerably longer and the mainmast is of the lattice type.

Displacement full load, tons: 1,900. (1,870 Yugoslavia).
Length, feet (metres): 316.3 (96.4). (317.3 (12.8), (Yugoslavia).
Beam, feet (metres): 41.3 (12.6). (42 (12.8), Yugoslavia).
Draught, feet (metres): 11.5 (3.5). (13.7 (4.2) Yugoslavia).
Speed, knots: 27.
Range, miles: 1,800 at 14 kts.

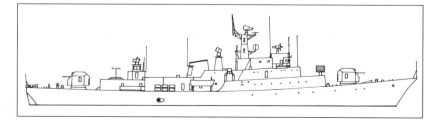

Koni/Mourad Rais class

RAIS KELLICH

Missiles: SSM — 4 SS-N-2C Styx. (Libyan (2 twin) and Yugoslav ships). (Not Algerian, Bulgarian or Cuban units). SAM - SA-N-4 Gecko twin launcher.
Guns: 4 3 in (76 mm)/60 (2 twin). (1 mounting in Yugoslav 33 and 34). 4 - 30 mm/65 (2 twin).
Torpedoes: 4 406 mm (2 twin tubes), USET-95. (Libya only).
A/S mortars: 2 RBU 6000, 12-barrel, trainable. (1 RBU 6000, Libya only).
Depth charges: 2 racks. (Not Yugoslav ships).
Mines: Rails. Capacity 22.
Decoys: 2 — PK 16 chaff launchers. (Algerian, Bulgarian, Cuban and Libyan units). 2 Wallop Barricade double layer chaff launchers, (Yugoslav ships).

Radars:
Air/surface search — Strut Curve.
Surface search — Plank Shave (Libya only).
Navigation — Don 2.
Fire control — Hawk screech.(Owl Screech in Yugoslav ships) Drum Tilt. Pop Group.
Sonars: Herkules (MG 322), or Bull Nose (Yugoslav 33 and 34) Hull-mounted.

Krivak I, (Burevestnik) (Type 1135)/
Krivak II (Type 1135M)/ Krivak III (Nerey) (Type 1135MP)/
Improved Krivak III (Type 1135.6) Classes

Country: INDIA, RUSSIA, UKRAINE
Country of origin: RUSSIA
Ship type: FRIGATES
Class: KRIVAK I (BUREVESTNIK) (TYPE 1135) (FFG)
Active: 9 (Russia), 2 (Ukraine)
RUSSIA
Name (Pennant Number): DRUZHNY, RAZUMNY, ZADORNY, ZHARKY, LADNY. Modified Krivak 1 — LEGKY (ex-Leningradsky Komsomolets), LETUCHY, PYLKY, STOROZHEVOY.
UKRAINE
Name (Pennant Number): NIKOLAYEV (ex-Bezzavetny) (U 133), DNIPROPETROVSK (ex-Bezukoriznenny) (U 134).

Class: KIRVAK II (TYPE 1135M) (FF)
Active: 3 (Russia), 1 (Ukraine)
RUSSIA
Name (Pennant Number): NEUKROTIMY (ex-Komsomolets Litvii), PYTLIVY, REZVY.
UKRAINE
Name (Pennant Number): SEVASTOPOL (ex-Razitelny) (U 132).

Class: KRIVAK III (TYPE 1135MP) (FFH)
Active: 7 (Russia), 1 (Ukraine)
RUSSIA
Name (Pennant Number): MENZHINSKY. DZERZHINSKY, OREL (ex-Imeni XXVII, Sesda KPSS), PSKOV (ex-Imeni LXX, Letiya VCHK-KGB), ANADYR (ex-Imeni LXX, Letiya Pogranvoysk), KEDROV, VOROVSKY.
UKRAINE
Name (Pennant Number): HETMAN

SAGAIDACHNY (U 130, ex-201).
Class: IMPROVED KRIVAK III (TYPE 1135.6) (FFH)
Active: 0
Building: 1 + 5 (India).

Recognition features: Krivak I
- Long forecastle with, from forward, Raduga SS-N-14 Silex A/S curved missile launcher, SA-N-4 Gecko SAM launcher and SS-N-25 SSM launcher.
- Forward superstructure with, at after end, complex of three lattice masts forming the mainmast structure with large air search radar aerial atop.
- Single, low profile funnel well aft of midships.
- Pop Group and Owl Screech fire control radar aerials mounted on complex structure between mainmast and funnel.
- 3 in gun mountings ('Y' and 'X' positions).

Note 1 - Most obvious identification of Krivak II/III is RBU 6000 A/S mortar mounting in place of SSM launcher on forecastle. Krivak III has a 3.9 gun mounting ('A' position) and a flight deck, replacing gun mountings in 'X' and 'Y' positions.

Note 2 - Indian Improved Krivak III will have a much more massive, continuous superstructure and squat mainmast.

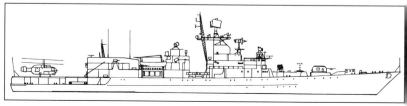

Krivak I, (Burevestnik) (Type 1135)/
Krivak II (Type 1135M)/ Krivak III (Nerey) (Type 1135MP)/
Improved Krivak III (Type 1135.6) Classes

Displacement full load, tons: 3,650.
Length, feet (metres): 405.2 (123.5).
Beam, feet (metres): 46.9 (14.3).
Draught, feet (metres): 16.4 (5).
Speed, knots: 32.
Range, miles: 4,600 at 20 kts.

Missiles: SSM — Zvezda SS-N-25
    Sapless (Kh 35 Uran) (2 quad); (Krivak
    I after modernisation). SAM - 2 SA-N-
    4 Gecko twin launchers (1 in Krivak
    III). A/S — Raduga SS-N-14 Silex
    quad launcher (not in Krivak III);
    payload nuclear or Type E53-72
    torpedo.
Guns: 4   3 in (76 mm)/60 (2 twin) (Krivak
    I). 2   3.9 in (100 mm)/59 (Krivak II) (1
    in Krivak III). 2   30 mm/65 (Krivak III).
Torpedoes: 8   21 in (533 mm) (2 quad)
    tubes.
Mines: Capacity for 20.
A/S mortars: 2 RBU 6000 12-tubed; (not
    modernised Krivak I).
Decoys: 4   PK 16 or 10 PK 10 chaff
    launchers. Towed torpedo decoy.

KRIVAK

Radars:
Air search — Head Net C, 3D, or Top Plate (Krivak I mod. And Krivak III).
Surface search — Don Kay or Palm Frond or Don 2 or Spin Trough and Peel
    Cone (Krivak III).
Fire control — 2 Eye Bowl (not in Krivak III). 2 Pop Group (1 in Krivak III). Owl

Screech (Krivak I). Kite Screech (Krivak II and III). Bass Tilt (Krivak III).
Sonars: Bull Nose (MGK 335MS); hull-mounted, active search/attack. Mare
    Tail or Steer Hide (some Krivak Is after modernisation); VDS.

Helicopters: 1 Kamov Ka-25 Hormone or Ka-27 Helix (ASW). (Krivak III).

Neustrashimy (Jastreb) (Type 1154) Class

Country: RUSSIA
Country of origin: RUSSIA
Ship type: FRIGATES
Class: NEUSTRASHIMY (JASTREB) (TYPE 1154) (FFG)
Active: 1
Building: 1
Name (Pennant Number): NEUSTRASHIMY, YAROSLAVL MUDRY (ex-Nepristupny)

Recognition features:

- Elegant profile with front of long forecastle slightly depressed.
- 3.9 in gun mounting ('A' position).
- SA-N-9 Gauntlet (Klinok) SAM VLS tubes just aft of forward mounting.
- RBU 12000 A/S mortar mounting ('B' mounting position).
- Forward superstructure has short forward mast at its after end supporting Cross Sword fire control radar aerial.
- Twin funnels. Forward one aft of forward superstructure, after one aft of mainmast.
- Large, pyramid mainmast well aft of midships with distinctive Top Plate air/surface radar aerial atop.
- CADS-N-1 SAM/Guns mounting at after end of after superstructure, just forward of flight deck.
- VDS towing array right aft.

Note 1 - Class slightly larger than Krivak. Helicopter deck extends across the full width of the ship.

Note 2 - After funnel is unusually flush decked, therefore not obvious in profile.

Displacement full load, tons: 4,250.
Length, feet (metres): 430.4 (131.2) oa.
Beam, feet (metres): 50.9 (15.5).
Draught, feet (metres): 15.7 (4.8).
Speed, knots: 30.
Range, miles: 4,500 at 16 kts.

Missiles: SSM - Fitted for, but not with 8 SS-N-25 Sapless (Kh 35 Uran). SAM - 4 SA-N-9 Gauntlet (Klinok) sextuple vertical launchers. SAM/Guns 2 CADS-N-1 (Kortik/Kashtan); each has a twin 30 mm Gatling combined with 8-SAN-11 Grisson and Hot Flash/Hot Spot fire control radar/optronic director. A/S - SS-N-15/16. Type 40 torpedo or nuclear warhead, fired from torpedo tubes.
Guns: 1 3.9 in (100 mm)/59.
Torpedoes: 6 21 in (533 mm) tubes combined with A/S launcher. Can fire SS-N-15/16 missiles or anti-submarine torpedoes.
A/S mortars: 1 RBU 12000; 10-tubed, trainable.
Mines: 2 rails.
Decoys: 8 PK 10 and 2 PK 16 chaff launchers.

Radars:
Air/surface search — Top Plate, 3D.
Navigation — 2 Palm Frond.
Fire control — Cross Sword. Kite Screech.
Sonars: Ox Yoke and Whale Tongue; hull-mounted. Ox Tail VDS or towed sonar array.

Helicopters: 1 Kamov Ka-27PL Helix (ASW).

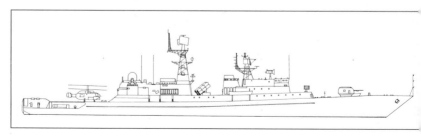

NEUSTRASHIMY

Parchim I and II (Type 1331) Class

Country: INDONESIA, RUSSIA
Country of origin: RUSSIA
Ship type: FRIGATES
Class: PARCHIM I (TYPE 1331) (KAPITAN PATIMURA) (FS)
Active: 16 (Indonesia)
Name (Pennant Number): KAPITAN PATIMURA (ex-Prenzlau), (371, ex-231), UNTUNG SUROPATI (ex-Ribnitz) (372, ex-233), NUKU (ex-Waren) (373, ex-224), LAMBUNG MANGKURAT (ex-Angermünde) (374, ex-214), CUT NYAK DIEN (ex-Lübz) (375, ex-P 6169, ex-221), SULTAN THAHA SYAIFUDDIN (ex-Bad Doberan) (376, ex-222), SUTANTO (ex-Wismar) (377, ex-P 6170, ex-241), SUTEDI SENOPUTRA (ex-Parchim) (378, ex-242), WIRATNO (ex-Perleberg) (379, ex-243), MEMET SASTRAWIRIA (ex-Bützow) (380, ex-244), TJIPTADI (ex-Bergen), (381, ex-213), HASAN BASRI (ex-Güstrow) (382, ex-223), IMAN BONJOL (ex-Teterow) (383, ex-P 6168, ex-234), PATI UNUS (ex-Ludwiglust) (384, ex-232), TEUKU UMAR (ex-Grevesmühlen) (385, ex-212), SILAS PAPARE (ex-Gadebusch) (386, ex-P 6167, ex-211).

Class: PARCHIM II (TYPE 1331) (FFL)
Active: 12 (Russia)
Name (Pennant Number): (MPK 67), (MPK 99), (MPK 105), (MPK 192), (MPK 205), (MPK 213), (MPK 216), (MPK 219), (MPK 223), (MPK 224), (MPK 228), KALMYKIA (MPK 229).

Recognition features:
- High bow, short forecastle.
- Low main superstructure with high central superstructure atop.
- 30mm/65 AK 630 CIWS mounting at forward end of main superstructure.
- RBU 6000 A/S mortar mounting forward of bridge.
- Substantial lattice mainmast atop central superstructure. Small 'Y' shaped (in profile)

lattice mast protruding aft.
- Large Cross Dome air/surface search radome atop mainmast.
- SA-N-5 Grail quad SAM launcher at after end of forward superstructure.
- Large, enclosed aftermast supporting distinctive drum-shaped Bass Tilt fire control radar aerial.
- 3 in gun mounting ('Y' position).

Note - Most obvious differences between Parchim I and II are conventional air/surface search radar aerial atop mainmast in Indonesian units and much smaller, shorter enclosed aftermast supporting Muff Cob fire control radar aerial.

Displacement full load, tons: 960. (769, Parchim I).
Length, feet (metres): 246.7 (75.2).
Beam, feet (metres): 32.2 (9.8).
Draught, feet (metres): 14.4 (4.4). (11.5 (3.5), Parchim I).
Speed, knots: 26. (24, Parchim I).

Missiles: SAM - 2 SA-N-5 Grail quad launchers. (Also in some Parchim I units).
Guns: 1 - 3 in (76 mm)/66 AK 176. 1 - 30 mm/65 AK 630 6 barrels. (Parchim II). 1 USSR 57 mm/80 (twin) automatic, 2 - 30 mm (twin), (Parchim I).
Torpedoes: 4 - 21 in (533 mm) (2 twin) tubes. 4 - 400 mm tubes, (Parchim I).

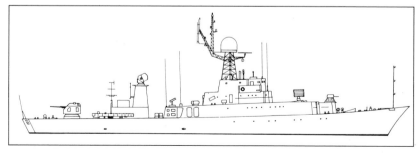

Parchim I and II (Type 1331) Class

PARCHIM

A/S mortars: 2 RBU 6000 12-tubed, trainable.
Depth charges: 2 racks.
Mines: Rails fitted.
Decoys: 2 PK 16 chaff launchers.

Radars:
Air/surface search — Cross Dome. (Strut Curve in Indonesian ships).
Navigation — TSR 333 or Nayala or Kivach III.
Fire control — Bass Tilt. (Muff Cob in Indonesian ships).
Sonars: Bull Horn, (MGT 332T) hull-mounted. Lamb Tail, helicopter type VDS.
   (Elk Tail VDS on starboard side in some Indonesian hulls).

Baptista de Andrade/João Coutinho Class

Country: PORTUGAL
Country of origin: SPAIN
Ship type: FRIGATES
Class: BAPTISTA DE ANDRADE/JOÃO COUTINHO (FF)
Active: 4 (Baptista de Andrade), 6 (João Coutinho)
Name (Pennant Number): BAPTISTA DE ANDRADE (F 486), JOÃO ROBY (F 487), AFONSO CERQUEIRA (F 488), OLIVEIRA E CARMO (F 489).
Name (Pennant Number): ANTONIO ENES (F 471), JOÃO COUTINHO (F 475), JACINTO CANDIDO (F 476), GENERAL PEREIRA D'ECA (F 477), AUGUSTO DE CASTILHO (F 484), HONORIO BARRETO (F 485).

Recognition features:

● Stepped forecastle with 3.9 in gun mounting ('A' position). (3 in twin mounting in João Coutinho class).
● Tall lattice mainmast just forward of midships with large distinctive Plessey ASW 2 air/surface search radar aerial atop.(AWS 2 absent from João Coutinho class, replaced by smaller Kelvin Hughes.)
● Large, single, black-capped funnel with sloping after end.
● 40 mm/70 mounting atop superstructure aft of funnel. (Substituted with 40 mm/60 twin mountings in João Coutinho class).
● Torpedo tubes right aft on quarterdeck. (absent from João Coutinho class).

Displacement full load, tons: 1,380.
Length, feet (metres): 277.5 (84.6).
Beam, feet (metres): 33.8 (10.3).
Draught, feet (metres): 10.2 (3.1), (10.8 (3.3) in João Coutinho class).
Speed, knots: 22.
Range, miles: 5,900 at 18 kts.

Guns: 1 Creusot-Loire 3.9 in (100 mm)/55 Mod 1968. US 3 in (76mm)/50 (twin) Mk 33 in João Coutinho class. 2 Bofors 40 mm/70. (2 Bofors 40 mm/60 (twin) in João Coutinho class).
Torpedoes: 6 324 mm US Mk 32 (2 triple) tubes. Honeywell Mk 46. (Baptista de Andrade class only).

Radars:

Air/surface search — Plessey AWS 2. (Kelvin Hughes in João Coutinho class).
Navigation — Decca RM 316P. (Racal Decca RM 1226C in João Coutinho class).
Fire control — Thomson-CSF Pollux. (Western Electric SPG-34 in João Coutinho class).
Sonars: Thomson-Sintra Diodon; hull-mounted, active search/attack. (Baptista de Andrade class only).

Helicopters: Platform only for 1 Westland Super Lynx Mk 95.

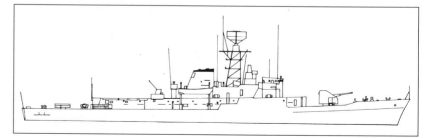

JOÃO ROBY

Descubierta/Modified Descubierta Class

Country: EGYPT, MOROCCO, SPAIN
Country of origin: SPAIN
Ship type: FRIGATES
Class: DESCUBIERTA/MODIFIED DESCUBIERTA (FFG)
Active: 2 (Egypt), 1 (Morocco, Modified Descubierta), 6 (Spain)
EGYPT
Name (Pennant Number): ABU QIR (ex-Serviola) (F 946), EL SUEZ (ex-Centinela) (F 941).
MOROCCO
Name (Pennant Number): LIEUTENANT COLONEL ERRAHAMANI (501).
SPAIN
Name (Pennant Number): DESCUBIERTA (F 31), DIANA (F 32), INFANTA ELENA (F 33), INFANTA CRISTINA (F 34), CAZADORA (F 35), VENCEDORA (F 36)

Recognition features:
- Short forecastle with 3 in gun mounting ('A' position).
- Bofors 375 mm A/S mortar mounting forward of bridge ('B' mounting position).
- Short forward superstructure with pyramid mainmast at after end. WM22/41 or WM25 fire control radome atop.
- Harpoon SSM angled launchers between mainmast and funnels, (Spain and Egypt; MM38 Exocet in Moroccan ship.).
- Unusual, black-capped 'V' formation funnels amidships with a large aerial atop each one.
- Short aftermast aft of funnels supporting DA05 air/surface search radar aerial.
- Two 40 mm/70 gun mountings, on two levels, aft of aftermast. (Breda/Bofors turrets, Morocco).
- Aspide SAM Albatros box launcher on afterdeck ('Y' mounting position).

Displacement full load, tons: 1,666. (Spain). 1,479, (Egypt, Morocco).
Length, feet (metres): 291.3 (88.8).

Beam, feet (metres): 34 (10.4).
Draught, feet (metres): 12.5 (3.8).
Speed, knots: 25.
Range, miles: 4,000 at 18 kts.

Missiles: SSM - 8 McDonnell Douglas Harpoon (2 quad) launchers. Normally 2 pairs are embarked. (MM38 Exocet, Morocco). SAM - Selenia Albatros octuple launcher, Aspide.
Guns: 1 OTO Melara 3 in (76 mm)/62 Compact. 1 or 2 Bofors 40 mm/70, (Spain). 2 Bofors 400 mm/70, (Egypt). 2 Breda Bofors 40 mm/70, (Morocco).
Torpedoes: 6   324 mm US Mk 32 (2 triple) tubes. Honeywell Mk 46 Mod 5, (Spain). (Mod 1 (Morocco). Marconi Stingray, (Egypt).
A/S mortars: 1 Bofors 375 mm twin-barrel, trainable launcher.
Decoys: 2 Loral Hycor SRBOC 6-barrel Mk 36. US Prairie Masker; blade rate suppression, (Spain and Egypt). 2 CSEE Dagaie double trainable launcher, (Morocco).

Radars:
Air/surface search — Signaal DA05/2.
Navigation — Signaal ZW 06.
Fire control — Signaal WM 22/41 or WM 25 system.
Sonars: Raytheon DE 1160B; hull-mounted.

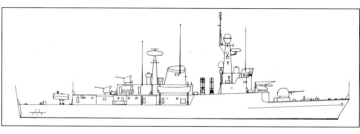

DIANA

Alvand (Vosper Mk 5) Class

Country: IRAN
Country of origin: UNITED KINGDOM
Ship type: FRIGATES
Class: ALVAND (VOSPER MARK 5) (FFG)
Active: 3
Name (Pennant Number): ALVAND (ex-Saam) (71), ALBORZ (ex-Zaal) (72), SABALAN (ex-Rostam) (73).

Recognition features:

- Similar hull and superstructure profile to Pakistani British 'Type 21' frigates.
- Long forecastle with 4.5 in gun mounting ('A' position).
- Short pyramid mainmast just forward of midships.
- Low profile, sloping funnel, well aft with distinctive gas turbine air intakes forward of funnel, port and starboard. AWS 1 air/surface radar aerial immediately forward of funnel.
- Sited on afterdeck, from forward to aft, YJ-2 or Sea Killer II SSM launcher; Limbo A/S mortar and 35 mm/90 twin gun turret mounting.

Displacement full load, tons: 1,350.
Length, feet (metres): 310 (94.5).
Beam, feet (metres): 36.4 (11.1).
Draught, feet (metres): 14.1 (4.3).
Speed, knots: 29.
Range, miles: 3,650 at 18 kts.

Missiles: SSM — YJ-2 (C-802, CSS-N-8 Saccade) (2 twin) (Alborz and Sabalan). 1 Sistel Sea Killer II quin launcher, (Alvand). (Top row of cassettes removed to incorporate BM-21 multiple rocket launcher.)
Guns: 1 Vickers 4.5 in (114 mm)/55 Mk 8. 2 Oerlikon 35mm/90 (twin). 3 Oerlikon GAM-BO1 20 mm. 2 12.7 mm MGs.
A/S mortars: 1 3-tubed Limbo Mk 10.
Decoys: 2 UK Mk 5 rocket flare launchers.

Radars:

Air/surface search — Plessey AWS 1.
Surface search — Racal Decca 1226.
Navigation — Decca 629.
Fire control — 2 Contraves Sea Hunter.
Sonars: Graseby 174; hull-mounted, active search. Graseby 170; hull-mounted, active attack.

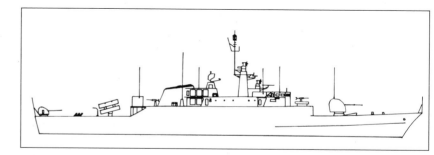

Alvand (Vosper Mk 5) Class

ALVAND

Amazon (Tariq) Type 21 Class

Country: PAKISTAN
Country of origin: UNITED KINGDOM
Ship type: FRIGATES
Class: AMAZON (TARIQ) (TYPE 21) (DDG/DD/FFG/FF)
Active: 6
Name (Pennant Number): TARIQ (ex-Ambuscade) (D 181 (ex-F 172), BABUR (ex-Amazon) (D 182, ex-F 169), KHAIBAR (ex-Arrow) (D 183, ex-F 173), BADR (ex-Alacrity) (D 184, ex-F 185), TIPPU SULTAN (ex-Avenger) (D 185, ex-F 185), SHAHJAHAN (ex-Active) (D 186, ex-F 171).

Recognition features:
- Long forecastle with raised bows.
- 4.5 in gun mounting in 'A' position.
- Harpoon being fitted in 'B' position or forward of funnel in D 186, D 184 and D 182.
- Low superstructure with tall enclosed mast aft of bridge, topped by Type 992R air/surface search radar; being replaced by Signaal DA08 in D 185, D 181, D 183 and D 182.
- Low, squat funnel with sloping top from forward to aft.
- Slim black-painted aftermast immediately forward of funnel.
- LY 60N SAM launcher atop aft end of hangar (replacing Seacat SAM in D 185, D 181 and D 183. Vulcan Phalanx CIWS substituted for Seacat in D 186, D 184 and D182).
- Short helicopter flight deck, with break down to very short quarterdeck.

Displacement full load, tons: 3,700.
Length, feet (metres): 384 (117) oa.
Beam, feet (metres): 41.7 (12.7).
Draught, feet (metres): 19.5 (5.9) screws.
Speed, knots: 30.
Range, miles: 4,000 at 17 kts.

Missiles: SSM — Harpoon 1C in D 182, 184 and 186. SAM — China LY 60N replacing Short Bros. Seacat in D 181, 183 and 185.
Guns: Vickers 4.5 in (114 mm)/55 Mk 8. 4 25 mm/60 (2 twin). 20 mm Vulcan Phalanx Mk 15 replacing Seacat in D 182, 184 and 186. 2 or 4 Oerlikon 20 mm Mk 7A or 1 MSI DS 30B 30 mm/75 and 2 GAM-B01 20 mm.
Torpedoes: 6 324 mm Plessey STWS Mk 2 (2 triple) tubes in D 184 and 186. All to be fitted with Bofors Type 43X2 single or quad launchers.
Decoys: 2 Vickers Corvus 8-tubed trainable launchers. SRBOC Mk 36 launchers being fitted in D 181, 183 and 185. Graseby Type 182 towed torpedo decoy.

Radar:
Air/surface search — Marconi Type 992R; replaced by Signaal DA08 in D 181-3, 185.
Surface search — Kelvin Hughes Type 1006. (Type 1007 in D 182).
Fire control — 2 Selenia Type 912 (RTN 10X).
Sonars: Graseby Type 184P hull-mounted, active search/attack. Kelvin Hughes Type 162M, hull-mounted. Thomson-Marconi ATAS, active.

Helicopters: 1 Westland Lynx HAS 3 (ASW/ASV).

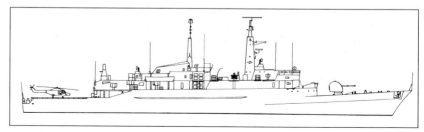

Country: BRAZIL, UNITED KINGDOM
Country of origin: UNITED KINGDOM
Ship type: FRIGATES
Class: BROADSWORD (TYPE 22) (BATCH 1 and 2) (FFG)
Active: 4 Brazil, 6 United Kingdom

Batch 1: BRAZIL

Name (Pennant Number): GREENHALGH (ex-Broadsword) (F 46, ex-F 88), DODSWORTH (ex-Brilliant) (F 47, ex-F 90), BOSISIO (ex-Brazen) (F 48, ex-F 91), RADEMAKER (ex-Battleaxe) (F 49, ex-F 89).

Batch 2: UNITED KINGDOM

Name (Pennant Number): BOXER* (F 92), BEAVER* (F 93), BRAVE† (F 94), LONDON* (ex-Bloodhound) (F 95), SHEFFIELD (F 96), COVENTRY† (F 98)

* Boxer, Beaver and London to be paid off in 1999 following the UK Government's Strategic Defence Review.

†Brave and Coventry will be paid off in 2000 and 2001 respectively.

Recognition features:

- Blunt bow with short forecastle.(Sharper bow in Batch 2).
- Exocet SSM box launcher ('A' mounting position).
- Seawolf SAM six-barrel launcher ('B' mounting position).
- Raised central maindeck section giving high freeboard.
- High enclosed mainmast at after end of forward superstructure.
- Large funnel, aft of midships, with sloping top and black exhausts just protruding at top.
- SATCOM dome atop superstructure just forward of funnel, (UK ships only).
- Large enclosed black-topped aftermast aft of funnel. This mast is only slightly shorter, and similar in size, to the mainmast.
- After superstructure has Type 910/11 fire control radar aerial atop raised forward section and Seawolf SAM 6-barrel launcher atop hangar.
- Flight deck aft with open quarterdeck below.

Note 1 - Batch 2 are some 14 m longer than Batch 1

and have high sweeping bow profile.

Note 2 - Last four Batch 2 have enlarged flight decks to take Sea King or EH 101 Merlin helicopters.

Displacement full load, tons: 4,400. (Batch 1), 4,800 (Batch 2).
Length, feet (metres): 430 (131.2) oa (Batch 1), 485.5 (145.0) oa.,(F 92-93), 480.5 (146.5) oa., (F 94-96, 98)
Beam, feet (metres): 48.5 (14.8).
Draught, feet (metres): 19.9 (6) (Batch 1), 21 (6.4) (Batch 2) (screws).
Speed, knots: 30.
Range, miles: 4,500 at 18 kts.

Missiles: SSM - 4 Aerospatiale MM 38 Exocet, (UK ships). MM 40 Block II Exocet (Brazilian ships). SAM - 2 British Aerospace 6-barrel Seawolf GWS 25 Mod 0 or Mod 4 (except F 94-96 and 98). 2 British Aerospace Seawolf GWS 25 Mod 3 (F 94-96 and 98).
Guns: 4 Oerlikon/BMARC GCM-A03 30 mm/75 (2 twin). 2 Oerlikon/BMARC 20 mm GAM-B01, (UK ships). 2 Bofors 40 mm/70, 2 Oerlikon/BMARC 20 mm GAM-B01, (Brazilian ships).
Torpedoes: 6 324 mm Plessey STWS Mk 2 (2 triple) tubes. Marconi Stingray.
Decoys: 4 Marconi Sea Gnat 130 mm/102 mm 6-barrel fixed launchers. Graseby Type 182; towed torpedo decoy.

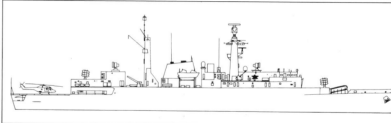

Broadsword Class Type 22 (Batch 1 and 2)

BATTLEAXE

Radars:
Air/surface search — Marconi Type 967/968 (Type 967M in F 94).
Navigation — Kelvin Hughes Type 1006 or Type 1007.
Fire control — 2 Marconi Type 911 or Type 910.
Sonars: Plessey Type 2016 or Ferranti/Thomson-Sintra Type 2050; hull-
  mounted. Dowty Type 2031Z (Batch 2 only) towed array.

Helicopters: 2 Westland Lynx HMA 3/8 (in Batch 2I); or 1 Westland Sea King
HAS 5/6 (or Westland/Agusta EH 101 Merlin HAS 1) (F 94-96 and 98).
(ASW/ASV). (UK ships). 2 Westland Super Lynx SAH-11 (HAS 21).
(ASW/ASV). (Brazilian ships).

Country: UNITED KINGDOM
Country of origin: UNITED KINGDOM
Ship type: FRIGATES
Class: BROADSWORD (TYPE 22) (BATCH 3) (FFG)
Active: 4
Name (Pennant Number): CORNWALL (F 99), CUMBERLAND (F 85), CAMPBELTOWN (F 86), CHATHAM (F 87)

Recognition features:

- Similar in profile to Broadsword class Type 22 Batch 2. Major identification differences are as follows:
- Steeper angle stern profile.
- 4.5 gun mounting ('A' position).
- Harpoon SSM angled launchers forward of mainmast.
- Signaal/GE Goalkeeper CIWS immediately forward of mainmast.

Displacement full load, tons: 4,900.
Length, feet (metres): 485.9 (148.1).
Beam, feet (metres): 48.5 (14.8).
Draught, feet (metres): 21 (6.4).
Speed, knots: 30.
Range, miles: 4,500 at 18 kts.

Missiles: SSM - 8 McDonnell Douglas Harpoon Block 1C (2 quad) launchers. SAM - 2 British Aerospace Seawolf GWS 25 Mod 3.
Guns: 1 Vickers 4.5 in (114 mm)/55 Mk 8. 1 Signaal/General Electric 30 mm 7-barrel Goalkeeper. 2 DES/MSI DS 30B 30 mm/75.
Torpedoes: 6 324 mm Plessey STWS Mk 2 (2 triple) tubes. Marconi Stingray.
Decoys: 4 Marconi Sea Gnat 6-barrel 130 mm/102 mm fixed launchers. Graseby Type 182; towed torpedo decoy.

Radars:

Air/surface search — Marconi Type 967/968.
Navigation — Kelvin Hughes Type 1007.
Fire control — Two Marconi Type 911.
Sonars: Ferranti/Thomson-Sintra Type 2050; hull-mounted, active search/attack. Dowty Type 2031; towed array.

Helicopters: 2 Westland Lynx HMA 3/8; or 1 Westland Sea King HAS 5 (or Westland/Agusta EH 101 Merlin HAS 1 in due course). (ASW/ASV).

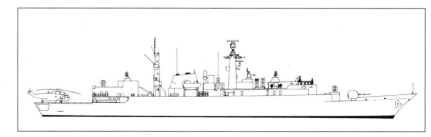

Broadsword Class Type 22 (Batch 3)

CORNWALL

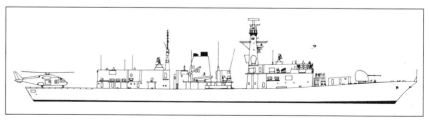

Duke Class (Type 23)

Country: UNITED KINGDOM
Country of origin: UNITED KINGDOM
Ship type: FRIGATES
Class: DUKE (TYPE 23) (FFG)
Active: 13
Building: 2
Proposed: 1
Name (Pennant Number): NORFOLK (F 230), ARGYLL (F 231), LANCASTER (F 229, ex-F 232), MARLBOROUGH (F 233), IRON DUKE (F 234), MONMOUTH (F 235), MONTROSE (F 236), WESTMINSTER (F 237), NORTHUMBERLAND (F 238), RICHMOND (F 239), SOMERSET (F 82), GRAFTON (F 80), SUTHERLAND (F 81), KENT (F 78), PORTLAND (F 79), ST ALBANS (F 83).

Recognition features:

- High bow with continuous maindeck through to stern.
- Three major weapons sited on forecastle from the bow aft, 4.5 in gun mounting, Seawolf SAM VLS launchers, Harpoon SSM angled launchers.
- Forward superstructure has large enclosed mainmast at after end with distinctive SATCOM domes, port and starboard, on wing platforms at its base.
- Unusual square section funnel amidships with two large black exhausts protruding from the top forward edge.
- Square profile after superstructure with short pyramid mast at forward edge.
- Flight deck aft.

Note - All vertical surfaces have a 7o slope and rounded edges to reduce IR emissions.

Displacement full load, tons: 4,200.
Length, feet (metres): 436.2 (133).
Beam, feet (metres): 52.8 (16.1).
Draught, feet (metres): 18 (5.5) (screws)

Speed, knots: 28.
Range, miles: 7800 at 15 kts.

Missiles: SSM - McDonnell Douglas Harpoon (2 quad) launchers. SAM - British Aerospace Seawolf GWS 26 Mod 1 VLS.
Guns: 1 Vickers 4.5 in (114 mm)/55 Mk 8. 2 DES/MSI 30B 30 mm/75.
Torpedoes: 4 Cray Marine 324 mm (2 twin) tubes. Marconi Stingray.
Decoys: 4 Marconi Sea Gnat 6-barrel 130 mm/102 mm launchers. Graseby Type 182; towed torpedo decoy.

Radars:

Air/surface search — Plessey Type 996(1), 3D.
Navigation — Kelvin Hughes Type 1007 or Racal Decca Type 1008.
Fire control — 2 Marconi Type 911.
Sonars: Ferranti/Thomson-Sintra Type 2050; bow-mounted, active search/attack. Dowty Type 2031Z; towed array. (F 229-239). To be replaced by Type 2087 from 2003.

Helicopters: 1 Westland Lynx HMA 3/8 or Westland/Agusta EH 101 Merlin HAS 1. (ASV/ASW).

NORFOLK

Leander/Broad-beamed Leander class

Country: CHILE, ECUADOR, INDIA, NEW ZEALAND, PAKISTAN
Country of origin: UNITED KINGDOM
Ship type: FRIGATES
Class: LEANDER/LEANDER BROAD-BEAMED /NILGIRI (FF/FFG)
Active: 4 Chile, (Leander/FFG). Ecuador, (Leander/FFG). India, (Nilgiri/FF). New Zealand, (Broad-beamed Leander/FF). 2 Pakistan, (Broad-beamed Leander/FF)

CHILE
Name (Pennant Number): CONDELL (06), LYNCH (07), MINISTRO ZENTENO (ex-Achilles) (08, ex-F 12), GENERAL BAQUEDANO (ex-Ariadne) (09, ex-F 72).

ECUADOR
Name (Pennant Number): PRESIDENTE ELOY ALFARO (ex-Penelope) (FM 01, ex-F 127), MORAN VALVERDE (ex-Danae) (FM 02 (ex-F 47).

INDIA
Name (Pennant Number): HIMGIRI (F 34), UDAYGIRI (F 35), DUNAGIRI (F 36), TARAGIRI (F 41), VINDHYAGIRI (F 42).

NEW ZEALAND
Name (Pennant Number): WELLINGTON (ex-Bacchante) (F 69), CANTERBURY (F 421).

PAKISTAN
Name (Pennant Number): ZULFIQUAR (ex-Apollo) (F 262), SHAMSHER (ex-Diomede) (F 263).

Recognition features
- High forecastle, break at after end of bridge with continuous maindeck to stern
- 4.5 in gun twin mounting at 'A' position. (Shorts Seacat SAM and MM 38 Exocet SSM launchers on forecastle in Ecuadorian ships).
- Substantial midships superstructure with tall enclosed mainmast aft of bridge.
- Single funnel just aft of bridge. (Extensions fitted to funnel uptakes on Canterbury).

- After superstructure has large enclosed aftermast atop. (Chilean ships have MM 40 Exocet launchers adjacent to after superstructure (F 06, 07) and alongside funnel (F 08 and 09).
- Larger hangars for Chetak or Sea King helicopters in Indian ships Taragiri and Vindhyagiri.
Note 1 - India acquired Broad-beamed Leander frigate Andromeda in 1995 from UK and converted her into the training ship Krishna, (F 46). Armament reduced.
Note 2 - The six Ahmad Yani (Van Speijk) class FFGs of the Indonesia Navy based on Leander design) and acquired 1986-90 from the Netherlands.
Note 3 - Australia has 1 'River' class frigate, Torrens, a design based on the 'Leander' class.

Displacement, full load, tons: 3,200. 2,945 (Broad-beamed); 2,962, (Chilean, Pakistan and Indian ships).
Length, feet (metres): 372 (113.4) oa.
Beam, feet (metres): 41 (12.5). 43 (13.1), (Broad-beamed).
Draught, feet (metres): 18 (5.6) (screws).
Speed, knots: 28 (29, Chile).
Range, miles: 5,500 at 15 kts. (NZ) 4,000 at 15 kts (Ecuador, Pakistan).

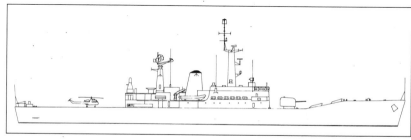

Leander/Broad-beamed Leander class

Missiles: SSM - MM 38/40 Exocet (Chile). MM 38 Exocet (Ecuador). SAM — Short Bros Seacat GWS 22 quad launchers in Chilean and Ecuadorian units, (non-operational in the latter.) No missiles fitted in Indian, NZ and Pakistan ships.

Guns: Vickers 4.5 in (114 mm)/45 Mk 6 (twin) semi-automatic. (Not Ecuador). 2 Bofors 40 mm/60 Mk 9 (Ecuador); 1 GE/GD 20 mm Vulcan Phalanx CIWS Mk 15, Mod 11, (NZ). 4 30 mm/65 (2 twin) AK 630, (India). 6 25 mm/60 (3 twin), (Pakistan). 2 Oerlikon/BMARC 20 mm GAM-B01 (Ecuador). 4 Oerlikon 20 mm Mk 9 (2 twin), (Chile). 2 Oerlikon 20 mm/70, (India). 4 or 6 12.7 mm MGs, (NZ).

A/S mortars: UK MoD Mortar Mk 10, 3-barrel. (Pakistan). 1 Limbo Mk 10 triple-tubed launcher (India —except Taragiri and Vindhyagiri which have Bofors 375 mm twin-tubed launcher). (No mortars in other units).

Torpedoes: 6 324 mm Mk 32 (2 triple) Honeywell Mk 46, Mod 2, (Chile and NZ only).

Decoys: 2 Loral Hycor SRBOC Mk 36 6-barrel launchers. (NZ). Graseby Type 182 towed torpedo decoy, (Ecuador, NZ and Pakistan). Graseby Type 738 towed torpedo decoy, (India). 2 Vickers Corvus 8-barrel chaff launchers. (Chile, Ecuador, Pakistan). Wallop Barricade double layer chaff launchers, (Chile).

ANDROMEDA

Radars:

Air Search — Marconi Type 965/966 (Chile, Ecuador, Pakistan). Signaal LW08 (India, NZ).

Surface search — Marconi Type 992 Q or Plessey Type 994 (F 08), (Chile). Plessey Type 994, (Ecuador). Plessey Type 993 (NZ, Pakistan). Signaal ZW06, (India).

Navigation — 1 Kelvin Hughes Type 1006 (Chile, Ecuador, NZ, Pakistan). Decca 1226, Signaal M 45, (India).

Fire control — RCA TR 76 (NZ). Plessey Type 903/904, (Chile, Ecuador, Pakistan).

Sonars: Graseby Type 184M/P, hull-mounted, active search/attack; Graseby Type 170 B, hull-mounted, active; Kelvin Hughes Type 162M hull-mounted, sideways-looking, (Chile, Pakistan). Graseby Type 184P/Kelvin Hughes Type 162M, (Ecuador, Pakistan). Westinghouse SQS-505/Graseby 750 (India). Westinghouse VDS in first three Indian ships. Graseby Type750/Kelvin Hughes Type 162M (NZ).

Helicopters: 1 Bell 206B JetRanger (ASW) or Nurtanio NAS 332C Cougar (ASV/ASW) (Chile, F 06 and 07.) Bell 206B JetRanger (Ecuador). 1 HAL SA 319B Chetak (Alouette III) (ASW) in first three Indian ships; 1 Sea King Mk 42A (ASW) in Taragiri and Vindhyagiri. 1 Kaman SH-2G. Seasprite, (NZ). 1 Aerospatiale SA 319B Alouette III (ASW), (Pakistan).

Country: MALAYSIA
Country of origin: UNITED KINGDOM
Ship type: FRIGATES
Class: LEKIU (FFG)
Active: 2
Name (Pennant Number): LEKIU (30), JEBAT (29)

Recognition features:

- High bow with straight leading edge sloping down towards bridge.
- 57 mm gun mounting ('A' position).
- Seawolf VLS SAM launchers immediately forward of bridge ('B' position).
- Raised angular bridge structure with all-round windows.
- Large enclosed mainmast amidships with sloping forward edge and vertical after edge.
- Distinctive DA08 air search radar aerial atop aftermast.
- Very large square section funnel with shallow sloping after edge abaft aftermast.
- Steeply sloping hangar doors down to large, low profile flight deck.

Displacement full load, tons: 2,270.
Length, feet (metres): 346 (105.5) oa.
Beam, feet (metres): 42 (12.8).
Draught, feet (metres): 11.8 (3.6).
Speed, knots: 28.
Range, miles: 5,000 at 14 kts.

Missiles: SSM - 8 Aerospatiale MM 40 Exocet, Block 2. SAM - British Aerospace VLS Seawolf.
Guns: 1 Bofors 57 mm/70 SAK Mk 2. 2 MSI Defense Systems 30 mm/75 DS 30B.
Torpedoes: 6 Whitehead B 515 324 mm (2 triple) tubes.
Decoys: 2 Super Barricade 12-barrel launchers. Graseby Sea Siren torpedo decoy.

Radars:
Air search — Signaal DA08.
Surface search — Ericsson Sea Giraffe 150HC.
Navigation — Racal.
Fire control — 2 Marconi 1802.
Sonars: Thomson-Sintra Spherion; hull-mounted, active search/attack.

Helicopters: 1 Westland Wasp HAS 1.

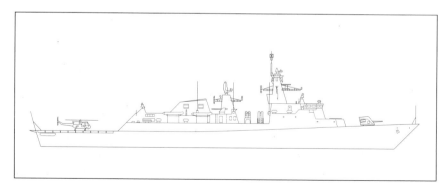

JEBAT

Country: BANGLADESH
Country of origin: UNITED KINGDOM
Ship type: FRIGATES
Class: LEOPARD (TYPE 41) (FF)
Active: 2
Name (Pennant Number): ABU BAKR (ex-Lynx) (F 15), ALI HAIDER (ex-Jaguar) (F 17)

Recognition features:

- Raised forecastle with break down to 4.5 in gun mounting.
- Type 275 fire control director atop after end of bridge roof.
- Two masts, lattice foremast immediately aft of fire control director, enclosed mainmast supporting single bedstead Type 965 air search radar aerial.
- Engine exhausts from short funnel inside lattice mainmast and at top after end of aftermast.
- 4.5 in gun mounting ('Y' position).
- Break in maindeck down to very short quarterdeck.

Displacement full load, tons: 2,520.
Length, feet (metres): 339.8 (103.6).
Beam, feet (metres): 40 (12.2).
Draught, feet (metres): 15.5 (4.7) (screws).
Speed, knots: 24.
Range, miles: 7,500 at 16 kts.
Guns: 4 Vickers 4.5 in (115 mm)/45 (2 twin) Mk 6. 1 Bofors 40 mm/60 Mk 9.

Radars:

Air search — Marconi Type 965 with single AKE 1 array.
Air/surface search — Plessey Type 993.
Navigation — Decca Type 978; Kelvin Hughes Type 1007.
Fire control — Type 275.

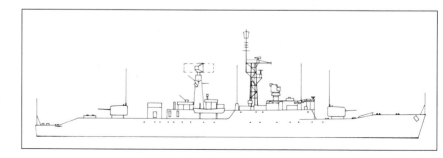

Leopard Class

ALI HAIDER

Niteroi Class

Country: BRAZIL
Country of origin: UNITED KINGDOM
Ship type: FRIGATES
Class: NITEROI
Active: 6
Name (Pennant Number): NITEROI (F 40), DEFENSORA (F 41), CONSTITUIÇÃO (F 42*), LIBERAL (F 43*), INDEPENDÊNCIA (F 44), UNIÃO (F 45)

*General Purpose design. Remainder are anti-submarine configuration.

Recognition features:

- General Purpose design -
- Short forecastle with 4.5 in gun mounting ('A' position) and Bofors 375 mm A/S mortar launcher ('B' mounting position).
- High forward superstructure flush with ship's side.
- Foremast at after end of forward superstructure.
- Pyramid mainmast immediately forward of funnel supporting air/surface search radar aerial.
- Squat, wide, black-capped funnel sited just aft of midships. Funnel has sloping top from forward to aft.
- Flight deck on maindeck level with break down to long quarterdeck with 4.5 in mounting ('Y' position). Liberal has Albatros octuple launcher for Aspide SAM.
- Ships boats, in davits, port and starboard, adjacent to funnel.

Note 1 - AIS design hulls have longer flight deck (hence shorter quarterdeck) and Ikara A/S missile launcher (Y mounting position).

Note 2 - Modified Niteroi class Brasil serves as training ship with pennant number U 27. Only 2 Bofors 40mm/70 are carried, together with 4 saluting guns.

Displacement full load, tons: 3,707.
Length, feet (metres): 424 (129.2).
Beam, feet (metres): 44.2 (13.5).
Draught, feet (metres): 18.2 (5.5) (sonar).
Speed, knots: 30.
Range, miles: 5,300 at 17 kts.

Missiles: SSM - Aerospatiale MM 40 Exocet (2 twin) launchers. SAM - 2 Short Bros Seacat triple launchers. Being replaced by Albatros octuple launcher for Aspide. A/S - 1 Ikara launcher (Branik standard) (A/S version); payload Mk 46 torpedoes.
Guns: 1 or 2 Vickers 4.5 in (115 mm)/55 Mk 8 (GP version). A/S version only has 1 mounting. 2 Bofors 40 mm/70. Being replaced by Bofors SAK 40mm/70 Mk 3.
Torpedoes: 6 324 mm Plessey STWS-1 (2 triple) tubes. Honeywell Mk 46 Mod 5.
A/S mortars: 1 Bofors 375 mm rocket launcher (twin-tube).
Depth charges: 1 rail; 5 charges (GP version).
Decoys: 2 Plessey Shield chaff launchers.

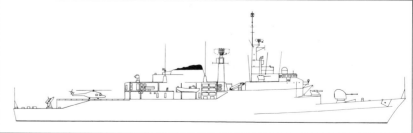

Niteroi Class

DEFENSORA

Radars:
Air/surface search — Plessey AWS 3.
Surface search — Signaal ZW06.
Fire control — 2 Selenia Orion RTN 10X.

Sonars: EDO 610E Mod 1; hull-mounted active search/attack. EDO 700E VDS (F 40 and 41).

Helicopters: 1 Westland Super Lynx SAH-11. (ASW).

Salisbury Class

Country: BANGLADESH
Country of origin: UNITED KINGDOM
Ship type: FRIGATES
Class: SALISBURY (TYPE 61) (FF)
Active: 1
Name (Pennant Number): UMAR FAROOQ (ex-Llandaff) (F 16)

Recognition features:
- Raised forecastle with break down to 4.5 in gun mounting ('A' position).
- Low superstructure with Type 275 fire control director at after end of bridge.
- Two large, black-topped mast and funnel combined structures, aftermast supporting double bedstead Type 965 air search radar aerial.
- Engine exhausts at top after end of masts.
- Short lattice mast supporting Type 278M height finder radar aerial between forward mast and fire control director.
- 40 mm/60 gun mounting ('Y' position).
- Break down to short quarterdeck.

Displacement full load, tons: 2,408.
Length, feet (metres): 339.8 (103.6).
Beam, feet (metres): 40 (12.2).
Draught, feet (metres): 15.5 (4.7).
Speed, knots: 24.
Range, miles: 7,500 at 16 kts.

Guns: 2 Vickers 4.5 in (115 mm)/45 (twin) Mk 6. 2 Bofors 40 mm/60 Mk 9.
A/S mortars: 1 triple-barrelled Squid Mk 4.

Radars:
Air search — Marconi Type 965 with double AKE 2 array.
Air/surface search — Plessey Type 993.
Height finder — Type 278M.
Navigation — Decca Type 978.
Fire control — Type 275.
Sonars: Type 174; hull-mounted, active search/attack. Graseby Type 170B; hull-mounted.

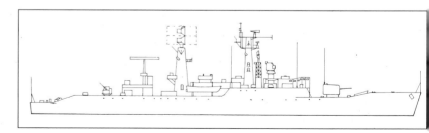

UMAR FAROOQ

Tribal/Khristina Tiyahahu Class

Country: INDONESIA
Country of origin: UNITED KINGDOM
Ship type: FRIGATES
Class: TRIBAL/KHRISTINA TIYAHAU (FFG)
Active: 3
Name (Pennant Number): MARTHA KRISTINA TIYAHAHU (ex-Zulu) (331), WILHELMUS ZAKARIAS YOHANNES (ex-Gurkha) (332), HASANUDDIN (Ex-Tartar) (333)

Recognition features:

- 4.5 in gun mounting ('A' position).
- Large lattice mainmast, forward of midships, supporting single Type 965 bedstead air search radar.
- Twin funnels, after one slightly shorter.
- Limbo A/S mortar mounting between after funnel and hangar.
- Helicopter landing pad, on hangar roof, forward of after 4.5 in mounting ('Y' position).

Note - Helicopter descends to hangar by flight deck lift and is covered by portable panels.

Displacement full load, tons: 2,700.
Length, feet (metres): 360 (109.7) oa.
Beam, feet (metres): 42.5 (13).
Draught, feet (metres): 12.5 (3.8) (keel).
Speed, knots: 25.
Range, miles: 5,400 at 12 kts.

Missiles: SAM - 2 Matra Simbad twin launchers for Mistral.
Guns: 2 Vickers 4.5 in (114 mm). 2 Oerlikon 20 mm. 2 12.7 mm MGs.
A/S mortars: 1 Limbo 3-tubed Mk 10.
Decoys: 2 Knebworth Corvus 8-tubed chaff launchers.

Radars:
Air search — Marconi Type 965.
Surface search — Type 993.
Navigation — Decca 978.
Fire control — Plessey Type 903.
Sonars: Graseby Type 177; hull-mounted active search. Graseby Type 170 B; hull-mounted, active attack. Kelvin Hughes Type 162.

Helicopters: 1 Westland Wasp HAS Mk 1 (ASW)

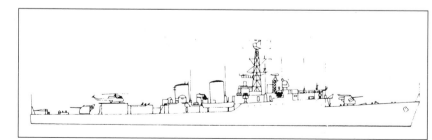

Tribal/Khristina Tiyahahu Class

WILHELMUS ZAKARIAS YOHANNES

Knox/Baleares (F 70) Class

Country: EGYPT, GREECE, MEXICO, SPAIN, TAIWAN, THAILAND, TURKEY
Country of origin: USA/SPAIN
Ship type: FRIGATES
Class: KNOX/EPIRUS/BALEARES (F 70)/TEPE CLASS (FF/FFG)
Active: 2 Egypt, 3 Greece (Epirus class), 2 Mexico (FF), 8 Taiwan, 2 Thailand, 8 Turkey (Tepe class), 5 Spain (Baleares class)

EGYPT
Name (Pennant Number): DAMYAT (ex-Jesse L Brown) (961, ex-FF 1089), RASHEED (ex-Moinester) (966, ex-FF 1097).

GREECE
Name (Pennant Number): EPIRUS (ex-Connole) (F 456, ex-FF 1056), THRACE (ex-Trippe) (F 457, ex-FF 1075), MAKEDONIA (ex-Vreeland) (F 458, ex-FF 1068).

MEXICO
Name (Pennant Number): — (ex-Stein) (—, ex-FF 1065), — (ex-Marvin Shields) (—, ex-FF 1066).

TAIWAN
Name (Pennant Number): CHIN YANG (ex-Robert E Peary) (932, ex-FF 1073), FONG YANG (ex-Brewton) (933, ex-FF 1086), FENG YANG (ex-Kirk) (934, ex-FF 1087), LAN YANG (ex-Joseph Hewes) (935, ex-FF 1078), HAE YANG (ex-Cook) (936, ex-FF 1083), HWAI YANG (ex-Barbey) (937 ex-FF 1088), — (ex-Downes) (938, ex-FF 1070), — (ex-Aylwin) (939, ex-FF 1081).

THAILAND
Name (Pennant Number): PHUTTHAYOTFA CHULALOK (ex-Truett) (461, ex-FF 1095), PHUTTHALOETLA NAPHALAI (ex-Ouellet) (462, ex-FF 1077).

TURKEY
Name (Pennant Number): MUAVENET (ex-Capodanno) (F 250, ex-FF 1093), ADATEPE (ex-Fanning) (F 251, ex-FF 1076), KOCATEPE (ex-Reasoner) (F 252, ex-FF 1063), ZAFER (ex-Thomas C Hart) (F 253, ex-FF 1092) TRAKYA (ex-McCandless) (F 254, ex-FF

1084), KARADENIZ (ex-Donald B Beary) (F 255, ex-FF 1085), EGE (ex-Ainsworth) (F 256, ex-FF 1090), AKDENIZ (ex-Bowen) (F 257, ex-FF 1079).

SPAIN
Name (Pennant Number): BALEARES (F 71), ANDALUCÍA (F 72), CATALUÑA (F 73), ASTURIAS (F 74), EXTREMADURA (F 75)

Recognition features:
- Long forecastle with 5 in gun mounting well forward of ASROC A/S box missile launcher.
- Very unusual large cylindrical mast and funnel combined amidships; air search radar aerial at forward end and short lattice mast atop after end supporting large surface search radar aerial.
- Baleares class has Harpoon launchers atop aft low superstructure, immediately aft of short lattice mast omitted from other 'Knox' class units.
- CIWS in 'Y' position on 'Knox' class ships. Standard SAM launch in 'X' position at aft end of superstructure in Baleares class.
- Flight deck aft, 'Knox' class ships.

Note - Baleares class built in Spain after very close co-operation between Spain and the USA. 'Knox' class units transferred from the US Navy.

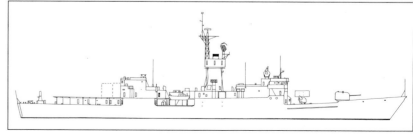

Knox/Baleares (F 70) Class

Displacement full load, tons: 4,177 (Baleares class). 4,260 ('Knox' class).
Length, feet (metres): 438 (133.6), (Baleares class) 439.6 (134), ('Knox' class).
Beam, feet (metres): 46.9 (14.3), (Baleares class). 46.8 (14.3), ('Knox' class).
Draught, feet (metres): 15.4 (4.7), (Baleares class) 15 (4.6), ('Knox' class).
Speed, knots: 28, (Baleares class). 27, ('Knox' class).
Range, miles: 4, 000 at 22 kts

Missiles: SSM - 8 McDonnell Douglas Harpoon (4 normally carried).   SAM - 16 GDC Pomona Standard SM-1MR; Mk 22 Mod 0 launcher.   A/S - Honeywell ASROC Mk 112 octuple launcher; payload Mk 46 torpedoes, (Baleares class). SSM - McDonnell Douglas Harpoon. (Not Mexican units).A/S — ASROC Mk 16 octuple launcher (with 2 cells modified to fire Harpoon), ('Knox' class). Greek ships have Stinger or Redeye SAM posts fitted.
Guns: 1 FMC 5 in (127 mm)/54 Mk 42 Mod 9, (all ships). 2 Bazan 20 mm/120 12-barrel Meroka, (Baleares class). 1 GE/GD 20 mm/76 Vulcan Phalanx Mk 15, ('Knox' class). 2 Rheinmetall 20 mm; 4 12.7 mm MGs, (Greek ships). 4 Type 75 20 mm (Taiwanese ships).
Torpedoes: 4 324 mm US Mk 32 (2 twin) tubes. Honeywell Mk 46 Mod 5. (all ships). 2 484 mm US Mk 25 stern tubes. Westinghouse Mk 37; no longer used. (Baleares class).
Mines: Rail for 8 mines can be fitted in Greek ships.
Decoys: 4 Loral Hycor SRBOC 6-barrelled Mk 36, (all ships). T Mk-6 Fanfare/SLQ-25 Nixie torpedo decoy. Prairie Masker hull and blade rate noise suppression, ('Knox' class).

Radars:
Air search — Hughes SPS-52B, 3D. (Baleares class) Lockheed SPS-40B/D ('Knox' class).

BALEARES

Surface search — Raytheon SPS-10 (Baleares class). SPS-10 or Norden SPS-67. ('Knox' class).
Navigation — Raytheon Marine Pathfinder, (Baleares class). Marconi LN66 ('Knox' class).
Fire control — Western Electric SPG-53B. Raytheon SPG-51C. Selenia RAN 12L. 2 Sperry VPS 2, (Baleares class). SPG-53A/D/F ('Knox' class).
Sonars: Raytheon SQS-56 (DE 1160); hull-mounted. EDO SQS-35V; VDS, (Baleares class). EDO/GE SQS-26CX ('Knox' class).

Helicopters: 1 Kaman SH-2G Seasprite, (Egyptian ships). 1 Agusta AB 212 (ASW), (Greek ships).   1 MBB BO 105CB (Patrol), (Mexico). 1 Kaman SH-2F Seasprite LAMPS 1 , (Taiwan). 1 Bell 212, (Thai ships). 1 Agusta AB 212 (ASW) (Turkish ships).

Oliver Hazard Perry/Adelaide/Santa María/
Cheng Kung/Gaziantep Class

Country: AUSTRALIA, BAHRAIN, EGYPT, SPAIN, TAIWAN, TURKEY, UNITED STATES OF AMERICA

Country of origin: UNITED STATES OF AMERICA

Ship type: FRIGATES

Class: OLIVER HAZARD PERRY/ADELAIDE /SANTA MARÍA/CHENG KUNG/GAZIANTEP (FFGs)

Active: 6 Australia, 1 Bahrain, 4 Egypt, 6 Spain (Santa María class), 7 Taiwan (Cheng Kung class), Turkey (Gaziantep class)*, 39 USA

*A further three US Oliver Hazard Perry class ships may possibly be transferred to Turkey in 1999. These are Tisdale (FFG 27), Reid (FFG 30) plus Duncan (FFG 10) for spares.

AUSTRALIA

Name (Pennant Number): ADELAIDE (01), CANBERRA (02), SYDNEY (03), DARWIN (04), MELBOURNE (05), NEWCASTLE (06).

BAHRAIN

Name (Pennant Number): SABHA (ex-Jack Williams) (90, ex-FFG 24).

EGYPT

Name (Pennant Number): MUBARAK (ex-Copeland) (F 911, ex-FFG 25), TABA (ex-Gallery) (F 916, ex-FFG 26), EL ARISH (ex-Fahrion) (——, ex-FFG 22), ———, (ex-Lewis B Puller), (——, ex-FFG 23).

SPAIN

Name (Pennant Number): SANTA MARÍA (F 81), VICTORIA (F 82), NUMANCIA (F 83), REINA SOFÍA (ex-América) (F 84), NAVARRA (F 85), CANARIAS (F 86).

TAIWAN

Name (Pennant Number): CHENG KUNG (1101), CHENG HO (1103), CHI KUANG (1105), YUEH FEI (1106), TZU-I (1107), PAN CHAO (1108), CHANG CHIEN (1109).

TURKEY

Name (Pennant Number): GAZIANTEP (ex-Clifton Sprague) (F 490, ex-FFG 16), GIRESUN (ex-Antrim) (F 491, ex-FFG 20), GEMLIK (ex-Flatley) (F 492, ex-FFG 21).

USA

Name (Pennant Number): McINERNEY (FFG 8), WADSWORTH (FFG 9), CLARK (FFG 11), GEORGE PHILIP (FFG 12), SAMUEL ELIOT MORISON (FFG 13), JOHN H SIDES (FFG 14), ESTOCIN (FFG 15), JOHN A MOORE (FFG 19), BOONE (FFG 28), STEPHEN W GROVES (FFG 29), REID (FFG 30), STARK (FFG 31), JOHN L HALL (FFG 32), JARRETT (FFG 33), UNDERWOOD (FFG 36), CROMMELIN (FFG 37), CURTS (FFG 38), DOYLE (FFG 39), HALYBURTON (FFG 40), McCLUSKY (FFG 41), KLAKRING (FFG 42), THACH (FFG 43), De WERT (FFG 45), RENTZ (FFG 46), NICHOLAS (FFG 47), VANDEGRIFT (FFG 48), ROBERT G BRADLEY (FFG 49), TAYLOR (FFG 50), GARY (FFG 51), CARR (FFG 52), HAWES (FFG 53), FORD (FFG 54), ELROD (FFG 55), SIMPSON (FFG 56), REUBEN JAMES (FFG 57), SAMUEL B ROBERTS (FFG 58), KAUFFMAN (FFG 59), RODNEY M DAVIS (FFG 60), INGRAHAM (FFG 61)

Recognition features:

- High bow with raised, solid sides to forward end of forecastle.
- Standard/Harpoon SAM/SSM launcher in 'A' mounting position. (Hsiung Feng SSM angled launchers between masts in Taiwanese ships. SAM launcher only in 'A' position).

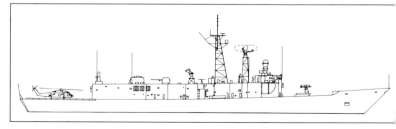

Oliver Hazard Perry/Adelaide/Santa María/ Cheng Kung/Gaziantep Class

- Slab-sided, box-like superstructure running from forecastle to flight deck.
- Distinctive WM28 fire control radar dome atop the bridge (RCA Mk 92 in Spanish ships; Unisys Mk 92 in Taiwanese units) with the lattice foremast immediately aft supporting large curved SPS-49 air search radar aerial.
- Large lattice mainmast just forward of midships.
- 3 in gun mounting forward of funnel.
- Low single funnel just showing towards after end of superstructure.
- After end of superstructure flush with ship's side.
- Vulcan Phalanx CIWS mounting atop after end of hangar roof, (Meroka CIWS in Spanish ships).
- Bofors 40mm/70 gun mountings on sponsons outboard of superstructure just forward of funnel. (Taiwanese ships only).

Displacement full load, tons: 4,100, (4,105, Taiwan). 3,638, (Bahrain, Egypt, Turkey, US FFG 9, 11-14, 19, 30-31, 33.) 3,969, (Spain).
Length, feet (metres): 453 (138.1). 445 (135.6), (Bahrain, Egypt, Turkey, US FFG 9, 11-14, 19, 30-31, 33). 451.2 (137.7), (Spain).
Beam, feet (metres): 45 (13.7). 46.9 (14.3), (Spain).
Draught, feet (metres): 14.8 (4.5).
Speed, knots: 29.
Range, miles: 4,500 at 20 kts.

Missiles: SSM - McDonnell Douglas Harpoon. SAM - GDC Pomona Standard SM-1MR. Mk 13 Mod 4 launcher for both SAM and SSM systems. (Hsiung Feng II (2 quad) SSM in Taiwanese ships). RAM fitted to US ships in due course.
Guns: 1 OTO Melara 3 in (76 mm)/62 Mk 75 Compact.1 GE/GD 20 mm/76 Mk 15 Vulcan Phalanx. Up to 6 - 12.7 mm MGs, (not Taiwan). (1 Bazán 20 mm/120 12-barrel Meroka Mod 2A or 2B CIWS, Spain). (2 additional Bofors 40mm/70; and 3 20 mm Type 75 on hangar roof, when fitted, Taiwan only). (2 McDonnell Douglas 25 mm Mk 38 can be fitted amidships in US ships).
Torpedoes: 6 324 mm Mk 32 (2 triple) tubes. Honeywell Mk 46 Mod 5.

Decoys: 2 Loral Hycor SRBOC 6-barrel Mk 36. SLQ-25 Nixie; towed torpedo decoy. (Prairie Masker hull noise/blade rate suppression in Spanish ships). (4 Kung Fen 6 chaff launchers, Taiwan only).

STARK

Radars:
Air search — Raytheon SPS-49(V)4 or 5.
Surface search/navigation — ISC Cardion SPS-55. (Raytheon SPS-55 in Spanish ships).
Navigation — Furuno. (Raytheon 1650/9 or SPS-67 in Spanish ships).
Fire control — Lockheed STIR (Modified SPG-60). Sperry Mk 92 (Signaal WM 28). (RCA Mk 92 Mod 2/6, Signaal STING, Selenia RAN 30L/X (RAN 12L + RAN 30X) in Spanish ships). (USN UD 417 STIR, Unisys Mk 92 Mod 6 in Taiwanese ships).
Sonars: Raytheon SQS-53B, hull-mounted, active search/attack. Gould SQR-18A passive towed array, (Turkish ships). Raytheon SQS-56 hull-mounted, (Australia/Bahrain/Egypt). Raytheon SQS-56 (DE 1160) hull-mounted and Gould SQR-19(V)2 tactical towed array, (Spanish ships). Raytheon SQS-56/DE 1160P and SQR-18A(V)2 passive towed array or BAe/Thomson-Sintra ATAS towed array, Taiwan). Raytheon SQQ-89(V)2; hull-mounted, active search/attack, (US ships).

Helicopters: 2 Sikorsky S-70B-2 Seahawks, or 1 Seahawk and 1 Aerospatiale AS 350B Squirrel, (Australia). 2 (normally only 1 embarked), Sikorsky SH-70L Seahawk (LAMPS III, Spain). 2 Sikorsky S-70C(M) Thunderhawks (only 1 embarked), (Taiwan). 2 Kaman SH-2G Seasprite (LAMPS 1) (Egypt/US) or 2 Sikorsky SH-60B LAMPS III. (ASW/ASV/OTHT). (US ships).

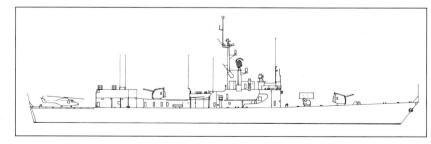

Pará Class

Country: BRAZIL
Country of origin: UNITED STATES OF AMERICA
Ship type: FRIGATES
Class: PARÁ (ex-US GARCIA) (FF)
Active: 4
Name (Pennant Number): PARÁ (ex-Albert David) (D 27, ex-FF 1050), PARAÍBA (ex-Davidson) (D 28, ex-FF 1045), PARANÁ (ex-Sample) (D 29, ex-FF 1048), PERNAMBUCO (ex-Bradley) (D 30, ex-FF 1041)

Recognition features:

- Very long forecastle with continuous maindeck line from stem to stern.
- 5 in gun mounting on forecastle approximately mid-point between bow and bridge.
- ASROC A/S missile box launcher between forward mounting and bridge.
- Single black-capped funnel amidships.
- Mast and funnel combined with pole mast atop after end. Large air search radar aerial at forward end of funnel.
- 5 in gun mounting atop after superstructure forward of hangar.
- Flight deck right aft.

Displacement full load, tons: 3,560.
Length, feet (metres): 414.5 (126.3).
Beam, feet (metres): 44.2 (13.5).
Draught, feet (metres): 14.5 (4.4) keel.
Speed, knots: 27.5.
Range, miles: 4,000 at 20 kts.

Missiles: A/S - Honeywell ASROC Mk 112 octuple launcher.
Guns: 2 USN 5 in (127 mm)/38 Mk 30.
Torpedoes: 6 324 mm Mk 32 (2 triple) tubes. 14 Honeywell Mk 46 Mod 5 Neartip.
Decoys: 2 Loral Hycor Mk 33 RBOC 6-tubed launchers. Mk T-6 Fanfare; torpedo decoy system. Prairie/Masker; hull/blade rate noise suppression.

Radars:
Air search — Lockheed SPS-40B.
Surface search — Raytheon SPS-10C.
Navigation — Marconi LN 66.
Fire control — General Electric Mk 35.
Sonars: EDO/General Electric SQS-26 AXR (D 29 and 30) or SQS-26B; bow-mounted.

Helicopters: Westland Super Lynx SAH-11.

PERNAMBUCO

Inhaúma Class

Country: BRAZIL
Country of origin: BRAZIL
Ship type: CORVETTES
Class: INHAÚMA (FSG)
Active: 4
Name (Pennant Number): INHAÚMA (V 30), JACEGUAY (V 31), JULIO DE
NORONHA (V 32), FRONTIN (V 33)

Recognition features:

- Apart from forecastle and quarterdeck, unusually high freeboard superstructure, flush with ship's side.
- 4.5 in gun mounting ('A' position).
- Steep fronted, high forward superstructure.
- Large enclosed mainmast at after end of forward superstructure topped by slender lattice mast.
- Lattice aftermast atop forward end of after superstructure.
- Squat, tapered, black-capped funnel aft of midships atop after superstructure.
- 40 mm/70 gun mountings at after end of superstructure, port and starboard.
- Flight deck on maindeck level forward of break down to quarterdeck.

Displacement full load, tons: 1,970.
Length, feet (metres): 314.2 (95.8).
Beam, feet (metres): 37.4 (11.4).
Draught, feet (metres): 12.1 (5.3).
Speed, knots: 27.**Range, miles:** 4,000 at 15 kts.

Missiles: SSM - 4 Aerospatiale MM 40 Exocet.
Guns: 1 Vickers 4.5 in (115 mm) Mk 8. 2 Bofors 40 mm/70.
Torpedoes: 6 324 mm Mk 32 (2 triple) tubes. Honeywell Mk 46 Mod 5 Neartip.
Decoys: 2 Plessey Shield chaff launchers.

Radars:
Surface search — Plessey ASW 4.
Navigation — Kelvin Hughes Type 1007.
Fire control — Selenia Orion RTN 10X.
Sonars: Atlas Elektronik DSQS-21C; hull-mounted, active.

Helicopters: 1 Westland Super Lynx SAH-11 (ASW/ASV) or Aerospatiale UH-12 Ecureuil (support).

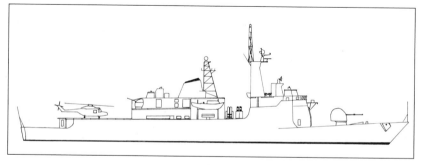

FRONTIN

Country: CROATIA
Country of origin: CROATIA
Ship type: CORVETTES
Class: KRALJ (TYPE R-03) (FSG)
Active: 2
Name (Pennant Number): KRALJ PETAR KRESIMIR IV (ex-Sergej Masera) (11), KRALJ TOMISLAV (ex-Milan Spasic) (12).

Recognition features:
- Smooth, rounded hull with low forecastle and continuous maindeck from stem to stern.
- 57 mm/70 gun mounting ('A' position).
- Long, central superstructure, raised in bridge area and at aft end.
- Pyramid shaped, lattice mainmast aft of bridge.
- 30 mm/65 AK 630 mounting on raised platform at aft end of superstructure.
- Saab RBS 15 SSM angled box launchers on afterdeck, port and starboard, trained forward.

Note - Derived from the 'Koncar' fast attack (missile) class with a stretched hull and a new superstructure. Mine rails may be removed in favour of increasing SSM capability to 8 missiles.

Displacement full load, tons: 385.
Length, feet (metres): 175.9 (53.6).
Beam, feet (metres): 27.9 (8.5).
Draught, feet (metres): 7.5 (2.3).
Speed, knots: 36.
Range, miles: 1,500 at 20 kts.

Missiles: SSM - Saab RBS 15 (2 or 4 twin).
Guns: 1 Bofors 57 mm/70. (Launchers for illuminants on side of mounting.) 1 - 30 mm/65 AK 630; 2 Oerlikon 20 mm or 2 12.7 mm MGs.
Decoys: 2 Wallop Barricade chaff/IR launcher.

Radars:
Surface search — Racal BT 502.
Navigation — Racal 1290A.
Fire control — BEAB 9LV 249 Mk 2.
Sonars: RIZ PP 10M; hull-mounted, active search.

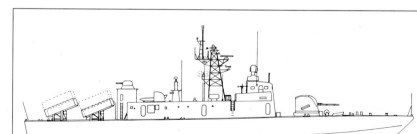

Kralj (Type R-03) Class

KRALJ PETAR KRESIMIR IV

Country: FINLAND
Country of origin: FINLAND
Ship type: CORVETTES
Class: TURUNMAA (FS)
Active: 2
Name (Pennant Number): TURUNMAA (03), KARJALA (04)

Recognition features:

- Long forecastle with 4.7 in gun mounting ('A' position).
- High superstructure running from after end of forecastle to quarterdeck.
- Distinctive WM22 fire control radome mounted atop superstructure aft of bridge.
- Very slim, tapered pole mainmast amidships.
- Small tapered, pole mast just forward of mainmast.
- 2 40 mm/70 gun mountings, one central on after superstructure, second right aft.
- RBU 1200 A/S mortars mounted inside maindeck superstructure abaft the pennant number.

Note - The exhaust system is trunked on either side of the quarterdeck.

Displacement full load, tons: 770.
Length, feet (metres): 243.1 (74.1).
Beam, feet (metres): 25.6 (7.8).
Draught, feet (metres): 7.9 (2.4).
Speed, knots: 35.
Range, miles: 2,500 at 14 kts.

Guns: 1 Bofors 4.7 in (120 mm)/46. 103 mm rails for illuminants are fitted on the side of the mounting. 2 Bofors 40 mm/70. 4 USSR 23 mm/87 (2 twin).
A/S mortars: 2 RBU 1200 5-tubed fixed launchers.
Depth charges: 2 racks.
Decoys: Wallop Barricade double chaff launcher.

Radars:

Surface search — Terma 20T 48 Super.
Navigation — Raytheon ARPA.
Fire control — Signaal WM22.
Sonars: Simrad, hull-mounted.

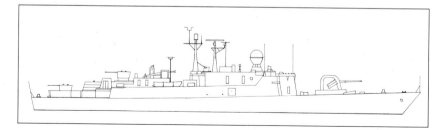

TURUNMAA

Al Manama/Victory/Muray Jib Class

Country: BAHRAIN, SINGAPORE, UNITED ARAB EMIRATES (UAE)
Country of origin: GERMANY
Ship type: CORVETTES
Class: AL MANAMA/VICTORY/MURAY JIB (LÜRSSEN MGB 62) (FSG)
Active: 2 Bahrain (Al Manama class), 6 Singapore (Victory class), 2 UAE (Muray Jib class)

BAHRAIN
Name (Pennant Number): AL MANAMA (50), AL MUHARRAQ (51).
SINGAPORE
Name (Pennant Number): VICTORY (P 88), VALOUR (P 89), VIGILANCE (P 90), VALIANT (P 91), VIGOUR (P 92), VENGEANCE (P 93).
UAE
Name (Pennant Number): MURAY JIB (CM 01, ex-P 6501), DAS (CM 02, ex-P 6502).

Recognition features:
- Continuous maindeck from stem to stern.
- Low freeboard.
- Forward superstructure has enclosed mainmast centrally sited atop. Singapore ships' mainmast more massive and taller with angled pole-mast atop. Upper portion of UAE ships' mast latticed.
- 3 in gun mounting ('A' position).
- Flat-topped after superstructure with helicopter platform atop, (Bahrain and UAE units).
- No deck house with helicopter platform on Singapore ships. SATCOM dome atop short pole-mast aft of Harpoon SSM angled launchers with torpedo tubes outboard in these units.
- 40 mm/70 mountings ('Y' position), (Bahrain ships).
- Goalkeeper CIWS immediately aft of mainmast in UAE ships.
- Exocet SSM launchers between main superstructure and helicopter platform in Bahrain/UAE ships.

Displacement full load, tons: 632, (Bahrain). 630, UAE). 595, (Singapore).
Length, feet (metres): 206.7 (63), (Bahrain and UAE). 204.7 (62.4) oa, (Singapore).
Beam, feet (metres): 30.5 (9.3), (Bahrain and UAE). 27.9 (8.5), (Singapore).
Draught, feet (metres): 9.5 (2.9), (Bahrain). 8.2 (2.5), (UAE). 10.2 (3.1), (Singapore).
Speed, knots: 32, (Bahrain and UAE). 35, (Singapore).
Range, miles: 4,000 at 16 kts., (Bahrain and UAE). 4,000 at 18 kts., (Singapore).

Missiles: SSM - 4 Aerospatiale MM 40 Exocet (2 twin) launchers, (Bahrain and UAE). 8 McDonnell Douglas Harpoon, (Singapore only). SAM — Thomson-CSF modified Crotale Navale octuple launcher, (UAE). IAI/Rafael Barak 1, 2 octuple launchers, (Singapore).

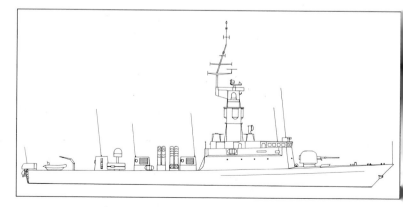

Al Manama/Victory/Muray Jib Class

Guns: 1 OTO MELARA 3 in (76 mm)/62 Compact. (Super Rapid, Singapore). 2 Breda 40 mm/70 (twin). 2 Oerlikon GAM-BO1 120 mm/93, (Bahrain). 1 Signaal Goalkeeper CIWS 30 mm, (UAE). 4 CIS 50 12.7 mm MGs, (Singapore).

Torpedoes: 6 324 mm Whitehead B 515 (2 triple tubes), Whitehead A 244S. (Singapore ships only).

Decoys: CSEE Dagaie. (Bahrain and UAE). 2 Plessey Shield chaff launchers, (Singapore).

Radars:

Air/surface search — Ericsson Sea Giraffe 50/150HC.

Navigation — Racal Decca 1226. (Bahrain, UAE). Kelvin Hughes 1007, (Singapore).

Fire control — CelsiusTech 9LV 331, (gun and SSM), (Bahrain and UAE). Thomson-CSF DRBV 51C (Crotale, UAE ships). 2 Elta EL/M-2221(X), (Singapore).

Sonars: Thomson-Sintra TSM 2064; VDS. (Singapore only).

Helicopters: 1 Eurocopter BO 105, (Bahrain). 1 Aerospatiale SA 316 Alouette, (UAE).

MURAY JIB

Niki (Thetis) (Type 420) Class

Country: GREECE
Country of origin: GERMANY
Ship type: CORVETTES
Class: NIKI (THETIS) (TYPE 420) (FS/PG)
Active: 5
Name (Pennant Number): NIKI (ex-Thetis) (P 62, ex-P 6052), DOXA (ex-Najade) (P 63, ex-P 6054), ELEFTHERIA (ex-Triton) (P 64, ex-P 6055), CARTERIA (ex-Hermes) (P 65, ex-P 6053), AGON (ex-Andreia, ex-Theseus) (P 66, ex-P 6056).

Recognition features:
● 40 mm/70 gun twin mounting ('A' position).
● High, smooth, forward superstructure with tripod mainmast at after end.
● Black-capped, sloping-topped funnel amidships.
● Torpedo tubes, port and starboard, on maindeck outboard of after superstructure.
● 40 mm/70 gun twin mounting at after end of after superstructure.
Note - Doxa has a deckhouse forward of bridge for sick bay.

Displacement full load, tons: 732.
Length, feet (metres): 229.7 (70).
Beam, feet (metres): 26.9 (8.2).
Draught, feet (metres): 8.6 (2.7).
Speed, knots: 19.5.
Range, miles: 2,760 at 15 kts.

Guns: 4 Breda 40 mm/70 (2 twin), 2 12.7 mm machine guns.
Torpedoes: 4   324 mm single tubes. 4 Honeywell Mk 46.
Depth charges: 2 rails.

Radars:
Surface search — Thomson-CSF TRS 3001.
Navigation — Kelvin Hughes 14/9.
Sonars: Atlas Elektronik ELAC 1 BV; hull-mounted, active search/attack.

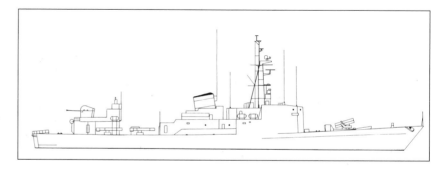

Niki (Thetis) (Type 420) Class

NIKI

Khukri Class

Country: INDIA
Country of origin: INDIA
Ship type: CORVETTES
Class: KHUKRI (PROJECTS 25 and 25A) (FSG)
Active: 5
Building: 3
Name (Pennant Number): KHUKRI (P 49), KUTHAR (P 46), KIRPAN (P 44), KHANJAR (P 47), KORA (—), KIRCH (—), KULISH (—), KARMUKH (—).

Recognition features:
● High bow with steep sloping forecastle.
● 3 in gun mounting mid-forecastle.
● Styx/Sapless SSM launchers forward of bridge, port and starboard.
● Unusual curved sloping front up to bridge windows.
● Midships superstructure has large lattice mainmast at after end.
● Distinctive Positive E/Cross Dome air search radome atop mainmast.
● Low funnel, with three pipe exhausts, aft of mainmast.
● 30 mm/65 gun mountings on platforms, port and starboard, immediately aft of funnel.
● Raised flight deck forward of short quarterdeck.

Displacement full load, tons: 1,350.
Length, feet (metres): 298.9 (91).
Beam, feet (metres): 34.4 (10.5).
Draught, feet (metres): 13.1 (4).
Speed, knots: 25.
Range, miles: 4,000 at 16 kts.

Missiles: SSM - 4 SS-N-2D Styx (1 or 2 twin) launchers, (first four hulls). Zvezda SS-N-25 (Kh 35 Uran) Sapless (2 quad), (last four hulls). SAM - SA-N-5 Grail.
Guns: 1 USSR AK 176 3 in (76 mm)/60. 2 30 mm/65 (twin) AK 630.
Decoys: 2 PK 16 chaff launchers. NPOL (Cochin); towed torpedo decoy.

Radars:
Air search — Positive E/Cross Sword.
Air/surface search — Plank Shave.
Navigation — Bharat 1245.
Fire control — Bass Tilt.

Helicopters: Platform only for HAL SA 319B Chetak, (Alouette III).

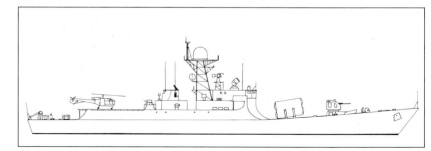

KHUKRI

Eithne Class

Country: IRELAND
Country of origin: REPUBLIC OF IRELAND
Ship type: CORVETTES
Class: EITHNE (OPV)
Active: 1
Name (Pennant Number): EITHNE (P 31)

Recognition features:
- High freeboard with high central superstructure.
- Short forecastle with 57 mm/70 gun mounting ('B' position).
- Large, solid based lattice mainmast atop superstructure aft of bridge.
- Tall tapered funnel at after end of superstructure.
- Long flight deck with break down to short quarterdeck.
- Distinctive flight deck overhang.
- Ship's boats in davits high up superstructure, amidships.

Displacement full load, tons: 1,910.
Length, feet (metres): 265 (80.8).
Beam, feet (metres): 39.4 (12).
Draught, feet (metres): 14.1 (4.3).
Speed, knots: 20+.
Range, miles: 7,000 at 15 kts.

Guns: 1 Bofors 57 mm/70 Mk 1. 2 Rheinmetall 20 mm/20. 2 Wallop 57 mm launchers for illuminants.

Radars:
Air/surface search — Signaal DA05 Mk 4.
Navigation — Two Racal Decca 1629C.
Sonars: Plessey PMS 26; hull-mounted.

Helicopters: 1 Aerospatiale SA 365F Dauphin 2.

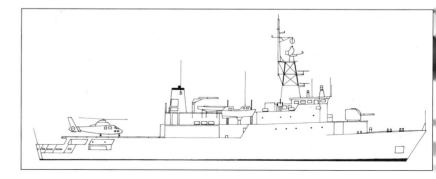

EITHNE

Eilat (Saar 5) Class

Country: ISRAEL
Country of origin: ISRAEL
Ship type: CORVETTES
Class: EILAT (SAAR 5) (FSG)
Active: 3
Name (Pennant Number): EILAT (501), LAHAV (502), HANIT (503)

Recognition features:
- High bow, short sloping forecastle.
- 3 in gun mounting or Vulcan Phalanx CIWS on raised forecastle position.
- High, bulky forward slab-sided superstructure with tall pole mainmast atop.
- Harpoon SSM angled launchers immediately aft of forward superstructure.
- Squat, black-capped funnel with unusual sloping forward edge.
- Barak I SAM VLS launcher immediately aft of funnel.
- Substantial angular after superstructure with after pole mast atop.
- Large Elta EL/M-2218S air search radar aerial atop after superstructure.
- Flight deck right aft.

Displacement full load, tons: 1,227.
Length, feet (metres): 283.5 (86.4) oa.
Beam, feet (metres): 39 (11.9).
Draught, feet (metres): 10.5 (3.2).
Speed, knots: 33.
Range, miles: 3,500 at 17 kts.

Missiles: SSM - McDonnell Douglas Harpoon (2 quad) launchers. SAM - 2 IAI/Rafael Barak I (vertical launch).
Guns: OTO MELARA 3 in (76 mm)/62 Compact. Interchangeable with a Bofors 57 mm gun or Vulcan Phalanx CIWS. 2 Sea Vulcan 25 mm CIWS.
Torpedoes: 6 324 mm Mk 32 (2 triple) tubes. Honeywell Mk 46.
Decoys: 3 Elbit/Deseaver chaff launchers. Rafael ATC-1 towed torpedo decoy.

Radars:
Air search — Elta EL/M-2218S.
Surface search — Cardion SPS-55.
Fire control — 3 Elta EL/M-2221 GM STGR.
Sonars: EDO Type 796 Mod 1; hull-mounted. Rafael towed array.

Helicopters: 1 Aerospatiale SA 366G Dauphin.

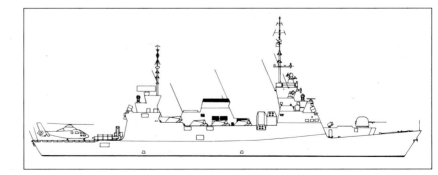

EILAT

Country: ECUADOR, IRAQ, MALAYSIA
Country of origin: ITALY
Ship type: CORVETTES
Class: ASSAD/ESMERALDAS/LAKSAMANA (FSG)
Active: 6 Ecuador (Esmeraldas class), 2 Iraq (Assad class)*, 4 Malaysia (Laksamana class)
* Iraqi ships moored at La Spezia shipbuilding yard, flying the Iraqi flag and with reduced Iraqi crews. Malaysian ships formerly built for Iraq.

ECUADOR
Name (Pennant Number): ESMERALDAS (CM 11), MANABI (CM 12), LOS RIOS (CM 13), EL ORO (CM 14), LOS GALAPAGOS (CM 15), LOJA (CM 16)

IRAQ
Name (Pennant Number): MUSSA BEN NUSSAIR (F 210), TARIQ IBN ZIAD (F 212).

MALAYSIA
Name (Pennant Number): LAKSAMANA HANG NADIM (ex-Khalid Ibn Al Walid) (F 134, ex-F 216), LAKSAMANA TUN ABDUL GAMIL (ex-Saad Ibn Abi Waccade) (F 135, ex-F 218), —— (ex-Abdulla Ben Abi Sarh) (F 136, ex-F 214), —— (ex-Salahi Ad Deen Alayoori) (F 137, ex-F 220).

Recognition features:
- High bow with sweeping continuous maindeck aft to stern.
- 3 in gun mounting ('A' position).
- Square profile main superstructure with raised bridge area, (Ecuador only) (Iraqi and Malaysian ships have flatter roofs to bridge with slight slope in line with superstructure).
- Pyramid mainmast atop centre of main superstructure.
- Prominent Aspide SAM Albatros box launcher atop after end of main superstructure.
- 2 Exocet SSM launchers immediately aft of forward superstructure and 40 mm/70 gun turret in 'Y' position, (Ecuador). 40 mm/70 gun turret mounting on superstructure, just aft of midships, with angled Otomat Teseo SSM launchers, facing port and starboard, on maindeck after of superstructure. (Malaysian ships)
- Raised helicopter landing platform aft of SSM launchers (Ecuador and Iraq, not Malaysian ships). (Telescopic hangar, Iraqi ships).

Displacement full load, tons: 685. (Ecuador and Iraq). (705, Malaysian ships).
Length, feet (metres): 204.4 (62.3).
Beam, feet (metres): 30.5 (9.3).
Draught, feet (metres): 8 (2.5).
Speed, knots: 37.
Range, miles: 4,000 at 18 kts., (Ecuador). 2,300 at 18 kts., (Malaysia)

Missiles: SSM - 6 Aerospatiale MM 40 Exocet (2 triple) launchers, (Ecuador). 6 OTO MELARA/Matra Otomat Teseo Mk 2 (TG 2) (3 twin) (Iraq, Malaysia). SAM - Selenia Elsag Albatros quad launcher, Aspide.
Guns: 1 OTO MELARA 3 in (76 mm)/62 Compact, (Ecuador, Iraq), Super Rapid, (Malaysia). 2 Breda 40 mm/70 (twin). (Not Iraqi ships)
Torpedoes: 6 324 mm ILAS-3 (2 triple) tubes. Whitehead Motofides A244S (Not Iraqi ships).
Decoys: 1 or 2 Breda 105 mm SCLAR chaff/illuminants launcher.

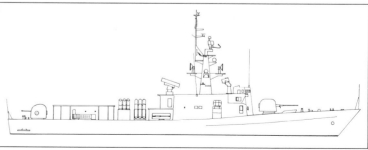

Assad/Esmeraldas/Laksamana Class

ESMERALDAS

Radars:
Air/surface search — Selenia RAN 10S. (Ecuador) RAN 12L/X (Iraq, Malaysia).
Navigation — SMA SPN-703 (3 RM 20), (Ecuador, Iraq). Kelvin Hughes 1007, (Malaysia).

Fire control — 2 Selenia Orion 10X.
Sonars: Thomson Sintra Diodon; hull-mounted. (Ecuador). Atlas Elektronik ASO 84-41, hull-mounted, (Iraq, Malaysia).

Helicopters: 1 Bell 206B (platform only), (Ecuador). 1 Agusta AB 212, (Iraq).

Minerva Class

Country: ITALY
Country of origin: ITALY
Ship type: CORVETTES
Class: MINERVA (FS)
Active: 8
Name (Pennant Number): MINERVA (F 551), URANIA (F 552), DANAIDE (F 553), SFINGE (F 554), DRIADE (F 555), CHIMERA (F 556), FENICE (F 557), SIBILLA (F 558)

Recognition features:

- Continuous maindeck from bow to break down to quarterdeck.
- Long forecastle with 3 in gun mounting at mid-point.
- Isolated forward superstructure with short pole mast at after end.
- Midships enclosed mainmast supporting distinctive SPS-774 air/surface search radar aerial.
- Tapered black-capped funnel atop central after superstructure with unusual forward sloping top.
- Aspide SAM Albatros box launcher at after end of after superstructure.
- Low freeboard quarterdeck.

Displacement full load, tons: 1,285.
Length, feet (metres): 284.1 (86.6).
Beam, feet (metres): 34.5 (10.5).
Draught, feet (metres): 10.5 (3.2).
Speed, knots: 24.
Range, miles: 3,500 at 18 kts.

Missiles: SSM - Fitted for but not with 4 or 6 Teseo Otomat between the masts. SAM - Selenia Elsag Albatros octuple launcher, Aspide.
Guns: 1 OTO Melara 3 in (76 mm)/62 Compact.
Torpedoes: 6 324 mm Whitehead B 515 (2 triple) tubes. Honeywell Mk 46.
Decoys: 2 Wallop Barricade double layer launchers. SLQ-25 Nixie; towed torpedo decoy.

Radars:

Air/surface search — Selenia SPS-774 (RAN 10S).
Navigation — SMA SPN-728(V)2.
Fire control — Selenia SPG-76 (RTN 30X).
Sonars: Raytheon/Elsag DE 1167; hull-mounted.

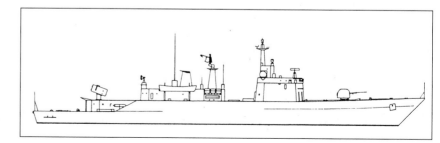

Minerva Class

DRIADE

Po Hang Class

Country: KOREA, SOUTH
Country of origin: SOUTH KOREA
Ship type: CORVETTES
Class: PO HANG (FS/FSG)
Active: 24
Name (Pennant Number): PO HANG (756), KUN SAN (757), KYONG JU (758), MOK PO (759), KIM CHON (761), CHUNG JU (762), JIN JU (763), YO SU (765), JIN HAE (766), SUN CHON (767), YEE REE (768), WON JU (769), AN DONG (771), CHON AN (772), SONG NAM (773), BU CHON (775), JAE CHON (776), DAE CHON (777), SOK CHO (778), YONG JU (779), NAM WON (781), KWAN MYONG (782), SIN HUNG (783), KONG JU (785).

Recognition features:
- 3 in gun mounting ('A' position). Breda 40 mm/70 twin gun mounting in 'B' position 761 onwards; Emerson Electric 30 mm twin mounting in 'B' position in 756-759.
- High forward superstructure with enclosed mainmast at after end.
- WM28 fire control radome atop mainmast.
- Large funnel well aft of midships with gas turbine air intakes immediately forward.
- Ship's boats in davits at funnel level outboard of air intakes.
- Exocet SSM box launchers at after end of after superstructure in 756-759. Replaced by 40 mm/70 gun turret mounting 761 onwards.
- Twin 30 mm or OTO MELARA 3 in gun mounting on afterdeck.

Displacement full load, tons: 1,220.
Length, feet (metres): 289.7 (88.3).
Beam, feet (metres): 32.8 (10).
Draught, feet (metres): 9.5 (2.9).
Speed, knots: 32.
Range, miles: 4,000 at 15 kts.

Missiles: SSM - 2 Aerospatiale MM 38 Exocet (756-759 only).
Guns: 1 or 2 OTO Melara 3 in (76 mm)/62 Compact. 4 Emerson Electric 30 mm (2 twin) (756-759). 4 Breda 40 mm/70 (2 twin), (761 onwards).
Torpedoes: 6 324 mm Mk 32 (2 triple) tubes (761 onwards). Honeywell Mk 46.
Depth charges: 12 (761 onwards).
Decoys: 4 MEL Protean fixed launchers. 2 Loral Hycor SRBOC 6-barrel Mk 36 (in some).

Radars:
Surface search — Marconi 1810 and/or Raytheon SPS-64. Fire control - Signaal WM28; or Marconi 1802.
Sonars: Signaal PHS 32 (761 onwards); hull-mounted.

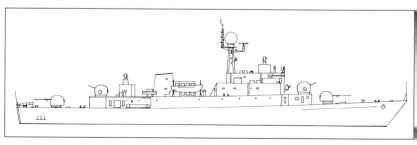

Po Hang Class

PO HANG

Nanuchka I/II/III/IV Class

Country: ALGERIA/INDIA/LIBYA/RUSSIA
Country of origin: RUSSIA
Ship type: CORVETTES
Class: NANUCHKA (BURYA/VETER/NAKAT/DURG) (TYPE 1234) (FSG)
Active: 3 Algeria (Nanuchka II/Burya), 3 India (Nanuchka II /'Durg' class), 3 Libya (Nanuchka II/Burya).

Russia - 6 Nanuchka I (Burya); 17 Nanuchka III (Veter); 1 Nanuchka IV (Nakat)

ALGERIA
Name (Pennant Number): RAIS HAMIDOU (801), SALAH RAIS (802), RAIS ALI (803).

INDIA
Name (Pennant Number): VIJAYDURG (K 71), SINDHUDURG (K 72), HOSDURG (K 73).

LIBYA
Name (Pennant Number): TARIQ IBN ZIYAD (ex-Ean Mara) (416), EAN AL GAZALA (417), EAN ZARA (418).

RUSSIA
Name (Pennant Number): Nanuchka 1 - SKVAL, STORM, METL, GROM, VOLNA, BURYA. Nanuchka III - METEOR, PRILIV, URAGAN, PASSAT, PRIBOY, SMERCH, MIRAS, SHTYL, VETER, MOROZ, RAZLIV, AJSBERG, ZYB, LIVEN, BURUN, TUCHA, PEREKAT. Nanuchka IV — NAKAT.

Recognition features:
- Continuous maindeck from stem to stern with raised bow.
- SA-N-4 Gecko SAM launcher ('A' mounting position).
- Fire control radar forward of bridge.
- High central superstructure with lattice mainmast at after end.
- Large, distinctive Square Tie air/surface search radome atop bridge, forward of mainmast. (Band Stand datalink for SS-N-9 Siren SSM in Russian units).
- Forward pointing tubular Styx/Siren SSM launchers on maindeck adjacent to bridge, port and starboard.
- 57 mm/80 gun mounting ('Y' position) in Nanuchka I; 3 in/60 in III and IV.

Note 1 - Obvious differences between I and III: larger lattice mainmast in III, 30 mm/65 gun mounting ('X' position) in III, 3 in gun mounting ('Y' position) in III, air/surface search radar dome atop bridge in III.
Note 2 - Nanuchka IV similar to III except she is trials vehicle for possible 300 km range version of SS-CX-5.

Displacement full load, tons: 660.
Length, feet (metres): 194.5 (59.3).
Beam, feet (metres): 38.7 (11.8).
Draught, feet (metres): 8.5 (2.6).
Speed, knots: 33.
Range, miles: 2,500 at 12 kts.

Missiles: SSM — 4 SS-N-2C Styx (Durg/Nanuchka II). 6 Chelomey SS-N-9 Siren (Malakhit) (2 triple) launchers. (Russian ships). SAM - SA-N-4 Gecko twin launcher.
Guns: 2 - 57 mm/80 twin automatic (Nanuchka I/II). 1 - 3 in (76 mm)/60 (Nanuchka III and IV). 1 - 30 mm/65 (Nanuchka III and IV).
Decoys: 2 - PK 16 (Nanuchka I/II) or PK 10 (Nanuchka III) chaff launchers.

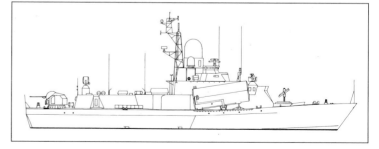

Nanuchka I/II/III/IV Class

NANUCHKA

Radars:
Air/surface search —Peel Pair. (Plank Shave in later Nanuchka IIIs).
Surface search — Square Tie (Nanuchka II)

Navigation — Nayada (Russian units). Don 2 (Burya/Durg class).
Fire control — Pop Group, (SA-N-4). Muff Cob (Nanuchka I/II). Bass Tilt
   (Nanuchka III).

Tarantul I/II/III Class

Country: BULGARIA, INDIA, POLAND, ROMANIA, RUSSIA, UKRAINE, VIETNAM, YEMEN

Country of origin: RUSSIA

Ship type: CORVETTES

Class: TARANTUL I (TYPE 1241.1) (ZBORUL), (GORNIK, VEER, TYPE 1241RE). TARANTUL II (TYPE 1241.1M), (VEER, TYPE 1241RE). TARANTUL III (TYPE 1241.1MP). MODIFIED TARANTUL III (TYPE 1242.1) (MOLNIYA) (FSG).

Active: 1 Bulgaria (Tarantul II), 13 India (Tarantul I/'Veer' class), 4 Poland (Tarantul I/'Gornik' class), 3 Romania (Tarantul I/'Zborul' class) Russia - 1 Tarantul I; 17 II; 26 III; 1 Mod Tarantul III, 2 Ukraine (Tarantul I) (May not be operational). 2 Vietnam (Tarantul I), 1 + 1 Reserve. Yemen. (Tarantul I)

BULGARIA
Name (Pennant Number): MULNIYA (101).

INDIA
Name (Pennant Number): VEER (K 40), NIRBHIK (K 41), NIPAT (K 42), NISHANK (K 43), NIRGHAT (K 44), VIBHUTI (K 45), VIPUL (K 46), VINASH (K 47), VIDYUT (K 48), NASHAK (K 83) — (K 93), PRAHAR (K 98)

POLAND
Name (Pennant Number): GORNIK (434), HUTNIK (435), METALOWIEC (436), ROLNIK (437).

ROMANIA
Name (Pennant Number): ZBORUL (188), LASTUNUL (189), PESCARUSUL (190).

RUSSIA
Name (Pennant Number): (Not available).

UKRAINE
Name (Pennant Number): NICOPOL (U 155), KREMENCHUK (U 156).

VIETNAM
Name (Pennant Number): HQ 371, HQ 372.

YEMEN
Name (Pennant Number): 971, 976.

Recognition features:
- Continuous maindeck from stem to stern with sweeping lines down from high bow to midships, then gently sloping up to slightly higher stern.
- 3 in gun mounting mid-forecastle.
- High central superstructure with mainmast atop. Some Russian Tarantul II/III units have radomes atop bridge and/or mainmast.
- Distinctive, forward pointing Styx SSM tubular launchers, two port two starboard, on maindeck adjacent mainmast.
- 30 mm/65 mountings, port and starboard, on after end of after superstructure.

Note - The above features generally apply to all three types.

Displacement full load, tons: 455. (450, Vietnam, 580, Yemen ships)
Length, feet (metres): 184.1 (56.1).
Beam, feet (metres): 37.7 (11.5).
Draught, feet (metres): 8.2 (2.5).
Speed, knots: 36.
Range, miles: 1,650 at 14 kts.

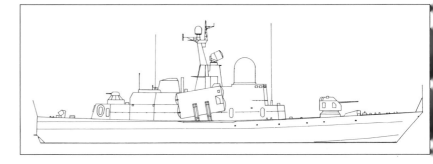

Tarantul I/II/III Class

TARANTUL

Missiles: SSM — Raduga SS-N-2C/D Styx (2 twin) launchers. SS-N-22 Sunburn (3M-82 Moskit) (2 twin) launchers (Tarantul III). SAM - SA-N-5 Grail quad launcher. SAM/Guns - CADS-N-1 (Kashtan) 30 mm Gatling/SA-N-11 mounting (1 Russian Tarantul II only).
Guns: 1 3 in (76 mm)/60. 2 30 mm/65 AK 630.
Decoys: 2 PK 16 or 4 PK 10 (Tarantul III) chaff launchers.

Radars:
Air/surface search — Plank Shave (Tarantul I), Band Stand (with Plank Shave) (Tarantul II and III).
Navigation — Spin Trough or Kivach II. (Mius, Indian ships). (Perchora 436, 437, Poland and Vietnam ships)
Fire control — Bass Tilt.
Sonars: Foal Tail, active. (Poland, Russia, Vietnam).

Göteborg Class

Country: SWEDEN
Country of origin: SWEDEN
Ship type: CORVETTES
Class: GÖTEBORG (FSG)
Active: 4
Name (Pennant Number): GÖTEBORG (K 21), GÄLVE (K 22), KALMAR (K 23), SUNDSVALL (K 24)

Recognition features:

- Continuous maindeck lines from stem to stern.
- 57 mm/70 gun mounting ('A' position).
- Saab Elma A/S mortar launchers ('B' mounting position).
- Long central superstructure with, midships, large enclosed mainmast atop.
- Torpedo tubes on maindeck outboard of bridge.
- Saab RBS 15 SSM angled twin box launchers, two port, two starboard, on maindeck at after end of superstructure.
- 40 mm/70 gun mounting or Sea Trinity CIWS on afterdeck.
- VDS towing equipment right aft.

Displacement full load, tons: 399.
Length, feet (metres): 187 (57).
Beam, feet (metres): 26.2 (8).
Draught, feet (metres): 6.6 (2).
Speed, knots: 30.

Missiles: SSM - Saab RBS 15 (4 twin) launchers.
Guns: 1 Bofors 57 mm/70 Mk 2. 1 Bofors 40 mm/70 (or Bofors Sea Trinity CIWS).
Torpedoes: 4 15.75 in (400 mm) tubes. Swedish Ordnance Type 43/45 or A244S.
A/S mortars: 4 Saab Elma LLS-920 9-tubed launchers.
Depth charges: On mine rails.
Decoys: 4 Philips Philax launchers. (A/S mortars adapted to fire IR/chaff decoys).

Radars:
Air/surface search — Ericsson Sea Giraffe 150HC.
Navigation — Terma PN 612.
Fire control — 2 Bofors Electronics 9GR 400.
Sonars: Thomson-Sintra TSM 2643 Salmon; VDS. Simrad SA 950; hull-mounted, active attack.

KALMAR

Stockholm Class

Country: SWEDEN
Country of origin: SWEDEN
Ship type: CORVETTES
Class: STOCKHOLM (FSG)
Active: 2
Name (Pennant Number): STOCKHOLM (K 11), MALMÖ (K 12)

Recognition features:

- Long forecastle with Saab Elma LLS-920 A/S mortar launcher at forward end and 57mm/70 gun mounting midpoint between bows and bridge.
- Short, high, central superstructure with lattice mainmast at after end.
- Distinctive RBS 15 SSM angled twin box launchers; two port two starboard, on maindeck at after end of superstructure.
- Short, slim lattice aftermast isolated, aft of SSM launchers.
- 40 mm/70 gun mounting right aft.

Note - Developed from 'Spica II' class.

Displacement full load, tons: 335.
Length, feet (metres): 164 (50).
Beam, feet (metres): 24.6 (7.5).
Draught, feet (metres): 6.9 (2.1).
Speed, knots: 32.

Missiles: SSM - Saab RBS 15 Mk II (4 twin) launchers.
Guns: 1 Bofors 57 mm/70 Mk 2. 1 Bofors 40 mm/70.
Torpedoes: 2 21 in (533 mm) tubes. FFV Type 613. 4 - 15.75 in (400 mm) tubes. Swedish Ordnance Type 43 or Whitehead A 244S Mod 2.
A/S mortars: 4 Saab Elma LLS-920 9-tubed launchers.
Depth charges: On mine rails.
Decoys: 2 Philips Philax launchers.

Radars:

Air/surface search — Ericsson Sea Giraffe 50HC.
Navigation — Terma PN 612.
Fire control — Philips 9LV 200 Mk 3.
Sonars: Simrad SA 950; hull-mounted, active attack. Thomson-Sintra TSM 2642 Salmon; VDS.

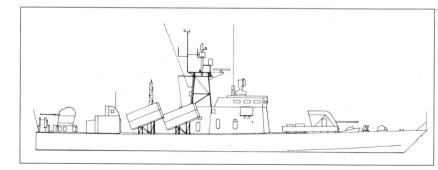

MALMÖ

Country: THAILAND
Country of origin: UNITED KINGDOM
Ship type: CORVETTES
Class: KHAMRONSIN (FS)
Active: 3
Name (Pennant Number): KHAMRONSIN (531, ex-1), THAYANCHON (532, ex-2), LONGLOM (533, ex-3)

Recognition features:

- Short forecastle with 76 mm/62 gun mounting ('A' position).
- High freeboard, slab sided superstructure running from forecastle to afterdeck.
- Lattice mainmast amidships, atop central superstructure.
- Squat, black-capped funnel with sloping top aft of mainmast.
- 30 mm/70 gun mounting ('X' position).
- Break down from maindeck to short quarterdeck.

Note 1 - Based on a Vosper Thornycroft Province class 56 m design stretched by increasing the frame spacing along the whole length of the hull.

Note 2 - Lightly armed version with different superstructure, active with marine police.

Displacement full load (tons): 630.
Length, feet (metres): 203.4 (62) oa.
Beam, feet (metres): 26.9 (8.2).
Draught, feet (metres): 8.2 (2.5).
Speed, knots: 25.
Range, miles: 2,500 at 15 kts.

Guns: 1 OTO MELARA 76 mm/62 Mod 7. 2 Breda 30 mm/70 (twin). 2 12.7 mm MG.
Torpedoes: 6 Plessey PMW 49A (2 triple) launchers. Marconi Stingray.

Radars:
Air/surface search — Plessey AWS 4.
Navigation — Racal Decca 1226.
Sonars: Atlas Elektronik DSQS-21C; hull-mounted, active search/attack.

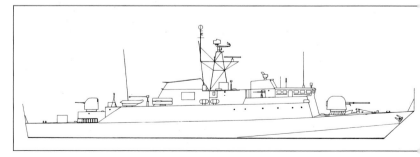

Khamronsin Class

KHAMRONSIN

Maritime Photographic

Qahir class

Country: OMAN
Country of origin: UNITED KINGDOM
Ship type: CORVETTES
Class: QAHIR (FSG)
Active: 2
Name (Pennant Number): QAHIR AL AMWAJ (Q 31), AL MUA'ZZER (Q 32)

Recognition features:
- Sloping straight-edged bow with long, gently sloping forecastle.
- 2 Exocet SSM launchers immediately forward of bridge, after one trained to port, forward one to starboard.
- 3 in gun mounting forward of SSM launchers.
- Large, smooth midships superstructure with angled surfaces for low reflective radar signature.
- Squat black-capped funnel immediately abaft mainmast.
- Crotale NG SAM box launcher at after end of superstructure immediately forward of flight deck.
- Long flight deck at after end of ship.

Displacement full load, tons: 1,450.
Length, feet (metres): 274.6 (83.7) oa.
Beam, feet (metres): 37.7 (11.5).
Draught, feet (metres): 11.8 (3.6).
Speed, knots: 28.
Range, miles: 4,000 at 10 kts.

Missiles: SSM - 8 Aerospatiale MM 40 Block II Exocet. SAM - Thomson-CSF Crotale NG, octuple launcher.
Guns: 1 OTO Melara 3 in (76 mm)/62 Super Rapid. 2 Oerlikon/Royal Ordnance 20 mm GAM-B01.
Torpedoes: 6 324 mm (2 triple tubes may be fitted).
Decoys: 2 Barricade 12-barrel chaff launchers.

Radars:
Air/surface search — Signaal MW08.
Navigation — Kelvin Hughes 1007.
Fire control — Signaal STING, Thomson CSF DRBV 51C.
Sonars: Thomson-Sintra/BAeSEMA ATAS towed array.

Helicopters: Platform for 1 Super Puma type.

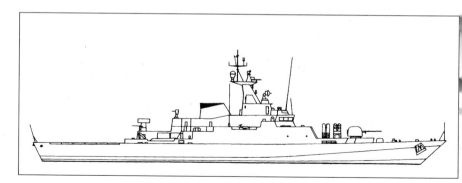

Qahir class

٣١ ق

QAHIR AL AMWAJ

Badr Class

Country: SAUDI ARABIA
Country of origin: UNITED STATES OF AMERICA
Ship type: CORVETTES
Class: BADR (FSG)
Active: 4
Name (Pennant Number): BADR (612), AL YARMOOK (614), HITTEEN (616), TABUK (618)

Recognition features:
- Long forecastle with 3 in gun mounting midpoint between bows and bridge.
- Centrally sited superstructure with fat central lattice mainmast with SPS-40Bair search radar and tall pole mast above.
- Sperry Mk 92 Fire control radome atop bridge roof.
- Short, black-capped funnel at after end of superstructure.
- Torpedo tubes on maindeck level at after end of superstructure.
- Harpoon SSM angled launchers on afterdeck.
- CIWS mounting right aft.

Displacement full load, tons: 1,038.
Length, feet (metres): 245 (74.7).
Beam, feet (metres): 31.5 (9.6).
Draught, feet (metres): 8.9 (2.7).
Speed, knots: 30.
Range, miles: 4,000 at 20 kts.

Missiles: SSM - McDonnell Douglas Harpoon (2 quad) launchers.
Guns: 1 FMC/OTO MELARA 3 in (76 mm)/62 Mk 75 Mod 0. 1 GE/GD 20 mm 6-barrel Vulcan Phalanx. 2 Oerlikon 20 mm/80. 1 81 mm mortar. 2 40 mm Mk 19 grenade launchers.
Torpedoes: 6 324 mm US Mk 32 (2 triple) tubes. Honeywell Mk 46.
Decoys: 2 Loral Hycor SRBOC 6-barrel Mk 36 fixed launchers.

Radars:
Air search — Lockheed SPS-40B.
Surface search — ISC Cardion SPS-55.
Fire control — Sperry Mk 92.
Sonars: Raytheon SQS-56 (DE 1164); hull-mounted, active search/attack.

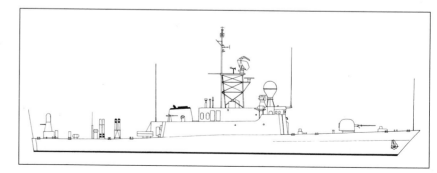

Badr Class

BADR

Bayandor/Tapi (PF 103) Class

Country: IRAN, THAILAND
Country of origin: UNITED STATES OF AMERICA
Ship type: CORVETTES
Class: BAYANDOR (FS)/TAPI (FF) (ex-US PF 103)
Active: 2 Iran (Bayandor class), 2 Thailand (Tapi class)

IRAN
Name (Pennant Number): BAYANDOR (81, ex-US PF 103), NAGHDI (82, ex-US PF 104)

THAILAND
Name (Pennant Number): TAPI (431, ex-5), KHIRIRAT (432, ex-6).

Recognition features:

- Unusual curved bow.
- Sloping forecastle with 3 in gun mounting ('A' position). (Not present in Thai units).
- 20 mm gun mounting ('B' position) in Iranian units. (OTO MELARA 3 in Thai ships).
- High, complex midships superstructure with sloping pole mainmast atop.
- Large SPS-6C (LW04, Thailand) air/surface search radar aerial on forward platform halfway up mainmast.
- Tall, sloping, black-capped funnel with curved after profile. (Straight after end to funnel profile in Thai ships).
- 3 in gun mounting ('Y' position) and 40 mm/60 mounting ('X' position), (Iranian ships). 40mm/70 gun mounting in 'Y' position in Thai ships.
- 20 mm mounting after end of quarterdeck in Iranian ships. (Torpedo tubes on quarterdeck in Thai ships).

Displacement full load, tons: 1,135, (Iran). 1,172 (Thailand).
Length, feet (metres): 275.6 (84.0), (Iran). 275 (83.8), (Thailand).
Beam, feet (metres): 33.1 (10.1), (Iran). (33 (10), Thailand).

Draught, feet (metres): 10.2 (3.1), (Iran). (10 (3), Thailand).
Speed, knots: 20.
Range, miles: 4,800 at 12 kts.

Guns: 2 US 3 in (76 mm)/50 Mk 3/4. 2 Bofors 40 mm/60 (twin). 2 Oerlikon GAM-BO1 20 mm. 2 - 12.7 mm MGs, (Iran). 1 OTO MELARA 3 in (76 mm)/62 Compact. 1 Bofors 40 mm/70. 2 Oerlikon 20 mm. 2 12.7 MGs, (Thailand).
Torpedoes: 6 324 mm UK Mk 32 (2 triple) tubes. Honeywell Mk 46. (Thai ships only).

Radars:

Air/surface search — Westinghouse SPS-6C. (Signaal LW04, Thailand).
Surface search — Racal Decca. (Raytheon SPS-53E, Thailand).
Navigation — Raytheon 1650, (Iran).
Fire control — Western Electric Mk 36, (Iran). Signaal WM22-61, (Thailand).
Sonars: EDO SQS-17A; hull-mounted, (Iran). Atlas Elektronik DSQS-21C, hull-mounted, active search/attack, (Thailand).

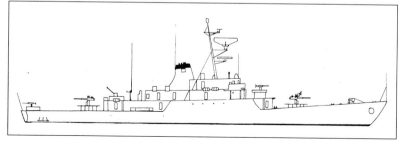

Bayandor/Tapi (PF 103) Class

NAGHDI

Rattanakosin Class

Country: THAILAND
Country of origin: UNITED STATES OF AMERICA
Ship type: CORVETTES
Class: RATTANAKOSIN (FSG)
Active: 2
Name (Pennant Number): RATTANAKOSIN (441, ex-1), SUKHOTHAI (442, ex-2)

Recognition features:
- High bow, short forecastle.
- 3 in gun mounting ('A' position).
- 40 mm/70 gun twin mounting ('B' position).
- Slab-sided high superstructure running from forecastle to afterdeck.
- Large, solid pyramid mainmast atop forward superstructure supportingWM25/41 fire control radome.
- Low, tapered funnel well aft of midships with curved after profile and twin exhaust protruding from top.
- Short, enclosed aftermast, immediately aft of funnel, supporting DA05 air/surface search radar aerial.
- Harpoon SSM angled launchers atop after end of superstructure.
- Aspide SAM Albatros launcher right aft on quarterdeck.

Displacement full load, tons: 960.
Length, feet (metres): 252 (76.8).
Beam, feet (metres): 31.5 (9.6).
Draught, feet (metres): 8 (2.4).
Speed, knots: 26.
Range, miles: 3,000 at 16 kts.

Missiles: SSM - McDonnell Douglas Harpoon (2 quad) launchers. SAM - Selenia Elsag Albatros octuple launcher, Aspide.
Guns: 1 OTO Melara 3 in (76 mm)/62. 2 Breda 40 mm/70 (twin). 2 Oerlikon 20 mm.
Torpedoes: 6 324 mm US Mk 32 (2 triple) tubes. Marconi Stingray.
Decoys: CSEE Dagaie 6 or 10-tubed trainable launchers.

Radars:
Air/surface search — Signaal DA05.
Surface search — Signaal ZW06.
Navigation — Decca 1226.
Fire control — Signaal WM 25/41.
Sonars: Atlas Elektronik DSQS-21C; hull-mounted, active search/attack.

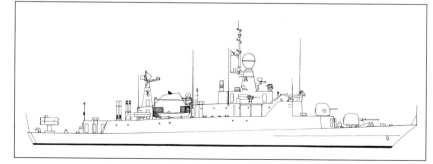

SUKHOTHAI

Grajaú Class

Country: BRAZIL
Country of origin: BRAZIL
Ship type: PATROL FORCES
Class: GRAJAÚ (LARGE PATROL CRAFT) (PG)
Active: 10
Proposed: 2
Name (Pennant Number): GRAJAÚ (P 40), GUAIBA (P 41), GRAÚNA (P 42), GOIANA (P 43), GUAJARÁ (P 44), GUAPORÉ (P 45), GURUPÁ (P 46), GURUPI (P 47), GUANABARA (P 48), GUARUJA (P 49)

Recognition features:
- Smooth, uncluttered lines from bow to stern.
- Small, flat fronted, central superstructure stepped down at after end.
- 40 mm/70 gun mounting ('A' position, P 40-43).
- Tall, lattice mainmast atop central superstructure.
- 20 mm gun mounting on afterdeck.

Note: Built to Vosper QAF design similar to Bangladesh 'Meghna' class.

Displacement full load, tons: 217.
Length, feet (metres): 152.6 (46.5).

Beam, feet (metres): 24.6 (7.5).
Draught, feet (metres): 7.5 (2.3).
Speed, knots: 22.
Range, miles: 2,000 at 12 kts.

Guns: 1 Bofors 40 mm/70. 2 Oerlikon 20 mm, (P 40-43). 2 Oerlikon/BMARC 20 mm GAM-B01 (P 44-51).

Radars:
Surface search — Racal Decca 1290A.

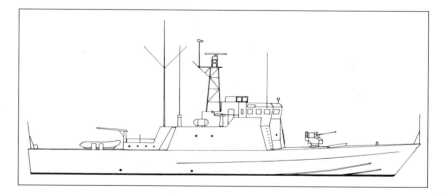

Grajaú Class

GURUPÁ

Van Gunderen collection

Hainan Class

Country: BANGLADESH, BURMA, CHINA, EGYPT, NORTH KOREA
Country of origin: CHINA
Ship type: PATROL FORCES
Class: HAINAN (DURJOY) (TYPE 037) (PC)
Active: 1 Bangladesh ('Durjoy' class), 10 Burma, 98 China, 8 Egypt, 6 North Korea, Bangladesh

BANGLADESH
Name (Pennant Number): NIRBHOY (P 812).

BURMA
Name (Pennant Number): YAN SIT AUNG (441), YAN MYAT AUNG (442), YAN NYEIN AUNG (443), YAN KHWIN AUNG (444), YAN MIN AUNG (445), YAN YE AUNG (446), YAN PAING AUNG (447), YAN WIN AUNG (448), YAN AYE AUNG (449), YAN ZWE AUNG (450).

CHINA
Name (Pennant Number): (275-285), (290), (302), (305), (609), (610), (618-622), (626-629), (636-687), (689-692), (695-699), (701), (707), (723-733), (740-742).

EGYPT
Name (Pennant Number): AL NOUR (430), AL HADY (433), AL HAKIM (436), AL WAKIL (439), AL QATAR (442), AL SADDAM (445), AL SALAM (448), AL RAFIA (451).

NORTH KOREA
Name (Pennant Number): (201-204), (292-293).

Recognition features:
- High bow, long sloping forecastle, low freeboard.
- RBU 1200 A/S mortars towards forward end of forecastle.
- 57 mm/70 gun twin mounting ('A' position).
- 25 mm/60 gun twin mounting ('B' position).
- Tall, angular midships superstructure.
- Small lattice mainmast atop after end of bridge.
- 57 mm/70 gun twin mounting ('Y' position).
- 25 mm/60 gun twin mounting ('X' position on raised platform).

Note 1 - A larger Chinese-built version of Soviet SO 1.
Note 2 - Missile launchers can be fitted in lieu of the after 57 mm mounting in Chinese units. Later Chinese and Burmese ships have a tripod foremast and a short stub mainmast.
Note 3 - 'Houxin' (Type 037/1G) class is a missile-armed version of the 'Hainan' class. See separate entry.

Displacement full load, tons: 392.
Length, feet (metres): 192.8 (58.8).
Beam, feet (metres): 23.6 (7.2).
Draught, feet (metres): 7.2 (2.2).
Speed, knots: 30.5.
Range, miles: 1,300 at 15 kts.

Missiles: Chinese units can be fitted with 4 YJ-1 (C-801) SSM launchers in lieu of after 57 mm gun.
Guns: China 57 mm/70 (2 twin). USSR 25 mm/60 (2 twin). (23 mm (2 twin) in Egyptian ships).
Torpedoes: 6 (322 mm) (2 triple) tubes in 2 of Egyptian class.
A/S mortars: 4 RBU 1200.
Depth charges: 2 BMB-2 projectors; 2 racks.
Mines: Rails fitted for 12.

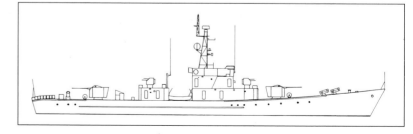

Hainan Class

HAINAN

Decoys: 2 PK 16 chaff launchers, (North Korea).

Radars:
Surface search — Pot Head or Skin Head.
Navigation — Raytheon Pathfinder (Burma). Decca, (Egypt).

Sonars: Stag Ear; hull-mounted. Thomson-Sintra SS 12 VDS on at least two of Chinese units. Tamir II, hull-mounted, (Bangladesh ships).

Hegu/Houku Class

Country: BANGLADESH, CHINA, EGYPT
Country of origin: CHINA
Ship type: PATROL FORCES
Class: HEGU/HOUKU (TYPE 024) (DURBAR) (PCFG)
Active: 5 Bangladesh ('Durbar' class), 30 China, Egypt,
BANGLADESH
Name (Pennant Number): DURBAR (P 8111), DURANTA (P 8112),
    DURVEDYA (P 8113), DURDAM (P 8114), UTTAL (P 8141).
CHINA
Name (Pennant Number): (1100) and (3100) series
EGYPT
Name (Pennant Number): (609), (611), (613), (615), (617), (619)

Recognition features:
- Low freeboard.
- 23 mm/60 or 25 mm/60 gun twin mounting ('A' position).
- Very small and low central superstructure.
- Stout, pole mainmast atop central superstructure.
- Square Tie air/surface search radar aerial atop mainmast.
- Two large, distinctive SSM launchers on quarterdeck, both raised at forward end and angled slightly outboard.

Note: Chinese variant of the Russian 'Komar' class.

Displacement full load, tons: 79.2.
Length, feet (metres): 88.6 (27).
Beam, feet (metres): 20.7 (6.3).
Draught, feet (metres): 4.3 (1.3).
Speed, knots: 37.5.
Range, miles: 400 at 30 kts.

Missiles: SSM - 2 SY-1, (CSS-N-1 Scrubbrush).
Guns: 2 USSR 25 mm/60 (twin). (2 23mm (twin), Egyptian units).

Radars:
Air/surface search — Square Tie.

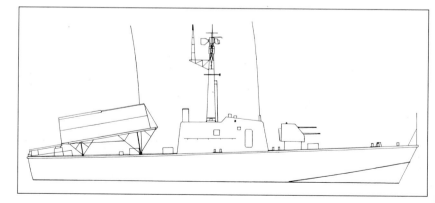

Hegu/Houku Class

Houjian/Huang Class

Country: CHINA
Country of origin: CHINA
Ship type: PATROL FORCES
Class: HOUJIAN/HUANG (TYPE 037/2) (PGG)
Active: 4
Name (Pennant Number): (770), (771), (772), (773).

Recognition features:

- High bow, sloping forecastle.
- 37 mm/63 gun twin mounting ('A' position).
- Main superstructure stepped down at after end.
- Tall, lattice mainmast at after end of bridge superstructure.
- Distinctive Rice Lamp fire control director atop bridge roof.
- Boxlike C-801 SSM launchers aft of forward superstructure, port and starboard, trained forward and slightly outboard.
- 2 30 mm/65 gun mountings ('Y' and 'X' positions).

Displacement standard, tons: 520.
Length, feet (metres): 214.6 (65.4).
Beam, feet (metres): 27.6 (8.4).
Draught, feet (metres): 7.9 (2.4).
Speed, knots: 32.
Range, miles: 1,800 at 18 kts.

Missiles: SSM - 6 YJ-1 (Eagle Strike) (C-801) (2 triple).
Guns: 37 mm/63 (twin) Type 76A. 30 mm/65 (2 twin) Type 69.

Radars:
Surface search — Square Tie.
Navigation — Type 765
Fire control — Rice Lamp.

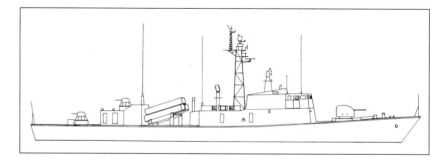

Houjian/Huang Class

HOUJIAN/HUANG

Houxin Class

Country: BURMA, CHINA, SRI LANKA
Country of origin: CHINA
Ship type: PATROL FORCES
Class: HOUXIN (TYPE 037/1G) (PGG/PCF)
Active: 6 Burma, 17 China, 1 Sri Lanka*
Building: 3 China
* Two more may have been acquired by Sri Lanka in 1998.
BURMA
Name (Pennant Number): (451-456)
CHINA
Name (Pennant Number): (751-760), (764-769), (653).
SRI LANKA
Name (Pennant Number): PARAKRAMABAHU (P 351).

Recognition features:
- High bow, long forecastle.
- 37 mm/63 gun twin mounting ('A' position).
- Long, central superstructure stepped down at after end.
- 2 14.5 mm MG mountings, port and starboard ('B' mounting position).
- Large lattice mainmast amidships with Square Tie surface search radar aerial atop.
- Small gap between forward and low after superstructure.
- 37 mm/63 gun twin mounting atop after superstructure ('X' position).
- 2 forward pointing (twin) SSM launchers, port and starboard, on quarterdeck. Both launchers angled up and slightly outboard.

Note: Missile armed version of 'Hainan' class. Some variations in the bridge superstructure of later Chinese ships.

Displacement full load, tons: 478.
Length, feet (metres): 203.4 (62.8).
Beam, feet (metres): 23.6 (7.2).
Draught, feet (metres): 7.5 (2.4).
Speed, knots: 28.
Range, miles: 1,300 at 15 kts.

Missiles: SSM - 4 YJ-1 (Eagle Strike)(C-801) (2 twin). (Not Sri Lanka unit).
Guns: 37 mm/63 Type 76A (2 twin), 4 14.5 mm MGs Type 69 (2 twin).
A/S mortars: 2 Type 87 6-tube launchers, (Sri Lanka only).

Radars:
Surface search — Square Tie, (Burmese and Chinese ships).
Navigation — Anritsu RA 723
Fire control — Rice Lamp.
Sonars: Stag Ear, hull-mounted active search/attack, (Sri Lankan ship only).

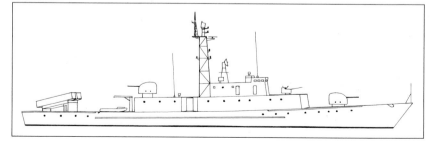

Houxin Class

HOUXIN

Flyvefisken Class

Country: DENMARK
Country of origin: DENMARK
Ship type: PATROL FORCES
Class: FLYVEFISKEN (PG/MHC/MLC/AGSC)
Active: 14
Name (Pennant Number): FLYVEFISKEN (P 550), HAJEN (P 551), HAVKATTEN (P 552), LAXEN (P 553), MAKRELEN (P 554), STØREN (P 555), SVAERDFISKEN (P 556), GLENTEN (P 557), GRIBBEN (P 558), LOMMEN (P 559), RAVNEN (P 560), SKADEN (P 561), VIBEN (P 562), SØLØVEN (P 563)

Recognition features:
- 3 in gun mounting ('A' position).
- High freeboard with break down to afterdeck adjacent to funnel.
- High, angular central superstructure flush with ship's side.
- Tall enclosed mainmast amidships with AWS 6 or TRS-3D (P557-563) air/surface search radar aerial atop.
- Very low profile, black-capped funnel aft of mainmast with sloping after end.
- 2 Harpoon SSM angled launchers, athwartships in crossover configuration, aft of funnel adjacent to break in maindeck.
- 2 torpedo tubes, one port one starboard, outboard of SSM launchers.
- **Note** - The overall design allows ships to change as required to the attack, patrol, MCMV or minelayer roles. Requirement is to be able to change within 48 hours.

Displacement full load, tons: 480.
Length, feet (metres): 177.2 (54).
Beam, feet (metres): 29.5 (9).
Draught, feet (metres): 8.2 (2.5).
Speed, knots: 30.
Range, miles: 2,400 at 18 kts.

Missiles: SSM - 8 McDonnell Douglas Harpoon. SAM — 3 Mk 48 Mod 3 twin launchers, Sea Sparrow. (Fitted for attack/MCM/minelaying roles).
Guns: 1 OTO Melara 3 in (76 mm)/62 Super Rapid. 2 12.7 mm MGs.
Torpedoes: 2 21 in (533 mm) tubes. FFV Type 613.
Mines: 60 (minelaying role only).
Decoys: 2 Sea Gnat DL-6T 6-barrel chaff launcher.

Radars:
Air/surface search — Plessey AWS 6 (P 550-P 556). Telefunken System Technik TRS-3D (P 557-P 563)
Surface search — Terma Scanter Mil.
Navigation — Furuno.
Fire control — Celsius Tech 9LV 200.
Sonars: Thomson-Sintra TSM 2640 Salmon; VDS. CelsiusTech CTS-36/39; hull-mounted.

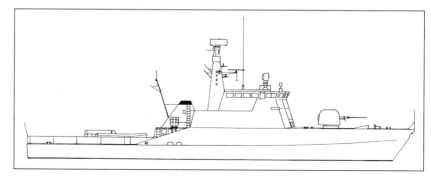

STØREN

Country: FINLAND
Country of origin: FINLAND
Ship type: PATROL FORCES
Class: HELSINKI (PCFG)
Active: 4
Name (Pennant Number): HELSINKI (60), TURKU (61), OULU (62), KOTKA (63)

Recognition features:
- Short forecastle with 57 mm/70 gun mounting ('A' position).
- High rounded superstructure forward of midships.
- Tall, slender, enclosed mainmast atop superstructure aft of bridge.
- 2 23 mm/87 gun mountings on wings at after end of superstructure. (Can be replaced by Sadral/Mistral SAM launcher)
- 4 twin RBS 15 SSM launchers on afterdeck; 2 port, 2 starboard, trained forward and angled outboard.

Note - See also Rauma class which was developed from this design.

Displacement full load, tons: 300.
Length, feet (metres): 147.6 (45).
Beam, feet (metres): 29.2 (8.9).
Draught, feet (metres): 9.9 (3).
Speed, knots: 30.

Missiles: SSM - 8 Saab RBS 15. SAM — 2 sextuple Sadral launchers; Mistral
Guns: 1 Bofors 57 mm/70. Sako 23 mm/87 (2 twin) (in place of Sadral launcher).
Depth charges: 2 rails.
Decoys: Philax chaff launcher.

Radars:
Surface search — 9GA 208.
Fire control — CelsiusTech 9LV 225.
Navigation — Raytheon ARPA.
Sonars: Simrad Marine SS 304. Finnyards Sonac/PTA towed array.

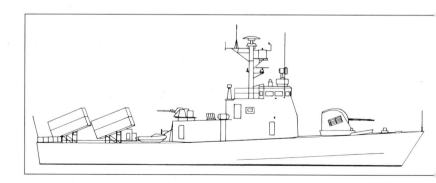

KOTKA (with 23 mm gun)

Rauma Class

Country: FINLAND
Country of origin: FINLAND
Ship type: PATROL FORCES
Class: RAUMA (PCFG)
Active: 4
Name (Pennant Number): RAUMA (70), RAAHE (71), PORVOO (72), NAANTALI (73)

Recognition features:

- High bow with long forecastle.
- 40 mm/70 gun mounting mid-forecastle.
- Saab Elma LLS-920 A/S mortar between mounting and forward superstructure.
- Central, angular, stepped superstructure.
- 9LV 225 fire control radar aerial atop bridge roof.
- Short, robust pole mainmast amidships.
- 9GA 208 surface search radar aerial atop mainmast.
- 2 RBS 15 SSM launchers outboard of after end of superstructure with second two right aft on the port and starboard quarter.

Note - SAM and 23 mm guns are interchangeable within the same barbette.

Displacement full load, tons: 248.
Length, feet (metres): 157.5 (48).
Beam, feet (metres): 26.2 (8).
Draught, feet (metres): 4.5 (1.5).
Speed, knots: 30.

Missiles: SSM - 6 Saab RBS 15SF. SAM - Matra Sadral sextuple launcher; Mistral.
Guns: Bofors 40 mm/70; (6 103 mm rails for rocket illuminants). Sako 23 mm/87 (twin) can be fitted instead of Sadral.
A/S mortars: 4 Saab Elma LLS-920 9-tubed launchers.
Depth charges: 1 rail.
Decoys: Philax chaff launcher.

Radars:

Surface search — 9GA 208.
Fire control — CelsiusTech 9LV 225.
Navigation — Raytheon ARPA.
Sonars: Simrad Subsea Toadfish sonar. Finnyards Sonac/PTA towed array.

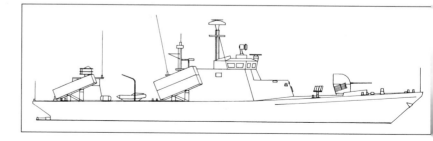

ORVOO

La Combattante I/Um Almaradim class

Country: KUWAIT
Country of origin: FRANCE
Ship type: PATROL FORCES
Class: LA COMBATTANTE I (UM ALMARADIM) (PCFG)
Active: 5
Building: 3
Name (Pennant Number): UM ALMARADIM (P 3711), OUHA (P 3713), FAILAKA (P 3715), MASKAN (P 3717), AL-AHMADI (P 3719), ALFAHAHEEL (P 3721), GAROH (P 3723), — (P 3725).

Recognition features
- Continuous maindeck from stem to stern.
- Angled, slab-sided superstructure with enclosed mast with slim pole atop, aft of midships. Whip aerial above bridge.
- 40 mm/70 gun mounting immediately forward of bridge superstructure.
- Sadral/Mistral SAM sextuple launcher atop superstructure immediately aft of mast.
- Sea Skua SSM box launchers right aft.

Displacement, full load, tons: 245.
Length, feet (metres): 137.8 (42) oa.
Beam, feet (metres): 26.9 (8.2).
Draught, feet (metres): 5.9 (1.8).
Speed, knots: 30.
Range, miles: 1,350 at 14 kts.

Missiles: SSM — BAe Sea Skua (2 twin). SAM — Sadral sextuple launcher, Mistral.
Guns: 1 OTOBreda 40 mm/70; 1 Giat 20 mm M 621, (in lieu of SSM); 2 12.7 mm MGs.
Decoys: 2 Dagaie Mk 2 chaff launchers.

Radars:
Air/surface search — Thomson-CSF MRR
Navigation — Racal Decca
Fire control — BAe Seaspray Mk 3.

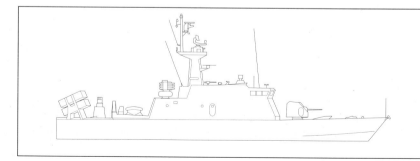

UM ALMARADIM

CMN Cherbourg

La Combattante II/IIA/Perdana Class

Country: CHILE, GERMANY, GREECE, IRAN, LIBYA, MALAYSIA,
Country of origin: FRANCE
Ship type: PATROL FORCES
Class: LA COMBATTANTE II/IIA (RIQUELME, TIGER, ANNINOS, VOTSIS, KAMAN, PERDANA) (PGF/PCFG)
Active: 4 Chile ('Riquelme' class Type 148), 10 Germany ('Tiger' class, Type 148), 4 Combattante II, ('Anninos') 4 Combattante IIA ('Votsis' class), Greece., 10 Iran ('Kaman' class), 4 + 5 reserve Libya, 4 Malaysia ('Perdana' class)

CHILE
Name (Pennant Number): GUARDIAMARINA RIQUELME (ex-Wolf) (LM 36, ex-P 6149), TENIENTE ORELLA (ex-Elster) (LM 37, ex-P 6154), —— (ex-Tiger) (LM 38, ex-P 6141), —— (ex-Luchs) (LM 39, ex-P 6143).

GERMANY
Name (Pennant Number): LEOPARD (P 6145), FUCHS (P 6146), JAGUAR (P 6147), LÖWE (P 6148), PANTHER (P 6150), ALK (P 6155), DOMMEL (P 6156), WEIHE (P 6157), PINGUIN (P 6158), REIHER (P 6159).

GREECE
Name (Pennant Number): 'Anninos' class - ANTHIPOPLOIARHOS ANNINOS (ex-Navsithoi) (P 14), IPOPLOIARHOS ARLIOTIS (ex-Evniki) (P 15), IPOPLOIARHOS KONIDIS (ex-Kymothoi) (P 16), IPOPLOIARHOS BATSIS (ex-Calypso) (P 17)
'Votsis' class — IPOPLIARHOS VOTSIS (ex-Iltis) (P 72, ex-P 51), ANTIPLIARHOS PEZOPOULOS (ex-Storch) (P 73, ex-P 30), PLOTARHIS VLAHAVAS (ex-Marder) (P 74), PLOTARHIS MARIDAKIS (ex-Häher) (P 75).

IRAN
Name (Pennant Number): KAMAN (P 221), ZOUBIN (P 222), KHADANG (P 223), FALAKHON (P 226), SHAMSHIR (P 227), GORZ (P 228), GARDOUNEH (P 229), KHANJAR (P 230), NEYZEH (P 231), TARBARZIN (P 232).

LIBYA
Name (Pennant Number): SHARABA (ex-Beir Grassa) (518), WAHAG (ex-Beir Gzir) (522), SHEHAB (ex-Beir Gtifa) (524), SHOUAIA (ex-Beir Algandula) (528), SHOULA (ex-Beir Ktitat) (532), SHAFAK (ex-Beir Alkrarim) (534), BARK (ex-Beir Alkardmen) (536), RAD (ex-Beir Alkur) (538), LAHEEB (ex-Beir Alkuefat) (542).

MALAYSIA
Name (Pennant Number): PERDANA (3501), SERANG (3502), GANAS (3503), GANYANG (3504).

Recognition features:
- Small bridge superstructure forward of midships.
- 35 mm/90 gun mounting ('A' position), Greek 'Anninos' class. (57 mm/70 gun in Malaysian ships, OTO MELARA 3 in, Chilean, German, Greek 'Votsis' class, Libyan and Iranian ships).
- Tall lattice mainmast at after end of superstructure. (Fire control radome atop in Iranian ships).
- Fire control radar aerial atop bridge roof, (not Iranian ships).
- SSM launchers aft of superstructure, forward two immediately aft of superstructure trained forward and to starboard, after two trained forward and to port. (2 Exocet launchers only in Malaysian ships. 2 twin Harpoon/2 or 4 C-802 SSM in Iranian ships).

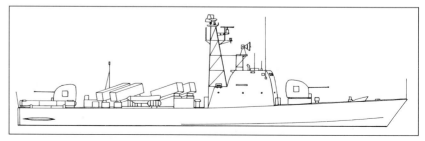

La Combattante II/IIA/Perdana Class

● 35 mm/90 gun mounting aft in 'Y' position, (Greek 'Anninos' class). 40 mm/70 in same position in Malaysian ships and in some Iranian units (some with 20 mm). (Chilean, German, Greek 'Votsis' class and Libyans with 40 mm/70 turret mounting).

Displacement full load, tons: 255, (Greek 'Anninos' class); 311 (Libya), 265 (Chile, Germany, Greek 'Votsis' class and Malaysia), 275, (Iran).
Length, feet (metres): 154.2 (47). (160.7 (49), Libya).
Beam, feet (metres): 23.3 (7.1). (23.1 (7), Chile, Germany, Greek 'Votsis' class and Malaysia).
Draught, feet (metres): 8.2 (2.5), Greek 'Anninos' class. (6.2, (1.9), Iran). (6.6 (2), Libya). (12.8 (3.9), Malaysia). (8.9 (2.7), Chile, Germany, Greek 'Votsis' class).
Speed, knots: 36.5.
Range, miles: 850 at 25 kts.

Missiles: SSM - 4 Aerospatiale MM 38 Exocet, (Chile, Germany, Greece, 2 only in Malaysian ships). OTO MELARA/Matra Otomat Mk 2 (TG 1), (Libya). 2 or 4 Chinese C-802 (1 or 2 twin) or Harpoon (2 twin), (Iranian ships).
Guns: Oerlikon 35 mm/90 (2 twin), (Greek 'Anninos'). 1 OTO MELARA 3 in(76mm)/62 Compact, 1 Breda Bofors 40 mm/70 (some have 20 mm or 23 mm gun in place of 40 mm) and 2 12.7 MGs (Iran). 1 OTO MELARA 3 in(76mm)/62 Compact, 1 Breda/Bofors 40 mm/70 (twin), (Chile, Germany, Greek 'Votsis' class, Libya). 1 Bofors 57 mm/70; 1 Bofors 40 mm/70, (Malaysia)
Torpedoes: 2 21 in (533 mm) tubes AEG SST-4, (Greek 'Anninos' only).

Radars:
Surface search — Thomson-CSF Triton, (Chile, German, Greek ships, Libyan and Malaysian ships).
Surface search/fire control — Signaal WM28 (Iran).
Navigation — Decca 1226C, (Greek 'Anninos', Iran). Racal Decca 616 (Malaysia). SMA 3 RM 20, (Chile, Germany, Greek 'Votsis' class).
Fire control — Thomson-CSF Pollux, (Greek 'Anninos' and Malaysian ships). Thomson-CSF Castor IIB, (Chile, Germany, Greek 'Votsis' class and Libya).

La Combattante III/IIB Class

Country: GREECE, NIGERIA, QATAR, TUNISIA
Country of origin: FRANCE
Ship type: PATROL FORCES
Class: LA COMBATTANTE III (LASKOS, DAMSAH) (PCFG)
Active: 9 Greece ('Laskos' class), 2 Nigeria (Combattante IIIB), 3 Qatar ('Damsah' class), 3 Tunisia

GREECE
Name (Pennant Number): ANTIPLOIARHOS LASKOS (P 20), PLOTARHIS BLESSAS (P 21), IPOPLOIARHOS MIKONIOS (P 22), IPOPLOIARHOS TROUPAKIS (P 23), SIMEOFOROS KAVALOUDIS (P 24), IPOPLOIARHOS DEGIANNIS (P 26), SIMEOFOROS XENOS (P 27), SIMEOFOROS SIMITZOPOULOS (P 28), SIMEOFOROS STARAKIS (P 29)

NIGERIA
Name (Pennant Number): AYAM (P 182), EKUN (P 183).

QATAR
Name (Pennant Number): DAMSAH (Q 01), AL GHARIYAH (Q 02), RBIGAH (Q 03).

TUNISIA
Name (Pennant Number): LA GALITÉ (501), TUNIS (502), CARTHAGE (503).

Recognition features:
- Low freeboard craft with 3 in gun mounting ('A' position).
- Low profile, rounded superstructure well forward of midships.
- Fire control radar aerial mounted on lattice structure atop bridge roof.
- Tall lattice mainmast atop mid-superstructure.
- Surface search radar aerial atop mainmast.
- 2 30 mm gun mountings, one port one starboard, atop after end of superstructure.
- Low profile after superstructure forward of 3 in gun mounting ('Y' position), (Greek ships only. 40 mm/70 twin mounting in Nigerian, Qatar and Tunisian units).
- SSM launchers between forward and after superstructures.
- 2 single torpedo tubes trained aft and sited outboard either side of after mounting. (Greek ships only).

Displacement full load, tons: 425 (Greece, P 20-23, Tunisia); 429 (Greece, P 24-29). 395 (Qatar). 430 (Nigeria).
Length, feet (metres): 184 (56.2), (Greece, Nigeria). 183.7 (56), (Qatar, Tunisia).
Beam, feet (metres): 26.2 (8), (Greece). 26.9 (8.2), (Qatar, Tunisia). 24.9 (7.6), (Nigeria).
Draught, feet (metres): 7 (2.1), (Greece, Nigeria). 7.2 (2.2), (Qatar, Tunisia).
Speed, knots: 36 (Greece, P 20-23); 32.5 (Greece, P 24-29). 38 (Nigeria, Qatar, Tunisia)
Range, miles: 2,700 at 15 kts. (Greece). 2,000 at 15 kts. (Remainder).

Missiles: SSM - 4 Aerospatiale MM 38 Exocet (Greece, P 20-23, Nigeria). MM 40 Exocet (2 quad), (Qatar, Tunisia).   6 Kongsberg Penguin Mk 2 (Greece, P 24-29).

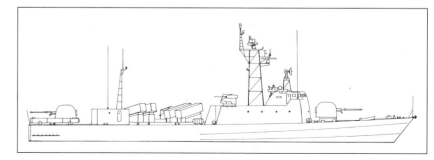

La Combattante III/IIB Class

RBIGAH

Guns: 2 OTO Melara 3 in (76 mm)/62 Compact; 4 Emerson Electric 30 mm (2 twin), (Greece). 1 OTO MELARA 3 in (76 mm)/62; 2 Breda 40 mm/70 (twin), (Nigeria, Qatar, Tunisia). 4 Emerson Electric 30 mm (2 twin), (Nigeria). 4 Oerlikon 30 mm/75 (2 twin), (Qatar, Tunisia).
Torpedoes: 2   21 in (533 mm) aft tubes. AEG SST-4. (Greece only).
Decoys: Wegmann launchers, (Greece). CSEE Dagaie single trainable launcher, (Qatar, Tunisia).

Radars:
Air/surface search — Thomson-CSF Triton.
Navigation — Decca 1226C, (Greece, Qatar). Racal Decca TM 1226, (Nigeria).
Fire control — Thomson-CSF Castor II/Thomson-CSF Pollux.

P 400 Class

Country: FRANCE, GABON, OMAN
Country of origin: FRANCE
Ship type: PATROL FORCES
Class: P 400 (PATRA/AL BUSHRA) (PC/OPV)
Active: 10 France, 2 Gabon ('Patra' class), 3 Oman ('Al Bushra' class OPV)

FRANCE
Name (Pennant Number): L'AUDACIEUSE (P 682), LA BOUDEUSE (P 683), LA CAPRICIEUSE (P 684), LA FOUGUEUSE (P 685), LA GLORIEUSE (P 686), LA GRACIEUSE (P 687), LA MOQUEUSE (P 688), LA RAILLEUSE (P 689), LA RIEUSE (P 690), LA TAPAGEUSE (P 691)

GABON
Name (Pennant Number): GÉNÉRAL d'ARMÉE BA-OUMAR (P 07), COLONEL DJOUE-DABANY (P 08).

OMAN
Name (Pennant Number): AL BUSHRA (B 1), AL MANSOOR (B 2), AL NAJAH (B 3).

Recognition features:
- 40 mm/60 gun mounting ('A' position). (OTO MELARA 76 mm/62 Super Rapid being fitted in Omani units from 1998).
- High, angular, midships superstructure.
- Pole mainmast, angled aft, atop superstructure amidships. (Lattice mast in Omani ships).
- Very unusual twin funnels aft of superstructure at outboard extremities of hull. Funnels are of square section, black-capped, and angled aft. Omani ships have single tapered funnel with tall whip aerial at forward end.

Note: Gabon P 08 has second 20 mm in place of 57 mm/70 mounting.

Displacement full load, tons: 477. (475 Oman, 446 Gabon.).
Length, feet (metres): 178.6 (54.5).
Beam, feet (metres): 26.2 (8).
Draught, feet (metres): 8.5 (2.5) (8.9 (2.7), Oman).
Speed, knots: 24.5
Range, miles: 4,200 at 15 kts.

Guns: 1 Bofors 40 mm/60. 1 Giat 20F2 20 mm. 2 - 12.7 mm MGs, (France.) 1 Bofors 57 mm/70 SAK 57 Mk 2 (P 07); 2 Giat 20F2 20 mm (twin) (P 08), (Gabon). In Omani ships, 40 mm/60 is to be replaced by OTO MELARA 76 mm/62 Super Rapid; 2 Oerlikon/Royal Ordnance 20 mm GAM-B01 20 mm and 2 12.7 mm MGs also in Omani ships.
Torpedoes: 4 16 in (406 mm) (2 twin tubes) to be fitted in Omani ships from 2000.

Radars:
Surface search — Racal Decca 1226. (French, Gabon ships). Kelvin Hughes 1007 ARPA (Oman).

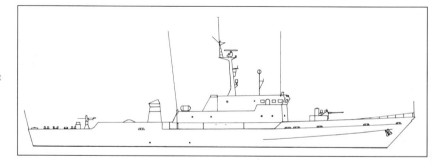

P 400 Class

LA TAPAGEUSE

PR-72P Velarde Class

Country: PERU
Country of origin: FRANCE
Ship type: PATROL FORCES
Class: VELARDE (PR-72P) (CM/PCF)
Active: 6
Name (Pennant Number): VELARDE (CM 21), SANTILLANA (CM 22), DE LOS HEROS (CM 23), HERRERA (CM 24), LARREA (CM 25), SANCHEZ CARRILLON (CM 26)

Recognition features:
- Unusual, downturned forward end of forecastle.
- 3 in gun mounting ('A' position).
- High rounded main superstructure forward of midships.
- Large lattice mainmast atop central superstructure supporting Triton surface search radar aerial.
- Castor II fire control radar aerial atop bridge.
- 4 Exocet SSM launchers aft of superstructure. Forward pair angled to starboard, after pair to port.
- 40 mm/70 gun twin mounting right aft.

Note - Morocco operates two PR 72 class ('Okba') PCs and Senegal one PR 72M PC which are similar in appearance, although smaller in dimensions and displacement.

Displacement full load, tons: 560.
Length, feet (metres): 210 (64).
Beam, feet (metres): 27.4 (8.4).
Draught, feet (metres): 5.2 (2.6).
Speed, knots: 37.
Range, miles: 2,500 at 16 kts.

Missiles: SSM - 4 Aerospatiale MM 38 Exocet. SAM — SA-N-10 launcher may be fitted on the stern.
Guns: 1 OTO Melara 3 in (76 mm)/62 Compact; 2 Breda 40 mm/70 (twin).

Radars:
Surface search — Thomson-CSF Triton.
Navigation — Racal Decca 1226.
Fire control — Thomson-CSF Castor II.

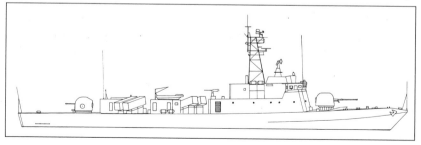

HERRERA

Country: GERMANY
Country of origin: GERMANY
Ship type: PATROL FORCES
Class: ALBATROS (TYPE 1438B) (PCFG)
Active: 10
Name (Pennant Number): ALBATROS (P 6111), FALKE (P 6112), GEIER (P 6113), BUSSARD (P 6114), SPERBER (P 6115), GREIF (P 6116), KONDOR (P 6117), SEEADLER (P 6118), HABICHT (P 6119), KORMORAN (P 6120)

Recognition features:
- Long forecastle, prominent breakwater forward of 3 in gun mounting ('A' position).
- Narrow central superstructure, stepped down aft of bridge.
- Lattice structure aft of bridge supporting distinctive WM27 surface search/fire control radome.
- Tall tripod mainmast at after end of superstructure.
- Exocet SSM launchers aft of superstructure, trained forward and to port and immediately aft, trained forward and to starboard.
- 3 in gun mounting aft of SSM launchers ('Y' position).
- 2 torpedo tubes outboard of after gun mounting, trained aft.

Displacement full load, tons: 398.
Length, feet (metres): 189 (57.6).
Beam, feet (metres): 25.6 (7.8).
Draught, feet (metres): 8.5 (2.6).
Speed, knots: 40.
Range, miles: 1,300 at 30 kts.

Missiles: SSM - Aerospatiale MM 38 Exocet (2 twin) launchers.
Guns: 2 OTO Melara 3 in (76 mm)/62 Compact; 2 12.7 mm MGs may be fitted.
Torpedoes: 2 21 in (533 mm) aft tubes. AEG Seeal.
Decoys: Buck-Wegmann Hot Dog/Silver Dog chaff/IR flare dispenser.

Radars:
Surface search/fire control — Signaal WM 27.
Navigation — SMA 3 RM 20.

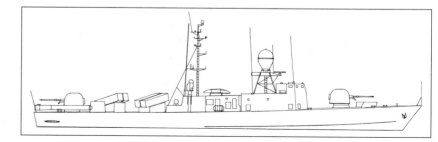

Albatros Class

SEEADLER

Country: GERMANY
Country of origin: GERMANY
Ship type: PATROL FORCES
Class: GEPARD (TYPE 143 A) (PCFG)
Active: 10
Name (Pennant Number): GEPARD (P 6121), PUMA (P 6122), HERMELIN (P 6123), NERZ (P 6124), ZOBEL (P 6125), FRETTCHEN (P 6126), DACHS (P 6127), OZELOT (P 6128), WIESEL (P 6129), HYÄNE (P 6130)

Recognition features:
- Long forecastle with 3 in gun mounting ('A' position).
- Central superstructure with high forward end, stepped down aft of bridge.
- Distinctive surface WM27 search/fire control radome atop after end of bridge.
- Tall tripod mainmast at after end of superstructure.
- 2 Exocet SSM launchers aft of superstructure trained forward and to port and 2 further aft trained forward and to starboard.

Displacement full load, tons: 391.
Length, feet (metres): 190 (57.6).
Beam, feet (metres): 25.6 (7.8).
Draught, feet (metres): 8.5 (2.6).
Speed, knots: 40.
Range, miles: 2,600 at 16 kts.

Missiles: SSM - 4 Aerospatiale MM 38 Exocet. SAM - GDC RAM 21 cell point defence system. **Guns:** 1 OTO Melara 3 in (76 mm)/62 Compact.
Decoys: Buck-Wegmann Hot Dog/Silver Dog chaff/IR flare dispenser.

Radars:
Surface search/fire control — Signaal WM 27.
Navigation — SMA 3 RM 20.

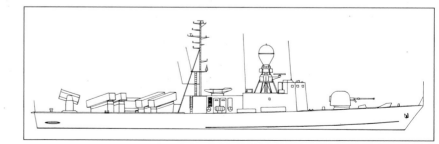

Gepard Class

ZOBEL (with RAM)

TNC 45 (Intrepida/Ahmad El Fateh/ Quito /Jerong/Sea Wolf /Prabparapak/Ban Yas) Class

Country: ARGENTINA, BAHRAIN, ECUADOR, GHANA, KUWAIT, MALAYSIA, SINGAPORE, THAILAND, UNITED ARAB EMIRATES (UAE).

Country of origin: GERMANY

Ship type: PATROL FORCES

Class: INTREPIDA, AHMAD EL FATEH, QUITO, JERONG, SEA WOLF, PRABPARAPAK, BAN YAS (TNC 45) (PCF/PCFG),

Active: 2 Argentina ('Intrepida' class), 4 Bahrain ('Ahmad el Fateh' class), 3 Ecuador ('Quito' class), 2 Ghana, 1 Kuwait, 6 Malaysia ('Jerong' class), 6 Singapore ('Sea Wolf' class), 3 Thailand ('Prabparapak' class), 6 UAE ('Ban Yas' class)

ARGENTINA
Name (Pennant Number): INTREPIDA (P 85), INDOMITA (P 86)

BAHRAIN
Name (Pennant Number): AHMAD EL FATEH (20), AL JABIRI (21), ABDUL RAHMAN AL FADEL (22), AL TAWEELAH (23)

ECUADOR
Name (Pennant Number): QUITO (LM 21), GUAYAQUIL (LM 23), CUENCA (LM 24).

GHANA
Name (Pennant Number): DZATA (P 26), SEBO (P 27).

KUWAIT
Name (Pennant Number): AL SANBOUK (P 4505)

MALAYSIA
Name (Pennant Number): JERONG (3505), TODAK (3506), PAUS (3507), YU (3508), BAUNG (3509), PARI (3510).

SINGAPORE
Name (Pennant Number): SEA WOLF (P 76), Sea LION (P 77), SEA DRAGON (P 78), SEA TIGER (P 79), SEA HAWK (P 80), SEA SCORPION (P 81).

THAILAND
Name (Pennant Number): PRABPARAPAK (311, ex-1), HANHAK SATTRU (312, ex-2), SUPHAIRIN (313, ex-3).

UAE
Name (Pennant Number): BAN YAS (P 4501), MARBAN (P 4502), RODQM (P 4503), SHAHEEN (P 4504), SAGAR (P 4505), TARIF (P 4506).

Recognition features:
- Sweeping bow, low freeboard. Continuous maindeck from stem to stern.
- 3 in gun mounting ('A' position), except Ghana, (Bofors 40 mm/70), Malaysia, Singapore and Thailand, (Bofors 57 mm/70).
- High superstructure forward of midships. (Deckhouse extended aft, Ghana ships).
- Open bridge atop enclosed bridge.
- Lattice mainmast aft of bridge with short pole mast at after end.
- Large radome with 2 smaller radomes on short mast atop bridge, (Singapore).

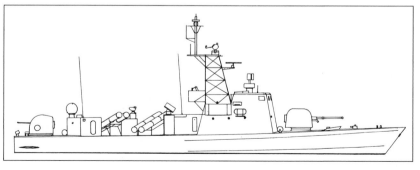

TNC 45 (Intrepida/Ahmad El Fateh/Quito /Jerong/Sea Wolf /Prabparapak/Ban Yas) Class

- 4 Exocet SSM launchers, 2 trained to port, 2 to starboard in crossover configuration aft of superstructure. (MM 40 Exocet fitted in Argentine ships 1997/98). (No missiles, Ghana or Malaysia). Harpoon SSM in crossover configuration aft of superstructure in Singapore units.
- 40 mm/70 mounting right aft. (2 in Intrepida class) (1 Oerlikon 35 mm/90 twin mounting in 'Y' position, Ecuador ships). (Breda 40 mm/70 twin mounting in 'Y' position, Bahrain, Kuwait and UAE units).

Displacement full load, tons: 259, (Bahrain). 268, (Argentina, Thailand). 269, (Ghana). 255, (Ecuador, Kuwait). 244, (Malaysia). 254, (Singapore). 260, (UAE).

Length, feet (metres): 147.3 (44.9). 147.6 (45), (Ecuador). (149 (45.4), Thailand).

Beam, feet (metres): 22.9 (7) (Bahrain). 24.3 (7.4), (Argentina, Thailand). 23 (7), (Ecuador, Ghana, Kuwait, Malaysia, Singapore, UAE).

Draught, feet (metres): 8.2 (2.5). (7.5 (2.3), Kuwait, Thailand). (8.9 (2.7), Ghana).

Speed, knots: 40. (32, Malaysia, 35 Singapore, 27 Ghana).

Range, miles: 1,800 at 16 kts.

Missiles: SSM - 4 Aerospatiale MM 40 Exocet (2 twin) launchers. (MM 38 in Ecuador ships) (No missiles in Ghana, Malaysia ships). McDonnell Douglas Harpoon (2 twin) 4 IAI Gabriel (Singapore). IAI Gabriel (1 triple, 2 single), (Thailand). SAM — Matra Simbad twin launcher, Mistral, (Singapore only).

Guns: 1 OTO MELARA 3 in (76 mm)/62, (all, except Ghana, Malaysia, Singapore and Thailand.); 2 Bofors 40 mm/70, (Ghana); 1 Bofors 57 mm/70, (Malaysia, Singapore, Thailand). 1 Bofors 40 mm/70, (Malaysia, Thailand); 1 or 2 Bofors 40 mm/70 in (Argentina); 2 Oerlikon 35 mm/90 (twin), (Ecuador); 2 Breda 40 mm /70, (Bahrain, Kuwait, UAE). 3 7.62 mm MGs, (Bahrain); 2 7.62 mm MGs, (UAE).

Decoys: CSEE Dagaie launcher. (Bahrain, Kuwait, UAE). 2 Hycor Mk 137 sextuple RBOC chaff launchers; 4 Rafael (2 twin) long-range chaff launchers, (Singapore).

Torpedoes: 2 21 in (533 mm) tubes. AEG SST-4. (Argentine ships only).

Radars:

Air/surface search — Ericsson Sea Giraffe 150 (Bahrain, Kuwait, UAE). Decca 626 (Argentina) Thomson-CSF Triton (Ecuador). Racal Decca 1226 (Malaysia, Singapore).

Surface search — Kelvin Hughes Type 17. (Thailand).

Navigation — Racal Decca 1226, (Bahrain, Ecuador, Malaysia, UAE). Decca TM 1226C (Ghana).

Fire control — CelsiusTech 9LV 226/231 (Bahrain). CelsiusTech 9LV 200 (Kuwait, UAE). Thomson-CSF Pollux, (Ecuador). Signaal WM28/5, (Singapore, Thailand).

AL TAWEELAH

Lürssen FPB 57/Singa/Kakap/Ekpe/Dogan Class

Country: GHANA, INDONESIA, KUWAIT, NIGERIA, TURKEY
Country of origin: GERMANY
Ship type: PATROL FORCES
Class: LÜRSSEN FPB 57 (SINGA), (KAKAP) (EKPE) (DOGAN) (PC/PCF/PCFG)
Active: 2 Ghana; 4 'Singa' class (PC), 4 'Kakap' class (PC), Indonesia, 1 Kuwait, 2 Nigeria ('Ekpe' class), 8 Turkey ('Dogan' class PCFG)

GHANA
Name (Pennant Number): ACHIMOTA (P 28), YOGAGA (P 29).
INDONESIA
Name (Pennant Number): 'Singa' class - SINGA (651), AJAK (653), PANDRONG (801), SURA (802). 'Kakap' class — KAKAP (811), KERAPU (812), TONGKOL (813), BARAKUDA (ex-Bervang) (814).
KUWAIT
Name (Pennant Number): ISTIQLAL (P 5702).
NIGERIA
Name (Pennant Number): EKPE (P 178), AGU (P 180).
TURKEY
Name (Pennant Number): DOGAN (P 340), MARTI (P 341), TAYFUN (P 342), VOLKAN (P 343), RÜZGAR (P 344), POYRAZ (P 345), GURBET (P 346), FIRTINA (P 347)

Recognition features:
- Long forecastle with 3 in or Bofors SAK 57 mm/70 gun mounting or Bofors 40 mm/60 ('A' position).
- Low freeboard.
- Rounded, short superstructure forward of midships stepped down at after end. (Longer superstructure in Ghanaian and Kuwait units)
- Raised helicopter platform extending aft from superstructure in Indonesia 'Kakap' class.
- Short, square profile lattice mainmast at after end of superstructure.

- Surface search radome atop mainmast, (Not Ghanaian or Indonesian 'Kakap' units).
- SSM launchers in 'V' formation on afterdeck. (No missiles, Ghana, Indonesia, Nigeria).
- 35 mm/70 mounting right aft ('Y' position). (40 mm/70, Ghana and Indonesian 'Singa' but absent in Indonesian 'Kakap' class.) Twin Breda 40 mm/70 turret in this position in Kuwaiti and Nigerian units.

Note - The new Turkish 'Yildiz' class is based on the 'Dogan' class hull.

Displacement full load, tons: 389 (Ghana). 410, (Kuwait). 423, (Indonesian 'Kakap' class). 428 (Indonesia 'Singa' class). 436. (Turkey). 444, (Nigeria).
Length, feet (metres): 190.6 (58.1)
Beam, feet (metres): 25. (7.6) (24.9 7.6), Kuwait, Nigeria).
Draught, feet (metres): 8.8 (2.7) Turkey. (8.9 2.7), Kuwait). (9.2 (2.8), Ghana, Indonesia). (10.2 (3.1), Nigeria).
Speed, knots: 42, Nigeria. (38, Turkey). (30, Ghana). (27, Indonesia).

Missiles: SSM - McDonnell Douglas Harpoon (2 quad) launchers, (Turkey). 4 Exocet MM 40, (Kuwait). (No missiles, Ghana, Indonesia, Nigeria)

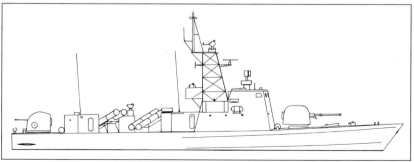

MARTI

Guns: 1 OTO MELARA 3 in (76 mm)/62 Compact. 2 Oerlikon 35 mm/90 (twin), (Turkish ships). 1 OTO MELARA 3 in (76 mm)/62 Compact, 1 Breda 40 mm/70, (Ghana, Kuwait, Nigeria). 1 Bofors SAK 57 mm/70 Mk 2; 1 Bofors SAK 40 mm/70; 2 Rheinmetall 20 mm (Indonesia 'Singa' class). 1 Bofors 40 mm/60; 2 12.7 mm MGs, (Indonesian 'Kakap' class).

Torpedoes: 2 21 in (533 mm) Toro tubes; AEG SUT. (Some Indonesian 'Singa' units only).

Decoys: 2 multi-barrelled launchers. (Not Ghana, Nigeria or Indonesian Kakap).

Radars:
Surface search — Racal Decca 1226, (Turkish, Nigerian ships). Thomson-CSF Canopus A (Ghana). Racal Decca 2459 (Indonesia). Marconi S 810 (Kuwait).
Navigation — Decca TM 1226C (Ghana, Kuwait). Kelvin Hughes 1007, (Indonesian 'Kakap' class).
Fire control — Signaal WM28/41, (Turkish, Nigerian ships). WM22, (Indonesia 'Singa' class). Philips 9LV 200, (Kuwait).

Sonars: Signaal PMS 32 (Some Indonesian 'Singa' units).

Helicopters: Platform for Nurtanio NBO 105C or Westland Wasp HAS Mk 1, (Indonesian 'Kakap' class only).

Willemoes Class

Country: DENMARK
Country of origin: GERMANY
Ship type: PATROL FORCES
Class: WILLEMOES (PGFG)
Active: 10
Name (Pennant Number): BILLE (P 540), BREDAL (P 541), HAMMER (P 542), HUITFELD (P 543), KRIEGER (P 544), NORBY (P 545), RODSTEEN (P 546), SEHESTED (P 547), SUENSON (P 548), WILLEMOES (P 549)

Recognition features:

- Long forecastle with visible breakwater just forward of 3 in gun mounting ('A' position).
- Low rounded superstructure from midships aft to quarterdeck.
- Torpedo tubes, port and starboard, adjacent to 'A' mounting.
- Short lattice mainmast mid-superstructure with taller tripod mast immediately aft supporting 9GA 208 air/surface search radar aerial.
- 9LV 200 fire control radar aerial on pedestal immediately aft of bridge.
- Harpoon SSM angled launchers mounted right aft on quarterdeck pointing forward and angled upwards and outboard.

Note - Some similarities to Swedish 'Spica II' class.

Displacement full load, tons: 260.
Length, feet (metres): 151 (46).
Beam, feet (metres): 24 (7.4).
Draught, feet (metres): 8.2 (2.5).
Speed, knots: 38.

Missiles: SSM - 4 or 8 McDonnell Douglas Harpoon. SAM — Dual Stinger mounting can be fitted.
Guns: 1 OTO Melara 3 in (76 mm)/62 Compact; 2 triple 103 mm illumination rocket launchers.
Torpedoes: 2 or 4 21 in (533 mm) tubes. FFV Type 61.
Decoys: Sea Gnat DL-6T 6-barrel chaff/IR launchers.

Radars:

Air/surface search — 9GA 208.
Navigation — Terma Elektronik 20T 48 Super.
Fire control — CelsiusTech 9LV 200.

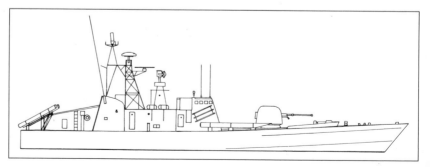

Willemoes Class

BREDAL

Dabur/Baradero/Grumete Diaz/Vai Class

Country: ARGENTINA, CHILE, FIJI, ISRAEL, NICARAGUA
Country of origin: Israel
Ship type: PATROL FORCES
Class: DABUR (BARADERO), (GRUMETE DIAZ), (VAI), (PC)
Active: 4 Argentina ('Baradero' class), 10 Chile ('Grumete Diaz' class), 4 Fiji ('Vai' class), 17 Israel, 3 Nicaragua

ARGENTINA
Name (Pennant Number): BARADERO (P 61), BARRANQUERAS (P 62), CLORINDA (P 63), CONCEPCIÓN DEL URUGUAY (P 64).

CHILE
Name (Pennant Number): GRUMETE DIAZ (1814), GRUMETE BOLADOS (1815), GRUMETE SALINAS (1816), GRUMETE TELLEZ (1817), GRUMETE BRAVO (1818), GRUMETE CAMPOS (1819), GRUMETE MACHADO (1820), GRUMETE JOHNSON (1821), GRUMETE TRONCOSO (1822), GRUMETE HUDSON (1823).

FIJI
Name (Pennant Number): VAI (301), OGO (302), SAKU (303), SAQA (304).
ISRAEL
Name (Pennant Number): 860-920 series.
NICARAGUA
Name (Pennant Number): (None available).

Recognition features:
- Low sleek hull
- Low compact superstructure with open bridge and slim enclosed mast aft of bridge.
- Guns forward and aft of superstructure

Note: Similar in profile to 'Dvora/Super Dvora' classes, which are derived from 'Dabur' class. 'Dabur' class has shorter deck aft of superstructure.

Displacement full load, tons: 39.
Length, feet (metres): 64.9 (19.8).
Beam, feet (metres): 18 (5.5).

Draught, feet (metres): 5.8 (1.8).
Speed, knots: 19.
Range, miles: 450 at 13 kts.

Guns: 2 Oerlikon 20 mm; 2 12.7 mm MGs; Carl Gustav 84 mm portable rocket launchers, (Israel). 2 Oerlikon 20 mm, (Chile). 2 Oerlikon 20 mm; 4 12.7 mm MGs, (Argentina). 2 Oerlikon 20 mm; 2 7.62 mm MGs, (Fiji). 2 Oerlikon 20 mm or 2 12.7 mm MGs, (Nicaragua).
Torpedoes: 2 324 mm tubes, Honeywell Mk 46, (Israel only).

Radars:
Surface search — Decca 101, (Argentina, Nicaragua`). Racal Decca Super 101 Mk 3, (Chile, Fiji, Israel).
Sonars: Active search/attack, (Israel only).

Dabur/Baradero/Grumete Diaz/Vai Class

GRUMETE SALINAS

Dvora/Hai Ou Class

Country: PARAGUAY, SRI LANKA, TAIWAN
Country of origin: ISRAEL
Ship type: PATROL FORCES
Class: DVORA (HAI OU) (PCFG)
Active: 2 Paraguay ('Modified Hai Ou' class), 3 Sri Lanka ('Dvora' class), 48 'Hai Ou' class, 2 'Dvora' class, Taiwan.

PARAGUAY
Name (Pennant Number): CAPITAN ORTIZ (P 06), TENIENTE ROBLES (P 07).

SRI LANKA
Name (Pennant Number): P 420 (ex-P 453), P 421 (ex-P 454), P 422 (ex-P 455).

TAIWAN
Name (Pennant Number): FABG 5-12, FABG 14-21, FABG 23-30, FABG 32-39, FABG 41-58.

Recognition features:

- Low, rounded bridge structure with square profile lattice mainmast at after end. (Paraguay boats have tall, slim enclosed mast).
- Surface search and fire control radar aerials atop mainmast.
- SSM launcher athwartships immediately aft of mainmast, (Taiwan units only).
- 20 mm gun mounting forward of bridge, (Sri Lanka).
- 20 mm gun mounting right aft, (Sri Lanka, Taiwan).

Note 1 The first Taiwanese series had an enclosed mainmast and the missiles were nearer the stern. Second Taiwanese series changed to a lattice mainmast and moved the missiles further forward allowing room for 20 mm mounting.

Note 2 See Super Dvora entry.

Displacement full load, tons: 47.
Length, feet (metres): 70.8 (21.6).
Beam, feet (metres): 18 (5.5).
Draught, feet (metres): 3.3 (1). (5.8 (1.8), Sri Lanka).
Speed, knots: 36.
Range, miles: 700 at 32 kts.

Missiles: SSM - 2 Hsiung Feng I, (Taiwan only).
Guns: 1 Oerlikon 20 mm Type 75; 2 12.7 mm MGs, (Paraguay and Taiwan). 2 Oerlikon 20 mm and 2 12.7 mm MGs., (Sri Lanka).
Decoys: 4 Israeli AV2 chaff launchers, (Taiwan only)

Radars:
Surface search — Marconi LN 66, (Taiwan). Anritsu 721UA, (Sri Lanka)
Fire control — RCA R76 C5.

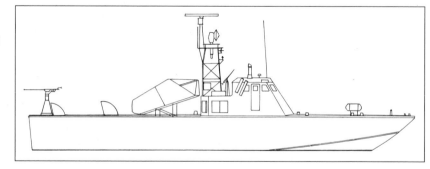

Dvora/Hai Ou Class

TAIWAN FABG

Hetz (Saar 4.5) Class

Country: ISRAEL
Country of origin: ISRAEL
Ship type: PATROL FORCES
Class: HETZ (SAAR 4.5) (PGF)
Active: 5
Name (Pennant Number): ROMAT, KESHET, HETZ (ex-Nirit), KIDON, YAFFO

Recognition features:
- Long sleek hull, low freeboard.
- Vulcan Phalanx CIWS mounting ('A' position) with distinctive domed top.
- Short superstructure well forward of midships.
- Massive enclosed mainmast at after end of superstructure.
- Neptune air/surface search radar aerial atop mainmast.
- Harpoon SSM tubular launchers aft of superstructure and forward of after mounting. Gabriel II box launchers immediately aft.
- 3 in gun mounting right aft.

Note 1 - Easily confused with the Saar 4 class. Nirit upgrade continues on Saar 4 to convert into Saar 4.5. Yaffo latest conversion in July 1998.

Note 2 - Two 'Aliya' Class (Saar 4.5), (Aliya and Geoula) operated by Israel. Of same basic hull design with substantially different weapons fits (CIWS in the eyes of the ships) and large slab-side superstructure aft.

Displacement full load, tons: 488.
Length, feet (metres): 202.4 (61.7).
Beam, feet (metres): 24.9 (7.6).
Draught, feet (metres): 8.2 (2.5).
Speed, knots: 31.
Range, miles: 3,000 at 17 kts.

Missiles: SSM - 4 Harpoon plus 6 IAI Gabriel II. SAM - Israeli Industries Barak I (vertical launch or pack launchers).
Guns: 1 OTO MELARA 3 in (76 mm)/62; 2 Oerlikon 20 mm; 1 GE/GD Vulcan Phalanx; 2 or 4 12.7 mm (twin or quad) MGs.
Decoys: Elbit Deseaver 72-barrel chaff/IR launchers.

Radars:
Air/surface search — Thomson-CSF TH-D 1040 Neptune.
Fire control — Elta EL/M-222 1 GM STGR.

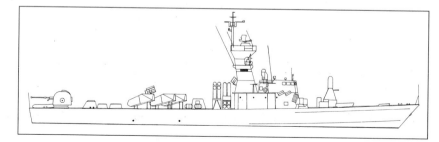

Hetz (Saar 4.5) Class

HETZ (SAAR 4.5)

Country: CHILE, ISRAEL, SOUTH AFRICA

Country of origin: ISRAEL

Ship type: PATROL FORCES

Class: RESHEF (SAAR 4), (CASMA, WARRIOR (EX-MINISTER) (PCFG)

Active: 4 Chile ('Casma' class), 4 Israel ('Reshef' class), 5 + 3 reserve South Africa ('Warrior', ex-'Minister' class)

CHILE

Name (Pennant Number): CASMA (ex-Romah) (LM 30), CHIPANA (ex-Keshet) (LM 31), ANGAMOS (ex-Reshef) (LM 34), PAPUDO (ex-Tarshish) (LM 35).

ISRAEL

Name (Pennant Number): NITZHON, ATSMOUT, MOLEDT, KOMEMIUT

SOUTH AFRICA

Name (Pennant Number): SHAKA (ex-P W Botha) (P 1562), ADAM KOK (ex-Frederic Creswell) (P 1563), SEKHUKUNE (ex-Jim Fouché) (P 1564), ISAAC DYOBHA (ex-Frans Erasmus) (P 1565), RENÉ SETHREN (ex-Oswald Pirow) (P 1566), GALESHEWE (ex-Hendrik Mentz) (P 1567), JOB MASEKO (ex-Kobie Coetsee) (P 1568), MAKHANDA (ex-Magnus Malan) (P 1569).

Recognition features:

- Long sleek hull, low freeboard.
- CIWS mounting ('A' position) with distinctive domed top, (Israeli ships). 3 in gun mounting forward of bridge in Chilean and South African units.
- Short superstructure well forward of midships.
- Large complex lattice mainmast at after end of superstructure.
- Air/surface search radar aerial atop mainmast.
- Combination of Harpoon and Gabriel SSM launchers aft of superstructure and forward of after mounting, (Israeli ships). Gabriel/Skerpioen SSM launchers in Chilean and South African ships.

- 3 in gun mounting ('Y' position).

Note 1 - Easily confused with the 'Saar 4.5' class. Israeli Nirit upgrade continues with conversion to Saar 4.5. Yaffo latest to be completed in July 1998. Now in Saar 4.5 class.

Note 2 - Photograph and line diagram have slightly different weapons fits illustrating different modification states.

Displacement full load, tons: 450, (Israeli and Chilean ships). 430 (South Africa).

Length, feet (metres): 190.6 (58). (204 (62.2), South Africa).

Beam, feet (metres): 25 (7.8).

Draught, feet (metres): 8 (2.4).

Speed, knots: 32.

Range, miles: 4,000 at 17.5 kts.

Missiles: SSM - McDonnell Douglas Harpoon (twin or quad) launchers; 4-6 IAI Gabriel II, (Israel). 4 Gabriel I or II, (Chile). 8 Skerpioen (licence-built Gabriel II), (South Africa).

Guns: 1 or 2 OTO Melara 3 in (76 mm)/62 Compact; 2 Oerlikon 20 mm; 1 GE/GD Vulcan Phalanx Mk 15; 2 12.7 mm MGs, (Israel). 2 OTO MELARA 3 in(76 mm)/62 Compact, (Chile, South Africa.) 2 Oerlikon 20

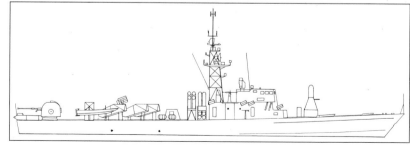

Reshef (Saar 4) Class

RESHEF (SAAR 4)

mm, (Chile). 2 LIW Vektor 35 mm (twin) may have replaced 1 76 mm gun in 1 South African hull for trials in 1998, plus 2 LIW Mk 1 20 mm and 2 12.7 mm MGs, (South Africa).

Decoys: 1 45-tube, 4 or 6 24-tube, 4 single tube chaff launchers, (Israel). 4 Rafael LRCR decoy launchers, (Chile). 4 ACDS chaff launchers, (South Africa).

Radars:
Air/surface search — Thomson-CSF TH-D 1040 Neptune, (Chile, Israel). Elta EL/M 2208, (South Africa.
Navigation — Raytheon 20X (Chile).
Fire control — Selenia Orion RTN 10X or Elta M-2221 in some Chilean ships.
Sonars: EDO 780; VDS; occasionally fitted in some of the Israeli ships.

Super Dvora/Super Dvora Mk II Class

Country: ERITREA, INDIA, ISRAEL, SLOVENIA, SRI LANKA
Country of origin: ISRAEL
Ship type: PATROL FORCES
Class: SUPER DVORA/SUPER DVORA MK II (PCF)
Active: 4 Eritrea (Mk II), 2 India (Mk II), 13 Israel (9 Mk I, 4 Mk II), 2 Slovenia (Mk II), 4 (Mk I), 4 (Mk II), Sri Lanka
Building: 4 (India, under licence).
Planned: 15 (India).
ERITREA
Name (Pennant Number): (None available).
INDIA
Name (Pennant Number): (None available).
ISRAEL
Name (Pennant Number): 811-819, (Mk I), 820-823, (Mk II).
SLOVENIA
Name (Pennant Number): ANKARAN (HPL 21), —— (——).
SRI LANKA
Name (Pennant Number): Mk I - P 440-443 (ex-P 465-468). Mk II - P 460 (ex-P 441), P 461 (ex-P 496), P 462 (ex-P497), P 463.

Recognition features:
- Low profile, compact craft.
- Slight raised bow with continuous maindeck from stem to stern. Low freeboard.
- Low profile superstructure with slim enclosed mast aft of open bridge.
- Gun mountings forward of bridge and right aft.

Displacement full load, tons: 54, (60, India, 58 Slovenia).
Length, feet (metres): 71 (21.6), (Mk I). 82 (25), (Mk II).
Beam, feet (metres): 18 (5.5), (Mk I). 18.4 (5.6), (Mk II).
Draught, feet (metres): 5.9 (1.8), (Mk I), 3.6 (1.1), (Mk II).
Speed, knots: 36, (Mk I), 40 (Mk II).
Range, miles: 1,200 at 17 kts.

Missiles: SSM — Hellfire, (sometimes carried, Israel only).
Guns: 2 Oerlikon 20mm/80 or Bushmaster 25 mm/87 Mk 96 or 3 Rafael Typhoon 12.7 mm (triple MG); 2 12.7 or 7.62 mm MGs; 1 84 mm rocket launcher, (Israel). 2 23 mm (twin); 2 12 mm MGs, (Eritrea). 1 Oerlikon 20 mm or 3 Rafael Typhoon 12.7 mm (triple) MGs; 2 12.7 mm MGs, (India). 2 Oerlikon 20 mm; 2 12.7 mm MGs, (Sri Lanka, Mk I). 1 Typhoon 20 mm, 2 12.7 mm MGs., (Sri Lanka, Mk II). 2 12.7 mm MGs, (Slovenia).

Radars:
Surface search — Raytheon, (Eritrea, Israel). Koden, (India, Slovenia, Sri Lanka, Mk II). Decca 926 (Sri Lanka, Mk I).

Super Dvora/Super Dvora Mk II Class

SUPER DVORA

Country: NORWAY
Country of origin: NORWAY.
Ship type: PATROL FORCES
Class: HAUK (PCFG)
Active: 14
Name (Pennant Number): HAUK (P 986), ØRN (P 987), TERNE (P 988), TJELD (P 989), SKARV (P 990), TEIST (P 991), JO (P 992), LOM (P 993), STEGG (P 994), FALK (P 995), RAVN (P 996), GRIBB (P 997), GEIR (P 998), ERLE (P 999)

Recognition features:
- Low profile, compact craft.
- 40 mm/70 gun open mounting ('A' position).
- Low superstructure centred just forward of midships.
- Forward pointing single torpedo tubes outboard of 'A' mounting, port and starboard.
- Short lattice mainmast atop after end of superstructure.
- 20 mm/20 gun mounting immediately aft of superstructure surrounded by high circular armoured breakwater.
- Distinctive Penguin SSM launchers mounted on afterdeck, 2 port, 2 starboard, angled outboard.

Note - Swedish 'Hugin/Kaparen' class similar to 'Hauk' class. See separate entry.

Displacement full load, tons: 160.
Length, feet (metres): 120 (36.5).
Beam, feet (metres): 20.3 (6.2).
Draught, feet (metres): 5.9 (1.8).
Speed, knots: 32.
Range, miles: 440 at 30 kts.

Missiles: SSM - 6 Kongsberg Penguin Mk 2 Mod 5. SAM - Twin Simbad launcher for Matra Mistral.
Guns: 1 Bofors 40 mm/70. 1 Rheinmetall 20 mm/20.
Torpedoes: 2 - 21 in (533mm) tubes. FFV Type 613.
Decoys: Chaff launcher

Radars:
Surface search/navigation — 2 Racal Decca TM 1226.
Sonars: Simrad; active search.

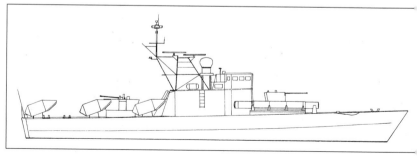

HAUK

Hugin/Kaparen Class

Country: SWEDEN
Country of origin: NORWAY
Ship type: PATROL FORCES
Class: HUGIN/KAPAREN (PCFG)
Active: 12
Name (Pennant Number): HUGIN (P 151), MUNIN (P 152), MODE (P 154), VIDAR (P 156), KAPAREN (P 159), VÄKTAREN (P 160), SNAPPHANEN (P 161), SPEJAREN (P 162), STYRBJÖRN (P 163), STARKODDER (P 164), TORDÖN (P 165), TIRFING (P 166)

Recognition features:

- Long forecastle with 57 mm/70 gun mounting ('A' position).
- Low profile, rounded midships superstructure.
- Short, tripod mainmast aft of bridge.
- Surface search radar aerial atop mainmast.
- 9LV 200 fire control radar aerial atop after end of bridge.
- Forward pointing SSM launchers on afterdeck, angled outboard, port and starboard.
- Short lattice aftermast with pole mast atop.
- Mine rails running from after end of bridge superstructure with an extension over the stern. (Cannot be used with missiles in place.)

Note - Norwegian 'Hauk' class similar. See separate entry.

Displacement full load, tons: 150 (170 after modernisation).
Length, feet (metres): 120 (36.6).
Beam, feet (metres): 20.7 (6.3).]
Draught, feet (metres): 5.6 (1.7).
Speed, knots: 36.

Missiles: SSM - 6 Kongsberg Penguin Mk 2.
Guns: 1 Bofors 57 mm/70 Mk 1. 57 mm illuminant launchers on either side of mounting.
A/S mortars: 4 Saab Elma 9-tube launchers.
Depth charges: 2 racks.
Mines: 24.

Radars:
Surface search — Skanter 16 in Mk 009.
Fire control — Philips 9LV 200 Mk 2.
Sonars: Simrad SA 950 (P 159-166) or SQ 3D/SF; hull-mounted. Simrad ST 570 VDS (P 159-166).

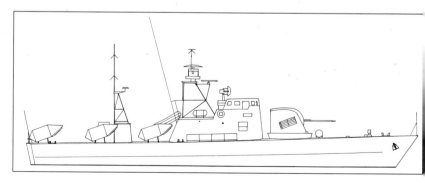

Hugin/Kaparen Class

KAPAREN

Storm Class

Country: ESTONIA, LATVIA, LITHUANIA, NORWAY
Country of origin: NORWAY
Ship type: PATROL FORCES
Class: STORM (PCF/PCFG)
Active: 1 Estonia (Border Guard), 1 Latvia, 1 Lithuania, 8 Norway
ESTONIA
Name (Pennant Number): TORM (ex-Arg) (PVL 105, ex-P 968).
LATVIA
Name (Pennant Number): BULTA (ex-Traust) (P 04, ex-P 973).
LITHUANIA
Name (Pennant Number): DZŪKAS (ex-Glimt) (P 31, ex-P 962).
NORWAY
Name (Pennant Number): BLINK (P 961), KJEKK (P 965), DJERV (P 966), SKUDD (P 967), STEIL (P 969), HVASS (P 972), BRASK (P 977), GNIST (P 979)

Displacement full load, tons: 138, (Norway). 135, (Estonia, Latvia, Lithuania).
Length, feet (metres): 120 (36.5).
Beam, feet (metres): 20.3 (6.2).
Draught, feet (metres): 5.9 (1.8).
Speed, knots: 32.

Missiles: SSM - Up to 6 Kongsberg Penguin Mk 1 Mod 7, (Norway only).
Guns: 1 Bofors 3 in (76 mm)/50; 1 Bofors 40 mm/70, (Norway). 1 12.7 mm MG, (Latvia and Lithuania). 25 mm/80 (twin); 14.5 mm (twin) MG, (Estonia).

Radars:
Surface search — Racal Decca TM 1226.
Fire control — Signaal WM 26, (Norway only).

Recognition features:
- Low profile, compact craft.
- 3 in gun mounting ('A' position), Norwegian boats. Twin 25 mm/80 on raised platform in Estonian boat.
- Low, rounded central superstructure.
- Central tripod mainmast supporting distinctive semi-spherical radar dome, (Norwegian boats).
- 40 mm/70 gun mounting aft of superstructure, (Norway only. Twin 14.5 mm MG on raised platform, Estonian unit).
- Distinctive SSM launchers mounted on afterdeck, 2 port, 2 starboard, angled outboard, (Norway only).

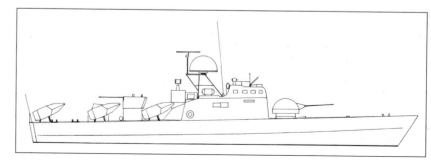

Storm Class

HVASS

Country: ALGERIA, BULGARIA, CROATIA, CUBA, EGYPT, ERITREA,
FINLAND, INDIA, IRAN, NORTH KOREA, LATVIA, LIBYA, POLAND,
ROMANIA, SYRIA, VIETNAM, YEMEN, YUGOSLAVIA.

Country of origin: RUSSIA

Ship type: PATROL FORCES

Class: OSA I (TYPE 205) (PUCK), OSA II (TYPE 205M) (PCFG)

Active: 9 Osa II, 2 Osa I, Algeria. 3 Osa II, 3 Osa I, Bulgaria. 1 Modified Osa I,
Croatia (PCF/ML)*. 1 Osa I, 11 Osa II, Cuba. 4 Osa I, Egypt. 2 Osa II,
Eritrea. 4 Modified Osa II, Finland ('Tuima' class, MLI). 5 Osa II, India. 1
Osa I, Iran.§. 8 Osa I, North Korea. 2 Osa I, Latvia (PCF). 6 + 6 reserve,
Osa II, Libya. 7 Osa I, Poland ('Puck' class). 3 Osa I, Romania. 8 Osa II,
Syria. 8 Osa II, Vietnam. 2 Osa II, Yemen. 5 Osa I, Yugoslavia.

* Captured from the Yugoslav Navy. § Escaped from Iraq in 1991, during Gulf
War.

ALGERIA
Name (Pennant Number): Osa I — 642-643. Osa II — 644-652.

BULGARIA
Name (Pennant Number): Osa I — BURYA (103), TYPFOON (112), SMERCH
(113). Osa II — URAGON (102), GRUM (104), SVETKAVITSA (111).

CROATIA
Name (Pennant Number): DUBROVNIK (ex-Mitar Acev) (OBM 41, ex-310).

CUBA
Name (Pennant Number): Osa I — 252. Osa II
- 256-262, 267, 271, 274.

EGYPT
Name (Pennant Number): 633, 637, 641, 643.

ERITREA
Name (Pennant Number): FMB 161, FMB 163.

FINLAND
Name (Pennant Number): TUIMA (11),
TUISKU (12), TUULI (14), TYRSKY (15).

INDIA
Name (Pennant Number): PRACHAND (K 90),
PRALAYA (K 91), PRABAL (K 93), CHAPAL
(K 94), CHATAK (K 96).

IRAN
Name (Pennant Number): (None available).

NORTH KOREA
Name (Pennant Number): (Not available).

LATVIA
Name (Pennant Number): ZIBENS (ex-Joseph Schares) (P 01, ex-753), ——
(ex-Fritz Gast) (P 02, ex-714).

LIBYA
Name (Pennant Number): AL KATUM (511), AL ZUARA (513), AL RUHA
(515), AL BAIDA (517), AL NABHA (519), AL SAFHRA (521), AL FIKAH
(523), AL MATHUR (525), AL MOSHA (527), AL SAKAB (529), AL BITAR
(531), AL SADAD (533)

POLAND
Name (Pennant Number): PUCK (427), USTKA (428), OKSYWIE (429),
DARLOWO (430), SWINOUJSCIE (431), DZIWNÓW (432),
WLADYSLAWOWO (433).

ROMANIA
Name (Pennant Number): VULTURUL (195), ERETELE (198), ALBATROSUL
(199).

SYRIA
Name (Pennant Number): 33-40.

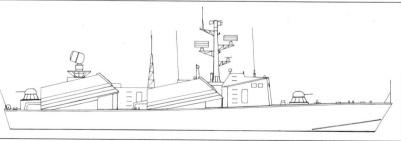

OSA I

VIETNAM
Name (Pennant Number): (Not available).
YEMEN
Name (Pennant Number): 122, 124.
YUGOSLAVIA
Name (Pennant Number): STEVAN FILIPOVIC STEVA (304), ZIKICA JOVANOVIC-SPANAC (305), NIKOLA MARTINOVIC (306), ZOSIP MAZAR SOSA (307), KRALO ROJC (308).

Recognition features:
- 30 mm/65 gun mounting ('A' position).
- Low profile rounded superstructure running from the forecastle almost to the stern.
- Pole mainmast just forward of midships with surface search radar aerial atop.
- Prominent raised pedestal aft supporting fire control radar aerial.
- 4 large distinctive Styx SSM launchers, two outboard of mainmast (1 port one starboard) and 2 outboard of fire control director (aft), (1 port, 1 starboard). Launchers tilted up at forward end and lying forward and aft. (Not Croatian, Finnish and Latvia units.)
- 30 mm/65 mounting right aft.

Note 1 - Similar 'Huangfen' class also operated by China (38), Bangladesh ('Durdharsha' class) (5), North Korea (4), Pakistan (4) and Yemen, (3).
Note 2 - Croatian unit converted to a minelayer in 1995. Finnish boats had similar conversion, 1993-96. Superstructure extended aft in Crotian, Finnish and Latvian units.
Note 3 - 'Matka' class hydrofoil PHGs, with similar hulls to 'Osa' operated by Russia, (2) and Ukraine, (5, as 'Vekhr' class).

Displacement full load, tons: 210 (Osa I), 245 (Osa II).
Length, feet (metres): 126.6 (38.6) (110.2 (33.6) Finnish units)
Beam, feet (metres): 24.9 (7.6).
Draught, feet (metres): 8.8 (2.7).

Speed, knots: 35 (Osa I), 37 (Osa II).
Range, miles: 400 at 34 kts (Osa I), 500 at 35 kts (Osa II).

Missiles: SSM - 4 SS-N-2A/B Styx (Osa I), 4 SS-N-2B/C Styx (Osa II). (Not Croatian, Finnish or Latvian units). SAM - SA-N-5 Grail (Egyptian Osa I). SA-N-5 Grail quad launcher, (Poland).
Guns: 30 mm/65 (2 twin). (Additional 2 12.7 mm MGs, Egypt.) Wrobel 23 mm Zu-23-2M (twin); 30 mm/65 AK 230, (twin), (Latvia).
Mines: 14-30, (Croatia only).

Radars:
Air/surface search — Kelvin Hughes, (Egypt only).
Surface search — Raytheon ARPA, (Finnish units), Square Tie.
Navigation — Racal Decca 916 (Egypt). SRN 207M, (Poland).
Fire control — Drum Tilt.

OSA CLASS

Pauk (Molnya) I/II/Reshitelni/ Improved Pauk/Ho-A Class

Country: BULGARIA, CUBA, INDIA, RUSSIA, UKRAINE, VIETNAM
Country of origin: RUSSIA
Ship type: PATROL FORCES
Class: PAUK I (TYPE 1241P) (RESHITELNI) (FS/PCF), PAUK II (TYPE 1241PE), (ABHAY), IMPROVED PAUK ('HO-A') (FS/FSG/PCF)
Active: 2 Bulgaria (Pauk I 'Reshitelni' class FS/PCF), 1 Cuba (Pauk II FS), 4 India (Pauk II, 'Abhay' class FS), 27 Pauk I, 3 Pauk II, Russia, 2 Pauk I, Ukraine, (plus 3, Border Guard), 1 Improved Pauk, Vietnam, ('Ho-A' class).

BULGARIA
Name (Pennant Number): RESHITELNI (13), BODRI (14).

CUBA
Name (Pennant Number): 321.

INDIA
Name (Pennant Number): ABHAY (P 33), AJAY (P 34), AKSHAY (P 35), AGRAY (P 36).

RUSSIA
Name (Pennant Number): (None available).

UKRAINE
Name (Pennant Number): UZHGOROD (U 207), KHMELNITSKY (U 208). Border Guard - 012-014.

VIETNAM
Name (Pennant Number): (None available)

Recognition features:
- High angled bow with long forecastle.
- 3 in gun mounting ('A' position).
- Large, central, stepped superstructure extending from forecastle to afterdeck.
- Prominent raised pedestal supporting fire control radar aerial sited amidships atop superstructure.
- Tall lattice mainmast well aft of midships with small lattice mast atop at after end.
- Torpedo tubes mounted on maindeck, two

port two starboard. One pair adjacent bridge, second pair adjacent mainmast. (Not Cuban ship).
- A/S mortars on maindeck, either side of forward superstructure.
- 30 mm/65 AK 630 gun mounting right aft ('X' position).

Note 1 - This appears to be an ASW version of the Tarantul class.
Note 2 - First three of Russian Pauk I have a lower bridge than successors.
Note 3 - Vietnam's Improved Pauk will have full load displacement of 517 tons, a length of 203.4 (62 metres), and a beam of 36 (11 metres). These ships will be armed with 8 Zvezda SS-N-25 (KH-35 Uran) SSMs, 1 3 in(76mm)/60 gun and 1 30 mm/65 AK 630, together with 2 12.7 mm MGs. The superstructure will be set back well aft, with a lattice mast supporting a Cross Dome radome, aft of midships with SSM angled launchers outboard.

Displacement full load, tons: 440. (485, Indian units).
Length, feet (metres): 195.2 (59.5), (Bulgaria). (189 (57.5), Cuba, India, Russia).
Beam, feet (metres): 33.5 (10.2)
Draught, feet (metres): 10.8 (3.3).(11.2 (3.3), Cuba).
Speed, knots: 32.
Range, miles: 2,200 at 18 kts.

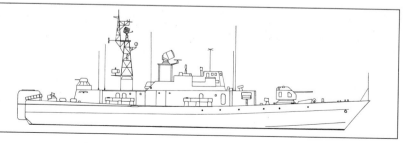

Pauk (Molnya) I/II/Reshitelni/
Improved Pauk/Ho-A Class

PAUK

Missiles: SAM - SA-N-5 Grail quad launcher.
Guns: 1 3 in (76 mm)/60. 1 30 mm/65 AK 630.
Torpedoes: 4 16 in (406 mm) tubes. Type 40, (Pauk I, not Cuban ship) or 4
   21 in (533 mm) (Pauk II). SET-65E , (India).
A/S mortars: 2 RBU 1200 5-tubed.
Depth charges: 2 racks, (not Cuban or Indian ships).
Decoys: 2 PK 16 or 24PK 10 chaff launchers.

Radars:
Air/surface search — Peel Cone (Pauk I), Positive E (Pauk II).
Surface search — Kivach. (Russia), Spin Trough, (Bulgaria).
Navigation — Pechora, (Cuba, India).
Fire control — Bass Tilt.
Sonars: Rat Tail; VDS (mounted on transom), (Cuba, India,). Foal Tail VDS
   (Bulgaria, Russia).

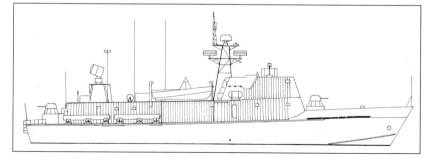

Stenka Class

Country: AZERBAIJAN, CAMBODIA, CUBA, RUSSIA, UKRAINE
Country of origin: RUSSIA
Ship type: PATROL FORCES
Class: STENKA (TYPE 205P) (PCF)
Active: 5 Azerbaijan, 2 Cambodia (Modified Stenka), 3 Cuba (Border Guard), 35 Russia, 10 Ukraine (Border Guard)

AZERBAIJAN
Name (Pennant Number): (None available).
CAMBODIA
Name (Pennant Number): 1133, 1134.
CUBA
Name (Pennant Number): (None available).
RUSSIA
Name (Pennant Number): (None available).
UKRAINE
Name (Pennant Number): Border Guard — 019-021, 023, 032-037.

Recognition features:

- Short high freeboard forecastle with 30 mm/65 or 23 mm/87 gun mounting ('A' position).
- Large superstructure, higher at forward end, extending to quarterdeck. Superstructure has vertical ribbed appearance.
- Complex tripod mainmast atop after end of bridge supporting surface search radar aerial.
- Distinctive Drum Tilt fire control radar aerial on pedestal at after end of superstructure.
- 30 mm/65 gun mounting on quarterdeck ('X' position).

Note 1 - 'Turya' class has similar 'ribbed' sides to superstructure.
Note 2 - Ukraine Border Guard vessels are dark grey with a thick yellow/thin blue diagonal line painted on the hull.

Displacement full load, tons: 253.
Length, feet (metres): 129.3 (39.4).
Beam, feet (metres): 25.9 (7.9).
Draught, feet (metres): 8.2 (2.5).
Speed, knots: 37. (34, Cuban ships).
Range, miles: 800 at 24 kts.

Guns: 30 mm/65 AK 230 (2 twin); 23mm/87 mm (twin). (2 Bofors 40 mm/60 (twin), Cambodia).
Torpedoes: 4 - 16 in (406 mm) tubes. (Not Cambodian or Cuban ships)
Depth charges: 2 racks. (Not Cambodian or Cuban ships).

Radars:
Surface search — Pot Drum or Peel Cone. (Racal Decca Bridgemaster, Cambodia).
Navigation — Palm Frond. (Racal Decca, Cambodia).
Fire control — Drum Tilt. (Muff Cobb, Cambodia, Cuba).
Sonars: Stag Ear or Foal Tail VDS. (Not Cambodia, Cuba).

Stenka Class

STENKA

Country: CAMBODIA, RUSSIA, VIETNAM
Country of origin: RUSSIA
Ship type: PATROL FORCES
Class: TURYA (TYPE 206M) (PC/PTH)
Active: 2 Cambodia (PC), 5 Russia, 7 Vietnam
CAMBODIA
Name (Pennant Number): (None available)
RUSSIA
Name (Pennant Number): (None available)
VIETNAM
Name (Pennant Number): HQ 331 (+ 6)

Recognition features:

- Blunt bow, short forecastle with 25 mm/80 gun twin mounting ('A' position).
- Angular central superstructure with raised open bridge just aft of enclosed bridge.
- Lattice mainmast aft of bridge with surface search radar aerial atop.
- Two torpedo tubes on maindeck each side of central superstructure, angled outboard, (not in all Vietnamese units, none in Cambodian units.).
- Pedestal supporting Muff Cob fire control radar aerial atop after end of superstructure.
- Prominent 57 mm/80 gun mounting right aft ('Y' position).

Note - Superstructure has similar 'ribbed' appearance as 'Stenka' class. Foils removed from Cambodian units.

Displacement full load, tons: 250.
Length, feet (metres): 129.9 (39.6).
Beam, feet (metres): 24.9 (7.6), (41 (12.5) over foils).
Draught, feet (metres): 5.9 (1.8), (13.1 (4) over foils)
Speed, knots: 40 foilborne.
Range, miles: 600 at 35 kts., foilborne, 1,450 at 14 kts hullborne.

Guns: 57 mm/80 (twin, aft); 25 mm/80 (twin, fwd); 1   14.5 mm MG.
Torpedoes: 4   21 in (533 mm) tubes. Type 53. (Not in all Vietnamese units; none in Cambodian units).
Depth charges: 1 rack.

Radars:
Surface search — Pot Drum.
Navigation — SRN 207.
Fire control — Muff Cob.
Sonars: Foal Tail VDS, (not in all Vietnamese units).

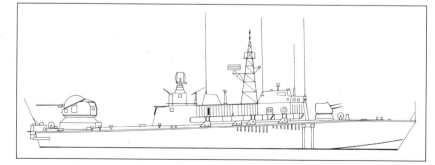

Turya Class

TURYA

Country: SPAIN
Country of origin: SPAIN
Ship type: PATROL FORCES
Class: SERVIOLA (OPV)
Active: 4
Name (Pennant Number): SERVIOLA (P 71), CENTINELA (P 72), VIGIA (P 73), ATALAYA (P 74)

Recognition features:

- High bow with break in profile forward of superstructure.
- High central freeboard adjacent to superstructure.
- 3 in gun mounting ('B' position).
- Tall, angular central superstructure.
- High, wide bridge set well aft from forward end of superstructure.
- Lattice mainmast atop after end of bridge.
- Large angular funnel at after end of superstructure, with wedge shaped, black smoke deflector atop.
- Large flight deck aft of superstructure.

Notes

1 Mexico operates 6 'Uribe' class PGs, ordered to a Halcon design with twin funnels and long open quarterdeck beneath a helicopter deck, similar to the 5 ships operated by the Argentine Prefectura Naval. Mexico also operates 4 larger 'Halzinger' class, a modified Halcon design.
2 Other 'Serviola' equipment fits could include four Harpoon SSM, Meroka CIWS, Sea Sparrow SAM or a Bofors 375 mm ASW rocket launcher.

Displacement full load, tons: 1,147.
Length, feet (metres): 225.4 (68.7)
Beam, feet (metres): 34 (10.4)
Draught, feet (metres): 11 (3.4)
Speed, knots: 19.
Range, miles: 8,000 at 12 kts.

Guns: 1 US 3 in (76 mm)/50 Mk 27; 2 12.7 MGs.

Radars:
Surface search — Racal Decca 2459.
Navigation — Racal Decca ARPA 2690 BT.

Helicopters: Platform for 1 Agusta AB-212, (surface search).

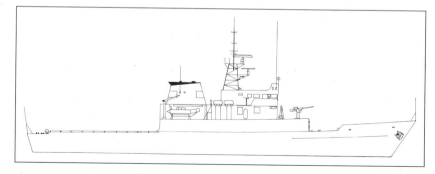

Serviola Class

CENTINELA

Norrköping Class

Country: SWEDEN
Country of origin: SWEDEN
Ship type: PATROL FORCES
Class: NORRKÖPING (PCFG)
Active: 6
Name (Pennant Number): NORRKÖPING (R 131), NYNÄSHAMN (R 132),
    PITEÅ (R 138), LULEÅ (R 139), HALMSTAD (R 140), YSTAD (R 142)

Recognition features:
- Exceptionally long forecastle with 57 mm/70 gun mounting just aft of
  midway between bows and bridge.
- Narrow superstructure centred well aft of midships.
- Complex lattice mainmast atop mid-superstructure.
- Sea Giraffe air/surface search radar aerial atop mainmast.
- 9LV 200 fire control radar aerial atop bridge roof.
- Single torpedo tubes outboard of gun mounting, port and starboard.
- Afterdeck can be fitted with any one of several combinations of torpedo
  tubes and SSM launchers.

Note - Similar to the original 'Spica' class from which they were developed.
    See separate entry.

Displacement full load, tons: 230.
Length, feet (metres): 143 (43.6).
Beam, feet (metres): 23.3 (7.1).
Draught, feet (metres): 7.4 (2.4).
Speed, knots: 40.5.
Range, miles: 500 at 40 kts.

Missiles: SSM - 8 Saab RBS 15.
Guns: 1 Bofors 57 mm/70 Mk 1, launchers for 57 mm illuminants on side of
    mounting.
Torpedoes: 6 21 in (533 mm) tubes (2-6 can be fitted at the expense of
    missile armament); Swedish Ordnance Type 613.
Mines: Minelaying capability.
Decoys: 2 Philips Philax launchers.

Radars:
Air/surface search — Ericsson Sea Giraffe 50HC.
Fire control — Philips 9LV 200 Mk 1.

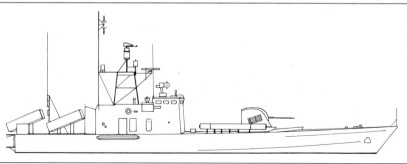

PITEÅ

Spica-M/Handalan Class

Country: MALAYSIA
Country of origin: SWEDEN
Ship type: PATROL FORCES
Class: SPICA-M (HANDALAN) (PCFG)
Active: 4
Name (Pennant Number): HANDALAN (3511), PERKASA (3512), PENDEKAR (3513), GEMPITA (3514)

Recognition features:

- 57 mm/70 gun mounting ('A' position).
- Main superstructure just forward of midships with tall lattice mainmast at after end.
- 9LV 212 fire control radar aerial atop bridge.
- 9GR 600 surface search radar aerial atop mainmast.
- 2, twin Exocet SSM launchers aft of bridge pointing forward and outboard in crossover formation forward pair to port after pair to starboard.
- 40 mm/70 gun mounting aft of SSM launchers on afterdeck.

Note 1 - Croatian and Yugoslav navies operate 'Koncar' class PCFGs, designed by the Naval Institute in Zagreb based on the 'Spica I' design. Bridge amidships like the Malaysian boats.

Note 2 - The Swedish Navy's 'Norrköping class PCFGs were developed from the original 'Spica' class. See separate entry.

Note 3 - Trinidad and Tobago operate two Type CG 40 PCs, with similar hulls to 'Spica' but with the bridge amidships.

Displacement full load, tons: 240.
Length, feet (metres): 142.6 (43.6).
Beam, feet (metres): 23.3 (7.1).
Draught, feet (metres): 7.4 (2.4) (screws).
Speed, knots: 34.5.
Range, miles: 1,850 at 14 kts.

Missiles: SSM - 4 Aerospatiale MM 38 Exocet.
Guns: 1 Bofors 57 mm/70; 1 Bofors 40 mm/70.

Radars:
Surface search — Philips 9GR 600.
Navigation — Decca 1226.
Fire control — Philips 9LV 212.

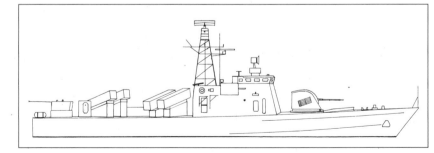

PENDEKAR

Azteca Class

Country: MEXICO
Country of origin: UNITED KINGDOM
Ship type: PATROL FORCES
Class: AZTECA (PC)
Active: 31

Name (Pennant Number): AZTECA (ex-Quintana) (P 01), GUAYCURA (ex-Cordova) (P 02), NAHUATL (ex-Arizpe) (P 03), TOTORAN (ex-Izazaga) (P 04), PAPAGO (ex-Bautista) (P 05), TARAHUMARA (ex-Rayon) (P 06), TEPEHUAN (ex-Rejon) (P 07), MEXICA (ex-Fuente) (P 08), ZAPOTECA (ex-Guzman) (P 09), HUASTECA (ex-Ramirez) (P 10), MAZAHUA (ex-Mariscal) (P 11), HUICHOL (ex-Jara) (P 12), SERI (ex-Mata) (P 13), YAQUI (ex-Romero) (P 14), TLAPANECO (ex-Lizardi) (P 15), TARASCO (ex-Mujica) (P 16), ACOLHUA (ex-Rouaix) (P 17), OTOMI (ex-Velazco) (P 18), MAYO (ex-Rojas) (P 19), PIMAS (ex-Macias) (P 20), CHICHIMECA (ex-Calderon) (P 21), CHONTAL (ex-Zaragoza) (P 22), MAZATECO (ex-Tamaulipas) (P 23), TOLTECA (ex-Yucatan) (P 24), MAYA (ex-Tabasco) (P 25), COCHIMIE (ex-Veracruz) (P 26), CORA (ex-Campeche) (P 27), TOTONACA (ex-Puebla) (P 28), MIXTECO (ex-Maza) (P 29), OLMECA (ex-Vicario) (P 30), TLAHUICA (ex-Ortiz) (P 31)

Recognition features:
- Continuous maindeck from stem to stern, high freeboard.
- 40 mm/70 gun mounting ('A' position).
- Rounded, low profile central superstructure.
- Small mast and funnel combined at after end of superstructure with radar aerial at its forward end.
- 20 mm gun mounting on afterdeck.

Displacement full load, tons: 148.
Length, feet (metres): 112.7 (34.4).
Beam, feet (metres): 28.3 (8.7).
Draught, feet (metres): 7.2 (2.2).
Speed, knots: 24.
Range, miles: 1,500 at 14 kts.

Guns: 1 Bofors 40 mm/70; 1 Oerlikon 20 mm or 1 7.62 mm MG.

Radar:
Surface search — Kelvin Hughes.

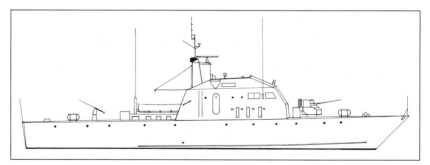

Azteca Class

TOTORAN

Castle Class

Country: UNITED KINGDOM
Country of origin: UNITED KINGDOM
Ship type: PATROL FORCES
Class: CASTLE (OPV)
Active: 2
Name (Pennant Number): LEEDS CASTLE (P 258), DUMBARTON CASTLE
(P 265)

Recognition features:
- High bow, long sweeping forecastle, high freeboard.
- 30 mm/75 gun mounting forward of bridge ('B' position).
- Prominent, angular midships superstructure, lower at forward end.
- High bridge set well aft from bows.
- Substantial enclosed mainmast, topped by pole mast, amidships supporting surface search and navigation radar aerials.
- Large flight deck aft.
- SATCOM on pole aft of mast.

Displacement full load, tons: 1,427.
Length, feet (metres): 265.7 (81).
Beam, feet (metres): 37.7 (11.5).
Draught, feet (metres): 11.8 (3.6).
Speed, knots: 19.5.
Range, miles: 10,000 at 12 kts.

Guns: 1 DES/MSI DS 30B 30 mm/75.
Decoys: Plessey Shield chaff launchers.

Radars:
Surface search — Plessey Type 944.
Navigation — Kelvin Hughes Type 1006.

Helicopters: Platform for operating Westland Sea King or Lynx.

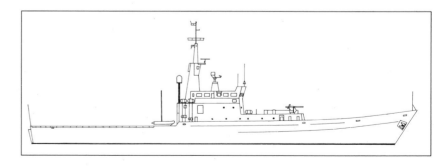

Castle Class

DUMBARTON CASTLE

Fremantle Class

Country: AUSTRALIA
Country of origin: UNITED KINGDOM
Ship type: PATROL FORCES
Class: FREMANTLE (LARGE PATROL CRAFT) (PC)
Active: 15
Name (Pennant Number): FREMANTLE (203), WARRNAMBOOL (204), TOWNSVILLE (205), WOLLONGONG (206), LAUNCESTON (207), WHYALLA (208), IPSWICH (209), CESSNOCK (210), BENDIGO (211), GAWLER (212), GERALDTON (213), DUBBO (214), GEELONG (215), GLADSTONE (216), BUNBURY (217)

Recognition features:
- Continuous maindeck from stem to stern.
- 40 mm/60 gun mounting ('A' position).
- Stepped, central superstructure.
- Sloping top to forward end of superstructure with bridge set back.
- Open bridge atop after end of enclosed bridge.
- Large whip aerial either side of forward end of superstructure.
- Pole mainmast amidships with small lattice structure supporting navigation radar just forward.
- Small ship's boat stowed at after end of superstructure.

Displacement full load, tons: 245.
Length, feet (metres): 137.1 (41.8).
Beam, feet (metres): 23.3 (7.1).
Draught, feet (metres): 5.9 (1.8).
Speed, knots: 30.
Range, miles: 1,450 at 30 kts.

Guns: 1 Bofors AN 4-40 mm/60; 1 81 mm mortar; 2   12.7 mm MGs.

Radars:
Navigation — Kelvin Hughes Type 1006.

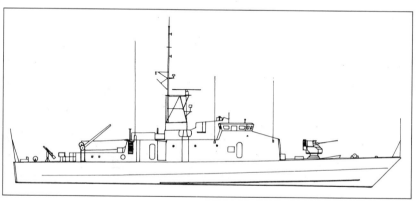

DUBBO

Island Class

Country: UNITED KINGDOM
Country of origin: UNITED KINGDOM
Ship type: PATROL FORCES
Class: ISLAND (OPV)
Active: 6
Name (Pennant Number): ANGLESEY (P 277), ALDERNEY (P 278), GUERNSEY (P 297), SHETLAND (P 298), ORKNEY (P 299), LINDISFARNE (P 300)

Recognition features:

- High bow profile with break down to lower level forward of bridge, high freeboard.
- Tall, substantial superstructure just aft of midships.
- 40 mm gun mounting on unusual raised barbette at after end of forecastle ('B' mounting position).
- Short, tripod mainmast atop mid-superstructure.
- Prominent funnel, with sloping after end, atop superstructure aft of mainmast.
- 2 small crane jibs at after end of superstructure, port and starboard.

Note - Also operated by Bangladesh as a training ship (Shaheed Ruhul Amin, (A 511) . ex-Jersey).

Displacement full load, tons: 1,260.
Length, feet (metres): 195.3 (59.5) oa.
Beam, feet (metres): 36 (11).
Draught, feet (metres): 15 (4.5).
Speed, knots: 16.5.
Range, miles: 7,000 at 12 kts.

Guns: 1 Bofors 40 mm Mk 3 or Oerlikon/BMARC 20 mm GAM-B01 or DES/MSI DS 30B 30 mm/75 Mk 1; 2   FN 7.62 mm MGs.

Radars:
Navigation — Kelvin Hughes Type 1006.

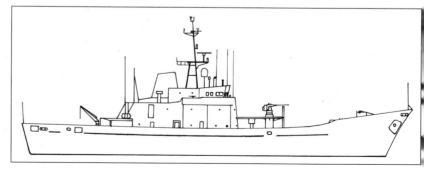

ORKNEY

Peacock/P41/Jacinto Class

Country: IRISH REPUBLIC, PHILIPPINES
Country of origin: UNITED KINGDOM
Ship type: PATROL FORCES
Class: PEACOCK/P41/JACINTO (PG/FS)
Active: 2 Irish Republic (PG), 3 Philippines (FS), Irish Republic
Name (Pennant Number): ORLA (ex-Swift) (P 41), CIARA (ex-Swallow) (P 42)
PHILIPPINES
Name (Pennant Number): EMILIO JACINTO (ex-Peacock) (—— ex-P 239), APOLINARIO MABINI (ex-Plover) (—— ex-P 240), ARTEMIO RICARTE (—— ex-P 241).

Recognition features:
- Low bow, low freeboard.
- 3 in gun mounting ('A' position).
- Superstructure amidships, stepped down aft of bridge.
- Lattice mainmast atop mid-superstructure.
- Squat, square-section funnel with sloping top atop after end of superstructure.
- Slender crane jib aft of funnel.

Displacement full load, tons: 712, (Irish units). 763, (Philippines ships).
Length, feet (metres): 204.1 (62.6).
Beam, feet (metres): 32.8 (10).
Draught, feet (metres): 8.9 (2.7).
Speed, knots: 25.
Range, miles: 2,500 at 17 kts.

Guns: 1 OTO Melara 3 in (76 mm)/62 Compact; 4 FN 7.62 mm MGs, (plus 2 12.7 mm MGs Irish ships).

Radars:
Navigation — Kelvin Hughes Type 1006, (Philippines). Kelvin Hughes Mk IV, (Irish ships).
Navigation — Kelvin Hughes 500A, (Irish ships).

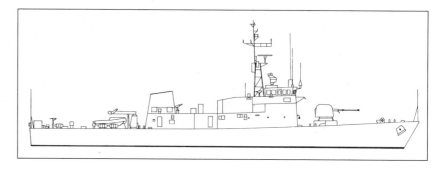

CIARA

Province (Dhofar/Nyayo) Class

Country: KENYA, OMAN
Country of origin: UNITED KINGDOM
Ship type: PATROL FORCES
Class: PROVINCE (NYAYO, DHOFAR) (PCFG)
Active: 2 Kenya ('Nyayo' class), 4 Oman ('Dhofar' class)
KENYA
Name (Pennant Number): NYAYO (P 3126), UMOJA (P 3127).
OMAN
Name (Pennant Number): DHOFAR (B 10), AL SHARQIYAH (B 11), AL BAT'NAH (B 12), MUSSANDAM (B 14)

Recognition features:
- Short forecastle, 3 in gun mounting ('A' position).
- High superstructure forward of midships. Superstructure is flush with craft's sides.
- Lattice mainmast centrally sited atop superstructure supporting AWS 4/6 air/surface search radar aerial.
- Two quadruple Exocet SSM launchers on maindeck aft of superstructure. Both launchers angled slightly forward. Forward launcher port side and after one starboard, (Oman). 4 Otomat box launchers aft of superstructure in Kenyan units.
- 40 mm/70 gun mounting right aft, (Oman). Twin 30 mm gun in same position in Kenyan boats.

Displacement full load, tons: 394, (Oman). 430, (Kenya).
Length, feet (metres): 186 (56.7).
Beam, feet (metres): 26.9 (8.2).
Draught, feet (metres): 7.9 (2.4).
Speed, knots: 38.
Range, miles: 2,000 at 18 kts.

Missiles: SSM - 8 Aerospatiale MM 40 Exocet, (Oman). OTO MELARA/Matra Otomat Mk 2 (2 twin), (Kenya).
Guns: 1 OTO Melara 3 in (76 mm)/62 Compact; Breda 40 mm/70 (twin); 2 12.7 mm MGs, (Oman). 1 OTO MELARA 3 in (76 mm)/62 Compact; Oerlikon/BMARC 30 mm GCM-A02 (twin); 2 Oerlikon/BMARC 20 mm A41A, (Kenya).
Decoys: 2 Wallop Barricade 3-barrel launchers, (Oman). 2 Wallop Barricade 18-barrel launchers, (Kenya).

Radars:
Air/surface search — Plessey AWS 4 or AWS 6.
Navigation — Racal Decca TM 1226C, (Oman). Decca AC 1226, (Kenya).
Fire control — Philips 9LV 307, (Oman). Marconi/Ericsson ST802, (Kenya).

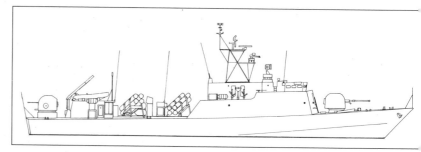

Province (Dhofar/Nyayo) Class

PROVINCE

Ramadan Class

Country: EGYPT
Country of origin: UNITED KINGDOM
Ship type: PATROL FORCES
Class: RAMADAN (PCFG)
Active: 6
Name (Pennant Number): RAMADAN (670), KHYBER (672), EL KADESSAYA (674), EL YARMOUK (676), BADR (678), HETTEIN (680)

Recognition features:
- Very short forecastle with 3 in gun mounting ('A' position).
- Main superstructure well forward of midships.
- Large, pyramid mainmast at after end of superstructure with pole mast atop the after end.
- Distinctive Marconi S 820 air/surface search radome atop mainmast.
- Small after superstructure supporting short enclosed mast with radome atop.
- Otomat SSM launchers sited between superstructures. Forward 2 trained to port, after 2 starboard. All launchers angled towards the bow.
- 40 mm/70 gun mounting ('Y' position).

Note - US Navy's 'Cyclone' PCFs based on 'Ramadan' design but of markedly different appearance. See separate entry.

Displacement full load, tons: 307.
Length, feet (metres): 170.6 (52).
Beam, feet (metres): 25 (7.6).
Draught, feet (metres): 7.5 (2.3).
Speed, knots: 40.
Range, miles: 1,600 at 18 kts.

Missiles: SSM - 4 OTO Melara/Matra Otomat Mk 1.
Guns: 1 OTO Melara 3 in (76 mm)/62 Compact; Breda 40 mm/70 (twin).
Decoys: 4 Protean fixed chaff launchers.

Radars:
Air/surface search — Marconi S 820.
Navigation — Marconi S 810.
Fire control — Two Marconi ST 802.

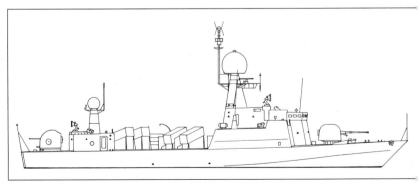

Ramadan Class

RAMADAN

Al Siddiq Class

Country: SAUDI ARABIA
Country of origin: UNITED STATES OF AMERICA
Ship type: PATROL FORCES
Class: AL SIDDIQ (PCFG)
Active: 9
Name (Pennant Number): AL SIDDIQ (511), AL FAROUQ (513), ABDUL AZIZ
(515), FAISAL (517), KHALID (519), AMYR (521), TARIQ (523), OQBAH
(525), ABU OBAIDAH (527)

Recognition features:
- High bow with sloping forecastle.
- 3 in gun mounting ('A' position).
- High central superstructure flush with ship's side.
- Large distinctive radome atop bridge roof.
- Slim tripod mainmast amidships.
- Angular, black-capped funnel with exhausts protruding at top aft of
  mainmast.
- Crossover Harpoon SSM tubular launchers on afterdeck, after 2 trained to
  port, forward 2 to starboard.
- Vulcan Phalanx CIWS mounting with distinctive white dome right aft.

Displacement full load, tons: 478.
Length, feet (metres): 190.5 (58.1).
Beam, feet (metres): 26.5 (8.1).
Draught, feet (metres): 6.6 (2).
Speed, knots: 38.
Range, miles: 2,900 at 14 kts.

Missiles: SSM - McDonnell Douglas Harpoon (2 twin) launchers.
Guns: 1 FMC/OTO MELARA 3 in (76 mm)/62 Mk 75 Mod 0; 1 GE/GD 20 mm
6-barrel Vulcan Phalanx CIWS; 2 Oerlikon 20 mm/80; 2 81 mm mortars;
2 40 mm Mk 19 grenade launchers.
Decoys: 2 Loral Hycor SRBOC 6-barrel Mk 36 fixed chaff/IR launchers.

Radars:
Surface search — ISC Cardion SPS 55.
Fire control — Sperry Mk 92.

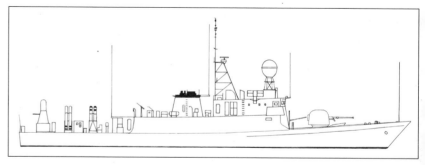

TARIQ

Cyclone Class

Country: UNITED STATES OF AMERICA
Country of origin: UNITED STATES OF AMERICA
Ship type: PATROL FORCES
Class: CYCLONE (PCF)
Active: 13
Building: 1
Name (Pennant Number): CYCLONE (PC 1), TEMPEST (PC 2), HURRICANE (PC 3), MONSOON (PC 4), TYPHOON (PC 5), SIROCCO (PC 6), SQUALL (PC 7), ZEPHYR (PC 8), CHINOOK (PC 9), FIREBOLT (PC 10), WHIRLWIND (PC 11), THUNDERBOLT (PC 12), SHAMAL (PC 13) — (PC 14)

Recognition features:
- Short forecastle with sloping forward edge to main superstructure.
- 25 mm gun mounting ('A' position).
- Raised bridge set well aft from bows.
- Continuous maindeck from stem to stern.
- Superstructure built in three distinct sections with catwalks between the tops of each section.
- Large lattice mainmast at after end of bridge supporting RASCAR surface search radar aerial atop.
- 25 mm gun mounting atop after section of superstructure ('X' position).

Note - The design is based on the Vosper Thornycroft 'Ramadan' class, modified to meet US Navy requirements.

Displacement full load, tons: 334.
Length, feet (metres): 170.3 (51.9).
Beam, feet (metres): 25.9 (7.9).
Draught, feet (metres): 7.9 (2.4)
Speed, knots: 35.
Range, miles: 2,500 at 12 kts.

Missiles: SAM - 1 sextuple Stinger mounting
Guns: 2 25 mm Mk 38; 1 Bushmaster 25 mm/87 Mk 96 (aft); 2 12.7 mm MGs; 2 40 mm Mk 19 grenade launchers (interchangeable with MGs).
Decoys: 2 Mk 52 sextuple chaff launchers; Wallop Super Barricade Mk 3 in PC 7 for trials.

Radars:
Surface search — Sperry RASCAR.
Navigation — Raytheon SPS-64(V)9.
Sonars: Wesmar; hull-mounted.

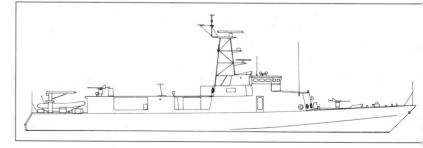

HINOOK

Country: FRANCE
Country of origin: FRANCE
Ship type: AMPHIBIOUS FORCES
Class: FOUDRE (TYPE TCD 90/LSD)
Active: 2
Name (Pennant Number): FOUDRE (L 9011), SIROCO (L 9012)

Recognition features:
- Short forecastle with high, distinctive superstructure set well forward.
- High freeboard.
- 40 mm/60 gun mounting immediately forward of bridge (Foudre) or 30 mm/70 (Siroco).
- Large complex mainmast atop main superstructure supporting air/surface search and surface search radar aerials.
- 2 Syracuse SATCOM domes, on pedestals, on after outboard edges of superstructure.
- 2 Simbad/Mistral SAM launchers at base of mainmast.
- Long flight deck aft of superstructure.
- Large crane derrick at after end of well deck.
- 2 20 mm gun mountings, port and starboard, aft of crane.

Note 1 - Designed to take a mechanised regiment of the Rapid Action Force and act as a logistic support ship.
Note 2 - Well dock 122 x 14.2 x 7.7 m, can dock a 400 ton ship.

Displacement full load, tons: 12,400. (17,200 flooded).
Length, feet (metres): 551 (168).
Beam, feet (metres): 77.1 (23.5).
Draught, feet (metres): 17 (5.2), (30.2 (9.2) flooded).
Speed, knots: 21.
Range, miles: 11,000 at 15 kts.

Missiles: SAM - 2 Matra Simbad twin launchers, Mistral.
Guns: 1 Bofors 40 mm/60 (Foudre); 2 Giat 20F2 20 mm; 3 Breda/Mauser 30 mm/70 (Siroco)

Radars:
Air/surface search — Thomson-CSF DRBV 21A Mars.
Surface search — Racal Decca 2459.
Navigation — 2 Racal Decca RM 1229.

Helicopters: 4 Aerospatiale AS 332F Super Puma or 2 Aerospatiale SA 321G Super Frelon.

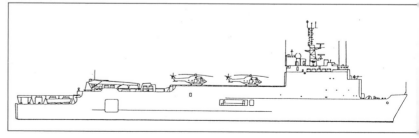

Foudre Class

FOUDRE

Ouragan Class

Country: FRANCE
Country of origin: FRANCE
Ship type: AMPHIBIOUS FORCES
Class: OURAGAN (TCD/LSD)
Active: 2
Name (Pennant Number): OURAGAN (L 9021), ORAGE (L 9022)

Recognition features:
- Very high freeboard section forward of midships.
- High distinctive bridge structure offset on starboard side of ship, well forward of midships.
- Large pole mainmast supporting radar aerials atop bridge roof.
- Flight deck aft of bridge.
- 2 medium-sized crane derricks aft at well deck.
- Small, black-capped funnel adjacent forward crane.

Note 1 - Three LCVPs can be carried.
Note 2 - Typical loads: 18 Super Frelon or 80 Alouette III helicopters or 120 AMX 13 tanks or 84 DUKWs or 340 Jeeps or 12 50 ton barges. 400 ton ship can be docked.

Displacement full load, tons: 8,500. (15,000, flooded).
Length, feet (metres): 488.9 (149).
Beam, feet (metres): 75.4 (23).
Draught, feet (metres): 17.7 (5.4) (28.5 (8.7),flooded).
Speed, knots: 17.
Range, miles: 9,000 at 15 kts.

Missiles: 2 Matra Simbad twin launchers; Mistral.
Guns: 2 4.7 in (120 mm) mortars; 4 Bofors 40 mm/60; 2 Breda/Mauser 30 mm/70; 4 12.7 mm MGs.

Radars:
Air/surface search — Thomson-CSF DRBV 51A.
Navigation — 2 Racal Decca 1226.

Helicopters: 4 Aerospatiale SA 321G Super Frelon or Super Pumas or 10 Aerospatiale SA 319B Alouette III.

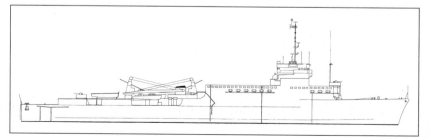

Ouragan Class

OURAGAN

Frosch I Class

Country: INDONESIA
Country of origin: GERMANY
Ship type: AMPHIBIOUS FORCES
Class: FROSCH (TYPE 108) (LSM)
Active: 12
Name (Pennant Number): TELUK GILIMANUK (ex-Hoyerswerda) (531, ex-611), TELUK CELUKAN BAWANG (ex-Hagenow) (532 ex-632), TELUK CENDRAWASIH (ex-Frankfurt/Oder) (533 ex-613), TELUK BERAU (ex-Eberswalde-Finow) (534 ex-634), TELUK PELENG (ex-Lübben) (535 ex-631), TELUK SIBOLGA (ex-Schwerin) (536 ex-612), TELUK MANADO (ex-Neubrandenburg) (537 ex-633), TELUK HADING (ex-Cottbus) (538 ex-614), TELUK PARIGI (ex-Anklam) (539 ex-635), TELUK LAMPUNG (ex-Schwedt) (540 ex-636), TELUK JAKARTA (ex-Eisenhüttenstadt) (541 ex-615), TELUK SANGKULIRANG (ex-Grimmen) (542 ex-616)

Recognition features:
- Wide bow ramp at forward end of forecastle with very distinctive wide, flat-topped bows.
- Crane at mid-foredeck.
- Large, stepped, slab-sided superstructure well aft of midships giving very high freeboard.
- Distinctive vertical-ribbed appearance to main superstructure.
- Large double-pole mainmast atop mid-superstructure supporting air/surface search and navigation radar aerials.
- Gun mountings fore and aft of superstructure.

Note - Former East German Navy ships transferred, unarmed, from Germany in August 1993.

Displacement full load, tons: 1,950.
Length, feet (metres): 321.5 (98).
Beam, feet (metres): 36.4 (11.1).
Draught, feet (metres): 9.2 (2.8).
Speed, knots: 18.

Guns: 37mm (2 twin).
Mines: Can lay mines through stern doors.

Radars:
Air/surface search — Strut Curve.
Navigation — TSR 333.

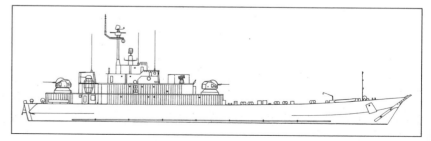

Frosch I Class

TELUK SANGKULIRANG

Country: GREECE
Country of origin: GREECE
Ship type: AMPHIBIOUS FORCES
Class: JASON (LST)
Active: 3
Building: 2
Name (Pennant Number): CHIOS (L 173), SAMOS (L 174), LESBOS (L 176), IKARIA (L 175), RODOS (L 177)

Recognition features:
- High forecastle with 76 mm/62 gun mounting at mid-point on raised platform
- Break, down from forecastle, to extensive well deck.
- High superstructure aft of well deck.
- Large tripod mainmast atop bridge roof supporting radar aerials.
- Distinctive twin funnels, side-by-side, at after end of superstructure. Funnels of square section, black-capped, with sloping tops.
- Large raised helicopter platform aft with stern overhang.

Note - Bow and stern ramps, drive-through design.

Displacement full load, tons: 4,400.
Length, feet (metres): 380.5 (116).
Beam, feet (metres): 50.2 (15.3).
Draught, feet (metres): 11.3 (3.4).
Speed, knots: 16.

Guns: 1 OTO MELARA 76 mm/62 Mod 9 Compact; Breda 40 mm/70 (2 twin) Compact. Rheinmetall 20 mm (2 twin).

Radars:
Surface search — CSF Triton.
Navigation — Kelvin Hughes Type 1007
Fire control — Thomson-CSF Pollux.

Helicopters: Platform for 1.

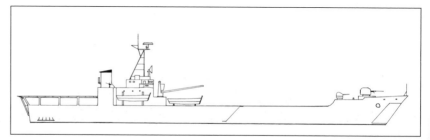

Jason Class

CHIOS

San Giorgio Class

Country: ITALY
Country of origin: ITALY
Ship type: AMPHIBIOUS FORCES
Class: SAN GIORGIO (LPDs)
Active: 3
Name (Pennant Number): SAN GIORGIO (L 9892), SAN MARCO (L 9893), SAN GIUSTO (L 9894)

Recognition features:

- Short forecastle with break up to aircraft carrier type flight deck, which continues to stern.
- Clean profile, high freeboard.
- 3 in gun mounting ('B' position).
- High, angular, square profile island superstructure sited starboard side, midships.
- Pole mainmast atop central island superstructure.
- 3 LCVPs carried in davits, 2 port side opposite island superstructure, 3rd starboard side forward of island superstructure.
- Small, square profile, raked funnel atop island superstructure.

Note 1 - Bow ramp (except San Giusto) for amphibious landings. Stern docking well 20.5 x 7 m. Fitted with a 30 ton lift and 2 40 ton travelling cranes for LCMs.

Note 2 - San Giusto is 285 tons heavier, of similar design except for a slightly longer island and different LCVP davit arrangement. Also no bow doors and therefore no beaching capability.

Displacement full load, tons: 7,665. (7,950, San Giusto).
Length, feet (metres): 437.2 (133.3). (449.5 (137), San Giusto).
Beam, feet (metres): 67.3 (20.5).
Draught, feet (metres): 17.4 (5.3).
Flight deck, feet (metres): 328.1 x 67.3 (100 x 20.5)
Speed, knots: 21.
Range, miles: 7,500 at 16 kts.

Guns: 1 OTO MELARA 3 in (76 mm)/62, (/62 Compact San Giusto); 2 Oerlikon 20 mm or 25 mm. 2 12.7 mm MGs.

Radars:
Surface search — SMA SPS-702.
Navigation — SMA SPN-748.
Fire control — Selenia SPG-70 (RTN 10X).

Helicopters: 3 Agusta-Sikorsky SH-3D Sea King or 5 Agusta-Bell AB 212.

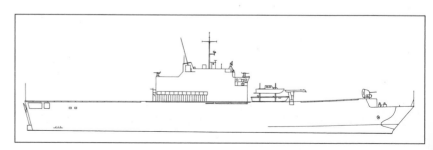

SAN GIORGIO

Osumi Class

Country: JAPAN
Country of origin: JAPAN
Ship type: AMPHIBIOUS FORCES
Class: OSUMI (LPD/LST)
Active: 1
Proposed: 1
Name (Pennant Number): OSUMI (LST 4001)

Recognition features:

- Short forecastle with sharp break up to aircraft carrier style flight deck, continuous to stern.
- Angular island sited starboard side, amidships.
- Enclosed pyramid mainmast with OPS-14C air search radar on projecting gantry forward.
- Square black funnel at aft end of superstructure with projecting exhausts and pole aerials.
- Large crane immediately aft of funnel.
- Vulcan Phalanx CIWS on platforms forward and aft of superstructure.

Note - Through deck and stern docking. Military lift — 330 troops; 2 LCAC; 10 Type 90 tanks or 1,400 tons cargo.

Displacement, standard, tons: 8,900.
Length, feet (metres): 584 (178).
Beam, feet (metres): 84.6 (25.8).
Draught, feet (metres): 19.7 (6).
Flight deck, feet (metres): 426.5 x 75.5 (130 x 23).
Speed, knots: 22.

Guns: 2 GE/GD Vulcan Phalanx Mk 15.

Radars:
Air search — Mitsubishi OPS-14C.
Surface search — JRC OPS-28D
Navigation — JRC OPS-20.

Helicopters: Platform for 2 Kawasaki/Boeing CH-47JA Chinook.

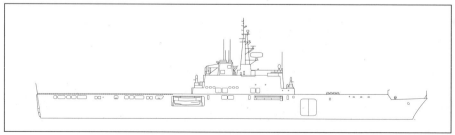

Osumi Class

OSUMI

Ivan Rogov (Yednorog) Class

Country: RUSSIA
Country of origin: RUSSIA
Ship type: AMPHIBIOUS FORCES
Class: IVAN ROGOV (YEDNOROG) (TYPE 1174) (LPD)
Active: 1
Name (Pennant Number): MITROFAN MOSKALENKO (O20)

Displacement full load, tons: 14,060.
Length, feet (metres): 516.7 (157.5).
Beam, feet (metres): 80.2 (24.5).
Draught, feet (metres): 21.2 (6.5). (27.8 (8.5), flooded).
Speed, knots: 19.
Range, miles: 7,500 at 14 kts.

Recognition features:

- Raised forecastle with 3 in gun twin mounting ('A' position).
- Long tank deck aft to very large superstructure, well aft of midships.
- Curved leading edge to high main superstructure with large pyramid mainmast atop supporting Top Plate A air/surface search radar aerial.
- Lattice mast atop after end of superstructure.
- 4 30 mm/65 gun mountings, 2 port, 2 starboard, outboard of mainmast and one deck down.
- Gecko SAM launcher at after end of superstructure.
- Short helicopter landing platform right aft with open quarterdeck below.

Note 1 - Has bow ramp with beaching capability leading from a tank deck. Stern doors open into a docking bay.
Note 2 - Helicopters can enter the hangar from both front and rear.
Note 3 - Two Pacific Fleet units paid off in 1996 and 1997. Reported that one might be transferred to Indonesia, but the Asian economic climate may have influenced this purchase.

Missiles: SAM - SA-N-4 Gecko twin launcher.   2 SA-N-5 Grail quad launchers.
Guns: 3 in (76mm)/60 (twin); 122 mm BM-21 (naval) rocket launcher; 2 20-barrel rocket launchers; 4 30 mm/65 AK 630.
Decoys: 16 PK 10 and 4 PK 16 chaff launchers.

Radars:
Air/surface search —Top Plate A
Navigation — 2 Don Kay or 2 Palm Frond.
Fire control — Owl Screech; 2 Bass Tilt; Pop Group.
Sonars: Mouse Tail VDS.

Helicopters: 4 Kamov Ka-29 Helix B (assault).

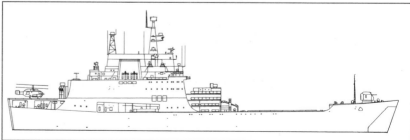

Ivan Rogov (Yednorog) Class

IVAN ROGOV

Polnochny A/B/C/D Class

Country: ALGERIA, AZERBAIJAN, BULGARIA, EGYPT, INDIA, LIBYA, RUSSIA, SYRIA, UKRAINE, VIETNAM
Country of origin: RUSSIA
Ship type: AMPHIBIOUS FORCES
Class: POLNOCHNY GROUP A (TYPE 770) (LSM)
Active: 2 Bulgaria, 3 Egypt, 1 Vietnam.
BULGARIA
Name (Pennant Number): SIRIUS (ex-Ivan Zagubanski) (701), ANTARES (702).
EGYPT
Name (Pennant Number): 301, 303, 305.
VIETNAM
Name (Pennant Number): HQ 512

Class: POLNOCHNY GROUP B (TYPE 771) (LSM)
Active: 1 Algeria, 2 Azerbaijan, 1 Russia, 3 Syria, 2 Vietnam
ALGERIA
Name (Pennant Number): 471.
AZERBAIJAN
Name (Pennant Number): (None available).
RUSSIA
Name (Pennant Number): (None available).
SYRIA
Name (Pennant Number): 1-114, 2-114, 3-114.
VIETNAM
Name (Pennant Number): HQ 511, HQ 512, HQ 513.

Class: POLNOCHNY GROUP C (TYPE 773) (LSM)
Active: 4 India, 1 Ukraine
INDIA
Name (Pennant Number): GHORPAD (L 14), KESARI (L 15), SHARDUL (L 16), SHARBAH (L 17)
UKRAINE

Name (Pennant Number): KIROVOGRAD (U 401).
Class: POLNOCHNY GROUP D (TYPE 773U) (LSM)
Active: 4 India, 2 + 1 reserve, Libya.
INDIA
Name (Pennant Number): CHEETAH (L 18), MAHISH (L 19), GULDAR (L 21), KUMBHIR (L 22).
LIBYA
Name (Pennant Number): IBN AL HADRAMI (112), IBN UMAYAA (116), IBN AL FARAT (118).
Recognition features:
- This class varies in appearance to quite a large degree between groups and countries. Below are general common features.
- High bow with long deck aft to superstructure well aft of midships.
- Squared profile lower superstructure with bridge superstructure atop.
- Mainmast (lattice or tripod) at central superstructure.
- Low profile funnel aft of mainmast.
- Step down at after end of superstructure to short afterdeck.
- Have bow ramps only.
- Group D has a helicopter landing platform amidships.

Note - Poland operates 2 modified Polnochny C ships — Cedynia (810) is used as a transport and Grunwald (811), as an amphibious command vessel.

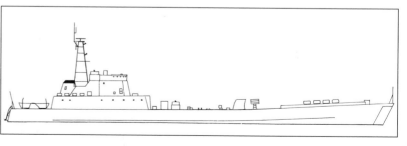

Polnochny A/B/C/D Class

POLOCHNY

Displacement full load, tons: 800, (Group A). 834, (Group B). 1,150, (Group C). 1,305 (Group D).
Length, feet (metres): 239.5 (73), (A). 246.1, (75), (B). 266.7 (81.3), (C/D). 257.3 (83.9) Libya D).
Beam, feet (metres): 27.9 (8.5), (A). 31.5 (9.6), (B). 31.8 (9.7), (C/D).
Draught, feet (metres): 5.8 (1.8), (A). 7.5 (2.3), (B). 7.9 (2.4), (C/D).
Speed, knots: 19, (A); 18, (B/C).
Range, miles: 1,000 at 18 kts. (Groups A and B); 2,000 at 12 kts. (Group C).

Missiles: SAM - 4 SA-N-5 Grail quad launchers (B and C, Russia and Ukraine only).

Guns: 30 mm/65 (twin), (A). 2 or 4 30 mm (1 or 2 twin) (B). 30 mm/65 (2 twin) (C). 2 140 mm 18-barrel rocket launchers (A, B and C).
Mines: Capacity to lay 100, (Libya 'D' only).

Radars:
Surface search — Spin Trough. (Bulgaria 'A,' Russia, Syria, Vietnam 'B', Ukraine 'C'); Decca, (Egypt 'A'). Radwar SRN 745, (Libya, 'D').
Navigation — Don 2 (B) or Don 2 or Krivach (SRN 745), (India 'C').
Fire control — Drum Tilt. (Not Bulgaria).

Helicopters: Platform only in Group D.

Ropucha Class

Country: RUSSIA, UKRAINE, YEMEN
Country of origin: RUSSIA
Ship type: AMPHIBIOUS FORCES
Class: ROPUCHA I (TYPE 775), ROPUCHA II (TYPE 775M) (LST)
Active: 17 'Ropucha I', 3 'Ropucha II' — Russia. 1 'Ropucha I' — Ukraine. 1 'Ropucha I' — Yemen.

RUSSIA
Name (Pennant Number): (Only 4 ships show names), ALEKSANDR SHABALIN (BDK 100), KONSTANTIN OLSHANSKY (BDK 56), TSESAR KUNIKOV (BDK 64), BOBRUISK (BDK 98).

UKRAINE
Name (Pennant Number): KONSTANTIN OLSHANSKY (U 402).

YEMEN
Name (Pennant Number): 139.

Recognition features:
- Unusual squared-off forward end to forecastle.
- 57 mm/80 (Ropucha I) or 76 mm/60 gun mounting (Ropucha II) at forward end of superstructure.
- Large superstructure centred aft of midships.
- Pole mast atop bridge roof.
- Large lattice mainmast atop mid-superstructure.
- Very wide square section funnels aft of mainmast.

Note 1 - A 'roll-on-roll-off' design with a tank deck running the whole length of the ship.
Note 2 - All have very minor differences in appearance. (See Guns and Missiles sections below.)
Note 3 - At least five Russian ships have rocket launchers at the after end of the forecastle.
Note 4 - 1 Ropucha II has a masthead radar dome.

Displacement full load, tons: 4,400.
Length, feet (metres): 369.1 (112.5). (370.7 (113), Ukraine).
Beam, feet (metres): 49.2 (15). (47.6 (14.5), Ukraine).
Draught, feet (metres): 12.1 (3.7). (11.5 (3.6), Ukraine).
Speed, knots: 17.5.
Range, miles: 6,000 at 12 kts.

Missiles: SAM - 4 SA-N-5 Grail quad launchers (in at least two Russian ships and Ukraine unit).
Guns: 4 57 mm/80 (2 twin) (Ropucha I). 1 76 mm/60 (Ropucha II). 2 30 mm/65 AK 630 (Ropucha II). 2 122 mm BM-21 (naval) (in some). 2 20-barrel rocket launchers.
Mines: 92 contact type. (Russia and Yemen only).

Radars:
Air/surface search — Strut Curve (Ropucha I) or Cross Dome (Ropucha II).
Navigation — Don 2 or Kivach. (Nayada, Yemen and some Russian units).
Fire control — Muff Cob (Ropucha I). Bass Tilt (Ropucha II).
Sonars: Mouse Tail VDS can be carried in Russian ships.

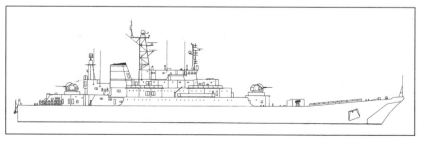

Ropucha Class

ROPUCHKA I

Fearless Class

Country: UNITED KINGDOM
Country of origin: UNITED KINGDOM
Ship type: AMPHIBIOUS FORCES
Class: FEARLESS (LPD)
Active: 1 + 1 reserve
Name (Pennant Number): FEARLESS (L 10), INTREPID (L 11)

Recognition features:
- Blunt bow, long forecastle, high freeboard.
- Long, high superstructure centred forward of midships.
- Short, enclosed foremast atop bridge roof.
- Large tall enclosed mainmast at mid-superstructure supporting surface search radar aerial.
- 2 distinctive, tall, slim funnels at after end of superstructure, 1 port, 1 starboard, staggered across the beam of the ship.
- 2 Vulcan Phalanx CIWS mountings between funnels and mainmast.
- Long helicopter platform aft of superstructure.
- Small break down to quarterdeck which houses lattice crane jib.

Note 1 - Landing craft are floated through the open stern by flooding compartments of the ship.
Note 2 - Intrepid in reserve as an amphibious transport, in theory at 30 days' readiness.

Displacement full load, tons: 12,120. (16,950 flooded).
Length, feet (metres): 500 (152.4) wl.
Beam, feet (metres): 80 (24.4).
Draught, feet (metres): 20.5 (6.2). 32 (9.8) (flooded)
Speed, knots: 21.
Range, miles: 5,000 at 20 kts.

Guns: 2 GE/GD 20 mm Mk 15 Vulcan Phalanx. 4 Oerlikon/BMARC 30 mm/75 GCM-AO3 (L 11). 2 Oerlikon/BMARC 20 mm GAM-BO1.
Decoys: 4 Sea Gnat 6-barrel fixed launchers.

Radars:
Surface search — Plessey Type 994.
Navigation — Kelvin Hughes Type 1006.

Helicopters: Platform for up to 4 Westland Sea King HC 4.

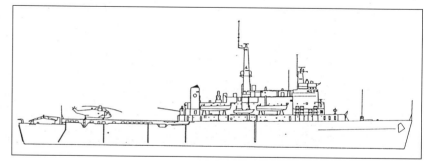

Fearless Class

INTREPID

Austin Class

Country: UNITED STATES OF AMERICA
Country of origin: UNITED STATES OF AMERICA
Ship type: AMPHIBIOUS FORCES
Class: AUSTIN (LPD)
Active: 11
Name (Pennant Number): AUSTIN (LPD 4), OGDEN (LPD 5), DULUTH (LPD 6), CLEVELAND (LPD 7), DUBUQUE (LPD 8), DENVER (LPD 9), JUNEAU (LPD 10), SHREVEPORT (LPD 12), NASHVILLE (LPD 13), TRENTON (LPD 14), PONCE (LPD 15)

Recognition features:
- High bow with wire aerial structure on forecastle.
- Large superstructure forward of midships creating very high freeboard.
- Two Vulcan Phalanx CIWS mountings, 1 forward end of main superstructure, the other atop superstructure, immediately aft of mainmast.
- Large tripod mainmast atop mid-superstructure.
- Unusual tall, slim twin funnels. Starboard funnel well forward of port one.
- Crane derrick between funnels.
- Long flight deck aft with telescopic hangar. (No hangar in LPD 4)

Note 1 - Enlarged version of 'Raleigh' class now paid off.
Note 2 - There are structural variations in the positions of guns and electronic equipment in different ships of the class.
Note 3 - Coronado (AGF 11) former class member, converted into command ship role.

Displacement full load, tons: 17,244.
Length, feet (metres): 570 (173.8).
Beam, feet (metres): 100 (30.5).
Draught, feet (metres): 23. (7).
Speed, knots: 21.
Range, miles: 7,700 at 20 kts.

Guns: 2 GE/GD 20 mm/76 Vulcan Phalanx Mk 15; 2 25 mm Mk 38; 8 12.7 mm MGs.
Decoys: 4 Loral Hycor SRBOC 6-barrel Mk 36.

Radars:
Air search — Lockheed SPS-40B/C.
Surface search — Norden SPS-67.
Navigation — Raytheon SPS-64(V)9.

Helicopters: Up to 6 Boeing CH-46D/E Sea Knight can be carried. Hangar for only 1 light (not in LPD 4).

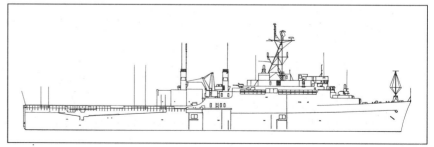

Austin Class

AUSTIN

Blue Ridge Class

Country: UNITED STATES OF AMERICA
Country of origin: UNITED STATES OF AMERICA
Ship type: AMPHIBIOUS FORCES
Class: BLUE RIDGE (LCC)
Active: 2
Name (Pennant Number): BLUE RIDGE (LCC 19), MOUNT WHITNEY (LCC 20)

Recognition features:
- Vulcan Phalanx CIWS mountings at forward end of forecastle and right aft on specially built platform.
- Numerous communications aerials and masts along length of maindeck, including tall lattice mast mid-way between bows and superstructure.
- Small superstructure amidships.
- Pole mainmast atop superstructure.
- Large, distinctive SPS-48C air search 3D radar aerial aft of mainmast atop superstructure.
- Twin, angled exhausts at top after end of superstructure.
- Very unusual flared hull midships section to protect stowages for LCPs and LCVPs.
- Large communications aerial mast mid-afterdeck.
- Tall, enclosed pyramid structure topped by white dome, further aft.

Note - Hull design similar to 'Iwo Jima' class.

Displacement full load, tons: 18,372 (LCC 19), 18,646 (LCC 20).
Length, feet (metres): 636.5 (194).
Beam, feet (metres): 107.9 (32.9).
Draught, feet (metres): 28.9 (8.8).
Speed, knots: 23.
Range, miles: 13,000 at 16 kts.

Guns: 2 GE/GD 20 mm/76 Vulcan Phalanx Mk 15.
Decoys: 4 Loral Hycor SRBOC 6-barrel Mk 36. SLQ-25 Nixie; torpedo decoy.

Radars:
Air search — ITT SPS-48C; Lockheed SPS-40E.
Surface search — Raytheon SPS-65(V)1.
Navigation — Marconi LN66; Raytheon SPS-64(V)9.

Helicopters: 1 Sikorsky SH-3G Sea King.

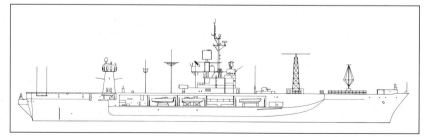

Blue Ridge Class

BLUE RIDGE

Country: UNITED STATES OF AMERICA
Country of origin: UNITED STATES OF AMERICA
Ship type: AMPHIBIOUS FORCES
Class: TARAWA (LHA)
Active: 5
Name (Pennant Number): TARAWA (LHA 1), SAIPAN (LHA 2), BELLEAU WOOD (LHA 3), NASSAU (LHA 4), PELELIU (ex-Da Nang) (LHA 5)

Recognition features:
● Similar outline to Wasp class but higher profile island with prominent crane aft of superstructure.
● Vulcan Phalanx CIWS mounting on platform at forward end of island.
● 2 masts atop island, slightly taller lattice mast forward and pole mast aft.
● Square SPS-52D air search 3D radar aerial atop after end of island, (forward end of island in Wasp class).
● 1 RAM SAM launcher on platform, below flight deck at stern, starboard side; second above bridge offset to port.
● Second CIWS mounting, below flight deck, at stern, port side.
Note - Floodable docking well beneath the after elevator (268 ft long and 78 ft wide) capable of taking four LCUs.

Displacement full load, tons: 39,967.
Length, feet (metres): 834 (254.2).
Beam, feet (metres): 131.9 (40.2).
Draught, feet (metres): 25.9 (7.9).
Flight deck, feet (metres): 820 x 118.1 (250 x 36).
Speed, knots: 24.
Range, miles: 10,000 at 20 kts.

Missiles: SAM - 2 GDC Mk 49 RAM.
Guns: 6 Mk 242 25 mm automatic cannons; 2 GE/GD 20 mm/76 Vulcan Phalanx Mk 15; 8 12.7 mm MGs.
Decoys: 4 Loral Hycor SRBOC 6-barrel Mk 36; AN/SLQ-25 Nixie; torpedo decoy; NATO Sea Gnat. SLQ-49 chaff buoys.

Radars:
Air search — Hughes SPS-52D; Lockheed SPS-40E; Hughes Mk 23 TAS.
Surface search — Raytheon SPS-67(V)3.
Navigation — Raytheon SPS 64(V)9.
Fire control — Lockheed SPG-60; Lockheed SPQ-9A.

Fixed wing aircraft: Harrier AV-8B VSTOL aircraft in place of helicopters as required.
Helicopters: 9 Sikorsky CH-53D Sea Stallion or 12 Boeing CH-46D/E Sea Knight.

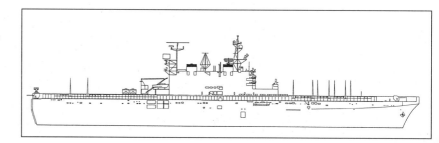

Tarawa Class

NASSAU

Wasp Class

Country: UNITED STATES OF AMERICA
Country of origin: UNITED STATES OF AMERICA
Ship type: AMPHIBIOUS FORCES
Class: WASP (LHD)
Active: 6
Building: 1
Name (Pennant Number): WASP (LHD 1), ESSEX (LHD 2), KEARSARGE
(LHD 3), BOXER (LHD 4), BATAAN (LHD 5), BONHOMME RICHARD
(LHD 6), IWO JIMA (LHD 7).

Recognition features:
- Effectively aircraft carrier style with continuous flight deck.
- Large starboard side island amidships.
- Two black-capped funnels, fore and aft atop island.
- 2 Sea Sparrow SAM box launchers, 1 at forward end of island, the other right aft on overhanging transom. (RAM SAM being fitted forward of Sea Sparrow on superstructure and at stern.)
- Two similar pole masts atop island, after one slightly the taller of the two.
- Vulcan Phalanx CIWS mountings, 1 immediately forward of bridge, 1 other on each quarter.
- 2 aircraft elevators, one to starboard and aft of the island and one to port amidships.

Note 1 - Stern doors with well deck of 267 x 50 ft to accommodate up to three LCACs.
Note 2 - Vehicle storage is available for five M1A1 main battle tanks, 25 LAV-25 APCs, eight M 198 155 mm howitzers, 68 trucks, 10 logistic vehicles and several service vehicles.

Displacement full load, tons: 40,532.
Length, feet (metres): 844 (257.3) oa.
Beam, feet (metres): 140.1 (42.7) oa.
Draught, feet (metres): 26.6 (8.1).
Flight deck, feet (metres): 819 x 106 (249.6 x 32.3).

Speed, knots: 22.
Range, miles: 9,500 at 18 kts.

Missiles: SAM - 2 Raytheon GMLS Mk 29 octuple launchers; Sea Sparrow. 2 GDC Mk 49 RAM being fitted forward of GMLS and at the stern.
Guns: 2 or 3 GE/GD 20 mm Vulcan Phalanx Mk 15; 3 25 mm Mk 38; 4 or 8 12.7 mm MGs.
Decoys: 4 or 6 Loral Hycor SRBOC 6-barrel Mk 36; SLQ-25 Nixie; torpedo decoy; NATO Sea Gnat; SLQ-49 chaff buoys.

Radars:
Air search — Hughes SPS-52C, 3D (LHD 1); ITT SPS-48E, (remainder); Raytheon SPS- 49(V)9; Hughes Mk 23 TAS.
Surface search — Norden SPS-67.
Navigation — SPS-64(V)9.

Fixed wing aircraft: 6-8 AV-8B Harriers or up to 20 in secondary role.
Helicopters: Capacity for 42 Boeing CH-46E Sea Knight. Capability to support Bell AH-1W SuperCobra, Sikorsky CH-53E Super Stallion, Sikorsky CH-53D Sea Stallion, Bell UH-1N Twin Huey, AH-1T SeaCobra, and Sikorsky SH-60B Seahawk.

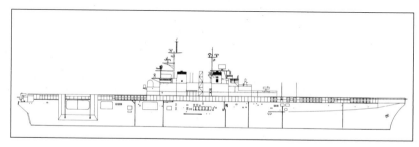

Wasp Class

ESSEX

Country: UNITED STATES OF AMERICA
Country of origin: UNITED STATES OF AMERICA
Ship type: AMPHIBIOUS FORCES
Class: WHIDBEY ISLAND (LSD)
Active: 8
Name (Pennant Number): WHIDBEY ISLAND (LSD 41), GERMANTOWN (LSD 42), FORT McHENRY (LSD 43), GUNSTON HALL (LSD 44), COMSTOCK (LSD 45), TORTUGA (LSD 46), RUSHMORE (LSD 47), ASHLAND (LSD 48).

Class: HARPERS FERRY (LSD-CV)
Active: 4
Name (Pennant Number): HARPERS FERRY (LSD 49), CARTER HALL (LSD 50), OAK HILL (LSD 51), PEARL HARBOR (LSD 52)

Recognition features:
- Short forecastle with wire aerial structure on forecastle.
- High superstructure well forward of midships.
- Large lattice mainmast atop mid-superstructure.
- 2 Vulcan Phalanx CIWS mountings atop main superstructure, 1 on bridge roof, 1 immediately forward of funnel.
- Large funnel with sloping after profile at after end of superstructure.
- 1 or 2 large cranes aft of funnel.
- Long afterdeck.

Note 1 - Based on the earlier 'Anchorage' class. 'Harpers Ferry' class cargo-carrying variants.
Note 2 - Well deck measures 440 x 50 ft (134.1 x 15.2 m) in the LSD but is shorter in the Cargo Variant (CV).
Note 3 - Approximately 90% commonality between the two variants.

Displacement full load, tons: 15,726 (LSD 41-48), 16,740 (LSD 49 onwards)
Length, feet (metres): 609.5 (185.8).
Beam, feet (metres): 84 (25.6).
Draught, feet (metres): 20.5 (6.3).
Speed, knots: 22.
Range, miles: 8,000 at 18 kts.

Missiles: SAM - 1 or 2 GDC Mk 49 RAM being fitted.
Guns: 2 GE/GD 20 mm/76 Vulcan Phalanx Mk 15; 2 20 mm Mk 38; 8   12.7 mm MGs.
Decoys: 4 Loral Hycor SRBOC 6-barrel Mk 36; SLQ-25 Nixie towed torpedo decoy.

Radars:
Air search — Raytheon SPS-49(V)5.
Surface search — Norden SPS-67V.
Navigation — Raytheon SPS-64(V)9.

Helicopters: Platform only for 2 Sikorsky CH-53D Sea Stallion.

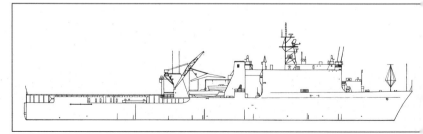

TORTUGA

Frankenthal Class

Country: GERMANY
Country of origin: GERMANY
Ship type: MINE WARFARE FORCES
Class: FRANKENTHAL (TYPE 332) (MHC)
Active: 12
Name (Pennant Number): FRANKENTHAL (M 1066), WEIDEN (M 1060), ROTTWEIL (M 1061), BAD BEVENSEN (M 1063), BAD RAPPENAU (M 1067), GRÖMITZ (M 1064), DATTELN (M 1068), DILLINGEN (M 1065), HOMBURG (M 1069), SULZBACH-ROSENBERG (M 1062), FULDA (M 1058), WEILHEIM (M 1059).

Recognition features:
- High freeboard forward with break down to maindeck level amidships.
- 40 mm/70 gun mounting ('A' position).
- Tall, substantial superstructure stepped down aft of midships.
- Small lattice foremast atop bridge.
- Tall, slim, tripod mainmast amidships.
- Small crane on quarterdeck.

Note 1 - Same hull, similar superstructure as 'Hameln' class, Type 343.

Note 2 - Equipped with 2 STN Systemtechnik Nord Pinguin-B3 drones with sonar and TV cameras.

Displacement full load, tons: 650.
Length, feet (metres): 178.8 (54.5).
Beam, feet (metres): 30.2 (9.2).
Draught, feet (metres): 8.5 (2.6).
Speed, knots: 18.

Missiles: SAM - 2 Stinger quad launchers.
Guns: 1 Bofors 40 mm/70.

Radars:
Navigation — Raytheon SPS-64.
Sonars: Atlas Elektronik DSQS-11M; hull-mounted.

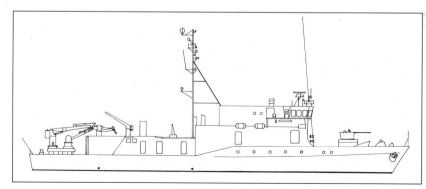

Frankenthal Class

FRANKENTHAL

Hameln Class

Country: GERMANY
Country of origin: GERMANY
Ship type: MINE WARFARE FORCES
Class: HAMELN (TYPE 343) (MSC/MHC)
Active: 10
Name (Pennant Number): HAMELN* (M 1092), ÜBERHERRN (M 1095), LABOE (M 1097), PEGNITZ* (M 1090), KULMBACH (M 1091), SIEGBURG (M 1098), ENSDORF* (M 1094), PASSAU (M 1096), HERTEN (M 1099), AUERBACH* (M 1093)
* Converted to control improved Troika minesweeping drones

Recognition features:
- Very similar profile to 'Frankenthal' class with main distinguishing differences as follows: -
- Latticed, pyramid shaped mainmast atop bridge roof supporting WM20/2 surface search/fire control radome.
- 40 mm/70 gun turret mounting forward of bridge.
- 40 mm/70 gun mounting aft ('X' position).
- Long sweep deck aft of superstructure.
- Sweep gear gantries right aft.

Displacement full load, tons: 635.
Length, feet (metres): 178.5 (54.4).
Beam, feet (metres): 30.2 (9.2).
Draught, feet (metres): 8.2 (2.5).
Speed, knots: 18.

Missiles: SAM - 2 Stinger quad launchers.
Guns: 2 Bofors 40 mm/70.
Mines: 60.
Decoys: 2 Silver Dog chaff rocket launchers.

Radars:
Surface search/fire control — Signaal WM 20/2.
Navigation — Raytheon SPS-64.
Sonars: Atlas Elektronik DSQS-11M; hull-mounted.

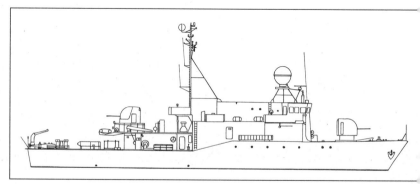

Hameln Class

KULMBACH

Kondor II Class

Country: INDONESIA, LATVIA, URUGUAY
Country of origin: GERMANY
Ship type: MINE WARFARE FORCES
Class: KONDOR II (TYPE 89) (MSC/PC)
Active: 9 Indonesia, 2 Latvia, 4 Uruguay
INDONESIA
Name (Pennant Number): PULAU ROTE (ex-Wolgast) (721 ex-V 811), PULAU RAAS (ex-Hettstedt) (722 ex- 353), PULAU ROMANG (ex-Pritzwalk) (723 ex-325), PULAU RIMAU (ex-Bitterfeld) (724 ex-332, ex-M 2672), PULAU RONDO (ex-Zerbst) (725 ex-335), PULAU RUSA (ex-Oranienburg) (726 ex-341), PULAU RANGSANG (ex-Jüterbog), (727 ex-342), PULAU RAIBU (ex-Sömmerda) (728 ex-311, ex-M 2670), PULAU REMPANG (ex-Grimma) (729 ex-336).

LATVIA
Name (Pennant Number): VIESTURS (ex-Kamenz) (M 01 ex-351), IMANTA (ex-Röbel) (M 02 ex-324).

URUGUAY
Name (Pennant Number): TEMERAIRO (ex-Riesa) (31), VALIENTE (ex-Eilenburg) (32), FORTUNA (ex-Bernau) (33), AUDAZ (ex-Eisleben) (34).

Recognition features:
- Low freeboard with continuous maindeck from stem to stern.
- High, stepped, smooth contoured superstructure centred well forward of midships.
- Sturdy pole mainmast immediately aft of bridge, supporting radar aerials.
- Squat, square sectioned funnel with sloping top sited midships.
- 2 25 mm/80 twin gun mountings mounting on sponsons aft of funnel in Indonesian ships. (Absent, Latvian and Uruguayan units).
- Small square structure on afterdeck.
- Sweep gear right aft.
- Kondor II some 16 ft longer than Kondor I.

- Kondor I has square profile funnel with sloping top. Kondor II has rounded funnel with wedge shaped smoke deflector at its after edge.
Note - Estonia operates 2 Kondor I class (Vambola (M 411) and Sulev (M 412) as OPVs. Malta operates 4 Kondor I (P 30, P 31, P 29 La Valette, and a further, as yet, unnamed ship), as coastal patrol craft. Guinea-Bissau operates 1 Kondor I (V 814), transferred, unarmed, from Germany in 1990, as a coastal patrol craft. Tunisian coastguard operates 5 Kondor I class as patrol craft.

Displacement standard, tons: 410.   377, Kondor I.
Length, feet (metres): 186 (56.7), Kondor II. 170.3 (51.9), Kondor I.
Beam, feet (metres): 24.6 (7.5), Kondor II. 23.3 (7.1), Kondor I.
Draught, feet (metres): 7.9 (2.4), Kondor II, 7.2 (2.2), Kondor I.
Speed, knots: 17.

Guns: 25 mm/80 (3 twin), (Indonesia).   Wrobel 23 mm (twin), (Latvia). 1 Bofors 40 mm/60, (Uruguay).
Mines: 2 rails, (Indonesia, Uruguay only).

Radars:
Surface search — Racal Decca (Latvia).
Navigation — TSR 333 or Raytheon 1900.
Sonars: Bendix AQS-17(V) VDS, (Indonesia).

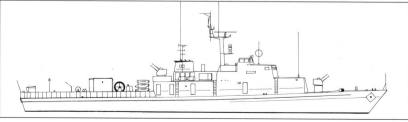

Kondor II Class

VIESTURS

Tripartite Minehunter Class

Country: BELGIUM, FRANCE, INDONESIA, NETHERLANDS, PAKISTAN
Country of origin: INTERNATIONAL
Ship type: MINE WARFARE FORCES
Class: TRIPARTITE MINEHUNTERS (FLOWER, ÉRIDAN, PULAU RENGAT, ALKMAAR, MUNSIF) (MHC)
Active: 7 Belgium ('Flower' class), 13 France ('Éridan' class), 2 Indonesia ('Pulau Rengat' class), 15 Netherlands ('Alkmaar' class), 3 Pakistan ('Munsif' class)

BELGIUM
Name (Pennant Number): ASTER (M 915), BELLIS (M 916), CROCUS (M 917), LOBELIA (M 921), MYOSOTIS (M 922), NARCIS (M 923), PRIMULA (M 924)

FRANCE
Name (Pennant Number): ÉRIDAN (M 641), CASSIOPÉE (M 642), ANDROMÈDE (M 643), PÉGASE (M 644), ORION (M 645), CROIX DU SUD (M 646), AIGLE (M 647), LYRE (M 648), PERSÉE (M 649), SAGITTAIRE (M 650), VERSEAU (ex-Iris) (M 651), CÉPHÉE (ex-Fuchsia), (M 652), CAPRICORNE (ex-Dianthus) (M 653).

INDONESIA
Name (Pennant Number): PULAU RENGAT (711), PULAU RUPAT (712).

NETHERLANDS
Name (Pennant Number): ALKMAAR (M 850), DELFZYL (M 851), DORDRECHT (M 852), HAARLEM (M 853), HARLINGEN (M854), SCHEVENINGEN (M 855), MAASSLUIS (M 856), MAKKUM (M 857), MIDDELBURG (M 858), HELLEVOETSLUIS (M 859), SCHIEDAM (M 860), URK (M 861), ZIERIKZEE (M 862), VLAARDINGEN (M 863), WILLEMSTAD (M 864).

PAKISTAN
Name (Pennant Number): MUNSIF (ex-Sagittaire) (M 166), MUHAFIZ (M 163), MUJAHID (M 164).

Recognition features:
- High bow and high freeboard.
- Continuous maindeck aft to break down to low freeboard quarterdeck.
- 20 mm/20 gun mounting ('A' position).
- Low superstructure from forecastle aft to quarterdeck.
- Pole mainmast atop after end of bridge.
- Squat, tapered, black-capped funnel with sloping top, atop superstructure.
- Small crane on quarterdeck.
- SATCOM on pole aft end of superstructure, (Dutch ships).

Displacement full load, tons: 595, (605, French ships), (568, Indonesian ships).
Length, feet (metres): 168.9 (51.5).
Beam, feet (metres): 29.2 (8.9).
Draught, feet (metres): 8.5 (2.6), Dutch ships. 8.2 (2.5), Belgian, Indonesian, French. 9.5 (2.9), Pakistan.
Speed, knots: 15.
Range, miles: 3,000 at 12 kts.

Guns: 1 DCN 20 mm/20. 1 12.7 mm MG, (Belgium). 1 Giat 20F2 20 mm,

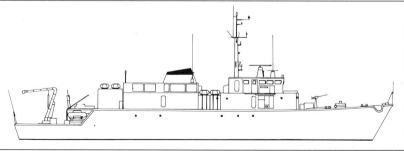

(France, Netherlands, Pakistan). 1 12.7 mm MG, (France, Pakistan). 2 Rheinmetall 20 mm (Indonesia. Matra Simbad/Mistral SAM launcher may be added for patrol duties or a third 20 mm gun).

Countermeasures: MCM - 2 PAP 104 remote-controlled mine locators. Mechanical sweep gear (medium depth). (AP-4 acoustic sweep, France). (Elesco MKR 400 acoustic sweep, MRK 960 magnetic sweep, Pakistan). (Fiskars F-82 magnetic sweep and SA Marine AS 203 acoustic sweeps, Indonesia).

PRIMULA

Radars:
Navigation — Racal Decca 1229, (Belgium, France, Pakistan). Racal Decca TM 1229C (Indonesia, Netherlands).
Sonars: Thomson-Sintra DUBM 21A/B or 21D; hull-mounted; (Thomson-Sintra TSM 2022, Indonesia), minehunting.

Lerici and Gaeta Class

Country: AUSTRALIA, ITALY, MALAYSIA, NIGERIA, THAILAND
Country of origin: ITALY
Ship type: MINE WARFARE FORCES
Class: LERICI (MAHAMIRU) (MHC/MSC)
Active: 4 Italy, 4 Malaysia ('Mahamiru' class), 2 Nigeria

ITALY
Name (Pennant Number): LERICI (M 5550), SAPRI (M 5551), MILAZZO (M 5552), VIESTE (M 5553).

MALAYSIA
Name (Pennant Number): MAHAMIRU (11), JERAI (12), LEDANG (13), KINABALU (14)

NIGERIA
Name (Pennant Number): OHUE (M 371), MARABAI (M 372).

Class: GAETA (HUON), (LAT YA) (MHC/MSC)
Active: 1 Australia ('Huon' class), 8 Italy, 2 Thailand ('Lat Ya' class)
Building: 2 Australia
Proposed: 3 Australia

AUSTRALIA
Name (Pennant Number): HUON (82), HAWKESBURY (83), NORMAN (84), GASCOYNE (85), DIAMANTINA (86), YARRA (87).

ITALY
Name (Pennant Number): GAETA (M 5554), TERMOLI (M 5555), ALGHERO (M 5556), NUMANA (M 5557), CROTONE (M 5558), VIAREGGIO (M 5559), CHIOGGIA (M 5560), RIMINI (M 5561)

THAILAND
Name (Pennant Number): LAT YA (633), THA DIN DAENG (634).

Recognition features:
- High bow, high freeboard. Sloping break, aft of funnel, down to sweep deck.
- 20 mm/70 mounting ('A' position). (40 mm/70 in Malaysian ships, 30 mm (twin) mounting in Nigerian

ships. MSI DS 30B 30 mm in Australian and Thai ships).
- High bridge superstructure with forward sloping bridge windows.
- SATCOM dome atop aft end of bridge in Australian ships.
- Tapered funnel with unusual, wedge shaped, smoke deflector atop.

Note 1 - Two types easily distinguished by large pole mainmast sited immediately aft of bridge (Lerici) and immediately forward of funnel (Gaeta).

Note 2 - 12 of much larger, modified Lerici design built by the USA as 'Osprey' class.

Note 3 - Italian ships fitted with telescopic crane for launching Callegari diver boats.

Displacement full load, tons: 620. (697 Gaeta onwards). 610 (Malaysian ships). 640, (Nigerian). 680 (Thailand). 720, (Australia).
Length, feet (metres): 164. (50), (172.1 (52.5) Gaeta class, and Australia, Thailand. 167.3 (51), Malaysian and Nigerian ships).
Beam, feet (metres): 32.5 (9.9).
Draught, feet (metres): 8.6 (2.6). (9.2 (2.8), Malaysian and Nigerian ships). (9.8 (3), Australia).
Speed, knots: 15.

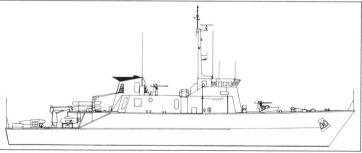

LERICI

Range, miles: 2,500 at 12 kts.

Guns: 1 Oerlikon 20 mm/70 (Lerici) or 2 Oerlikon/70 (twin) (Gaeta class), (Italy). 1 MSI DS 30B 30 mm/75, (Australia, Thailand). 1 Bofors 40 mm/70 (Malaysian ships). Emerson Electric 30 mm (twin); 2 Oerlikon 20 mm GAM-B01 (Nigeria).

Countermeasures: Minehunting - 1 MIN 77 or MIN Mk 2 (Gaeta class); 1 Pluto mine destruction system. Minesweeping - Oropesa Mk 4 wire sweep, (Italy). 2 Bofors SUTEC Double-Eagle Mk 2 mine disposal vehicles; ADI Oropesa mechanical sweep, (Australia). Thomson-CSF IBIS II minehunting system; 2 Improved PAP 104 remotely operated vehicles, (Malaysia). 2 Pluto systems; Oropesa 'O' Mis 4 and IBIS V control

system, (Nigeria). Atlas MWS 80-6 minehunting system; magnetic, acoustic and mechanical sweeps; 2 Pluto Plus ROVs, (Thailand).

Decoys: 2 Super Barricade chaff launchers, (Australia only).

Radars:

Navigation — SMA SPN-728V(3), (Italy). Kelvin Hughes 1007, (Australia). Racal Decca 1226; Thomson-CSF Tripartite III, (Malaysia,). Racal Decca 1226, (Malaysia and Nigeria). Atlas Elektronik 9600M (ARPA), (Thailand).

Sonars: FIAR SQQ-14(IT) VDS (lowered from keel fwd of bridge), (Italy). Thomson-Sintra TSM 2022, minehunting, (Malaysia, Nigeria). GEC Marconi Type 2093 VDS, (Australia). Atlas Elektronik DSQS-11M, hull-mounted, active, (Thailand).

Hatsushima and Uwajima Class

Country: JAPAN
Country of origin: JAPAN
Ship type: MINE WARFARE FORCES
Class: HATSUSHIMA (MHC/MSC)
Active: 16
Class: UWAJIMA (MHC/MSC)
Active: 9
Name (Pennant Number): Hatsushima class - YAKUSHIMA (MSC 656), NARUSHIMA (MSC 657), CHICHIJIMA (MSC 658), TORISHIMA (MSC 659), HAHAJIMA (MSC 660), TAKASHIMA (MSC 661), NUWAJIMA (MSC 662), ETAJIMA (MSC 663), KAMISHIMA (MSC 664), HIMESHIMA (MSC 665), OGISHIMA (MSC 666), MOROSHIMA (MSC 667), YURISHIMA (MSC 668), HIKOSHIMA (MSC 669), AWASHIMA (MSC 670), SAKUSHIMA (MSC 671). Uwajima class - UWAJIMA (MSC 672), IESHIMA (MSC 673), TSUKISHIMA (MSC 674), MAEJIMA (MSC 675), KUMEJIMA (MSC 676), MAKISHIMA (MSC 677), TOBISHIMA (MSC 678), YUGESHIMA (MSC 679) NAGASHIMA (MSC 680).

Recognition features:
- Continuous deck from bow aft to break adjacent to funnel, down to lower deck level.
- Small bridge superstructure well forward of midships.
- Tall tripod mainmast midships.
- Tall, black-capped cylindrical funnel aft of mainmast at deck break.
- Slender aftermast forward of sweep deck.
- Sweeping gantries at after end of sweep deck.

Displacement full load, tons: 510.
Length, feet (metres): 180.4 (55), (189.3 (57.7) MSC 670 on).
Beam, feet (metres): 30.8 (9.4).
Draught, feet (metres): 7.9 (2.4).
Speed, knots: 14.

Guns: 1 JM-61 20 mm/76 Sea Vulcan 20.

Radars:
Surface search — Fujitsu OPS-9 or OPDS-39 (MSC 674 onwards).
Sonars: Nec/Hitachi ZQS 2B or ZQS 3 (MSC 672 onwards); hull-mounted; minehunting.

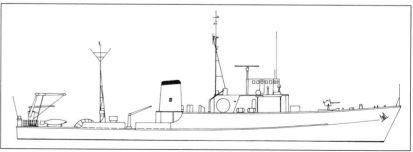

AWASHIMA

Country: NORWAY
Country of origin: NORWAY
Ship type: MINE WARFARE FORCES
Class: OKSØY/ALTA (MHC/MSC)
Active: 9
Name (Pennant Number): MHC - OKSØY (M 340), KARMØY (M 341),
  MÅLØY (M 342), HINNØY (M 343). MSC -ALTA (M 350), OTRA (M 351),
  RAUMA (M 352), ORKLA (M 353), GLOMMA (M 354)

Recognition features:

- Unusual blunt, flat-fronted bow.
- Twin-hulled.
- Flat, uncluttered forecastle forward of stepped, substantial
  superstructure.
- Bridge just forward of midships set atop superstructure.
- Lattice mainmast atop after end of bridge.
- Unusual, square section twin funnels at after end of main superstructure.
- Deck aft of funnels drops down to small sweep deck.
- Distinctive, modern design ship with clean, smooth lines and high
  freeboard.

Displacement full load, tons: 375.
Length, feet (metres): 181.1 (55.2).
Beam, feet (metres): 44.6 (13.6).
Draught, feet (metres): 8.2 (2.5)
Speed, knots: 20.5.
Range, miles: 1,500 at 20 kts.

Missiles: SAM — Matra Sadral; twin launcher; Mistral.
Guns: 1 or 2 Rheinmetall 20 mm. 2 12.7 mm MGs.
Countermeasures: Minehunters - 2 Pluto submersibles. Minesweepers -
  Mechanical and influence sweeping equipment.

Radars:

Navigation — 2 Racal Decca.
Sonars: Thomson Sintra/Simrad TSM 2023N; hull-mounted (minehunters).
  Simrad Subsea SA 950; hull-mounted (minesweepers).

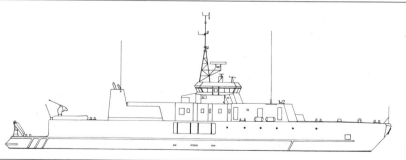

Oksøy/Alta Class

OKSØY

Natya I/II Class

Country: INDIA, LIBYA, RUSSIA, SYRIA,YEMEN
Country of origin: RUSSIA
Ship type: MINE WARFARE FORCES
Class: NATYA I (TYPE 266M) (PONDICHERRY) (AKVAMAREN) (MSO)
Active: 12 India ('Pondicherry' class), 8 Libya, 23 Russia ('Akvamaren'), 1 Yemen

INDIA
Name (Pennant Number): PONDICHERRY (M 61), PORBANDAR (M 62), BEDI (M 63), BHAVNAGAR (M 64), ALLEPPEY (M 65), RATNAGIRI (M 66), KARWAR (M 67), CANNANORE (M 68) CUDDALORE (M 69), KAKINADA (M 70), KOZHIKODA (M 71), KONKAN (M 72).

LIBYA
Name (Pennant Number): AL ISAR (ex-Ras El Gelais) (111), AL TIYAR (ex-Ras Hadad) (113), RAS AL HAMMAN (115), RAS AL FULAIJAH (117), RAS AL QULA (119), RAS AL MADWAR (121), RAS AL MASSAD (123), RAS AL HANI (125).

RUSSIA
Name (Pennant Number): DIZELIST, ELEKTRIK, POLEMETCHIK, RADIST, NAVODCHIK, MOTORIST, SNAYPR, TURBINIST, ZENITCHIK, ZHUKOV, VINOGRADOV, VLASOV, SVYAZIST, SABANYEV, PERSHIN, RAZVEDCHIK, KOMENDOR, DESANTNIK, RAKETCHIK, SEMEN ROSHAL, DMITRY LYSENKR, MACHINIST, ZARYAD.

YEMEN
Name (Pennant Number): 201

Class: NATYA II (TYPE 266DM) (MSO)
Active: 1 Russia
Name (Pennant Number): STRELOK

Recognition features:
- High bow, short forecastle with slender mast at forward end.
- 30 mm/65 gun mounting ('A' position).
- Continuous maindeck aft to break down to sweep deck.

- Main superstructure well forward of midships.
- Large lattice mainmast atop after end of superstructure supporting distinctive radar aerial.
- Black-capped funnel with sloping top aft of midships.
- Ship's boat in davits, starboard side just forward of funnel.
- 30 mm/65 gun mounting ('X' position).
- Distinctive hydraulic gantries right aft (in some).

Note 1 - Natya II was built without minesweeping gear to make way for a lengthened superstructure.
Note 2 - Not all have Gatling 30 mm guns.

Displacement full load, tons: 804.
Length, feet (metres): 200.1 (61).
Beam, feet (metres): 33.5 (10.2).
Draught, feet (metres): 10.8 (3).
Speed, knots: 16.
Range, miles: 3,000 at 12 kts.

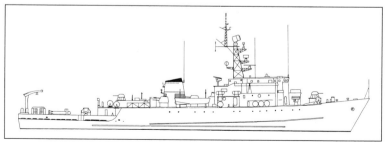

Natya I/II Class

NATYA I

Missiles: SAM - 2 SA-N-5 Grail quad launchers (in some Russian ships).
Guns: 4 30 mm/65 (2 twin) or 2 - 30 mm/65 AK 630 (Russian). 30 mm/65 (2 twin); 25 mm/80 (2 twin) (Natya I).
A/S mortars: 2 RBU 1200 5-tubed (Natya I).
Countermeasures: Capable of magnetic, acoustic and mechanical sweeping.

Radars:
Surface search — Don 2 or Low Trough.
Fire control — Drum Tilt (not in all).
Sonars: Hull-mounted; minehunting.

Landsort Class

Country: SINGAPORE, SWEDEN
Country of origin: SWEDEN
Ship type: MINE WARFARE FORCES
Class: LANDSORT (BEDOK) (MHC)
Active: 4 Singapore ('Bedok' class), 7 Sweden
SINGAPORE
Name (Pennant Number): BEDOK (M 105), KALLANG (M 106), KATONG (M 107), PUNGGOL (M 108).
SWEDEN
Name (Pennant Number): LANDSORT (M 71), ARHOLMA (M 72), KOSTER (M 73), KULLEN (M 74), VINGA (M 75), VEN (M 76), ULVÖN (M 77)

Recognition features:
● High freeboard with continuous maindeck from stem to stern.
● Main superstructure forward of midships.
● Bridge set atop mid-superstructure.
● 40 mm/70 gun mounting ('B' position).
● Sturdy pole mainmast at after end of main superstructure with twin funnels at its base.

Displacement full load, tons: 360.
Length, feet (metres): 155.8 (47.5).
Beam, feet (metres): 31.5 (9.6).
Draught, feet (metres): 7.3 (2.2).
Speed, knots: 15.
Range, miles: 2,000 at 12 kts.

Guns: 1 Bofors 40 mm/70 Mod 48. 2 7.62 mm MGs. (4 12.7 mm MGs in Singapore ships).
A/S mortars: 4 Saab Elma 9-tube launchers, (Sweden only).
Decoys: 2 Philips Philax launchers can be carried, (Sweden only).
Countermeasures: MCM - Fitted for mechanical sweeps for moored mines, magnetic and acoustic sweeps. (Possible to operate 2 - unmanned magnetic and acoustic sweepers, Sweden).

Radars:
Navigation — Thomson-CSF Terma, (Sweden). Norcontrol DB 2000, (Singapore).
Sonars: Thomson-CSF TSM-2022; hull-mounted; minehunting.

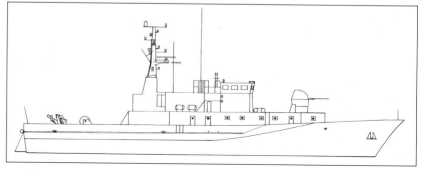

Landsort Class

VEN

Hunt Class

Country: UNITED KINGDOM
Country of origin: UNITED KINGDOM
Ship type: MINE WARFARE FORCES
Class: HUNT (MSC/MHC)
Active: 13
Name (Pennant Number): BRECON (M 29), LEDBURY (M 30), CATTISTOCK (M 31), COTTESMORE (M 32), BROCKLESBY (M 33), MIDDLETON (M 34), DULVERTON (M 35), BICESTER (M 36), CHIDDINGFOLD (M 37), ATHERSTONE (M 38), HURWORTH (M 39), BERKELEY (M 40), QUORN (M 41)

Recognition features:
- High freeboard maindeck.
- Continuous maindeck aft to sloping break down to sweep deck.
- 30 mm/75 gun mounting mid-forecastle.
- Midships superstructure has high bridge at forward end.
- Tapered, enclosed mainmast amidships.
- Navigation radar aerial atop bridge roof.
- Large, black-capped funnel aft of mainmast.
- Large structure on afterdeck housing various minehunting and minesweeping equipment.

Displacement full load, tons: 750.
Length, feet (metres): 197 (60) oa.
Beam, feet (metres): 32.8 (10).
Draught, feet (metres): 9.5 (2.9) (keel).
Speed, knots: 15.
Range, miles: 1,500 at 12 kts.

Guns: 1 DES/MSI DS 30B 30 mm/75; 2 Oerlikon/BMARC 20 mm GAM-CO1; 2 7.62 mm MGs.
Countermeasures: 2 PAP 104/105 remotely controlled submersibles; MS 14 magnetic loop; Sperry MSSA Mk 1 towed acoustic generator; conventional sweeps.
Decoys: 2 Wallop Barricade Mk III.

Radars:
Navigation — Kelvin Hughes Type 1006 or 1007.
Sonars: Plessey Type 193M Mod 1; hull-mounted; minehunting. Mil Cross mine avoidance sonar; hull-mounted. Type 2059 addition to track PAP 104/105.

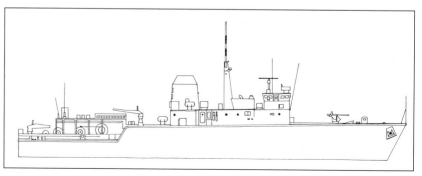

Hunt Class

COTTESMORE

Sandown Class

Country: SAUDI ARABIA, UNITED KINGDOM
Country of origin: UNITED KINGDOM
Ship type: MINE WARFARE FORCES
Class: SANDOWN (AL JAWF) (MHC)
Active: 3 Saudi Arabia ('Al Jawf'), 6 United Kingdom
Building: 3 United Kingdom
Proposed: 3 Saudi Arabia, 3 United Kingdom

SAUDI ARABIA

Name (Pennant Number): AL JAWF (420), SHAQRA (422) AL KHARJ (424), ONAIZAH (426), AL RAAS (428), AL BAHAN (430).

UNITED KINGDOM

Name (Pennant Number): SANDOWN (M 101), INVERNESS (M 102), CROMER (M 103), WALNEY (M 104), BRIDPORT (M 105), PENZANCE (M 106), PEMBROKE (M 107), GRIMSBY (M 108), BANGOR (M 109), RAMSEY (M 110), BLYTHE (M 111), SHOREHAM (M 112).

Recognition features:

- Short, sloping forecastle with 30 mm/75 gun mounting ('A' position).
- Long superstructure extending from forecastle to small quarterdeck.
- Most of superstructure is flush with ship's side giving a slab-sided effect.
- Bridge sited atop superstructure just forward of midships.
- Navigation radar aerial atop bridge roof.
- Tapered, enclosed mainmast amidships, with short pole mast atop.
- Square profile, black-capped funnel with sloping top, aft of mainmast.

Displacement full load, tons: 484, (480 Saudi Arabia).
Length, feet (metres): 172.2 (52.5). (172.9 (52.7), Saudi Arabia).
Beam, feet (metres): 34.4 (10.5).
Draught, feet (metres): 7.5 (2.3). (6.9 (2.1), Saudi Arabia).
Speed, knots: 13.
Range, miles: 3,000 at 12 kts.

Guns: 1 DES/MSI 30 mm/75 DS 30B, (UK). 30 mm (twin), (Saudi Arabia).
Countermeasures: ECA mine disposal system; 2 PAP 104 Mk 5.

Radars:
Navigation — Kelvin Hughes Type 1007.
Sonars: Marconi Type 2093 VDS; mine search and classification.

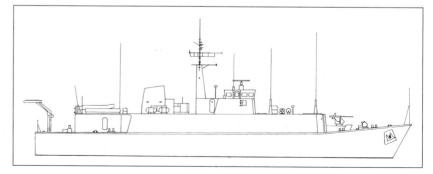

Sandown Class

INVERNESS

Avenger Class

Country: UNITED STATES OF AMERICA
Country of origin: UNITED STATES OF AMERICA
Ship type: MINE WARFARE FORCES
Class: AVENGER (MCM/MSO/MHO)
Active: 14
Name (Pennant Number): AVENGER (MCM 1), DEFENDER (MCM 2),
SENTRY (MCM 3), CHAMPION (MCM 4), GUARDIAN (MCM 5),
DEVASTATOR (MCM 6), PATRIOT (MCM 7), SCOUT (MCM 8), PIONEER
(MCM 9), WARRIOR (MCM 10), GLADIATOR (MCM 11), ARDENT (MCM
12), DEXTROUS (MCM 13), CHIEF (MCM 14)

Recognition features:
- High bow, sloping forecastle.
- Continuous maindeck profile from bow aft, with two breaks down aft of main superstructure.
- High superstructure extending from forecastle to sweep deck.
- Large, distinctive tripod mainmast on bridge roof with short pole mast atop.
- Very large tapered funnel aft of midships with sloping top and flat, sloping after end.
- Sweep cable reels and floats on sweepdeck.
- Unusually large for MCM craft.

Note - Japan operates 3 'Yaeyama' class MSOs (Yaeyama (MSO 301), Tsushima (MSO 302) and Hachijou (MS0 303), which appears to be a derivative of the 'Avenger' class. Hulls are slightly smaller, with a full load displacement of 1,275 tons. There is only one break in the maindeck down to the sweeping deck and the lattice mainmast is atop the after end of the superstructure. There is also a small radome atop the bridge roof in these vessels.

Displacement full load, tons: 1312.
Length, feet (metres): 224 (68.3).
Beam, feet (metres): 39 (11.9).
Draught, feet (metres): 12.2 (3.7).
Speed, knots: 13.5.

Guns: 2 12.7 mm Mk 26 MGs.
Countermeasures: MCM - 2 SLQ-48; ROV mine neutralisation system; SLQ-37(V)3; magnetic/acoustic influence sweep; Oropesa SLQ-38 Type 0 Size 1; mechanical sweep.

Radars:
Surface search — ISC Cardion SPS-55.
Navigation — Raytheon SPS-64(V)9 or LN66.
Sonars: General Electric SQQ-30 (Raytheon/Thomson-Sintra SQQ-32 (MCM 10 on) VDS; minehunting.

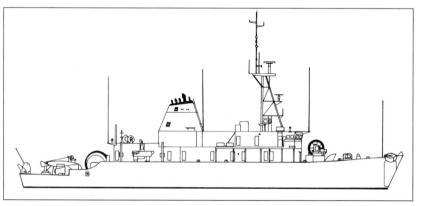

Avenger Class

AVENGER

Osprey Class

Country: UNITED STATES OF AMERICA
Country of origin: UNITED STATES OF AMERICA
Ship type: MINE WARFARE FORCES
Class: OSPREY (MHC)
Active: 12
Name (Pennant Number): OSPREY (MHC 51), HERON (MHC 52), PELICAN (MHC 53), ROBIN (MHC 54), ORIOLE (MHC 55), KINGFISHER (MHC 56), CORMORANT (MHC 57), BLACK HAWK (MHC 58), FALCON (MHC 59), CARDINAL (MHC 60), RAVEN (MHC 61), SHRIKE (MHC 62)

Recognition features:

● Continuous maindeck from bow, aft to break down to low freeboard afterdeck.
● Main superstructure extending from forecastle to break.
● High bridge at forward end of superstructure with unusual outward-sloping bridge windows.
● Bulky, square section, tapered funnel at after end of superstructure with wedge shaped smoke deflector Rad-Haz screen atop.
● Narrow, square section enclosed mainmast immediately forward of funnel.
● Large crane deck on afterdeck.

Note - Modified design based on 'Lerici' class, with much larger hull.

Displacement full load, tons: 930.
Length, feet (metres): 188 (57.3).
Beam, feet (metres): 35.9 (11).
Draught, feet (metres): 9.5 (2.9).
Speed, knots: 10.
Range, miles: 1,500 at 10 kts.

Guns: 2 12.7 mm MGs.
Countermeasures: MCM — Alliant SLQ-48 ROV mine neutralisation system.

Radars:
Navigation — Raytheon SPS-64(V)9 and R4 1XX.
Sonars: Raytheon/Thomson-Sintra SQQ-32 VDS; minehunting.

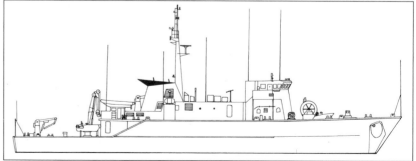

Osprey Class

BLACK HAWK

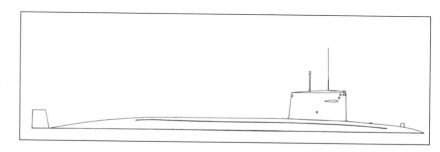

Han Class

Country: CHINA
Country of origin: CHINA
Ship type: SUBMARINES
Class: HAN (Type 091) (SSN)
Active: 5
Name (Pennant Number): (401), (402), (403), (404), (405).

Recognition features:
- Fin sited well forward of midships with diving planes at its forward edge, just above mid-height.
- Fin has vertical forward edge, top sloping down towards after end and sloping after edge, curved at the bottom.
- Tall rudder with sloping forward edge and vertical after edge.
- YJ 8-2 (C-801) SSM tubes fitted aft of the fin.

Displacement dived, tons: 5,550.
Length, feet (metres): 321.5 (98). (347.8 (106), 403 on).
Beam, feet (metres): 32.8 (10).
Draught, feet (metres): 24.2 (7.4).
Speed, knots: 25 dived, 12 surfaced.

Missiles: SSM - YJ8-2 (Eagle Strike) (C-801).
Torpedoes: 6 21 in (533 mm) bow tubes; Yu-3 (SET-65E) and Yu-1 (Type 63-51) combination.

Radars:
Surface search — Snoop Tray.
Sonars: Trout Cheek, hull-mounted, active/passive search and attack; DUUX-5.

Han Class

HAN

Agosta/Agosta B Class

Country: FRANCE, PAKISTAN, SPAIN
Country of origin: FRANCE
Ship type: SUBMARINES
Class: AGOSTA /AGOSTA B (HASHMAT, GALERNA) (SSK)
Active: 2 France, 2 Pakistan ('Hashmat' class), 4 Spain ('Galerna' class)
Building: 2 Pakistan (Agosta B class)
Proposed: 1 Pakistan (Agosta B class)
FRANCE
Name (Pennant Number): LA PRAYA (S 662), OUESSANT (S 623).
PAKISTAN
Name (Pennant Number): HASHMAT (ex-Astrant) (S 135), HURMAT (ex-Adventurous) (S 136). Agosta B - —— (S 137), —— (S 138), —— (S 139).

SPAIN
Name (Pennant Number): GALERNA (S 71), SIROCO (S 72), MISTRAL (S 73), TRAMONTANA (S 74).

Recognition features:
- Blunt, bull-nose bow with sonar pod atop forward end of casing.
- Wide fin with rounded surfaces. Fin has vertical leading edge with straight, sloping after edge. Distinctive protrusion at top after end of fin.
- Bow-mounted diving planes.
- Flat top to casing.
- Rudder has steeply sloping forward edge.

Displacement surfaced, tons: 1,510, (France, Pakistan). 1,570, (Agosta B). 1,490, (Spain).
Displacement dived, tons: 1,760, (France and Pakistan). 1,740, (Spain).
Length, feet (metres): 221.7 (67.7).
Beam, feet (metres): 22.3 (6.8).
Draught, feet (metres): 17.7 (5.4).
Speed, knots: 12 surfaced, 20 dived.
Range, miles: 8,500 at 9 kts. snorting; 350 at 3.5 kts. dived.

Missiles: SSM - Aerospatiale SM 39 Exocet; launched from 533 mm tubes, (France and Agosta B). McDonnell Douglas Sub-Harpoon, (Pakistan).
Torpedoes: 4 21 in (533 mm) bow tubes. ECAN L5 Mod 3 and ECAN F17 Mod 2.
Mines: Up to 36 in lieu of torpedoes, (France). Stonefish, (Pakistan). Up to 19, (Spain).

Radars:
Search — Thomson-CSF DRUA 33.
Sonars: Thomson-Sintra DSUV 22; DUUA 2D; DUUA 1D; DUUX 2; DSUV 62A towed array, (France). Thomson-Sintra TSM 2233, (Agosta B). Thomson-Sintra DSUV 2H, DUUA 2A/2B, DUUX 2A, DUUA 1D, (Pakistan). Thomson-Sintra DSUV 22, DUUA 2A/2B, DUUX 2A/5, DSUV-62 or Thomson Marconi Narama (S 73), (Spain).

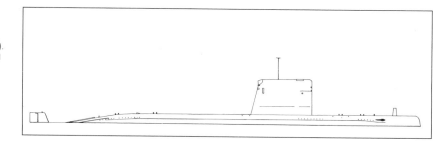

BEVEZIERS

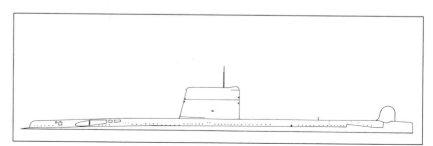

Daphné Class

Country: FRANCE, PAKISTAN, PORTUGAL, SOUTH AFRICA, SPAIN
Country of origin: FRANCE
Ship type: SUBMARINES
Class: DAPHNÉ (HANGOR, ALBACORA, DELFIN) (SSK)
Active: 1 France, 4 Pakistan ('Hangor' class), 3 Portugal ('Albacora' class), 3 South Africa, 4 Spain ('Delfin' class)

FRANCE
Name (Pennant Number): PSYCHÉ (S 650).

PAKISTAN
Name (Pennant Number): HANGOR (S 131), SHUSHUK (S 132), MANGRO (S 133), GHAZI (ex-Cachalote) (S 134).

PORTUGAL
Name (Pennant Number): ALBACORA (S 163), BARRCUDA (S 164), DELFIM (S 166).

SOUTH AFRICA
Name (Pennant Number): MARIA VAN RIEBEECK (S 97), EMILY HOBHOUSE (S 98), JOHANNA VAN DER MERWE (S 99).

SPAIN
Name (Pennant Number): DELFIN (S 61), TONINA (S 62), MARSOPA (S 63), NARVAL (S 64).

Recognition features:
- Pointed bow, flat fronted in profile.
- Large, distinctive sonar dome atop casing at bow. (Flatter, more elongated dome in Pakistan, Portugal and South Africa boats.).
- Slim fin with vertical leading edge and sloping after edge.
- Flat top to casing.
- Bow-mounted diving planes and rudder not visible.

Displacement surfaced, tons: 860, (France). 869, (remainder).
Displacement dived, tons: 1,038, (France), 1,043, (remainder).
Length, feet (metres): 189.6 (57.8).
Beam, feet (metres): 22.3 (6.8).
Draught, feet (metres): 15.1 (4.6).
Speed, knots: 13.5 surfaced; 16 dived.
Range, miles: 4,500 at 5 kts. surfaced; 3,000 at 7 kts. snorting.

Missiles: SSM — McDonnell Douglas Sub-Harpoon (Pakistan only).
Torpedoes: 12 21.7 in (550 mm) (8 bow, 4 stem) tubes.
Mines: Stonefish, (Pakistan only). (12 can be carried in lieu of torpedoes, Spain).

Radars:
Search — Thomson-CSF Calypso, (France, South Africa). Thomson-CSF DRUA 31, (Pakistan). Kelvin Hughes Type 1007, (Portugal). DRUA 31 or 33A, (Spain).
Sonars: Thomson-Sintra DSUV 2; DUUA 2; DUUX 2, (France, South Africa). DSUV 1; DUUA 1, (Pakistan). DSUV 2; DUUA 2, (Portugal). DSUV 22; DUUA 2A, (Spain).

Daphné Class

SIRENE

Country: FRANCE
Country of origin: FRANCE
Ship type: SUBMARINES
Class: L'INFLEXIBLE M4 (SNLE/SSBN)
Active: 3
Name (Pennant Number): L'INDOMPTABLE (S 613), LE TONNANT (S 614), L'INFLEXIBLE (S 615)*
*One of this class will pay off as each of the successor Le Triomphant SNLE-NG/SSBNs commissions.

Recognition features:
- Streamlined fin with diving planes at forward end towards its top.
- Large, flat-topped casing atop main pressure hull, housing the SLBM tubes.
- Slim, rounded fin with diving planes forward and protrusion at after end.
- Casing extends well aft of the fin and slopes down more steeply at its after end.
- Square-topped rudder with slightly sloping forward edge, right aft.

Displacement surfaced, tons: 8,080.
Displacement dived, tons: 8,920.
Length, feet (metres): 422.1 (128.7).
Beam, feet (metres): 34.8 (10.6).
Draught, feet (metres): 32.8 (10)
Speed, knots: 20 surfaced; 25 dived.
Range, miles: 5,000 at 4 kts. on auxiliary propulsion only.

Missiles: SLBM - 16 Aerospatiale M4/TN 70 or TN 71. SSM - Aerospatiale SM 39 Exocet, launched from 533mm torpedo tubes.
Torpedoes: 4 21 in (533 mm) tubes. ECAN L5 Mod 3 and ECAN F17 Mod 2.

Radars:
Navigation — Thomson-CSF DRUA 33.
Sonars: Thomson-Sintra DSUX 21, passive bow and flank arrays. DUUX 5. DSUV 61; towed array.

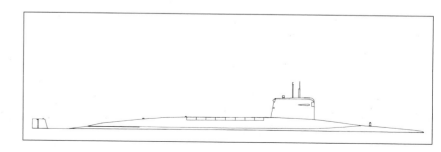

L'Inflexible M4 Class

L'INFLEXIBLE

Rubis Améthyste Class

Country: FRANCE
Country of origin: FRANCE
Ship type: SUBMARINES
Class: RUBIS AMÉTHYSTE (SSN)
Active: 6
Name (Pennant Number): RUBIS (S 601), SAPHIR (S 602), CASABIANCA (S 603), ÉMERAUDE (S 604), AMÉTHYSTE (S 605), PERLE (S 606)

Recognition features:

● Rounded, smooth lined hull.
● Small, prominent pod atop casing forward of fin.
● Rounded top to casing.
● Slim fin forward of midships with vertical leading edge and sloping after edge. Top of the fin is slightly rounded in profile and slopes down at the after end.
● Diving planes sited near the top of the fin at its leading edge.
● Rudder, right aft, has sloping forward edge.

Displacement surfaced, tons: 2,410.
Displacement dived, tons: 2,670.
Length, feet (metres): 241.5 (73.6).
Beam, feet (metres): 24.9 (7.6).
Draught, feet (metres): 21 (6.4).
Speed, knots: 25.

Missiles: SSM - Aerospatiale SM 39 Exocet, launched from 533 mm torpedo tubes.
Torpedoes: 4 21 in (533 mm) tubes. ECAN L5 Mod 3 and ECAN F17 Mod 2.
Mines: Up to 32 FG 29 in lieu of torpedoes.

Radars:

Navigation — Kelvin Hughes Type 1007.
Sonars: Thomson-Sintra DMUX 20 multi-function; DSUV 62C; towed array.

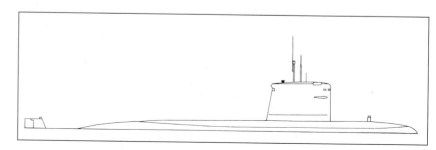

Rubis Améthyste Class

AMETHYSTE

Le Triomphant Class

Country: FRANCE
Country of origin: FRANCE
Ship type: SUBMARINES
Class: LE TRIOMPHANT (SNLE-NG/SSBN)
Active: 2
Building: 1
Proposed: 1
Name (Pennant Number): LE TRIOMPHANT (S 616), LE TÉMÉRAIRE (S 617), LE VIGILANT (S 618), — (S 619)

Recognition features:
- Very thin, tall fin with large diving planes at forward end towards its top.
- Rounded casing with flattened top with SLBM tubes aft of fin.
- Casing slopes down steeply at aft end to square-topped rudder.

Displacement, surfaced, tons: 12,640.
Displacement, dived, tons: 14,335.
Length, feet (metres): 453 (138).
Beam, feet (metres): 41 (12.5).
Draught, feet (metres): 41 (12.5).
Speed, knots: 25 dived.

Missiles: SLBM — 15 Aerospatiale M45/TN 75. SSM — Aerospatiale SM 39 Exocet.
Torpedoes: 4 21 (533 mm) tubes; ECAN L5 Mod 3.

Radars:
Search — Dassault.
Sonars: Thomson-Sintra DMUX 80 passive bow and flank arrays. Towed array.

Le Triomphant Class

LE TRIOMPHANT

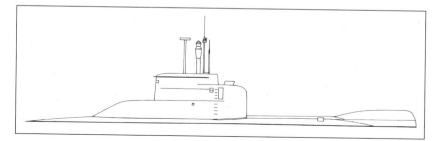

Type 206 Class

Country: GERMANY INDONESIA
Country of origin: GERMANY
Ship type: SUBMARINES
Class: TYPE 206 (SSK)
Proposed: 5, Indonesia.*
*Transfers from Germany. Because of the Asian economic crisis, these
transfers may not be completed.
Name (Pennant Number): NAGARANGSANG (ex-U 13) (403), NAGABANDA
(ex-U 14) (404), BRAMASTRA (ex-U 19), (405), CUNDAMANI (ex-U 21),
(406), ALUGORO (ex-U 20) (407).

Class: TYPE 206A
Active: 12
Name (Pennant Number): U 15 (S 194), U 16 (S 195), U 17 (S 196), U 18 (S
197), U 22 (S 171), U 23 (S 172), U 24 (S 173), U 25 (S 174), U 26 (S
175), U 28 (S 177), U 29 (S 178), U 30 (S 179)

Recognition features:

- Distinctive, bulbous bow narrowing down to slim casing.
- Large, bulky, irregular shaped fin with vertical forward edge, rounded at
  top. Fin is stepped at its after end with sloping after edge down to
  casing.
- Round top to casing of which very little is
  visible aft of the fin.
- Bow-mounted diving planes not visible.

Note 1 - Type 206A submarines have a slight
difference in superstructure shape.
Note 2 - Unusual GRP mine containers are
secured either side of the hull, forward of
the fin.

Displacement surfaced, tons: 450.
Displacement dived, tons: 498.
Length, feet (metres): 159.4 (48.6).
Beam, feet (metres): 15.1 (4.6).
Draught, feet (metres): 14.8 (4.5).
Speed, knots: 10 surfaced; 17 dived.
Range, miles: 4,500 at 5 kts. surfaced.

Torpedoes: 8 21 in (533 mm) bow tubes. STN Atlas DM 2A3, (Germany).
AEG DM 2A1 (Indonesia).
Mines: GRP container secured outside hull each side containing 12 each, in
addition to normal torpedo or mine armament.

Radars:

Surface search — Thomson-CSF Calypso II.
Sonars: Thomson-Sintra DUUX 2; Atlas Elektronik 410 A4 (Type 206); Atlas
Elektronik DBQS-21D (Type 206A).

U 21

Type 209 1100/1200/1300/1400/1500 Class

Country: ARGENTINA, BRAZIL, CHILE, COLUMBIA, ECUADOR, GREECE, INDIA, INDONESIA, SOUTH KOREA, PERU, TURKEY, VENEZUELA.
Country of origin: GERMANY
Ship type: SUBMARINES
Class: TYPE 209 (TYPES 1100, 1200, 1300, 1400 and 1500) (SALTA, TUPI, THOMSON, PIJAO, GLAVKOS, SHISHUMAR, CAKRA, CHANG BOGO, CASMA, ATILAY, PREVEZE, SABALO) (SSK)
Active: 1 Argentina ('Salta,' Type 1200, 3 Brazil ('Tupi' class, Type 1400), 2 Chile ('Thomson' class. Type 1300), 2 Colombia ('Pijao' class, Type 1200), 2 Ecuador (Type 1300), 8 Greece ('Glavkos' class, Types 1100 and 1200), 4 India ('Shishumar' class, Type 1500), 2 Indonesia ('Cakra' class, Type 1300), 7 South Korea ('Chang Bogo' class, Type 1200), 6 Peru ('Casma' class, Type 1200), 6 'Atilay' class, (Type 1200), 3 'Preveze' class, (Type 1400) Turkey, 2 Venezuela ('Sabalo' class, Type 1300).
Building: 1 Brazil (Type 1400). 2 South Korea (Type 1200). 1 Turkey (Type 1400).

ARGENTINA
Name (Pennant Number): SALTA (S 31).

BRAZIL
Name (Pennant Number): TUPI (S 30), TAMOIO (S 31), TIMBIRA (S 32), TAPAJÓ (S 33)

CHILE
Name (Pennant Number): THOMSON, (20), SIMPSON (21).

COLOMBIA
Name (Pennant Number): PIJAO (SS 28), TAYRONA (SS 29).

ECUADOR
Name (Pennant Number): SHYRI (S 101, ex-S 11), HUANCAVILCA (S 102, ex-S 12).

GREECE
Name (Pennant Number): GLAVKOS (S 110), NEREUS (S 111), TRITON (S 112), PROTEUS (S 113), POSYDON (S 116), AMPHITRITE (S 117), OKEANOS (S 118), PONTOS (S 119).

INDIA
Name (Pennant Number): SHISHUMAR (S 44), SHANKUSH (S 45), SHALKI (S 46), SHANKUL (S 47).

INDONESIA
Name (Pennant Number): CAKRA (401), NANGGALA (402).

SOUTH KOREA
Name (Pennant Number): CHANG BOGO (061), YI CHON (062), CHOI MUSON (063), PAKUI (065), LEE JONGMU (066) JEONGUN (067) — (068), — (069), — (071)

PERU
Name (Pennant Number): CASMA (SS 31), ANTOFAGASTA (SS 32), PISAGUA (SS 33), CHIPANA (SS 34), ISLAY (SS 35), ARICA (SS 36).

TURKEY
Name (Pennant Number): 'Atilay' class — ATILAY (S 347), SALDIRAY (S 348), BATIRAY (S 349), YILDIRAY (S 350), DOGANAY (S 351), DOLUNAY (S 352). 'Preveze' class — PREVEZE (S 353), SAKARYA (S 354), 18 MART (S 355), ANAFARTALAR (S 356).

VENEZUELA
Name (Pennant Number): SABALO (S 31, ex-S 21), CARIBE (S 32, ex-S 22).

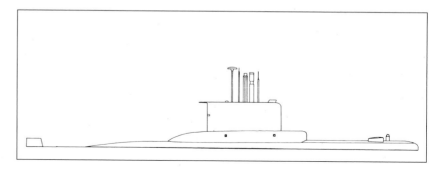

Type 209 1100/1200/1300/1400/1500 Class

Recognition features:
- Blunt bow profile with bow mounted diving planes not visible.
- Round top to casing.
- Low, long fin mounted on raised part of the casing on some, with blunt profile forward and sloping profile aft.
- Fin has vertical leading and after edges.
- Rudder just visible right aft.
- Type 1300/1400/1500 and South Korean Type 1200 have more streamlined curves to hull, without raised portion around fin.

Note - These are a singlehull design with two ballast tanks and forward and after trim tanks.

Displacement surfaced, tons: 980 (Turkey 'Atilay' class) 1,100 (Greece, South Korea). 1,180, (Colombia). 1,185 (Peru). 1,248 (Argentina). 1,260 (Brazil, Chile). 1,285 (Ecuador, Indonesia, Venezuela). 1,454 (Turkey 'Preveze' class). 1,660 (India).

Displacement dived, tons: 1,185 (Turkey 'Atilay' class). 1,285 (Colombia, Greece, South Korea). 1,290 (Peru). 1,390, (Chile, Ecuador, Indonesia). 1,440 (Argentina, Brazil). 1,585 (Turkey 'Preveze' class). 1,600 (Venezuela). 1,850, (India).

Length, feet (metres): 183.4 (55.9), (Argentina, Columbia, Greece). 183.7 (56), (South Korea, Peru). 195.2 (59.5), (Chile, Ecuador, Indonesia). 200.1 (61), (Brazil, Venezuela). 200.8 (61.2), (Turkey 'Atilay' class). 203.4 (62), (Turkey, 'Preveze' class). 211.2 (64.4), India.

Beam, feet (metres): 20.5 (6.3), (Argentina, Columbia, Ecuador). 20.3 (6.2) (Chile, Greece, Brazil, Indonesia, South Korea, Peru, Turkey, (both classes), Venezuela). 21.3 (6.5), (India).

Draught, feet (metres): 17.9 (5.5). 19.7 (6), (India).

Speed, knots: 11 surfaced; 21.5 dived

Missiles: McDonnell Douglas Sub-Harpoon. (Greece and Turkey, 'Preveze' class only).

Torpedoes: 8 21 in (533 mm) bow tubes. AEG SUT SST 4 Mod 1 (Argentina, Chile, Columbia Ecuador, India, Turkey 'Atilay' class, Venezuela). Mod 0, (Greece, Indonesia). Marconi Mk 24 Tigerfish Mod 1/2 (Brazil, Turkey, 'Preveze' class). SystemTechnik Nord (STN) SUT Mod 2, (South Korea). Whitehead A184, (Peru).

Radars:
Surface search — Thomson-CSF Calypso II/III (all, except Turkey 'Atilay' class). S 63B, (Turkey, 'Atilay' class) and Terma Scanter Mil (Venezuela).

Sonars: Atlas Elektronik CSU 83-90 (DBQS-21), (Greece S 110-113). CSU 83/1, (Brazil, India. South Korea, Turkey, 'Preveze' class). Atlas Elektronik PRS-3-4; passive ranging. Atlas Elektronik CSU 3-4 (Argentina, Chile, Columbia, Ecuador, Greece (S 116-119), Peru, Turkey, 'Atilay' class, Venezuela); hull-mounted. CSU 3-2 (Colombia, Indonesia). Atlas Elektronik TAS-3 towed array, (Turkey, 'Preveze' class). Thomson Sintra DUUX 2, (Argentina, Ecuador, Greece, Peru, Venezuela). DUUX 5 (India). DUUG 1 D (Argentina)

SAKARYA

Sauro (Type 1081)/Improved Sauro Class

Country: ITALY
Country of origin: ITALY
Ship type: SUBMARINES
Class: SAURO (TYPE 1081)/IMPROVED SAURO (SSK)
Active: 4 'Sauro' and 4 'Improved Sauro'.
Name (Pennant Number): 'Sauro' - NAZARIO SAURO (S 518), FECIA DI COSSATO (S 519), LEONARDO DA VINCI (S 520), GUGLIELMO MARCONI (S 521). 'Improved Sauro' — SALVATORE PELOSI (S 522), GIULIANO PRINI (S 523), PRIMO LONGOBARDO (S 524), GIANFRANCO GAZZANA PRIAROGGIA (S 525).

Recognition features:
● Blunt, rounded bow.
● Three sets of diving planes, one at bow, one on fin and one aft.
● Flat top to casing.
● Low profile, slim fin with vertical forward edge and sloping after edge. Diving planes just under midway up fin.
● Rudder visible right aft with vertical leading edge ('Sauro' — slopes in 'Improved Sauro') and sloping after edge.

Displacement surfaced, tons: 1,456, (Sauro). 1,476 (Improved Sauro. 1,653, S 524-5).
Displacement dived, tons: 1,631, (Sauro). 1,662 (Improved Sauro, 1,862, S 524-5).
Length, feet (metres): 210 (63.9). (211.2 (64.4), Improved Sauro; 217.8 (66.4), S 524-5).
Beam, feet (metres): 22.5 (6.8).
Draught, feet (metres): 18.9 (5.7). (18.4 (5.6), Improved Sauro).
Speed, knots: 11 surfaced; 12 snorting; 19 dived
Range, miles: 11,000 surfaced at 11 kts., 250 dived at 4 kts.

Torpedoes: 6 21 in (533 mm) bow tubes. 12 Whitehead A184.

Radars:
Search/navigation — SMA BPS-704.
Sonars: Selenia Elsag IPD 70/S. Selenia Elsag MD 100/100S.

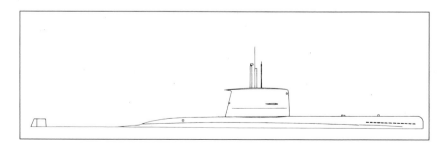

Sauro (Type 1081)/Improved Sauro Class

FECIA DI COSSATO

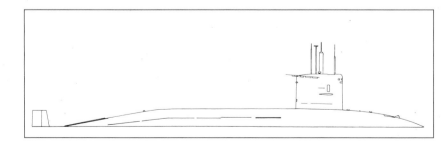

Harushio Class

Country: JAPAN
Country of origin: JAPAN
Ship type: SUBMARINES
Class: HARUSHIO (SSK)
Active: 7
Name (Pennant Number): HARUSHIO (SS 583), NATSUSHIO (SS 584),
 HAYASHIO (SS 585), ARASHIO (SS 586), WAKASHIO (SS 587),
 FUYUSHIO (SS 588), ASASHIO (SS 589)

Recognition features:
- Low profile bow.
- Rounded top to casing.
- Only short amount of casing visible forward of fin which is sited well
 forward of midships.
- Tall fin, tapered from forward to aft with vertical leading and after edges.
- Diving planes on fin at leading edge, just below mid-height.
- Curved, hump-back profile to hull.
- Rudder visible right aft with sloping forward edge.

Note - The slight growth in all dimensions and same basic shape suggests a
 natural progression from the 'Yuushio' class (active 10).

Displacement standard, tons: 2,450.
Displacement dived, tons: 2,750, (2,850, SS 589).
Length, feet (metres): 252.6 (77). (255.9 (78), SS 589).
Beam, feet (metres): 32.8 (10).
Draught, feet (metres): 25.3 (7.7).
Speed, knots: 12 surfaced; 20 dived

Missiles: SSM - McDonnell Douglas Sub-Harpoon, fired from torpedo tubes.
Torpedoes: 6 21 in (533 mm) tubes. Japanese Type 89.

Radars:
Surface search — JRC ZPS 6.
Sonars: Hughes/Oki ZQQ 5B; hull-mounted. ZQR 1 towed array similar to
 BQR 15.

Harushio Class

ARASHIO

Walrus Class

Country: NETHERLANDS
Country of origin: NETHERLANDS
Ship type: SUBMARINES
Class: WALRUS (SSK)
Active: 4
Name (Pennant Number): WALRUS (S 802), ZEELEEUW (S 803), DOLFIJN (S 808), BRUINVIS (S 810).

Recognition features:
- Low bow with small pod at forward end of casing.
- Flat top to casing.
- Large slender fin with leading edge sloping slightly aft and vertical after end.
- Diving planes at extreme forward edge of fin and just above mid-height.
- X rudders just visible right aft.

Note - These are improved 'Zwaardvis' class, upon which the Taiwanese 'Hai Lung' class (active 2) is based. Trial snort diffuser fitted to Zeeleeuw in 1996.

Displacement standard, tons: 1,900.
Displacement surfaced, tons: 2,465.
Displacement dived, tons: 2,800.
Length, feet (metres): 223.1 (67.7).
Beam, feet (metres): 27.6 (8.4).
Draught, feet (metres): 23 (7).
Speed, knots: 12 surfaced; 20 dived.
Range, miles: 10,000 at 9 kts. snorting

Missiles: SSM - McDonnell Douglas Sub-Harpoon.
Torpedoes: 4   21 in (533 mm) tubes. Honeywell Mk 48 Mod 4 and Honeywell NT 37D.

Radars:
Surface search — Signaal/Racal ZW07.
Sonars: Thomson-Sintra TSM 2272 Eledone Octopus; hull-mounted. GEC Avionics Type 2026; towed array. Thomson-Sintra DUUX 5.

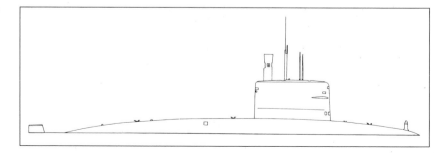

Walrus Class

BRUINVIS

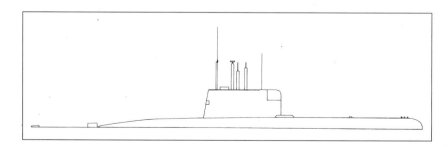

Ula Class

Country: NORWAY
Country of origin: NORWAY
Ship type: SUBMARINES
Class: ULA (SSK)
Active: 6
Name (Pennant Number): ULA (S 300), UREDD (S 305), UTVAER (S 303), UTHAUG (S 304), UTSTEIN (S 302), UTSIRA (S 301)

Recognition features:
- Blunt, high bow. Flat-topped casing slopes down from bow to water level right aft.
- Diving planes sited at bow, not visible.
- Fin sited just aft of midships.
- Fin is unusually low in profile with vertical leading edge and sharp, sloping after edge with notch cut out at mid-point.
- X rudders just visible right aft.

Displacement surfaced, tons: 1,040.
Displacement dived, tons: 1,150.
Length, feet (metres): 193.6 (59).
Beam, feet (metres): 17.7 (5.4).
Draught, feet (metres): 15.1 (4.6).
Speed, knots: 11 surfaced; 23 dived.
Range, miles: 5,000 at 8 kts.

Torpedoes: 8   21 in (533 mm) bow tubes. AEG DM 2A3.

Radars:
Surface search — Kelvin Hughes 1007.
Sonars: Atlas Elektronik CSU 83. Thomson-Sintra flank array.

Ula Class

UTSIRA

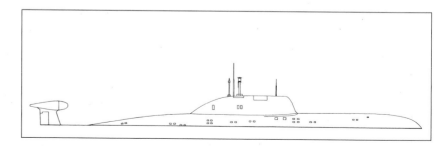

Akula I/II Class

Country: RUSSIA
Country of origin: RUSSIA
Ship type: SUBMARINES
Class: AKULA I/II (BARS) (TYPE 971/971M) (SSN)
Active: 10 Akula I; 1 Akula II.
Building: 2 Akula II.
Name (Pennant Number): Akula I - DOLPHIN (K 263), KASHALOT (K 322), KIT (K 391), PANTERA (K 317), NARWHAL (K 331), WOLF (K 461), MORZ (K 419), LEOPARD (K 328) TIGR (K 157), DRAKON (K 267). Akula II — VEPR (-), GEPARD (-), BISON (-).

Recognition features:
- Blunt, bull-nosed bow.
- Large diameter hull, flat-topped aft of fin.
- Very distinctive, low profile fin, unusually long sloping edge aft and has smoothly rounded hydrodynamic lines moulded into the casing.
- Retractable diving planes not visible.
- Large stern pod (towed array dispenser) on rudder.

Note 1 - Has the same broad hull as 'Sierra' class.
Note 2 - A number of non-acoustic sensors have begun to appear on the fin leading edge and on the forward casing.

Displacement surfaced, tons: 7,500.
Displacement, dived, tons: 9,100. (9,500 Akula II).
Length, feet (metres): 360.1 (110) oa.
Beam, feet (metres): 45.9 (14).
Draught, feet (metres): 34.1 (10.4).
Speed, knots: 10 surfaced; 28 dived.

Missiles: SLCM — Raduga SS-N-21 Sampson (RKV-500 Granat) fired from 533 mm tubes. SAM — SA-N-5/8 Strela portable launcher. A/S — Novator SS-N-15 Starfish fired from 533 mm tubes. SS-N-16 Stallion fired from 650 mm tubes; with 200 kT nuclear warhead or Veder Type 40 torpedoes.
Torpedoes: 4   21 in (533 mm) and 4   25.6 in (650 mm) tubes.

Radars:
Surface search — Snoop Pair or Snoop Half with back-to-back aerials on same mast as ESM.
Sonars: Shark Gill (Skat MGK-503); hull-mounted. Mouse Roar MG-519; hull-mounted. Skat 3 towed array.

Akula I/II Class

AKULA

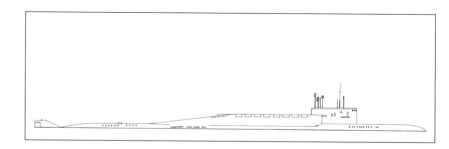

Delta IV (Delfin) Class

Country: RUSSIA
Country of origin: RUSSIA
Ship type: SUBMARINES
Class: DELTA IV (DELFIN) (TYPE 667BDRM) (SSBN)
Active: 7
Name (Pennant Number): K 51, K 84, K 64, K 114, K 117, K 18, K 407.

Recognition features:
- .Blunt, rounded, low bow.
- Low profile fin sited well forward.
- Large diving planes on fin at leading edge, about mid-height. ·
- Very large and distinctive raised flat-topped missile casing aft of the fin with its forward end moulded round after edge of fin. Missile casing runs straight for approximately half the distance to the stern where it smoothly tapers away.
- Rudder, with sloping forward edge, just visible right aft.

Note - Delta IV differs from III by being about 20 ft longer oa. and has a pressure-tight fitting on the after end of the missile tube housing. 9 Delta III 'Kalmar' class are active; the 4 Delta I 'Murena' class SSBNs were expected to pay off in 1998-9.

Displacement surfaced, tons: 10,800.
Displacement dived, tons: 13,500.
Length, feet (metres): 544.6 (166) oa.
Beam, feet (metres): 39.4 (12).
Draught, feet (metres): 28.5 (8.7).
Speed, knots: 14 surfaced; 24 dived

Missiles: SLBM — Makeyev SS-N-23 (RSM 54) Skiff. A/S — Novator SS-N-15 Starfish.
Torpedoes: 4   21 in (533 mm).

Radars:
Surface search — Snoop Tray MRP-25.
Sonars: Shark Gill (Skat MGK-503); hull-mounted. Mouse Roar MG-519; hull-mounted. Pelamida towed array.

Delta IV (Delfin) Class

DELTA IV

Country: ALGERIA, CHINA, INDIA, IRAN, POLAND, ROMANIA, RUSSIA
Country of origin: RUSSIA
Ship type: SUBMARINES
Class: KILO/KILO 4B (VASHAVYANKA) (TYPE 877E/877K/877M)
(SINDHUGHHOSH) (SSK)
Active: 2 Algeria (Type 877E), 4 China (Type 877EKM/636), 9 India
('Sindhughhosh' class, Type 877EM), 3 Iran (Type 877EKM), 1 Poland
(Type 877E), 1 Romania (Type 877E), 15 Russia (Type 877,877K,877M)

ALGERIA
Name (Pennant Number): RAIS HADJ MUBAREK (012), EL HADJ SLIMANE
(013)

CHINA
Name (Pennant Number): 364, 365, 366, 367.

INDIA
Name (Pennant Number): SINDHUGHOSH (S 55), SINDHUDHVAJ (S 56),
SINDHURAJ (S 57), SINDHUVIR (S 58) SINDHURATNA (S 59),
SINDHUKESARI (S 60), SINDHUKIRTI (S 61), SINDHUVIJAY (S 62),
SINDHURAKSHAK (S 63).

IRAN
Name (Pennant Number): TAREQ (901), NOOR (902), YUNES (903).

POLAND
Name (Pennant Number): ORZEL (291).

ROMANIA
Name (Pennant Number): DELFINUL (521).

RUSSIA
Name (Pennant Number): None available.

Recognition features:
- Blunt, rounded bow.
- Flat-topped casing, tapering towards after
  end.
- Long, low fin with vertical leading and after
  edges and flat top.
- Two windows either side at top, leading
  edge of fin.

- Hull-mounted diving planes not visible.
- Rudder just visible.

Displacement surfaced, tons: 2,325.
Displacement dived, tons: 3,076.
Length, feet (metres): 238.2 (72.6). (242.1 (73.8), China, Poland, Russia, Kilo
4B).
Beam, feet (metres): 32.5 (9.9).
Draught, feet (metres): 21.7 (6.6).
Speed, knots: 10 surfaced; 17 dived
Range, miles: 6,000 at 7 kts, surfaced; 400 at 3 kts. dived.
Missiles: SLCM — Novator SS-N-27 may be fitted from 1999 in Indian boats.
SAM — SA-N-8 Gremlin portable launcher, (India). SA-N-5/8 (Russia).
Torpedoes: 6 21 in (533 mm) tubes. Combination of TEST 71/96 and 53-
65.(TEST-71ME, Algeria only).

Radars:
Surface search — Snoop Tray MRP-25.
Sonars: MGK-400 Shark Teeth/Shark Fin; hull-mounted. Mouse Roar MG-519;
hull-mounted.

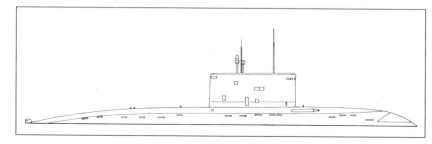

KILO 4B

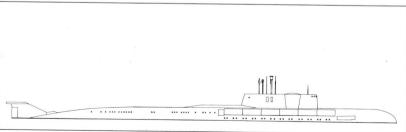

Oscar II Class

Country: RUSSIA
Country of origin: RUSSIA
Ship type: SUBMARINES
Class: OSCAR II (ANTYEY) (TYPE 949A) (SSGN)
Active: 11
Building: 1
Name (Pennant Number): KRASNODAR (K 148), IRKUTSK (K 132), VERONESH (K 119), TAMBOV (ex-Chelyabinsk) (K 173), SMOLENSK (K 410), PSKOV (K 442), WILIUCZINSK (ex-Kasatka) (K 456), OREL (ex-Severodvinsk) (K 266), OMSK (K 186), KURSK (K 141), TOMSK (K 512), BELGOROD (K 530).

Recognition features:
- Blunt, rounded low bow.
- Exceptionally large diameter hull with rounded top.
- Low, smooth profile fin forward of midships.
- Fin is tapered at the leading and after edges.
- Three windows at either side of top leading edge of fin.
- Retractable diving planes, not visible.
- Large rudder right aft.

Note 1 - Much shorter and much larger diameter than Delta IV.
Note 2 - SSM missile tubes are in banks of 12 either side and external to the 8.5 m diameter pressure hull.
Note 3 - All have a tube on the rudder fin as in Delta IV which may be used for dispensing a thin line towed sonar array.

Displacement surfaced, tons: 13,900.
Displacement dived, tons: 18,300.
Length, feet (metres): 505.2 (154).
Beam, feet (metres): 59.7 (18.2).
Draught, feet (metres): 29.5 (9).
Speed, knots: 15 surfaced; 28 dived.

Missiles: SSM — 24 Chelomey SS-N-19 Shipwreck (Granit). A/S — Novator SS-N-15 Starfish fired from 533 mm tubes. Novator SS-N-16 Stallion fired from 650 mm tubes; payload Type 45 Veder torpedo or Vodopad 200 kT nuclear weapon.
Torpedoes: 4 21 in (533 mm) and 4 25.6 in (650 mm) tubes. Type 53 and Type 65.

Radars:
Surface search — Snoop Pair (Albatros) or Snoop Half.
Sonars: Shark Gill (Skat MGK-503); hull-mounted; Shark Rib flank array; Mouse Roar MG-519; hull-mounted; Pelamida towed array.

Oscar II Class

OSCAR

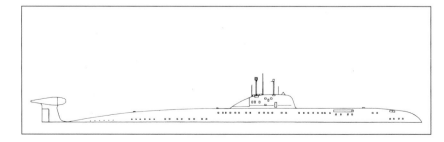

Country: RUSSIA
Country of origin: RUSSIA
Ship type: SUBMARINES
Class: VICTOR III (SCHUKA) (TYPE 671RTM) (SSN)
Active: 11
Name (Pennant Number): K 264, K 292, K 298, K 388, K 414, K 448, K 492, K 502, K 507, K 524, K 527.

Recognition features:
- Low, blunt bow.
- Retractable, hull-mounted diving planes.
- Large diameter, bulbous hull with a low profile.
- Rounded top to casing.
- Relatively small, rounded fin with slightly sloping leading edge and shallow sloping after edge.
- Distinctive, large, streamlined pod, housing towed array dispenser, mounted on rudder.

Note - Pennant numbers are now painted on the fin.

Displacement surfaced, tons: 4,850.
Displacement dived, tons: 6,300.
Length, feet (metres): 351.1 (107).
Beam, feet (metres): 34.8 (10.6).
Draught, feet (metres): 24.3 (7.4).
Speed, knots: 10 surfaced; 30 dived.

Missiles: SLCM - SS-N-21 Sampson (Granat) fired from 533 mm tubes. A/S — Novator SS-N-15 Starfish fired from 533 mm tubes. SS-N-16 Stallion fired from 650 mm tubes; payload Veder Type 40 torpedo or Vodopad 200 kT nuclear warhead.
Torpedoes: 2   21 in (533 mm) and 4 25.6 in (650 mm) tubes.

Radars:
Surface search — Snoop Tray (MRP-25).
Sonars: Shark Gill (Skat MGK-503); hull-mounted. Shark Rib flank array. Mouse Roar MG-519; hull-mounted. Skat 3 towed array.

Victor III Class

VICTOR III

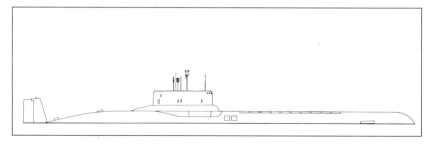

Country: RUSSIA
Country of origin: RUSSIA
Ship type: SUBMARINES
Class: TYPHOON (AKULA) (TYPE 941) (SSBN)
Active: 4 + 2 reserve
Name (Pennant Number): TK 208, TK 202, TK 12, TK 13, TK 17, TK 20.
Note Being deleted

Recognition features:

- Easily identified, the largest submarine built.
- Blunt, bull-nosed bows with huge cylindrical hull.
- Flat top to casing.
- Streamlined fin, with windows at the top forward edge, sited well aft of midships.
- The fin has a relatively low profile with the lower part being larger and rounded where it moulds onto the main casing.
- In profile the leading edge to the fin is vertical and the after edge has a slight slope.
- Retractable diving planes are not visible.
- The very large rudder at the after end gives this class an unmistakable profile.
- Missile tubes are mounted forward of the fin.

Displacement surfaced, tons: 18,500.
Displacement dived, tons: 26,500.
Length, feet (metres): 562.7 (171.5) oa.
Beam, feet (metres): 80.7 (24.6).
Draught, feet (metres): 42.7 (13).
Speed, knots: 12 surfaced; 25 dived.

Missiles: SLBM — Makeyev SS-N-20 (RSM 52/3M20) Sturgeon. SAM - SA-N-8 Gremlin capability when surfaced. A/S — Novator SS-N-15 Starfish fired from 533 mm tubes, payload, 200 kT Vodopad nuclear warhead or Veder Type 40 torpedo.
Torpedoes: 2 21 in (533 mm) and 4 25.6 in (650 mm) tubes.

Radars:
Surface search — Snoop Pair (Albatros).
Sonars: Shark Gill (Skat MGK-503); hull-mounted. Shark Rib flank array; Mouse Roar MG-519; hull-mounted; Pelamida towed array.

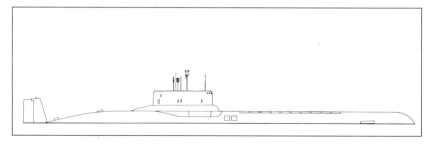

Typhoon Class

TYPHOON

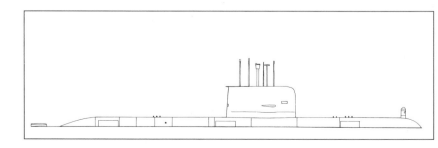

Collins Kockums Type 471 Class

Country: AUSTRALIA
Country of origin: SWEDEN
Ship type: SUBMARINES
Class: COLLINS (KOCKUMS TYPE 471) (SSK)
Active: 3
Building: 3
Name (Pennant Number): COLLINS (73), FARNCOMB (74), WALLER (75), DECHAINEUX (76), SHEEAN (77), RANKIN (78)

Recognition features:
- Blunt bow with prominent pod.
- Low, slim fin with forward edge sloping slightly aft.
- Unusual, flat extension to the top after end of the fin.
- Conventional diving planes low down on fin.
- Rounded top to casing.
- X rudders visible above waterline, aft.

Displacement surface, tons: 3,051.
Displacement dived, tons: 3,353.
Length, feet (metres): 255.2 (77.8).
Beam, feet (metres): 25.6 (7.8).
Draught, feet (metres): 23. (7).
Speed, knots: 10 surfaced; 10 snorting; 20 dived.
Range, miles: 9,000 at 10 kts. (snort).

Missiles: SSM - McDonnell Douglas Sub-Harpoon.
Torpedoes: 6 21 in (533 mm) forward tubes; Gould Mk 48 Mod 4.
Decoys: 2 SSE; torpedo decoys.

Radars:
Navigation — Kelvin Hughes Type 1007.
Sonars: Thomson-Sintra Scylla bow and flank arrays. GEC-Marconi Kariwara or Thomson Marconi Narama or Allied Signal TB 23 passive towed array.

COLLINS

Gotland (A 19) Class

Country: SWEDEN
Country of origin: SWEDEN
Ship type: SUBMARINES
Class: GOTLAND (A 19) (SSK)
Active: 3
Name (Pennant Number): GOTLAND (-), UPPLAND (-), HALLAND (-).

Recognition features:
- Blunt, bull-nosed rounded bow.
- Flat top to casing.
- Slim fin amidships with slightly sloped base, forward and aft.
- Diving plans midway up centre of fin.

Displacement, surfaced, tons: 1,240.
Displacement, dived, tons: 1,490.
Length, feet (metres): 198.2 (60.4).
Beam, feet (metres): 20.3 (6.2).

Draught, feet (metres): 18.4 (5.6).
Speed, knots: 10 surfaced, 20 dived.

Torpedoes: 4 21 in (533 mm) bow tubes; FFV Type 613/62. 2 15.75 in (400 mm) bow tubes; Swedish Ordnance Type 432/451.
Mines: Capability for 48 in external girdle or 12 Type 47 swim-out mines in lieu of torpedoes.

Radars:
Navigation — Terma Scanter.
Sonars: STN/Atlas Elektronik CSU 90-2, hull-mounted.

Gotland (A 19) Class

GOTLAND

Sjöormen Class

Country: SINGAPORE
Country of origin: SWEDEN
Ship type: SUBMARINES
Class: SJÖORMEN (A 12) (SSK)
Active: 1
Conversion: 3*
*Remaining trio being converted and being delivered from August 1999.
Name (Pennant Number): CHALLENGER (ex-Sjöbjörnen), — (ex-Sjöormen),
— (ex-Sjölejonet), — (ex-Sjöhunden)

Recognition features:
- Low, blunt bow.
- Low profile hull with smooth, sloping forward and after ends.
- Rounded top to casing.
- Bulky fin with unusual curves to leading edge. Vertical after edge, slightly flared at bottom.
- Fin-mounted diving planes sited at centre of fin and well below mid-height.

Note - Albacore hull. Twin-decked.

Displacement surfaced, tons: 1,130.
Displacement dived, tons: 1,210.
Length, feet (metres): 167.3 (51).
Beam, feet (metres): 20 (6.1).
Draught, feet (metres): 19 (5.8).
Speed, knots: 12 surfaced; 20 dived.

Torpedoes: 4 21 in (533 mm) bow tubes. FFV Type 613; 2 16 in (400 mm) tubes. FFV Type 431.

Radars:
Navigation — Terma.
Sonars: Plessey Hydra; hull-mounted.

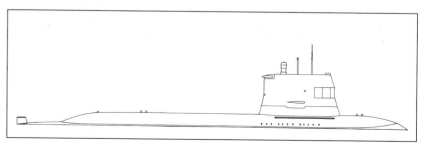

Sjöormen Class

SJÖLEJONET

Västergötland (A17) Class

Country: SWEDEN
Country of origin: SWEDEN
Ship type: SUBMARINES
Class: VÄSTERGÖTLAND (A 17) (SSK)
Active: 4
Name (Pennant Number): VÄSTERGÖTLAND (-), HÄLSINGLAND (-),
SÖDERMANLAND (-), ÖSTERGÖTLAND (-).

Recognition features:
- Rounded bow, small pod atop forward casing.
- Smooth, symmetrical casing with rounded top.
- Large, distinctive fin with sloping top at forward edge.
- Fin is slightly flared out (in profile) for the lower one third of its height.
- Fin-mounted diving planes, aft from forward edge below mid-height.

Note - Single hulled, with an X type rudder/after hydroplane design.

Displacement surfaced, tons: 1,070.
Displacement dived, tons: 1,143.
Length, feet (metres): 159.1 (48.5).
Beam, feet (metres): 20 (6.1).
Draught, feet (metres): 18.4 (5.6).
Speed, knots: 10 surfaced; 20 dived.

Torpedoes: 6   21 in (533 mm) tubes. FFV Type 613; 3 15.75 in (400 mm)
tubes. FFV Type 431/451.

Radars:
Navigation — Terma.
Sonars: Atlas Elektronik CSU 83; hull-mounted.

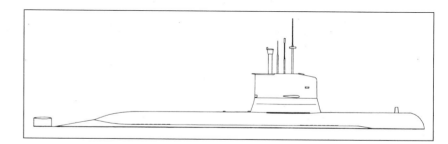

Västergötland (A17) Class

HÄLSINGLAND

Country: UNITED KINGDOM
Country of origin: UNITED KINGDOM
Ship type: SUBMARINES
Class: SWIFTSURE (SSN)
Active: 5
Name (Pennant Number): SOVEREIGN (S 108), SUPERB (S 109), SCEPTRE (S 104), SPARTAN (S 105), SPLENDID (S 106)

Recognition features:

- Submarine has hump-backed appearance in profile.
- The pressure hull maintains its diameter for most of the hull length.
- Retractable, hull-mounted diving planes.
- Prominent, slender sonar pod atop casing forward of fin.
- Fin mounted just forward of midships. Fin has vertical leading and after edges and is tapered to point at after end.
- Slopes steeply down at after end of hull compared with shallow slope at forward end.
- Large, flat-topped rudder with sloping forward edge at after end of casing.

Displacement standard, tons: 4,400.
Displacement dived, tons: 4,900.
Length, feet (metres): 272 (82.9).
Beam, feet (metres): 32.3 (9.8).
Draught, feet (metres): 28 (8.5).
Speed, knots: 30+ dived

Missiles: SLCM — Hughes Tomahawk Block III, (Splendid).   SSM - McDonnell Douglas UGM-84B Sub-Harpoon.
Torpedoes: 5   21 in (533 mm) bow tubes. Marconi Spearfish/Marconi Tigerfish Mk 24 Mod 2.
Decoys: 2 SSE Mk 6 launchers for torpedo decoys.

Radars:

Navigation — Kelvin Hughes Type 1006.
Sonars: Plessey Type 2074; hull-mounted. BAC Type 2007; hull-mounted; flank array. Ferranti Type 2046; towed array. Thomson-Sintra Type 2019 PARIS or THORN EMI 2082; Marconi Type 2077.

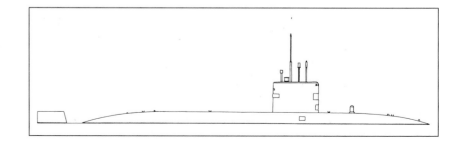

Swiftsure Class

SCEPTRE

Country: UNITED KINGDOM
Country of origin: UNITED KINGDOM
Ship type: SUBMARINES
Class: TRAFALGAR (SSN)
Active: 7
Name (Pennant Number): TRAFALGAR (S 107), TURBULENT (S 87), TIRELESS (S 88), TORBAY (S 90), TRENCHANT (S 91), TALENT (S 92), TRIUMPH (S 93)

Recognition features:
- Long, low hull with almost identical sloping profiles at the forward and after ends of the pressure hull.
- Rounded top to casing.
- Retractable, forward, hull-mounted diving planes.
- Prominent, slender sonar pod atop casing forward of fin.
- Fin is mounted just forward of midships. Fin has vertical leading and after edges and is tapered to point at after end.
- Large, flat-topped rudder at after end of casing.

Note 1 - Turbulent has a hump on the after casing housing a small winch.
Note 2 - The pressure hull and outer surfaces are covered with conformal anechoic noise reduction coatings.
Note 3 - Strengthened fins for under ice operations.

Displacement surfaced, tons: 4,740
Displacement dived, tons: 5,208.
Length, feet (metres): 280.1 (85.4).
Beam, feet (metres): 32.1 (9.8).
Draught, feet (metres): 31.2 (9.5).
Speed, knots: 32 dived.

Missiles: SLCM — Hughes Tomahawk Block III being fitted from 1998. SSM - McDonnell Douglas UGM-84B Sub-Harpoon Block IC.
Torpedoes: 5   21 in (533 mm) bow tubes. Marconi Spearfish/Marconi Tigerfish Mk 24 Mod 2.
Decoys: 2 SSE Mk 8 launchers for torpedo decoys.

Radars:
Navigation — Kelvin Hughes Type 1007.
Sonars: BAe Type 2007 AC or Marconi 2072; hull-mounted. Plessey Type 2020 or Marconi/Plessey 2074; hull-mounted. GEC Avionics Type 2026 or Ferranti Type 2046; towed array. Thomson-Sintra Type 2019 PARIS or THORN EMI 2082. Marconi Type 2077.

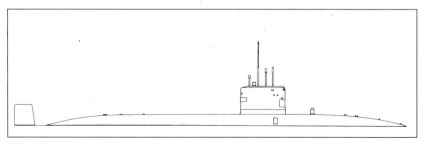

Trafalgar Class

TRENCHANT

Country: UNITED KINGDOM
Country of origin: UNITED KINGDOM
Ship type: SUBMARINES
Class: VANGUARD (SSBN)
Active: 3
Building: 1
Name (Pennant Number): VANGUARD (S 28), VICTORIOUS (S 29), VIGILANT (S 30), VENGEANCE (S 31)

Recognition features:
- Casing slopes down forward of fin to waterline.
- Slim, tapered fin well forward of midships.
- Hull-mounted diving planes approximately midway between fin and bow.
- Large, distinctive, flat-topped casing aft of fin, dropping down steeply at its after end. Casing houses SLBMs.
- Large rudder with curved top.

Note - The outer surface of the submarine is covered with conformal anechoic noise reduction coatings.

Displacement dived, tons: 15,900.
Length, feet (metres): 491.8 (149.9).
Beam, feet (metres): 42 (12.8).
Draught, feet (metres): 39.4 (12).
Speed, knots: 25 dived.

Missiles: SLBM - Lockheed Trident 2 (D5).
Torpedoes: 4   21 in (533 mm) tubes. Marconi Spearfish.
Decoys: 2 SSE Mk 10 launchers for torpedo decoys.

Radars:
Navigation — Kelvin Hughes Type 1007.
Sonars: Marconi/Plessey Type 2054; hull-mounted. Marconi/Ferranti Type 2046 towed array.

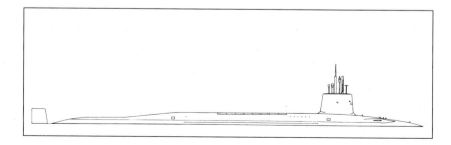

Vanguard Class

VIGILANT

Los Angeles Class

Country: UNITED STATES OF AMERICA
Country of origin: UNITED STATES OF AMERICA
Ship type: SUBMARINES
Class: LOS ANGELES (SSN)
Active: 53

Name (Pennant Number): LOS ANGELES (SSN 688), PHILADELPHIA (SSN 690), MEMPHIS (SSN 691), BREMERTON (SSN 698), JACKSONVILLE (SSN 699), DALLAS (SSN 700), LA JOLLA (SSN 701), BOSTON (SSN 703), CITY OF CORPUS CHRISTI (SSN 705), ALBUQUERQUE (SSN 706), PORTSMOUTH (SSN 707), MINNEAPOLIS-SAINT PAUL (SSN 708), HYMAN G RICKOVER (SSN 709), AUGUSTA (SSN 710), SAN FRANCISCO (SSN 711), ATLANTA (SSN 712), HOUSTON (SSN 713), NORFOLK (SSN 714), BUFFALO (SSN 715), SALT LAKE CITY (SSN 716), OLYMPIA (SSN 717), HONOLULU (SSN 718), PROVIDENCE (SSN 719), PITTSBURGH (SSN 720), CHICAGO (SSN 721), KEY WEST (SSN 722), OKLAHOMA CITY (SSN 723), LOUISVILLE (SSN 724), HELENA (SSN 725), NEWPORT NEWS (SSN 750), SAN JUAN (SSN 751), PASADENA (SSN 752), ALBANY (SSN 753), TOPEKA (SSN 754), MIAMI (SSN 755), SCRANTON (SSN 756), ALEXANDRIA (SSN 757), ASHEVILLE (SSN 758), JEFFERSON CITY (SSN 759), ANNAPOLIS (SSN 760), SPRINGFIELD (SSN 761), COLUMBUS (SSN 762), SANTA FE (SSN 763), BOISE (SSN 764), MONTPELIER (SSN 765), CHARLOTTE (SSN 766), HAMPTON (SSN 767), HARTFORD (SSN 768), TOLEDO (SSN 769), TUCSON (SSN 770), COLUMBIA (SSN 771), GREENEVILLE (SSN 772), CHEYENNE (SSN 773)

Recognition features:

- Blunt bow, very low profile pressure hull.
- Hull profile tapers gently and consistently down to water level from bow to stern.
- Slender fin, with vertical leading and after edges, is sited well forward of midships.
- Fin-mounted diving planes at mid-height. Diving planes have distinct swept wing appearance. (See Note 3).
- Tall rudder right aft with sloping forward edge.

Note 1 - From SSN 719 onwards, all are equipped with the Vertical Launch System.

Note 2 - From SSN 751 onwards the class have acoustic tile cladding to augment the 'mammalian' skin which up to then had been the standard USN outer casing coating.

Note 3 - From SSN 751 onwards the forward diving planes are hull-fitted forward instead of on the fin.

Note 4 - The towed sonar array is stowed in a blister on the side of the casing.

Displacement standard, tons: 6,082.
Displacement dived, tons: 6,927.
Length, feet (metres): 362 (110.3).
Beam, feet (metres): 33 (10.1).
Draught, feet (metres): 32.3 (9.9).
Speed, knots: 32 dived.

Missiles: SLCM — GDC/Hughes Tomahawk (TLAM-N). SSM — GDC/Hughes Tomahawk (TASM). McDonnell Douglas Harpoon.
Torpedoes: 4   21 in (533 mm) tubes midships. Gould Mk 48.
Decoys: Emerson Electric Mk 2; torpedo decoy.

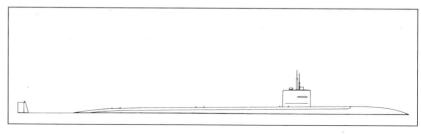

Los Angeles Class

PHILADELPHIA

Jane's/HM Steele

Radars:
Surface search/navigation/fire control — Sperry BPS 15A/16.
Sonars: IBM BQQ-5D/E. BQG—5D (flank array, SSN 710 and SSN 751
onwards). TB 23/29 thin line array or TB 16 and TB 93 passive towed
array. AMETEK BQS-15; MIDAS (mine and ice avoidance system) (SSN
751 on).

Sturgeon Class

Country: UNITED STATES OF AMERICA
Country of origin: UNITED STATES OF AMERICA
Ship type: SUBMARINES
Class: STURGEON (SSN)
Active: 8
Name (Pennant Number): POGY (SSN 647), HAWKBILL (SSN 666),
TREPANG (SSN 674), BILLFISH (SSN 676), WILLIAM H BATES (ex-
Redfish) (SSN 680), BATFISH (SSN 681), PARCHE (SSN 683), L MENDEL
RIVERS (SSN 686)

Recognition features:
- Bulbous pressure hull with unusually tall fin set well forward.
- Fin has vertical leading and after edges and is tapered at the forward and aft ends.
- Slender, fin-mounted diving planes at approximately mid-height. Diving planes have distinct swept wing appearance.
- Hull does not slope away until well aft of the fin.
- Large rudder right aft with slightly sloping forward edge.

Note 1 - Fin height is 20 ft 6 in above deck.
Note 2 - Fin-mounted diving planes rotate to vertical for breaking through ice when surfacing.
Note 3 - SSN 680-683 and 686 are 10 ft longer than remainder of class to accommodate BQQ-5 sonar.

Displacement standard, tons: 4,460.
Displacement dived, tons: 4,960. (7,800,
Parche, with special equipment for seabed operations).

Length, feet (metres): 302.2 (92.1). (Parche 100 (30) longer).
Beam, feet (metres): 31.8 (9.7).
Draught, feet (metres): 28.9 (8.8).
Speed, knots: 15 surfaced; 30 dived

Missiles: SLCM — GDC/Hughes Tomahawk (TLAM-N). SSM — GDC/Hughes
Tomahawk (TASM). McDonnell Douglas Harpoon.
Torpedoes: 4 21 in (533 mm) Mk 63 tubes midships. Gould Mk 48.
Decoys: Emerson Electric Mk 2; torpedo decoy.

Radars:
Surface search/navigation/fire control — Sperry BPS-15 or Raytheon BPS-14.
Sonars: IBM BQQ-5 (SSN 680 onwards) or Raytheon BQQ-2. EDO BQS-8 or
Raytheon BQS-14A, (ice detection). Raytheon BQS 13. BQR-15; towed
array.

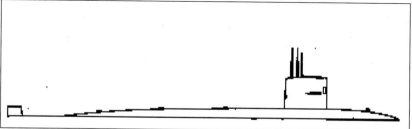

Sturgeon Class

L MENDEL RIVERS

Ohio Class

Country: UNITED STATES OF AMERICA
Country of origin: UNITED STATES OF AMERICA
Ship type: SUBMARINES
Class: OHIO (SSBN)
Active: 18
Name (Pennant Number): OHIO (SSBN 726), MICHIGAN (SSBN 727),
FLORIDA (SSBN 728), GEORGIA (SSBN 729), HENRY M JACKSON
(SSBN 730), ALABAMA (SSBN 731), ALASKA (SSBN 732), NEVADA
(SSBN 733), TENNESSEE (SSBN 734), PENNSYLVANIA (SSBN 735),
WEST VIRGINIA (SSBN 736), KENTUCKY (SSBN 737), MARYLAND
(SSBN 738), NEBRASKA (SSBN 739), RHODE ISLAND (SSBN 740),
MAINE (SSBN 741), WYOMING (SSBN 742), LOUISIANA (SSBN 743).

Recognition features:
- Very long, low profile pressure hull.
- Hull steeply sloped at the forward end with a long shallow slope down to
  the rudder aft.
- Comparatively small, slim fin sited well forward with vertical leading and
  after edges. After end of fin is tapered.
- Long, slender fin-mounted diving planes at mid-height.

Displacement surfaced, tons: 16,600.
Displacement dived, tons: 18,750.
Length, feet (metres): 560 (170.7).
Beam, feet (metres): 42 (12.8).
Draught, feet (metres): 36.4 (11.1).
Speed, knots: 24 dived.

Missiles: SLBM - Lockheed Trident I (C4) (726-733). Lockheed Trident II (D5)
(734 onwards).
Torpedoes: 4 21 in (533mm) Mk 68 bow tubes. Gould Mk 48.
Decoys: 8 launchers for Emerson Electric Mk 2; torpedo decoy.

Radars:
Surface search/navigation/fire control — BPS-15A.
Sonars: IBM BQQ-6. Raytheon BQS-13; spherical array for BQQ-6. AMETEK
BQS-15. Western Electric BQR-15 (with BQQ-9 signal processor).
Raytheon BQR-19.

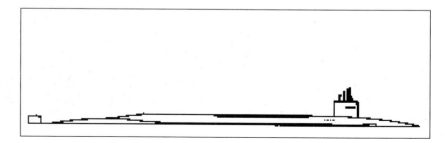

Ohio Class

OHIO

NATO STANAG DESIGNATORS FOR SHIPS

DESIGNATOR	REPORTING TITLE	DESCRIPTION
AA	Auxiliary type ship, general	General designator for all naval auxiliary type ships
AH	Hospital ship	Ship 40 m or more providing hospital services
AP	Personnel transport	Ship of 120 m or over to transport troops and supplies
CA	Cruiser, gun	A cruiser with 6 in guns or larger as main armament and carries no missiles
CC	Cruiser, general	Cruisers of 150 m and over
CG	Cruiser, guided missile	Cruiser having guided missiles as main armament
CGH	Cruiser, guided missile,	Guided missile cruiser with helicopter capability
CGN	Cruiser, guided missile, nuclear	As CG but with nuclear propulsion
CV	Aircraft carrier	Designator for aircraft carriers and multi-role aircraft carriers
CVG	Aircraft carrier, guided missile	Aircraft carrier with surface-to-air guided missiles
CVH	Aircraft carrier, VSTOL/helicopter	Carrier not fitted with arrest gear/catapult, operating VSTOL and/or helicopters which is not an amphibious or mine warfare vessel
CVN	Aircraft carrier, nuclear	As CV but with nuclear propulsion
CVS	Aircraft carrier, ASW	Carrier capable of operating VSTOL and/or helicopters in sustained ASW operations
DD	Destroyer, general	General designator for destroyer type ships in range of c.95 to 140 m
DDE	Destroyer, escort (Canada)	
DDG	Destroyer, guided missile	Destroyer fitted with surface-to-air guided missiles
DDH	Destroyer, helicopter (Canada)	
FF	Frigate/corvette general	General designator for frigate. Ship of 75 to 150 m. Generally lighter surface armament than DD
FFG	Frigate, guided missile	Frigate fitted with surface-to-air guided missiles
FFH	Frigate, helicopter	Frigate carrying helicopters
FFT	Frigate	Frigate which can be used as a training platform
FS	Corvette	Small escort of 60 to 100 m
FSG	Corvette (guided missile)	
LCC	Amphibious command ship	Command ship for amphibious taskforce and landing assault operations
LCM	Landing craft, mechanised	Landing craft of 15 to 25 m capable of carrying one tank or 50-200 troops. Must have landing ramp
LCP	Landing craft, personnel	Landing craft of 7.5 to 30 m personnel only
LCU	Landing craft, utility	All purpose landing craft of 25 to 55 m capable of handling 2-3 tanks or 300-450 troops. Must have landing ramp
LCVP	Landing craft, vehicle, personnel	Similar to LCP but capable of carrying light vehicle in place of troops
LHA	Amphibious general assault ship	Large general purpose amphibious assault ship for landing a force from helicopters or landing craft. Must have internal stowage, ramp and flooded well
LHD	Amphibious assault ship	Large multi-purpose amphibious ship for landing an assault force from helicopters, landing craft or amphibious vehicles. Can also conduct missions with VSTOL aircraft and ASW helicopters
LL	Amphibious vessel, general	General designator for amphibious vessels
LPA	Amphibious transport, personnel	Ship capable of carrying 1300-1500 troops and landing them in its own landing craft
LPD	Amphibious transport, dock	Capable of carrying 1000 troops up to 9 LCM. Must have helicopter platform
LPH	Amphibious assault ship	Large helicopter carrier for landing circa 1800 troops with its own aircraft
LSD	Landing ship, dock	Primarily tank and vehicle carrier, also capable of carrying 150-400 troops
LSM	Landing ship, medium	Of 45 to 85 m capable of beaching to land troops and tanks
LST	Landing ship, tank	Of 85 to 160 m to transport troops, vehicles and tanks for amphibious assault. Must have bow doors and/or ramps
MM	Mine warfare vessels, general	General designator for mine warfare vessels
MCM	Mine countermeasures vessel	Minehunter with mechanical and influence sweep capability
MH(I)(C)(O)	Minehunter, general	Fitted with equipment to hunt mines (Inshore) (Coastal) (Ocean). Ship of 25 to 60 m with enhanced minehunting capability.
MHS	Minehunter and sweeper, general	Ship designed to sweep mines
MLC	Minelayer (coastal)	
MSC	Minesweeper, coastal	Of 40 to 60 m
MSO	Minesweeper, ocean	Of 46 m or more
OPV	Offshore patrol vessel	
PC(F)	Patrol craft, general (fast).	General designator for patrol vessels
PG	Patrol ship, general	Of 45 to 85 m not designed to operate in open ocean. Must have at least 76 mm armament
PG (F) (G)	Patrol or gunship (fast) (guided missile)	
PHM	Patrol combatant, guided missile	High speed (hydrofoil) craft with SSM capability
PT (H)	Patrol/torpedo boat (hydrofoil)	High speed (35 kts) of 20 to 30 m. Anti-surface torpedo equipped.
SS	Submarine, general	General designator for submarines
SSA	Submarine, missile	Submarines fitted with underwater-to-surface guided missiles
SSBN	Submarine, ballistic missile, nuclear	Primary strategic nuclear submarine armed with ballistic missiles
SSGN	Submarine, attack, surface missile, nuclear	Nuclear submarine fitted with underwater or surface to surface missiles
SSK	Submarine, patrol	Non-nuclear long range patrol submarine may have anti-surface or anti-submarine role
SSN	Submarine, attack, nuclear	Nuclear attack submarine with both anti-submarine and anti-surface capability

Note: It should be noted that not all countries conform to the NATO STANAG codings for their ships. There are a number of ships in this publication whose designations will not be found in the above list (e.g. France).

GLOSSARY

AAW	Anti-air warfare.
ACDS	Advanced combat direction system.
ACV	Air cushion vehicle.
AEW	Airborne early warning.
ANV	Advanced naval vehicle.
A/S, ASW	Anti-submarine (warfare).
ASM	Air-to-surface missile.
ASROC/SUBROC	Rocket-assisted torpedo.
ASV	Anti-surface vessel.
AX/TD	Training ship.
BPDMS	Base point defence missile system
Cal./Calibre	Diameter of a gun barrel; also used for measuring the length of the barrel.
CIWS	Close-in weapons system.
CH	Helicopter cruiser.
cp	Controllable pitch propellers.
DCT	Depth charge thrower.
DE	Destroyer escort, (Japan).
DDK	Destroyer. (Japan).
DP	dual purpose.
Displacement	The weight of water displaced by a ship's hull when floating.
DUKW	Amphibious vehicle.
DSRV	Deep submergence recovery vehicle.
ECM	Electronic countermeasures.
ECCM	Electronic counter-countermeasures.
EHF	Extremely high frequency.
ELF	Extremely low frequency.
ELINT	Electronic intelligence.
ESM	Electronic support measures.
EW	Electronic warfare.
FAC	Fast attack craft.
FLIR	Forward looking infra-red radar.
FRAM	Fleet rehabilitation and modernisation programme.
fwd	forward
FY	fiscal year.
GFCS	Gun fire control system.
GMLS	Guided missile launch system.
GPS	Global positioning system.
GWS	Guided weapons system.
HF	High frequency.
IFF	Identification friend/foe.
kT	Kiloton. (Explosive power equivalent to 1,000 tons of TNT).
kts	Knots.(Speed of 1 nautical mile per hour)
LAMPS	Light airborne multipurpose system (helicopter).
LCA	Landing craft — assault.
LCAC	Landing craft — air cushion.
LCL	Landing craft — logistic, (UK).
LCM	Landing craft — mechanised load.
LCP	Landing craft — personnel.
LCT	Landing craft — tank.
LCU	Landing craft — utility.
LCVP	Landing craft — vehicles and personnel.
LF	Low frequency.
LMCR	Liquid metal cooled reactor
LRMP	Long-range maritime patrol.
LSM	Landing ship, medium.
MAD	Magnetic anomaly detector.
MCM/MCMV	Mine countermeasures/mine countermeasures vessel.
MF	Medium frequency.
MFCS	Missile fire control system.
MG	Machine gun.
MIRV	Multiple, independently targetable re-entry vehicle (Nuclear warhead).
MRV	Multiple re-entry vehicle. (nuclear warhead).
MSC	US Military Sealift Command.
MSC	Coastal minesweeper.
MW	Megawatt.
NBC	Nuclear, biological and chemical warfare.
nm	Nautical miles.
NTDS	Naval tactical direction system.
NTU	New threat upgrade.
oa	Overall length between extremities.
OTH	Over the horizon.
PAN	Aircraft carrier, nuclear-powered, (France).
PDMS	Point defence missile system.
PWR	Pressurised water reactor.
RAM	Rolling Airframe Missile.
RAM	Radar absorbent material.
RAS	Replenishment at sea.
RBU	Russian anti-submarine rocket launcher.
Ro-ro	Roll-on/roll-off.
ROV	Remote operated vehicle.
SAM	Surface-to-air missile.
SAR	Search and rescue.
SATCOM	Satellite communications.
SDV	Swimmer delivery vehicle.
SES	Surface effect ships.
SHF	Super high frequency.
SINS	Ship's inertial navigation system.
SLBM	Submarine-launched ballistic missile.
SLCM	Ship(submarine)-launched cruise missile.
SLEP	Service Life Extension Programme.
SNLE/SNLE-NG	Sous-Marins Nucléaires Lanceurs d'Engins. (French version of SSBN). NG stands for Nouvelle Génération.
SRBOC	Super rapid blooming offboard chaff.
SSDE/SSE	Submerged signal and decoy ejector.
SSM	Surface-to-surface missile.
SSTDS	Surface Ship Torpedo Defence System.
STIR	Surveillance Target Indicator Radar.
SURTASS	Surface Towed Array Surveillance System.
SUWN	Surface-to-underwater missile launcher.
SWATH	Small waterplane area twin hull.
TACAN	Tactical air navigation system.
TACTASS	Tactical Towed-Acoustic Sensor System.
TAS	Target Acquisition System.
TASS	Towed Array Surveillance System.
TCD	Landing ship, dock. (France).
ULF	Ultra-high frequency.
VDS	Variable depth sonar.
Vertrep	Vertical replenishment.
VLF	Very low frequency.
VLS	Vertical launch system.
VSTOL	Vertical or short take-off/landing (aircraft).
WIG	Wing-in-ground effect (aircraft).
wl	Water line. (measurement of length between extremities on the water-line.)

INDEX

INDEX

INDEX

508

INDEX

INDEX

Catherine Cookson was born in Tyne Dock, the illegitimate daughter of a poverty-stricken woman, Kate, whom she believed to be her older sister. She began work in service but eventually moved south to Hastings where she met and married Tom Cookson, a local grammar-school master. At the age of forty she began writing about the lives of the working-class people with whom she had grown up, using the place of her birth as the background to many of her novels.

Although originally acclaimed as a regional writer – her novel *The Round Tower* won the Winifred Holtby award for the best regional novel of 1968 – her readership soon began to spread throughout the world. Her novels have been translated into more than a dozen languages and more than 50,000,000 copies of her books have been sold in Corgi alone. Many of her novels have been made into successful television dramas, and more are planned.

Catherine Cookson's many bestselling novels established her as one of the most popular of contemporary women novelists. After receiving an ⬚⬚⬚⬚⬚⬚⬚⬚⬚⬚⬚⬚ ⬚kson was created a Dame ⬚⬚⬚⬚⬚⬚⬚⬚⬚⬚ She was appointed an Hono⬚⬚⬚⬚⬚⬚⬚⬚⬚⬚ ⬚, Oxford in 1997. For man⬚⬚⬚⬚⬚⬚⬚⬚⬚om lived near Newcastle-u⬚⬚⬚⬚⬚⬚⬚⬚⬚efore her ninety-second birt⬚⬚⬚⬚⬚⬚1996, ha⬚⬚⬚⬚⬚pleted 104 works, nine of wh⬚⬚⬚ e being published ⬚⬚⬚⬚ously.

'Catherine Cook⬚⬚⬚⬚⬚⬚⬚⬚⬚⬚⬚⬚⬚⬚ship, the intractability of l⬚⬚⬚⬚⬚⬚⬚⬚⬚⬚⬚⬚gle first to survive and next ⬚⬚⬚⬚⬚⬚⬚⬚⬚⬚⬚⬚. Humour, toughness, resolu⬚⬚⬚⬚ d generosity ar⬚⬚ virtues, in a world which s⬚⬚⬚⬚⬚⬚⬚⬚⬚⬚⬚⬚olent. Her novels are weigh⬚⬚⬚⬚⬚⬚⬚⬚⬚⬚⬚experiences of illegitimacy a⬚⬚ d poverty. This is w⬚⬚⬚⬚⬚⬚ n power. In the specialised w⬚⬚⬚⬚ of women's popular ⬚⬚⬚⬚⬚h, Cookson has created her own territory'

He⬚

BOOKS BY CATHERINE COOKSON

NOVELS

Kate Hannigan
The Fifteen Streets
Colour Blind
Maggie Rowan
Rooney
The Menagerie
Slinky Jane
Fanny McBride
Fenwick Houses
Heritage of Folly
The Garment
The Fen Tiger
The Blind Miller
House of Men
Hannah Massey
The Long Corridor
The Unbaited Trap
Katie Mulholland
The Round Tower
The Nice Bloke
The Glass Virgin
The Invitation
The Dwelling Place
Feathers in the Fire
Pure as the Lily
The Mallen Streak
The Mallen Girl
The Mallen Litter
The Invisible Cord
The Gambling Man
The Tide of Life
The Slow Awakening
The Iron Façade
The Girl
The Cinder Path
Miss Martha Mary Crawford
The Man Who Cried
Tilly Trotter
Tilly Trotter Wed
Tilly Trotter Widowed

The Whip
Hamilton
The Black Velvet Gown
Goodbye Hamilton
A Dinner of Herbs
Harold
The Moth
Bill Bailey
The Parson's Daughter
Bill Bailey's Lot
The Cultured Handmaiden
Bill Bailey's Daughter
The Harrogate Secret
The Black Candle
The Wingless Bird
The Gillyvors
My Beloved Son
The Rag Nymph
The House of Women
The Maltese Angel
The Year of the Virgins
The Golden Straw
Justice is a Woman
The Tinker's Girl
A Ruthless Need
The Obsession
The Upstart
The Branded Man
The Bonny Dawn
The Bondage of Love
The Desert Crop
The Lady on My Left
The Solace of Sin
Riley
The Blind Years
The Thursday Friend
A House Divided
Kate Hannigan's Girl
Rosie of the River

THE MARY ANN STORIES

A Grand Man
The Lord and Mary Ann
The Devil and Mary Ann
Love and Mary Ann

Life and Mary Ann
Marriage and Mary Ann
Mary Ann's Angels
Mary Ann and Bill

FOR CHILDREN

Matty Doolin
Joe and the Gladiator
The Nipper
Rory's Fortune
Our John Willie

Mrs Flannagan's Trumpet
Go Tell It To Mrs Golightly
Lanky Jones
Nancy Nutall and the Mongrel
Bill and the Mary Ann Shaughnessy

AUTOBIOGRAPHY

Our Kate
Catherine Cookson Country

Let Me Make Myself Plain
Plainer Still